Mary Tudor, England's first sovereign queen, is arguably also England's most vilified and misrepresented monarch. For centuries, she has been branded in popular and academic works as a vicious failure and superstitious tyrant. Infamous for burning hundreds of her subjects at the stake in a futile attempt to undo the English Reformation and restore Catholicism in England, she is widely remembered today as 'Bloody Mary'. In this volume, an outstanding team of international scholars trace and analyse the growth of the Bloody Mary myth, from the time of Elizabeth I through to the present day. Detailing the political, religious and gender assumptions on which the myth is based, they also attempt to recover the 'real' Mary – an educated, pragmatic and resourceful queen – underneath the myth of the villainous tyrant. Based on the very latest research, this book offers a truly revisionist and uniquely balanced portrait of Mary Tudor.

Essays by: Thomas Betteridge, Susan Doran, Thomas S. Freeman, Teresa Grant, Victor Houliston, Paulina Kewes, Aysha Pollnitz, Judith M. Richards, Andrew Taylor and William Wizeman

SUSAN DORAN is a Senior Research Fellow at Jesus College, University of Oxford, UK. She is the author of many books and articles on the Tudor period, including *Monarchy and Matrimony: The courtships of Elizabeth I, Elizabeth I* in the British Library Historic Lives series and *Mary Queen of Scots: An illustrated life.* She is the co-editor (with Thomas S. Freeman) of *The Myth of Elizabeth* and *Tudors and Stuarts on Film* (Palgrave Macmillan).

THOMAS S. FREEMAN was the Research Officer for the British Academy John Foxe Project and is now affiliated with the Faculty of Divinity at Cambridge University. He is the co-editor (with Thomas F. Mayer) of *Martyrs and Martyrdom in England, 1400–1700* and (with Susan Doran) of *The Myth of Elizabeth* and *Tudors and Stuarts on Film.* He is the co-author (with Elizabeth Evenden) of *Religion and the Book in Early Modern England: The making of Foxe's 'Book of Martyrs'.*

Also edited by Susan Doran and Thomas S. Freeman

THE MYTH OF ELIZABETH

TUDORS AND STUARTS ON FILM: HISTORICAL PERSPECTIVES

Mary Tudor

Old and New Perspectives

Edited by

SUSAN DORAN AND THOMAS S. FREEMAN

palgrave
macmillan

Selection and editorial matter © Susan Doran and Thomas S. Freeman 2011

Individual chapters (in order) © Thomas S. Freeman; Susan Doran, Victor Houlistan; Paulina Kewes; Teresa Grant; Thomas S. Freeman; Andrew W. Taylor; Aysha Pollnitz; Thomas Betteridge; William Wizeman; Thomas S. Freeman; Judith M. Richards.

First published 2011 by
PALGRAVE MACMILLAN

Palgrave Macmillan in the UK is an imprint of Macmillan Publishers Limited, registered in England, company number 785998, of Houndmills, Basingstoke, Hampshire RG21 6XS.

Palgrave Macmillan in the US is a division of St Martin's Press LLC, 175 Fifth Avenue, New York, NY 10010.

Palgrave Macmillan is the global academic imprint of the above companies and has companies and representatives throughout the world.

Palgrave® and Macmillan® are registered trademarks in the United States, the United Kingdom, Europe and other countries.

ISBN 978–0–230–00462–7 hardback
ISBN 978–0–230–00463–4 paperback

This book is printed on paper suitable for recycling and made from fully managed and sustained forest sources. Logging, pulping and manufacturing processes are expected to conform to the environmental regulations of the country of origin.

A catalogue record for this book is available from the British Library.

A catalog record for this book is available from the Library of Congress.

10   9   8   7   6   5   4   3   2   1
20   19   18   17   16   15   14   13   12   11

Printed and bound in China

TO CHRISTOPHER HAIGH
AND THE LATE FR. WILLIAM WIZEMAN:
FRIENDS, COLLEAGUES AND REVISIONISTS IN
THE STUDY OF MARY'S REIGN

Contents

List of Map and Figure

Map

Figure

Notes on the Contributors

Thomas Betteridge is Professor of early modern English literature and drama at Oxford Brookes University. His books include, *Literature and politics in the English Reformation* (2004), *Shakespearean fantasy and politics* (2005) and *Writing faith: Literature, religion and politics in the works of Thomas More* (2010).

Susan Doran is a Senior Research Fellow in history at Jesus College, Oxford and Lecturer at Regent's Park College, Oxford. She has written widely on the reign of Elizabeth I, and co-edited *The myth of Elizabeth* (2003), *Tudor England and its neighbours* (2005) and *Tudors and Stuarts on film* (2008) for Palgrave.

Thomas S. Freeman is an affiliated Lecturer at the Faculty of Divinity at the University of Cambridge. He is the co-editor of *The myth of Elizabeth* (2003), *Martyrs and martyrdom in England, 1400–1700* (2003) and *Tudors and Stuarts on film* (2008). He is the co-author of *Religion and the book in early modern England: The making of Foxe's 'Book of Martyrs'* (Cambridge, 2011).

Teresa Grant is Associate Professor in Renaissance theatre at the University of Warwick. She has published on early modern drama and culture, including essays on animals and on monarchs, and she co-edited *English historical drama, 1500–1660: Forms outside the canon* (2008) for Palgrave.

Victor Houliston is a full Professor of English at the University of the Witwatersrand, Johannesburg. His book on Robert Persons, *Catholic resistance in Elizabethan England*, appeared in 2007.

Paulina Kewes is a Fellow in English Literature at Jesus College Oxford and a Fellow of the Royal Historical Society. Her publications include *Authorship and appropriation: Writing for the stage in England, 1660–1710* (1998), *Drama, history, and politics in*

Elizabethan England (forthcoming), and, as editor or co-editor, *Plagiarism in early modern England* (2003), *The uses of history in early modern England* (2006), The *Oxford handbook to Holinshed's Chronicles* (forthcoming) and *The question of succession in late Elizabethan England* (forthcoming).

Aysha Pollnitz is a Lecturer in History at Rice University. She has been a Research Fellow of Trinity College, Cambridge and published essays on Tudor court culture, Shakespeare and political thought and humanist pedagogy. She is completing a monograph on princely education in sixteenth-century Britain.

Judith M. Richards is now a Research Associate of the History Programme at La Trobe University, Melbourne. She has published a number of essays in recent years on female monarchy in early modern England, and a biography, *Mary Tudor* (2008). She is currently working on a biography of Elizabeth I.

Andrew W. Taylor is Fellow and Director of Studies in English at Churchill College, Cambridge. He has recently published essays on Henry Howard, earl of Surrey (in the *Review of English Studies*), Nicolas Bourbon (in *Translation and Literature*), and John Bale (in *English historical drama, 1500–1660*). He has contributed essays on biblical translation and commentary to the *Oxford history of literary translation in English, Volume 2: 1550–1660* and on The Dialogue of Comfort to *The Cambridge companion to Thomas More*. He is co-editing 'Ovid' for the MHRA Tudor & Stuart Translations.

William Wizeman, SJ was the author of numerous articles as well as the monograph *The theology and spirituality of Mary Tudor's Church* (Ashgate 2006).

Abbreviations

A&M [1563]	John Foxe, *Actes and Monuments of these latter and perilous days* (London, 1563), STC 11222
A&M [1570]	John Foxe, *The first [second volume] of the ecclesiastical history containing the Actes and Monuments* (London, 1570), STC 11223
A&M [1583]	John Foxe, *Actes and Monuments of matters most speciall and memorables* (London, 1583) STC 11225
APC	*Acts of the Privy Council of England*, eds John Roche Dasent et al., new series (46 vols, London, 1890–1964)
BL	British Library
Cooper's chronicle	*Coopers chronicle . . . by me Thomas Cooper* (London, 1560), STC 15218
CPR	*Calendar of Patent Rolls*
Crowley's Chronicle	*An epitome of chronicles, containing the histories of England as al other countries, gathered out of most probable authors, first by T. Lanquet, from the beginning of the world to the incarnation of Christ, secondly to the reign of Edward the sixth, by T. Cooper, and thirdly to the reign of queen Elizabeth, by R. Crowley* (London, 1559) STC 15217.5
CSPD	*Calendar of State Papers Domestic*
CSPF	*Calendar of State Papers Foreign*
CSPSp	*Calendar of State Papers Spanish*
CSPVen	*Calendar of State Papers Venetian*
CWE	*Collected Works of Erasmus* (Toronto, 1969–)
Duffy and Loades (2006)	*The Church of Mary Tudor*, eds Eamon Duffy and David Loades (Aldershot, 2006)
ECL	Emmanuel College Library, Cambridge
EETS	Early English Texts Society
EHR	*English Historical Review*
GL	Guildhall Library, London
HJ	*Historical Journal*

Holinshed's Chronicles (1577)	Raphael Holinshed, *The Chronicles of England, Scotland and Ireland* (London, 1577) STC 13568.5
Holinshed's Chronicles (1587)	Raphael Holinshed, *The Chronicles of England, Scotland and Ireland* (London, 1587) STC 13569
HoP	*House of Commons, 1509–1558*, ed. S. T. Bindoff (3 vols., London, 1982).
LMA	London Metropolitan Archive
Loades (1965)	David Loades, *Two Tudor conspiracies* (Cambridge, 1965)
Loades (1979)	David Loades, *The reign of Mary Tudor: Politics, government and religion in England, 1553–1558* (London, 1979)
Loades (1989)	David Loades, *Mary Tudor: A life* (hardback, London, 1989)
Loades (1991)	David Loades, *The reign of Mary Tudor: Politics, government and religion in England, 1553–1558*, 2nd edn (London, 1991)
Loades (1992)	David Loades, *Mary Tudor: A life* (paperback, London, 1992)
Loades (2007)	David Loades, *Mary Tudor: The tragical history of the first queen of England* (London, 2007)
LP	*Letters and Papers, foreign & domestic of the reign of Henry VIII*, eds James Gairdner and R. H. Brodie (21 vols, 1846–1932)
LPL	Lambeth Palace Library
ODNB	*Oxford Dictionary of National Biography*
SCJ	*Sixteenth Century Journal*
STC	*A short-title catalogue of books . . . 1475–1640*, eds A.W. Pollard and G. R. Redgrave (3 vols, London, 1976–91)
STC [Wing]	*A short-title catalogue of books . . . 1641–1700*, ed. Donald Wing (3 vols, New York, 1945–51)
SWV	*Selected Works of J. L. Vives*, ed. C. Fantazziu and C. Matheeussen (8 vols, Leiden, 1987–2006)
TRHS	*Transactions of the Royal Historical Society*
TNA	The National Archives

Conventions

Throughout the volume the New Year is considered to have begun on 1 January. The spelling of book titles has been modernized in the text as has the punctuation in quotations. However, the original spelling has been retained in all quotations except for the letters i, j, u and v. We have anglicized foreign names. We have also used the phrase 'Edwardine' as the adjective referring to the reign of Edward VI.

Introduction

Susan Doran and Thomas S. Freeman

On 17 November 2008, the 450th anniversary of the death of Mary Tudor, the first sovereign queen of England, was commemorated in Westminster Abbey. Imagine for a moment, however, that the queen had lived for another decade (not on the face of it implausible, as she was only 42 when she died) and that the anniversary of her death would not occur until 2018. The world would then be very different from the one that we know today. Almost certainly, England would be Catholic and probably Scotland as well, since the Scottish Protestants would not have had the crucial backing from England that they received at the beginning of Elizabeth's reign. From this vantage point a world of alternative realities unfolds. Perhaps a union of England and Scotland under Mary Stuart, followed by a Catholic British Empire? A Europe in which the Spaniards with the support of the English were able to crush the Dutch Protestants, ultimately confining Calvinism to Geneva? These colourful vistas may be simply mirages; ultimately there is no way for anyone to know. Yet although counter-factual history is inherently inconclusive, it nevertheless serves a useful purpose; not so much in imagining plausible alternative realities, but in helping us to realize just how easily and completely the course of the history we take for granted could have been different. In the case of Mary, it helps awaken us to the possibility that, contrary to traditional historiography, her restoration of Catholicism was not an unrealistic endeavour and that the triumph of Protestantism in England, far from being either natural or inevitable, was the result of one woman's premature death. More than the winds that scattered the Spanish Armada or blew William of Orange safely to England, the microbes that took Mary Tudor's life would appear to be the decisive intervention of a Protestant deity into the course of British history.

Unquestionably, the success of the Catholic restoration in sixteenth-century England was dependent on a Catholic wearing the

1

crown, but how long could Mary have continued wearing it? Could she have retained power in the wake of the 'unpopular' burnings, epidemics, bad harvests and military defeat that marked the years 1556–8? G. R. Elton and A. G. Dickens, arguably the most eminent and influential Tudor historians in the second half of the twentieth century, were confident that she could not. Discussing the fall of Calais early in 1558, Elton concluded that: 'From that day her regime was doomed; even if she had lived, she had forfeited the loyalties which, less than five years before, had so easily brought her to the throne'.[1] As for Dickens, he could see no rational grounds for envisaging a beneficent outcome of Mary's survival: 'her reign must be judged a huge failure, but one likely to have become more monumental with every succeeding year'. He continued:

> By Mary's last year the supply of martyrs showed no sign of diminishing, and her further survival would surely have meant more exiles, more burnings, more conspiracies, very possibly even civil warfare on the subsequent Dutch and French models. People did not need to be rabid Protestants in order to reject such a persecution, while a government so burdened both by its own miscalculations and its undeserved misfortunes could not afford so divisive a luxury.[2]

Many historians, however, are now questioning this analysis. Eamon Duffy has observed that 'the supply of martyrs' did actually diminish.[3] Additionally, the problems that Mary confronted in 1558 were serious, but only temporary. Bad harvests do not last and neither do epidemics, while the shock of an unexpected defeat fades with time. Even without capable leadership, the situation would gradually and inexorably have improved. Had a rebellion arisen, would the supposedly disaffected conservative nobility and gentry have rallied behind Elizabeth – whose essentially evangelical sympathies were the worst kept secret of her sister's reign – or failed to support Mary? And would such a rebellion have succeeded? Early modern English monarchs were remarkably resilient, well able to weather prolonged periods of severe unpopularity. Had she lived in a democracy, Mary might not have survived an election in the 1550s, but then it is doubtful that Henry VIII would have been re-elected in the 1530s or Elizabeth in the 1590s.

What is more, historians today are aware that many of the earliest histories of Mary's reign were fashioned by Protestant historians who saw the triumph of Protestantism as inevitable. Consequently, as Christopher Haigh has observed:

Historians have often regarded Mary's reign as an aberration, an inconvenient disruption of the natural process of Reformation. Henry VIII's break with the pope and Edward VI's breach with the popish past seem to lead obviously to Protestant success in the reign of Elizabeth; Mary's Catholic regime was seeking to dam the tide of history, and it had to fail: doomed from the beginning and disintegrating at the end.[4]

Or in the trenchant words of what has some claim to be the definitive book on English history, 'Mary's reign was, however, a Bad Thing, since England was bound to be C of E'.[5] Put that baldly, the assumption that the restoration of Catholicism was an inevitable failure seems risible, but it is an assumption that has been surprisingly pervasive and enduring. As already seen, in the late 1980s Dickens rejected any suggestion that Mary could have succeeded in restoring Catholicism no matter how long she reigned;[6] and in the mid-1990s Andrew Pettegree warned, on similar grounds, that the success of the Marian restoration was unlikely even had the queen survived:

> The experience of both France and the Netherlands, where the central power remained unblinkingly loyal to Catholicism and yet could not prevent a major religious crisis, should caution against too glib an assumption of this sort. There is no assurance that Mary's regime would have ridden out the challenge posed by the rise of Calvinism in the early 1560s any better than these other regimes.[7]

It might be objected, however, that it is this equation of the situation in England with that on the Continent that is too glib. The Protestants in France were in a far stronger position in several respects than their English counterparts. By the 1560s the Huguenots were already a substantial majority in Nîmes and Montpellier, and a bare majority in La Rochelle. In the great city of Lyons, Protestants made up a third of the population.[8] The number of English Protestants in the mid-sixteenth century is virtually impossible to quantify. Nevertheless on one point there seems to be agreement: even in the south-east, their area of greatest numerical strength, English Protestants were in the minority.[9]

A closer look at the distribution of Protestants in south-eastern England reveals, moreover, significant vulnerabilities in their position. While the generalization of Protestant strength in Suffolk, Essex, Middlesex, Kent and Chichester is true relative to the anaemic Protestant presence in the rest of England, it does not take into account that in large areas of even these counties their numbers were negligible. Even where the Protestants were more numerous they were still a minority. Suffolk contained areas where the numbers of Protestants were at least as high as anywhere else in the kingdom: the Stour valley and the town of Ipswich as well as market towns of the central part of county, such as Mendlesham and Thorndon. But the western and north-eastern portions of Suffolk remained staunchly Catholic, and even in areas of relatively high Protestant numbers, evangelical dominance should not be assumed. John Craig's researches have shown that Hadleigh, which John Foxe extolled for its evangelical zeal and whose parish had been led for decades by egregiously evangelical rectors, was nevertheless deeply divided in its religious sympathies.[10]

The town of Colchester, in north-eastern Essex, was another area of Protestant strength, but once again, this strength should not be overestimated. Mark Byford has calculated that, at the time of Henry VIII's death, Protestants made up at most 10 per cent of Colchester's population.[11] Admittedly, their numbers very probably rose during Edward VI's reign, but even if they doubled, Protestants would have been a long way from equality, let alone dominance in Colchester. Elsewhere throughout Essex, particularly in the south and the east, the Protestants were widely, but thinly dispersed. In London, there was a sizeable Protestant minority, but their numbers appear to have been negligible in the rest of Middlesex. In Kent, there were small groups of Protestants in the city of Rochester and the towns of Dartford and Tonbridge, as well as in the Cinque Ports, particularly Hythe. But the major concentrations of Protestants in the county were in the towns of Maidstone and Ashford, and in the eastern and central Weald. The city of Canterbury, the most populous in the county, was staunchly Catholic, as were the areas north and east of the city, while most of the southern portions of the county were conservative in religion.[12] Overall, at the beginning of Mary's reign, Protestants probably formed a 'significant minority' of the Kentish population, but as one scholar has cautioned, the 'size and commitment of that minority must remain in doubt'.[13] In Sussex, Protestants were active in the eastern extremity of the county, a consequence of geographical and commercial links with the Weald, but they were very thin on the ground elsewhere.

Two important points can be gleaned from this survey. The first is that the Protestants, while spread across five south-eastern counties, and an important minority in at least four of them, were not a majority in a significant portion of any of them. In contrast to France and the Netherlands, there was no Protestant heartland in England, no area in which they were dominant. As Alec Ryrie observed, 'Even in the most reformist areas, sympathy for reform did not equate to majority support'.[14] The second is that, again in contrast to France and the Netherlands, a large number of English Protestants were based in the countryside. As already noted, there was a large Protestant minority in London and smaller minorities in Bristol and Norwich, yet English Protestants, unlike their Continental counterparts, lacked the military and political advantages that resulted from control of a major, or even minor, city.

Furthermore, in comparison to their English co-religionists, the French Protestants not only had the big battalions on their side, they also had the commanders of these battalions fighting in their cause. With all due respect to the second earl of Bedford, Protestant inroads into the ranks of the English aristocracy were negligible by 1558. In contrast, French Protestants could rely not only on the (admittedly wavering) support of Antoine de Bourbon, the king of Navarre, but also on the unwavering support of his wife, Jeanne d'Albret, and brother, Louis de Bourbon, prince de Condé. Of almost equal prominence were the Châtillon family, particularly, Gaspard de Coligny, the admiral of France, and later, Henri, duc de Rohan. The support of such magnates provided invaluable protection to Protestants on their vast estates. (It is not an accident that Protestantism flourished in Béarn, where Antoine de Bourbon held sway and in Normandy, where Gaspard de Coligny had extensive estates.) When the need arose, great nobles like Condé in Picardy, Coligny in Normandy and Rohan in Brittany were able to utilize their client networks to raise large numbers of troops for the Protestant cause. Noble families, moreover, provided a pool of experienced officers for the French Protestants.[15]

In the Netherlands the Protestants also had several advantages. For one thing, they benefited from the weakness of the central government and the relative independence of the towns and cities from the imperial authorities.[16] In sharp contrast to England, the major cities of the Netherlands, particularly when a number of them banded together, had the resources to defy the central authorities. In both France and the Netherlands there were contiguous Protestant heartlands: in the former, the southern part of the kingdom and in the Netherlands the north-western provinces. By contrast, English Protestants were dispersed over a fairly wide area and – to reiterate – apart from a few villages there was no place in which they were a majority. Moreover, the Protestant heartlands of France and the Netherlands were easily defensible. In France, the Huguenots defied their enemies in mountain strongholds stretching in an arc across southern France. In the Netherlands, the Protestant rebels were protected by dykes, canals and rivers, and sheltered in heavily fortified cities and islands.[17] The gentle rivers and rolling landscape of south-eastern England provided relatively poor defensive barriers for the Protestants even had they been able to rally support from their predominantly Catholic neighbours. In short, English Protestants were in no position to provoke a religious war, and had one broken out, it almost certainly would have ended in their rapid and complete defeat. If English Protestants were to challenge the policies of a Catholic monarch, it could not be through force, at least not successfully.

There were, of course, other ways of subverting a Catholic restoration, but how effective could these have been if the English state and Church remained Catholic? Here again, English Protestants were at a disadvantage compared with their Continental counterparts. The proximity of Geneva, both geographically and linguistically, to southern France made possible extensive Calvinist missionary activity and facilitated the dissemination of heretical literature. The cities of the Netherlands had extensive cultural and economic links with heretical regions such as northern Germany. England, however, was largely reached through ports under the control of Catholic powers. Of course, heretical literature circulated in England, conventicles met, and Protestant services were conducted clandestinely, but censorship and persecution made such activities sporadic and erratic as well as hazardous.

During Elizabeth's reign, Catholics mounted a mission to reclaim England for Catholicism, but had Mary remained on the throne, the ability of the Protestants to undertake a similar mission would have been limited. The city states of Germany and Switzerland could not have provided the logistical support that Spain and the papacy gave to the English exiles. Furthermore, the organization of the Catholic mission, no matter how imperfect, was superior to anything likely to have been established by different, sometimes contending, Protestant congregations scattered across the Netherlands, Germany and Switzerland. If the Catholics, with elite support that Marian Protestants could only have dreamed of, with the backing of the greatest power in Europe, and spearheaded by the Jesuits, failed to prevent the gradual conversion of England to Protestantism under Elizabeth, how could the Protestants have stopped the restoration of Catholicism under Mary, if of course Mary had lived?

Yet it must be admitted that the Marian regime had an Achilles' heel, which eventually proved fatal to the Catholic restoration. Pettegree pointedly asked, 'how secure could Mary's regime have been, dependant as it was on the health of an ageing, childless Queen for the continuance of Catholic rule?' Elsewhere he claimed that 'a cold assessment of the Queen's likely life expectancy militated against the rapid restoration of the fabric of traditional worship'.[18] This last observation is perhaps exaggerated; Mary was only 42 when she died and her Habsburg relatives lived into their mid-fifties. Still, Pettegree has put his finger on the major long-term threat to the successful restoration of Catholicism in England: the fact that Elizabeth, the heir presumptive to the childless queen, had widely known Protestant leanings. However, even this threat might well have receded over time, had Mary lived. On her death in November 1558, the strongest Catholic claimant to the throne, Mary Stuart, was married to the dauphin in France and not in a position to press her claim. Moreover, her candidacy was opposed by Mary Tudor's husband, Philip II, who was determined to prevent the accession of a queen so closely linked to his great enemy. Yet Mary Stuart's position might have been stronger in the 1560s when she was queen of a neighbouring country, Scotland. There was another Catholic claimant to the English throne whose position would also have improved the longer Mary Tudor lived: Henry, Lord Darnley. Although Mary Stuart's claim trumped his, Darnley possessed what, in the sixteenth century, was an enormous advantage: he was the only male candidate with a strong hereditary claim. Furthermore, his mother was on excellent terms with Mary Tudor, which might have helped persuade the queen to position him as her heir. Darnley was only 12 in 1558, which hamstrung his claim, but his position a few years later might have been formidable. And while one shudders at the thought of Darnley as king, he would almost certainly have reigned as a Catholic. In fact, Mary's death happened at the most opportune time for Elizabeth. There is a tendency to view Elizabeth's accession to the throne as inevitable, and in late 1558 this was nearly the case. But had Mary Tudor lived even a few years longer, her younger sister would very probably have faced serious challenges to her accession.

Even if Elizabeth had overcome these challenges, the net effect would have been to weaken her and quite possibly to have made it more difficult or even impossible for her to undo the Catholic restoration. For one thing, she might well have been more dependent on a religiously conservative aristocracy for support against rival claimants.

In 1559, the Act of Uniformity, establishing the Elizabethan religious settlement, only passed the House of Lords by a vote of 21 to 18, and this was with the ranks of the Marian episcopate decimated by illness and demoralized by the death of Cardinal Pole. Had Elizabeth tried to push this legislation through parliament against a full bench of bishops, under effective leadership, the result would probably have been quite different. And had Mary died even a few years later, that is exactly the kind of resistance Elizabeth would have encountered. Time would also have allowed Catholicism to become even more deeply entrenched in the universities and among the middle and lower ranks of the clergy. Under these circumstances Elizabeth might well have been forced to follow a policy of, at best incremental evangelical reform, and at worst grudging acceptance of a Catholic status quo.

Since most historians tended to believe that the restoration of Catholicism was doomed to failure, they formed a low opinion of the character and sagacity of the queen who attempted to implement it. Additionally Mary's gender associated her with the perceived 'feminine' attributes of irrationality and dependency.[19] So, while Elizabeth − the Protestant 'successful' ruler − was typically presented as 'unfeminine', indeed, masculine, Mary's varying representations throughout the centuries formed a montage of (negative) female archetypes ranging from a cruel, superstitious hag to a well-meaning but hysterical ruler, tragically ill-equipped to meet the challenges that she faced.[20] Elton's famous description of Mary as 'arrogant, assertive, bigoted, stubborn, suspicious, and (not to put too fine a point upon it) rather stupid' leaned towards the former description and revealed his preconceptions about the queen's religion and gender. Mary's Catholicism, Elton explained, owed nothing to intellectual thinking and everything to her emotional needs: 'she depended on the mass because it gave her emotional satisfaction'. Similarly, Mary's decision to marry into the Habsburg family was not based on political considerations but was the result of 'her deep feelings for her mother's family'.[21] Other historians characterized the queen as emotionally unstable, neurotic, even hysterical. Adapting the earlier verdict of James Froude and A. F. Pollard that Mary was 'hysterical', they rephrased it in the language appropriate to an era that reclines upon the psychiatrist's couch.[22] Dickens, for example, asserted that 'Mary was no sort of politician and suffered from a mental fibrosis almost unique among our former rulers. Her sorrowful memories, her "nerves", her romantic admiration for her mother's country swamped her natural intelligence.'[23] Mary's first academic biographer David Loades also found Mary to be emotionally unfit to rule, and described her as 'psychologically dependant', subject to fits of melancholy and prone to bouts of hysteria. According to his account, Mary, 'an amiable soul', was a figure more to be pitied than condemned, for she had been scarred by the 'prolonged period of psychological stress' during her troubled adolescence and damaged by long years in the wilderness when she was unable to marry and bear a child.[24]

These negative views of Mary's character and achievements owe a great deal to Elizabethan historiography. If, as is argued elsewhere in this volume, the myth of 'Bloody Mary' was not a creation of the triumphant Elizabethan Protestants, the equally enduring myth that Mary's reign was a series of ignominious failures was certainly their fabrication. Elizabethan MPs continuously, almost ritualistically, contrasted the political, economic and military failures of Mary's reign with the peace and prosperity her successor brought. Similarly, 'Elizabeth's ministers bolstered the legitimacy of her regime by continual reference to the weakness, poverty and false religion of Mary's reign'.[25] But the myth was given its definitive shape in Foxe's *Acts and Monuments* (popularly known as the 'Book of Martyrs'), particularly in a section towards the end of the book entitled 'A brief declaration shewing the unprosperous success of Queen Mary'.[26] Here Foxe listed the disasters, real and alleged, that Mary and her subjects endured – the failure to have Philip crowned, the loss of Calais, the lack of an heir, Philip's putative abandonment of the queen and her sudden death, and presented them as punishments inflicted on her by God. Above all, it was Foxe, in this section, who first related the story that Mary on her deathbed declared her embalmers would find the word 'Calais' written on her heart. As Susan Doran shows in her essay, Foxe's account was then incorporated into the second edition of Holinshed's *Chronicle*, for its editor, Abraham Fleming, was determined to present Elizabeth as a providential monarch whose rule was the antithesis of that of her half-sister.[27] Modern historians naturally removed providence from the equation, but they equally tended to exaggerate the extent of these misfortunes and retained the basic idea that Mary was somehow doomed to failure; they just shifted the blame from an angry deity to the character flaws of the queen herself: her obstinacy, bigotry, political insensitivity, and/or emotional instability. In Chapter 5, Thomas Freeman shows how the dominant Marian historiography came to be forged and developed from the late seventeenth century until modern times.

From the mid-1970s onwards, a few dissenting voices began to be heard against this prevailing historiography. Rex Pogson suggested that Mary's religious views were neither marginal nor unpopular, but instead reflected the preferences of the majority of her subjects; and he went on to conclude that the Marian restoration was fairly successful given all the problems it faced.[28] Jennifer Loach, meanwhile, challenged the dominant view (popularized by Pollard) that the sterility of the Marian regime was evident in its failure to exploit the press for propaganda purposes. In two articles – one of 1975 and the other of 1986 – she argued that the Marian regime was energetic and effective in its use of the press. Although producing propaganda was not its principal function, Loach demonstrated that Marian printers published a large number of primers, model sermons, homiletic works and Bonner's catechism, all of which assisted the clergy in their work of Catholic restoration.[29]

The process of re-evaluation continued with the publication in 1980 of *The mid-Tudor polity, c1540–1560*, a collection of essays edited by Loach and Robert Tittler, in which several contributors revised traditional accounts of Mary's reign and presented more favourable judgements of her government. Ann Weikel, for example, rebutted the long-established belief that the Marian privy council was so divided by faction that it was barely capable of managing the daily tasks of governance, and asserted that 'Not only was the Council more competent than traditionally thought, but, in addition, it was capable of important administrative initiative in domestic policy.'[30] In the same volume, C. S. Davies rewrote the story of the French war by demonstrating that it was by no means as unpopular as conventionally thought, and that the English army did well when fighting alongside Philip II at the battle of St Quentin.[31]

Three years later, Loach and Tittler individually produced books that pushed forward the revisionist agenda, at least as far as governance was concerned. In a monograph based on her earlier doctoral thesis, Loach demolished earlier accounts of the Marian regime's difficult relations with its parliaments. Far from seeing the government badly deadlocked in unsuccessful struggles with its parliaments, Loach cogently argued that the queen's management of her parliaments was capable and generally successful. At the same time, Loach questioned whether the French war was indeed the 'final disaster' of the reign by pointing to the readiness of MPs to become involved in the war effort and by demonstrating that Mary's last two parliamentary sessions were remarkably 'smooth'.[32]

Tittler's book, a short survey of Mary's reign originally designed for sixth-formers and undergraduates, was more cautiously revisionist, however. On the positive side, Tittler credited the queen and her councillors with having made good progress in establishing royal control over the localities, reforming the coinage, reviving the navy, and searching out new trade routes. Nonetheless, he was reluctant to abandon aspects of the traditionally negative picture of the reign: the Marian Church was repressive rather than intellectually or spiritually vibrant; the Spanish match was bitterly resented; and the final two years of the reign experienced a host of setbacks. The note of praise that ended Tittler's survey was so muted that it was almost grudging: 'Mary and her cohorts may therefore not have been doing so badly by the time their rule came to its abrupt and premature end.'[33]

Over the next few years, the prevailing assumption that Mary's attempt to restore Roman Catholicism to England was a doomed project and dismal failure came to be challenged in a provocative collection of essays edited by Christopher Haigh, and shattered by a pair of seminal works appearing almost in tandem in 1992.[34] Eamon Duffy's *The stripping of the altars* maintained that the ecclesiastical policies of the Marian regime were surprisingly innovative and successful, particularly in their provision for pastoral care and in the use of propaganda.[35] Haigh's *English Reformations* argued persuasively for the successes of Marian religious policies and the vigour of Catholicism throughout Marian England: 'The last years of Mary's reign were not a gruesome preparation for Protestant victory, but a continuing consolidation of Catholic strength.'[36]

Works published in the first decade of the twenty-first century have tended to reinforce the view of the Marian Church as innovative, energetic and successful in its mission. Thomas Mayer's biography of Cardinal Pole demonstrated the sophistication with which the Church was administered.[37] Two other studies, while disagreeing sharply on numerous points, concurred in emphasizing the Marian Church's theological sophistication and intellectual coherence. Lucy Wooding made claims for the insularity of the Marian Church and stressed its debt to Henrician humanism, whereas William Wizeman placed the Marian Church at the centre of European developments, contesting head-on Dickens' declaration that the Marian Church 'failed to discover the Counter-Reformation'.[38] A collection of essays edited by John Edwards and Ronald Truman and published in 2005 focused on the contribution of the Spanish friar Bartolomé Carranza to the restoration of Catholicism in England and his productive collaboration with Pole.[39] The following year another collection of essays, this time edited by Duffy and Loades, contained some contributions that highlighted the strengths and achievements of the Marian Church, including the able and unusually learned episcopal bench, the leadership of Cardinal Pole which remained intact even after his legatine status was revoked by Paul IV, and the successful restoration of Catholicism in the universities.[40] Then, in 2009, Duffy's *Fires of faith* presented a resounding defence of Marian religious policies and achievements. Duffy produced strong evidence that the Marian regime successfully recruited educated and committed clerics to run the Church, energetically promoted good preaching, skilfully handled the printing press, and established vibrant Catholic worship in the parishes. More controversially, he argued that England, under Pole's leadership, became a blueprint for later European Tridentine reform, and challenged the long-held conviction that the Marian burnings were unnecessary and unpopular. As far as the latter was concerned, he maintained that 'the vast majority of executions passed off quietly' and that there was no sign of any spreading religious disaffection during Mary's last years.[41]

Even while the achievements of Mary's reign were being re-evaluated, the view of Mary as politically inept, emotionally unstable and basically rather stupid persisted within academic circles. The process of rethinking and rehabilitating Mary only began with a pioneering essay of 1990 in which Elizabeth Russell argued for Mary's political skill in negotiating the reunion with Rome and the Spanish marriage.[42] In both matters, concluded Russell, Mary 'created her own reputation for weakness and lack of skill, in order to serve her own political ends', for by emphasizing her domestic difficulties, Mary was able to obtain the best possible deal in her negotiations with the Papacy and Habsburgs.[43] Russell's novel interpretation had little immediate impact. Nevertheless, it was afterwards taken up and extended by Judith M. Richards, who has consistently argued in essays and her 2008 biography for Mary's intelligence and political ability. Richards also threw doubts on the traditional accounts of Mary as psychologically damaged and hysterical, views that she develops in her essay for this volume.

At the same time, Richards brought a gender perspective to the study of the queen that had been lacking previously.[44] Until the publication of two articles by Richards in 1997, Elizabeth I had monopolized the scholarly activity of Tudor historians interested in gender issues. They had generally assumed that it was Elizabeth who

had overcome the obstacles associated with female rule, unlike Mary
who had proved unable or unwilling to move outside conventional
gender roles and assume monarchical power on the same terms as
a king. Richards convincingly proposed that Mary was just as capable as her Tudor male predecessors in projecting 'magnificence', in
upholding 'sacral monarchy', and in offering strong government. Her
marriage, claimed Richards, in no way diluted her authority, and
Philip did not operate in England as a king regnant but instead had
to carve out for himself a new role as king consort. It was Mary, not
her successor, who normalized queenship, and it was Elizabeth who
learned from Mary's example and built on her success.

R ichards's thoughtful reassessment of Mary has spawned other
modern treatments which also reject the earlier presentation of the
queen as politically naive and emotionally unbalanced. Jeri McIntosh's
study of Mary's pre-accession household shows that Mary was not an
ingénue when she succeeded to the throne, but on the contrary had
during Edward VI's reign assumed responsibility for her highly politicized household and operated as a regional magnate and patron.[45] In
two recent biographies – one by Linda Porter in 2007 and the other by
Anna Whitelock in 2009 – Mary is depicted as a pragmatic, moderate,
hard-working, courageous, decisive and skilful ruler.[46] Their Mary
is also successful: 'She ruled with the full measure of royal majesty
and achieved much of what she set out to do', wrote Whitelock.[47]
Her reign 'saw achievements that have long gone unacknowledged',
declared Porter. While some of these had indeed already been recognized by historians – the search for new markets abroad, social and
economic legislation, the reform of the exchequer, the new Book of
Rates, and plans for a re-coinage – Porter was able to bring them
to the attention of a popular readership. Porter also emphasized the
thriving and vibrant court culture under Mary, an aspect of her reign
that was often neglected by historians.[48]

Revisionism is therefore emerging as the dominant trend of current
Marian scholarship. Nonetheless, older interpretations continue to be
aired. As far as Mary herself is concerned, many biographers persist
in presenting her as a tragic figure. For Loades, 'Mary's real tragedy is
that she was born to be a royal consort, the pious and dutiful wife of a
powerful king. Instead she found that God had given her the duty of
ruling a realm.'[49] For Whitelock, her tragedy lay in her personal life:
although she triumphed as a queen, she suffered as a woman because
of her unwavering infatuation for a husband who did not return her
passion. 'Her life, always one of tragic contrast', writes Whitelock,

'ended in personal tragedy as Philip abandoned her, never to return, even as his Queen lay dying.'[50] Porter's biography avoided designating the queen a tragic figure, but she also emphasized Mary's personal unhappiness: her traumatic relationship with her father, her bouts of depression, and her grief at Philip's departure for the Netherlands in 1555.[51]

Equally, not all historians are convinced about Mary's abilities or success as a ruler. Loades started his 2006 biography with the judgment that 'In terms of her own ideas and purposes, Mary Tudor was a failure and nothing can conceal the fact.'[52] Though Loades admitted that not all the failures were her own fault (the weather and her childlessness for example), he did blame her for some serious weaknesses and errors: she had a 'lack of image consciousness'; she 'did not deal wisely with her council'; she should not have married Philip and she should not have allowed him to push through the reconciliation with Rome.[53] Another scholar writing in 2006 did not stray far from Elton when asserting, 'Unlike her younger sister, Mary has never been accused of being a subtle woman. Her strict Roman Catholic beliefs were both unpopular and undisguised, and she had not the capacity to dazzle'.[54] Eric Ives, in his 2009 study of the 1553 succession crisis, was also unimpressed with Mary's political abilities, claiming that she 'frequently displayed a naivety in affairs and a chronic lack of self-confidence'. Although she was admittedly 'not the total disaster which extreme Protestant propaganda portrayed', her reign, declared Ives, was arguably 'the most inglorious in English history' and the 'absence of popular mourning at her death in November 1558 said it all'.[55] Even where the Marian Church is concerned, some historians remain unconvinced that it was as dynamic and successful as revisionists have argued. In a 2004 article, Pettegree referred to the 'half-hearted' refoundations of the monasteries under Mary and asserted that:

> Revisionism has been generous to Mary. The misfortune of her death is often emphasized, but it hardly seems a sufficient answer to the question of how the regime would eventually have succeeded in creating a healthy, enduring Catholic culture – and what shape that Church would have taken.

As for the burnings, he went on:

> by 1556 the most visible sign of Catholic renewal was the burning of heretics. Mary was not a well-travelled woman, but her husband would have been able

to tell her that, as a means of building the faith, burning dissidents did not work; and that it put intolerable strains on the local communities required to take responsibility for carrying out such policies.[56]

Even the mainly revisionist volume edited by Duffy and Loades contains essays that write off the Marian bishops as mediocrities and treat the Marian persecutions as a failure.

So where does this present volume fit into present-day scholarship? Neither a biography of the queen nor a survey of her reign, our collection of essays centres on two topics. The first of these is the reputation of, and the historiography on, Mary Tudor from Mary's death in 1558 until the beginning of the last century. In it the contributors examine the origins and development of the myth of Mary as a cruel, superstitious tyrant whose reign was an almost continuous progression of misjudgements and misfortunes. This portion of our book bears a strong resemblance to an earlier volume we edited, *The myth of Elizabeth*, which examined the (much more favourable) posthumous reputation of Mary's sister and successor.[57] In addition to the essays of the two editors referred to above, Victor Houlistan reviews the references to Mary in Elizabethan Catholic writings; Paulina Kewes discusses how the question of the succession shaped the assessment of the accession crisis of 1553 and Mary's rule during Elizabeth's reign; and Teresa Grant looks at the dramatic representations of Mary in the early seventeenth century.

The second section of this book examines in more detail some of the areas of Mary's life and reign which were distorted by centuries of myth and misrepresentation and are now under reconsideration: her education, her decision to marry Philip, her hysterical pregnancies and the burnings. Here it is unashamedly revisionist. We start with Mary's education. As yet there is no consensus about her linguistic ability, her intellectual achievements and her exposure to humanism, and the essays by Andrew Taylor and Aysha Pollnitz focus on these contested areas surrounding her life. In Chapter 6, Taylor mediates between two polarized historical judgements: the older view that Mary was untouched by humanism and the newer one that she was an exemplary humanist princess. In his chapter he suggests how Mary's religious and political commitments seem to have both informed and limited her engagement with humanism. In Chapter 7, Pollnitz is more confident about Mary's humanism and reappraises her role in the translation of Erasmus's *Paraphrase on John*. This essay emphasizes the close relationship between Mary and her stepmother Katherine

Parr, offers insights into Mary's religious sensibilities in the 1540s and throws new light on Mary's linguistic skills and weaknesses. Both essays draw attention to the importance of Margaret Beaufort on the education and intellectual interests of the princess.

In Chapter 8 Thomas Betteridge analyses contemporary gendered interpretations of Mary's reign, focussing on John Heywood's *The spider and the fly* and William Forrest's poem, *The history of Grisild the second*. Then Chapters 9 and 10 consider Mary's religious policy. The late William Wizeman provides a summary and extension of the views he first expressed in his important monograph mentioned above. Thomas Freeman examines the burnings of Mary's reign and assesses their impact, both positive and negative, on the restoration of Catholicism. Finally Judith M. Richards examines the veracity of claims that Mary was hysterical or unstable, and argues trenchantly for the wisdom and success of the Habsburg marriage.

In order to rule successfully Mary had to face three challenges: she had to seize power from a rival claimant whose supporters occupied the capital city and included the greatest nobles in the kingdom; she had to reign as a female sovereign monarch (not merely as female regent) in a society where such an idea was without precedent; and finally she sought to restore Catholicism to a kingdom where it had been officially banned, much of its clerical hierarchy supplanted or disbanded, much of its property confiscated, its monasteries dissolved and its shrines razed. Her success in meeting the first challenge is indisputable, and it was no easy task. The odds were stacked against Mary, yet her seizure of the throne proved to be the only successful uprising against the central government in sixteenth century. Mary moved with decisiveness against the duke of Northumberland and Queen Jane. This same resoluteness was manifested when she was faced with an initially successful rebellion against her rule, and remained calm. While her advisors panicked, Mary rallied her forces, and she crushed it.

Mary's success in meeting the second challenge is also difficult to deny. Scholarship over the past 25 years has indicated that she reigned more effectively than she had previously been given credit for. Yet, more fundamentally, despite her gender (in sixteenth-century England eyes a considerable handicap), she reigned. In reigning as a female, she created a model and developed themes of propaganda and self-presentation which her sister readily appropriated.[58] Despite famine and epidemic – both, needless to say, outside of her control – her government was always in control and her kingdom never descended into chaos. Her authority was never successfully challenged and only Death pried the sceptre from her grasp.

Finally, Mary's accomplishments in restoring Catholicism were considerable. Within five years she had appointed an outstanding bench of bishops under whose leadership traditional worship was largely restored in the parishes. The Church over which she presided saw a rise in clerical morale and recruitment. She restored money to the Church and directly contributed to the restoration of monastic houses. She gave generously to the universities and must take some of the credit for the revival of Catholicism in them, particularly at Oxford.[59] Under the leadership of her trusted advisor Reginald Pole, a diligent programme of reform and preaching was implemented.[60] All of this activity had lasting effects: Mary and Pole provided the education and training of the leaders of the first generation of Elizabethan Catholics, and they fostered a parochial revival of Catholicism that took a generation at least to eradicate. It is reasonable to argue that success in the restoration of Catholicism only eluded the queen because her life was cut prematurely short. In her lifetime, Mary was compared to many Biblical figures: Deborah, Judith and the Virgin Mary herself. Yet perhaps her true antecedent was Deborah's adversary Sisera. Like Sisera, Mary strove valiantly and for a while carried all before her, but, in the end, the stars in their courses fought against her.

Acknowledgement

We would like to thank Dale Hoak, Peter Marshall and Alec Ryrie for reading and commenting on earlier drafts of this Introduction.

Part I

OLD PERSPECTIVES

1

A 'Sharp Rod' of Chastisement: Mary I through Protestant Eyes during the Reign of Elizabeth I

Susan Doran

> ... what English heart could forbeare Tears, and not inwardly sigh and lament the Misery? Which heavy infelicities the English Children yet unborn, shall weep at and wail to consider the same. If these be not severe Tokens and Proofs of God's heavy displeasure towards England, for so vilely despising his Word, his Light, his Religion, his Sacraments, his Institutions, what can be Shews of his Wrath and Indignation?[1]

This impassioned review and providential explanation of the misfortunes that took place under Mary I, written by Archbishop Matthew Parker, is an example of the standard Elizabethan Protestant response to the previous reign. Elizabethan chroniclers, preachers, poets and politicians all agreed that Edward VI's death and Mary's accession were God's punishment for England's sins. Like the trials Israel had faced in the Old Testament, England was put through its own ordeal in order to be given the chance to repent and gain redemption. God's hand could be seen most obviously in the plagues, 'pestilent agues', 'strange diseases' and freak weather conditions that afflicted England from 1555 to 1558.[2] But even the fall of Calais was thought by some Protestants to be the work of God. After all, as the chronicler John Stow explained, 'To many it semed strange, how that towne, which so many yeares had bene fortified with all munitions that could be devised, shold nowe in so shorte space be taken of our ennemies.' Stow also noted that:

> when the counsel of England raysed great power to have gone to the defence of that towne ... such tempest rose, as the like in many yeares had not ben sene, wherby no shyppe could broke the sea, and suche of the shyppes, as adventured, were wonderfully shaken, and forced by the saide tempest to returne agayne with great daunger.[3]

In accordance with this providential framework of thought, Mary's death and Elizabeth's accession were regarded as signs of God's infinite and mysterious mercy. Robert Crowley wrote in *The epitome of chronicles*, that deliverance came not because England had shown itself worthy of a divine reward but because 'Thus dyd the Lord of his mercy take from his people his sharpe rodde.'[4] In his Accession Day sermon of 1578, Edwin Sandys was equally grateful for a divine intervention that was unmerited : 'the Lorde in his mercie remembering us, when wee little hoped and less deserved, delivered us from the state of miserable servitude'.[5] And nine years later, Edward Hake continued the theme when he spoke of God's 'myraculous and extraordinary power and great mercy' which 'shortened those days' of England's desolation.[6]

The main lesson that Elizabeth's subjects had to learn from this experience was clear. They should repent their sins and amend their lives; otherwise, God would again purge and punish the nation. As to be expected, preachers were not slow to drive home this message, but it could also be found in more popular forms of print. So William Baldwin, in his verse, *The funerals of King Edward the Sixth*, declared:

> For if our sins send her [Elizabeth] to her brother
> Swift vengeance wil follow, let none looke for other.[7]

Similarly William Samuel warned in *The love of God*:

> se you repent your lyfe misspent
> Or els be sure and trust
> That God wyll strike, and strike again
> A sharper stroke then this.[8]

Consequently, when England suffered military defeat and the scourge of plague for a second time, in 1563, these calamities were interpreted as God's warning that the troubles of the previous reign would swiftly return if people did not perform atonement through public prayer and fasting.[9]

But the queen too was expected to take a lesson from the Marian experience. As God's handmaid she had responsibilities and duties to meet. So, time and again, preachers reminded Elizabeth that she owed her personal happiness, the peace and prosperity of the realm, and the love and loyalty of her subjects to God alone; and they cautioned her that what God gave he could equally well take away.[10] John Jewel's exhortation to the queen in an Accession Day sermon was but one of many to express these sentiments: '[God] hathe given you peace, happiness, the love and true hearts of your subiectes. Oh turn and employ these to the Glory of God, that God may confirm in your Grace the thing which he hath begun.'[11]

When Elizabeth failed to live up to such hopes and expectations, Protestants could be extremely critical, chastising her for failing to fulfil her providential role and threatening her with God's wrath if she did not improve her ways. Edward Dering did exactly this in his well-known sermon of 25 February 1570 before the queen. Highly critical of her treatment of non-conforming ministers, he used the memory of Mary's reign as a stick with which to beat his Protestant mistress. Reminding Elizabeth that it was only thanks to God's mercy that she could say, 'I have been a prisoner, I am a Princesse', he admonished her for showing ingratitude now that she was 'set in safetie', and urged her to ask 'What shall I give unto the Lord for al those benefits that he hath bestowed upon me?' instead of following Mary's example and cruelly persecuting godly preachers.[12]

As to be expected Elizabeth did not take kindly to sermons that drew attention to her duties and failings as a godly ruler. Nonetheless she fully embraced her providential status, although she could turn it on its head by reminding her subjects of the allegiance and thanks they owed her. In order to silence MPs who were petitioning for a settlement of the succession in 1563, she declared: 'I trust you do not forget that by me yow were delivered, whilest yow were hanging on the bowgh redy to fall into the mudde, yea to be drowned in the donge.'[13]

When issuing their providential warnings to the queen, Elizabethan Protestants were far from asserting that their own allegiance to her as monarch was conditional.[14] For all that 'puritans' appealed to their consciences in refusing to conform to the 1559 Prayer Book and presbyterians contested her governorship of the Church, Protestants on the whole did not challenge Elizabeth's authority to rule the state, whether on the grounds of her gender or her failure to conform to the godly ideal.[15] On the contrary, they were at pains to distance themselves from the various resistance theories produced by the radical fringe of Marian exiles. Hence, early-Elizabethan chroniclers condemned, as an unlawful act, the attempt to place Lady Jane Grey on the throne and implied their disapproval for Wyatt's rebellion, even when they were clearly sympathetic to the concerns that had prompted the rising. Elizabeth's horrified reaction to John Knox's *The first blast of the trumpet against the monstrous regiment of women* was an obvious reason for this general attitude, but another was the need to combat one of the justifications for rebellion against Elizabeth used by Catholic polemicists, namely that Protestants had previously claimed the same right against Mary.[16]

The rejection of radical resistance theories, however, created something of a predicament for those who supported the deposition of Mary Queen of Scots and favoured intervention on the side of the rebels in France and the Low Countries against their lawful Catholic rulers. Councillors like Burghley and Walsingham tended to argue for this kind of political programme on pragmatic grounds, and side-stepped the theoretical issues that had been raised by the Marian exiles. Thomas Bilson, however, addressed directly the apparent inconsistency and tried to square the circle. In *The true difference betweene Christian subiection and unchristian rebellion*, he asserted that subjects had no right of resistance at all against a hereditary and absolute sovereign (as in England), although they should indeed disobey the particular commands of a prince that were against God's law. But, where subjects owed their monarchs 'not simple subjection but respective homage' (as in France), they could legitimately take up arms to reform a tyrant. Furthermore, in elective monarchies (such as those in Germany), magistrates, argued Bilson, could be justly deposed 'by those that have authoritie to doe it'. In a short piece of dialogue dealing specifically with the Marian resistance thinkers, Bilson (through the voice of Theophilus) explained that Christopher Goodman had been 'beguiled' into calling for a rebellion against Mary by his erroneous reasoning that she was a 'violent intruder' and 'no lawful' prince, but no Protestant now accepted the argument within *How superior powers ought to be obeyed*, while Goodman himself 'hath long since disliked' it.[17]

As seen above, God's hand was detected in all Mary's failures. Nonetheless, most Elizabethans appreciated that human agency was

also at work, and consequently believed that some specific political lessons could be drawn from the Marian experience.[18] They
did not, however, always reach a consensus about what those lessons
might actually be. Take the question of Mary's marriage. In the main
it was viewed negatively, and blamed for a needless war and the
dishonourable loss of Calais. Some people also criticized the marriage for allowing foreigners to be 'over pryvye' to the secret affairs
of the state while permitting Spaniards to lord it over Englishmen.
Philip was meanwhile censured for being 'content to be pingling
with our purses' and emptying the Treasury.[19] Furthermore, a number
of Protestants implied that the policy of persecution was initiated or
encouraged by the Spaniards, for they were 'straungers moste cruell,
moste blodie, most unsufferable'.[20]

Not surprisingly, these perceived outcomes persuaded many Elizabethans that their queen would be extremely unwise to marry a
foreigner. Early in the reign, Sir Thomas Smith (through the voice
of Axenius or Homefriend in his 'Dialogue on the Queen's marriage') argued against a foreign match partly on the grounds that
the Habsburg marriage had resulted in 'nothing but fining, heading, hanging, quartering and burning; taxing, levying, and pulling
down of bulwarks at home and losing our strong holds abroad'.[21]
Later on (in 1579) Philip Sidney also had in mind Mary's Spanish
marriage when he opposed the Anjou match. According to Fulke
Greville's reminiscences of his conversations with Sidney, Mary's marriage 'was yet so fresh in memory — with so many inconveniences
of it — as, by comparing and paralleling these together, he [Sid-
ney] found credible instances to conclude neither of these foreign
alliances could prove safe for this kingdom'. Apart from foreign policy concerns, wrote Greville, Sidney had been especially troubled
about the impact of a Catholic prince upon England's religion, for
had Philip not been 'a fore-running hand in the change of religion
after King Edward's death? And had he not . . . so mastered us in our
own Church by his chaplain and concave of Rome?'[22] John Stubbs
concurred, although he concluded that England had escaped relatively lightly with Philip and might fare far worse under Anjou. If
Philip had been more settled in his own dominions and not waited
'to be warm in his bed here, the end would have been worse than
the beginning', Stubbs wrote. As England could not expect the same
degree of political distraction from Anjou, Elizabeth's marriage to
the French duke could well result in the absorption of England into
France.[23]

But, not all of Elizabeth's advisers were convinced that Mary's marriage should be invoked as a stark warning against a foreign husband for their queen. Men like the third earl of Sussex, who had served under Mary and Philip, were far from persuaded that the Spanish king had really been a threat to England's independence. They pointed out that Philip had made no attempt to bring in foreign laws during Mary's lifetime and had relinquished the realm on her death.[24] As for the war against France, these men took the line that England's involvement was the result of Mary's personal affection for Spain and devotion towards Philip, rather than the marriage itself. Such a view was actually quite widely held.[25] Because the matrimonial treaty of 1554 had contained the commitment that England would not enter the Habsburg war against the French, many writers – including a number of chroniclers – blamed Mary herself for 'tangling, contrary to promise, in hir husband's quarrel'.[26] Men who backed the Austrian and French matches trusted (or perhaps just hoped) that a fully English Elizabeth would, once married, put the interests of her country before those of her husband. From the very start of her reign, Elizabeth had been presented as a princess who (unlike Mary) 'never meaneth nor intendeth, for any private affection to advaunce the cause or quarrell of any forreigne power or potentate to the destruccion of her subiectes, to the losse of any her domynions, or to the impoverishing of her realmes';[27] and supporters of a foreign marriage thought that this characteristic together with the marriage treaty (which had also denied Philip a coronation and excluded him from exercizing patronage and power) would sufficiently safeguard the realm from a foreign yoke and expensive wars.

In discussions on the succession, there was similarly no agreement about what lessons could be learned from Mary's reign. On the one hand, Elizabeth insisted that her position as heir presumptive under Mary demonstrated clearly the dangers of naming a successor. When she was second to the throne, she said, the nobility and gentry had secretly given their loyalty to her rather than to the queen, while Wyatt's rebellion had sought to put her on the throne in Mary's place. On the other hand, many parliamentarians and most councillors contested this interpretation of past events. According to one unidentified MP in 1566, 'It is not the nature of such as seeke for advancement . . . to tarry or gape for dead men's shoes espetially when the prince is so bountifull, as was Queen Mary.' It was, he went on, 'generall misliking [of the queen] that brought so many perils to her sister, and not for that the successor was knowne'.[28] In

other words, Elizabeth had extrapolated the wrong principle from
the Marian experience since she had neglected to take into account
the particular circumstances related to the unpopularity of the queen.
This MP and others like him chose to take another lesson from the
previous reign. The persecution carried out by the Marian regime
demonstrated to them the importance of preventing another Catholic
monarch from succeeding to the throne and the necessity of the queen
or parliament naming a Protestant heir.

Just as Elizabethan Protestants did not speak with one voice about
these matters, so they approached the person of Mary in different
ways. A few writers condemned her unequivocally for the policies undertaken in her name and identified her as a member of the
False Church or an agent of Antichrist. Others avoided an explicit
attack on the late queen. Instead they deflected the main responsibility for her religious policies onto her bishops and even, in some
cases, commented positively about certain aspects of her character
and government. A third group adopted the strategy of airbrushing
the queen largely or entirely from their narratives of her reign.

In the first grouping can be placed John Aylmer. Although Aylmer
did not call the queen Jezebel or Athalia[29] in his *An harbour for faithful
and true subjects*, he made it perfectly clear that he held her personally responsible for 'the tormentes of Martyres, the murdrynge of
goodmen, The banishing of Christ, The receiving of Antechriste, the
spoyling of subiectes, the moving of warres, The losse of Englande's
honour'. Aylmer was prepared to admit that Mary might have been
influenced or even bewitched 'by Cardinall, Bishoppes and church-
men' because such 'rigour and extremitie' was unnatural to one
'bearinge, and wearinge a woman's hart'. Nevertheless, she remained
culpable in his eyes; and when it came to the exhumation and burning of the bones of the reformers, Paulius Fagius and Martin Bucer,
'Prince and Prelates deale it betwixt them.' As for the war and the
French capture of Calais, Mary was in Aylmer's judgement entirely
to blame. Had she followed the example of Tamyris, the legendary
Scythian queen (who had turned down the matrimonial proposal of
Cyrus and gone on to lead her troops to victory against him), argued
Aylmer, the pale would not have been lost. The war against France
occurred solely 'throug hir wylfulness'; a peace had been possible but
Mary insisted upon war 'because she wold shew her[self] a loving
worme and an obediente wife, rather than a careful governesse'.[30]

Aylmer's uncompromising condemnation of Mary reflected the
purpose of his book, which was to rebut Knox's arguments in *The*

first blast of the trumpet. Aylmer's central line of reasoning was that Knox had mistakenly generalized about women from the particular example of Mary Tudor. Knox had certainly been right to 'mislike the regiment from which such fruits did spring', contended Aylmer, but the Scot should have understood that the undoubted calamities of Mary's reign arose 'through the faulte of the persone, and not of the Sexe'.[31]

John Foxe followed Aylmer in denouncing Mary in print; indeed he was influenced by *An harbour*. For all his evident contempt for Stephen Gardiner and Edmond Bonner, there can be little doubt that Foxe also held the queen personally to blame for the miseries endured by Protestants during her reign.[32] Although David Loades has claimed that the martyrologist portrayed the queen as 'seduced by a clerical conspiracy' and 'misled, even betrayed, but never evil in herself', a close examination of the *Acts and Monuments* strongly suggests that Foxe painted a more complex picture.[33]

In his first edition, Foxe hints at Mary's reprobate status. When writing of the princess's stance during Edward VI's reign, for example, he concluded that 'in matters that concerned true fayth and doctrine she shewed her selfe so stiffe and obstinate, that there was no other hope of her to be conceived'.[34] 'Stiff and obstinate' were of course words associated with non-believers and others who cut themselves off from God's grace. Furthermore, as Megan Hickerson has demonstrated, in the first edition's story of Alice Driver's martyrdom, Foxe identified Mary as Jezebel. Driver had had her ears cut off for likening Mary to the Old Testament queen, and Foxe not only demonstrated his approval of Driver's words but indexed the incident as 'Quene Mary Jesabell'.[35] In the second and subsequent editions of his *Acts and Monuments*, moreover, Foxe made it even clearer that he held Mary directly responsible for the religious policies and persecutions pursued in her reign. Some of the glosses he introduced in 1570 spelled out his attitude: 'breach of promise in Q. Mary'; 'Religion here grounded upon the Queene's will'; 'Popishe Prelates intruded by Q. Mary'; 'Queene Mary will shewe no mercy but to the Pope's frendes'; 'Q Mary stirreth Boner to sheade innocent bloud', and 'A terrible proclamation of K. Phillip and Q. Mary against the poore servaunts and members of Christ'.[36] Equally significant, at the end of the narrative in the second edition, Foxe inserted a section entitled 'A briefe declaration shewing the unprosperous success of Queene Mary in persecutyng Gods people, and how mightily God wrought agaynst her in all her affaires'. There Foxe portrayed Mary as a member of the False Church: she had not only broken her promise 'with God and man' that she would make no change in religion, but she also refused to respond appropriately to God's 'manifold plagues and corrections' warning her to choose another path. Instead, to the very end she 'would not yet cease her persecution, but still continued more and more to revenge her Catholicke zeale upon the Lordes faithfull people'.[37] No wonder she died lonely, loveless, and in torment about the loss of Calais.

Borrowing heavily from the 1570 and later editions of the *Acts and Monuments*, Abraham Fleming in the 1587 edition of Holinshed's *Chronicles* was just as damning about the Catholic queen. Although he did not apply the glosses used by Foxe and reserved his abusive epithets for the figure of Gardiner, Fleming at the end of his narrative paraphrased Foxe's 'Declaration' condemning Mary as a member of the False Church.[38]

It was because of their strong belief in Mary's reprobate status that both Foxe and Fleming emphasized (with approval) the queen's personal unhappiness as well her political failures. As Thomas Betteridge explains elsewhere in this volume, Fleming effectively turned Mary's false pregnancies and barrenness into a metaphor for her inability to restore Catholicism. Foxe, meanwhile, linked the desolation Mary experienced through losing divine favour with that she felt at the loss of her husband's affection.[39] The message for readers of both works was explicit: first (in the words of Fleming), readers must 'learne withall, what the Lord can doo, when man's wilfulness needs resist him, and will not be ruled'. And, second, they could see for themselves the falsity of Mary's religion, for otherwise the queen would have had some degree of success.[40] This message was addressed as much to Elizabeth as to any of her subjects. As Thomas S. Freeman recently explained, Foxe (like Dering) was by 1570 thoroughly disillusioned with the queen, and his second edition was consequently designed 'to express his disapproval' of her religious policies and 'to spur her on to the thorough reformation for which he longed'.[41] Writing his text in the climate of Archbishop Whitgift's repression of the godly nonconformists, Fleming similarly took the example of Mary to serve as a lesson for Elizabeth.

Not all Elizabethan Protestants judged Mary so severely. Many of them chose, instead to present her as a fairly decent, if misguided, human being who had been manipulated by papist clerics. Arthur Goldyng in his *A brief treatise concerning the burning of Bucer and Phagius at Cambridge* declared that 'the cardinal and the rest of the bishops of England, miserablye abused [Queen Mary] to th'utter destruction of Christ's church'.[42] Addressing himself to Roman Catholics, John Bridges made the same point, declaring that 'your popishe byshops and priestes were the doers of all. And she good Lady, was but your instrument and meane.'[43] In several Elizabethan chronicles, the clergy was shown to be exercising undue influence over their queen, specifically in the matter of returning the ecclesiastical revenues and lands to the Church, but also by implication in other aspects of her religious policy.[44] More predictably, the anti-clerical *A new ballad* placed responsibility for the return to Rome firmly on the shoulders of the Marian clergy:

> Then came your syster, Quene Mary;
> And for five yeres that she did rayne,
> All that was done [by] Edward and Hary,
> Her wicked priestes made it but vaine:
> They brought in agayne the Romyshe lore . . .[45]

When it came to the persecutions, most of these Elizabethan Protestants found it difficult to accuse Mary of personal cruelty or hold her directly responsible for the burnings. 'Queen Marie', wrote Richard Bancroft, 'was of nature and disposition, very mild and pitifull', and her only fault was to permit 'such crueltie and superstition, to be practised and maintained in her day'.[46] John Clapham, in his *Certain observations concerning the life and reign of Elizabeth*, used similar words to describe his monarch's half-sister: 'she was a prince of noble nature, very bountiful, and in her own disposition, much inclined to pity and compassion, though much blood was shed in her time'.[47] Once again others were blamed for the cruelty: Thomas Brooke, in his broadsheet ballad marking the death of Edmund Bonner, pointed his finger directly at the bishop and away from the queen:

> Abusing much the lenitie, and mercy of the Queene:
> Such bloody broyles began to brue, as earst was never seene.[48]

Early chroniclers took a similar stance, taking care to draw attention to Mary's kind-hearted acts and elide over her role in the burnings. Thus, Thomas Lanquet's *Cooper's chronicle* noted that Mary had given Peter Martyr a safe conduct to leave the realm.[49] Richard Grafton stated that she had pardoned most of Northumberland's closest adherents in

1553, and repeated hearsay reports that she would have 'been content to have spared the said Duke's life as well as the rest, for the speciall favour that before time she did always beare unto him'. Grafton later went on to mention that Mary had spared Wyatt from the agonizing hanging and drawing that was the usual punishment for treason, permitting him to be beheaded instead.[50] Fabian's *Chronicle*, meanwhile, recorded that 'the quene, of her abundaunt and accustomed mercie' had pardoned 400 participants in Wyatt's rebellion.[51] The first edition of Holinshed claimed that had it not been for Suffolk's 'stirre and commotion in the Countrey', Lady Jane was 'lyke ynough to have beene pardoned'.[52]

These chroniclers generally downplayed Mary's involvement in the burnings, again leaving readers with the impression that the bishops were more at fault than the queen. It is true that Grafton, Stow and the first edition of Holinshed's *Chronicles* referred readers back to Foxe or even lifted some passages from the 1563 edition of the *Acts and Monuments*, but the emphasis in their texts was quite different from his, not least because his glosses and concluding summary about Mary introduced in the second edition were absent. Mary was also distanced from the individual burnings by the use these chroniclers made of the passive voice when recording them, in marked contrast to the active voice they applied whenever Mary was thought to have been the prime mover behind an action. To take a few examples, Thomas Lanquet, Robert Crowley and Richard Grafton between them gave Mary agency for depriving Edward's bishops, recalling Cardinal Pole, setting forth ecclesiastical injunctions, requesting the restoration of the pope, arranging her marriage, acting purposefully during Wyatt's rebellion, and causing 'open wars to be proclaimed between England and France'. However, they recorded the execution of Lady Jane, the apprehension of Elizabeth, and the burning of named martyrs in the passive voice without mentioning Mary's name at all.

Of course Mary was not thought totally blameless, but these chroniclers generally pointed an accusatory finger elsewhere, whether at Pole for sending down commissioners to examine Hugh Latimer and Thomas Cranmer, or at the bishops of Chester, Lincoln and Chichester for the burnings in Cambridge, or at the bishops in general for burning 67 men and women as late as 1557.[53] Even Crowley, who was the least inclined to exonerate the queen, did not turn her into a scapegoat. Although he bitterly commented that 'her byshops and she burned even to the laste breathe', it is noticeable that he mentioned the bishops first. Nor did Crowley remove responsibility from the laity who had remained in England and participated in the persecutions: 'the kyng, the quene, and all the commons', he recorded sternly, renewed the statutes 'for the punisshement of Christes people' and the advancement of Antichrist.[54]

At the same time, these Elizabethan chroniclers tried to be fair to the queen by recording her strengths as well as weaknesses. In particular, they described with evident approval the resourcefulness Mary had displayed during both her accession crisis and Wyatt's rebellion. At the latter time, she was depicted as acting purposefully as soon as reports of a rising had reached London: Crowley, Stow and Grafton noted that she immediately issued proclamations declaring Wyatt and Suffolk traitors; 'forthwith' ordered the city of London to provide 600 men; dispatched the duke of Norfolk to Kent 'with so much spede as might be'; and ordered the earl of Huntingdon to Leicestershire to withstand Suffolk.[55] Despite his strong Protestant credentials, Grafton seemed particularly impressed with Mary's courage during the crisis. He contrasted her behaviour with that of the Imperial ambassadors who were in London at that time, negotiating the Anglo–Spanish matrimonial treaty. While the ambassadors scurried away, Mary stood firm and rejected her council's advice that she should seek sanctuary in the Tower. Furthermore, to build up support in the city, she delivered her Guildhall speech which, reported Grafton, 'well satisfied' London's citizens. Finally, concluded Grafton, when the queen was told in error that Wyatt had won the day, she did not flinch but declared herself ready to enter the field of battle 'rather than to yelde one iote unto suche a traitor as Wyat, and prepared herself accordingly'. Grafton could not but admire her fortitude: 'more than marvayle it was to see that day, the invincible heart and constancie of the Queene her selfe, who beyng by nature a woman, and therefore commonly more feareful then men be, shewed her self in that case more stout then is credible'.[56] Grafton's words were repeated in both editions of Holinshed's *Chronicles*, but predictably Fleming tempered the praise by reminding his readers that Wyatt's sedition had only occurred in the first place because God had cursed Mary's reign.[57]

Why did Mary get off so lightly in the accounts of so many Elizabethan chroniclers, especially when it came to allocating responsibility for the unpopular religious policies and cruel burnings? It may be that some of them were merely following the long-standing convention of blaming evil councillors rather than their monarchs. Another possible reason is Mary's gender. At least until the St Bartholomew's Day massacre it was perhaps unthinkable to associate such cruelty with the stereotypical gentle and merciful woman. Aylmer's comment, quoted earlier, is relevant here. The most likely explanation, however, is that these men wanted to avoid offending Elizabeth by casting her half-sister in the role of Antichrist. Elizabeth's treatment of Knox provided a stark warning of the dangers of attacking Mary too directly and severely in print. Aylmer's lack of promotion during the early years of Elizabeth's reign may also have been noticed and attributed to his hard-hitting critique of her sister. Certainly Elizabeth preferred to pass over Mary's faults in silence, despite her readiness to be presented as a victim of her sister's government and to distance herself from Mary's style of queenship. In a speech to her first parliament Elizabeth recalled her treatment before her accession but refused to apportion blame for it, and declared that even 'if the whole cause were in my sister herself, I will not now burden her therewith, because I will not charge the dead'.[58] In all probability public loyalty to family and reverence towards monarchy lay behind Elizabeth's attitude, but so might have respect for Erasmus' dictum 'Rayle not upon him that is deade.'[59]

Fear of arousing Elizabeth's disapproval possibly persuaded other men to adopt a somewhat different tactic when writing about the persecutions. A number of ballad-writers and preachers preferred to excise Mary from their story altogether or to refer to her only very briefly, thereby apparently denying her any agency in the traumatic events of her reign. In a poem printed in 1569 to commemorate (or rather celebrate) Edmund Bonner's death, Lemake Avale blamed 'Butcher Bonner' for the burnings and omitted any reference to Mary's role in the persecutions; Avale treated the deprived bishop of London as an instrument of the pope and helper of the 'friars of Spain' but not the servant of the queen.[60] John Prime's Accession Day sermon of 1588 on the 23rd Psalm spoke of Elizabeth as the '*Tamquam Ovis*' saved by God from the 'butcher's hand', but he did not name the butcher. Likewise, he spoke of the persecutions and idolatry that followed 'when a Spanish Prince and an Italian Priest ruled England', but chose not to mention the Catholic queen.[61]

Mary made no appearance at all in John Rainold's sermon of 1584 delivered in Oxford, a sermon that included a brief history of the godly reformation. The preacher passed over in silence the Catholic interlude of Mary's reign, and told only of Henry setting forth the holy word, of Edward who 'began to purge England from Images, and Masses', and finally of Elizabeth who built on their work.[62] Thomas Brice similarly airbrushed Mary from history in his

1559 verse compendium listing and honouring the individual Marian martyrs. He even took steps to avoid using Mary's name in the title of his work, preferring to call her reign the period 'since the death of our famous Kyng of immortall memory Edwarde the sixte: to the entrance and beginning of the raign, of our souveraigne and derest Lady Elizabeth'.[63] But perhaps it was not only a wish to avoid offending Elizabeth that influenced men like Brice; a more subtle motivation may have been at work. Elizabethan Protestants memorialized the Marian martyrs by naming, wherever possible, each one of the individuals concerned, no matter what their social status. Conversely, by expunging Mary from their narratives, writers denied her the fame and commemoration usually accorded to monarchs, and attempted to efface her from public memory.

Elizabethan engravers, painters and their patrons took a similarly diverse approach to Mary in their depictions of the Tudor dynasty and monarchs of England. Gyles Godet's representation of her in his 'genealogie of all the Kynges of England' interestingly shows Mary alongside her husband but superior to him; so for example, on Philip's head is an open crown but on hers is the closed imperial crown, while the verse below points out that he 'raigned with hir as King, and yet was he/Not crownde'. More significantly perhaps, although the verse omits the encomia included under the portraits of the other Tudor monarchs, the tone is restrained and neutral: it maintains she 'allowed the Pope's authoritie/Erecting eke all Papistry agayne' but makes no mention of the burnings or military defeat that must have been uppermost in people's minds early in Elizabeth's reign when the woodcut was produced.[64] William Rogers's engraving of the Tudor dynasty produced in the 1590s is startlingly different. Based on an earlier painting, it follows its predecessor in presenting Philip and Mary as the paired opposite of Elizabeth who symbolizes true religion, good government, peace and prosperity; however, new verses are added to re-emphasize the contrast and condemn the Catholic queen:

> Queen Mary then the Royall Scepter swayd,
> With foraine blood she matcht and put down truth
> Which Englands' glory suddainly decayd
> Who brought in warre and discord by that deed,
> Which did in comon wealth great sorow breed.

Again no specific mention is made of the cruel burnings, but perhaps there was no need, as 'put down truth' and great sorow' said it all.

But at least Mary makes an appearance in this work: in an unattributed painting of 1597, Henry VIII, Edward VI and Elizabeth are depicted as 'Professors and Defenders of the True Catholicke Fyathe' while Mary – unsurprisingly given the inscription – is omitted altogether from the family portrait.[65]

Did one of the different views concerning Mary's involvement in the persecutions come to dominate her representation during the early Stuart period? Given the influence and popularity of the *Acts and Monuments* and Holinshed's *Chronicle*, we would expect, and indeed find, that Foxe and Fleming's condemnatory portrait of the queen prevailed. With Elizabeth dead, there remained no need for later writers to protect her sister's name. Furthermore, the popular hostility to the Spanish match in the 1620s and the fears of Catholicism engendered by the Thirty Years' War reignited negative writings about Mary and Philip.

Admittedly, apologists for Mary could be still found during James's reign, some of whom were widely read. William Camden, for example, described Mary as:

> A Princess never sufficiently to be commended of all men for her pious and religious Demeanour, her Commiseration towards the Poor, and her Munificence and Liberality towards the Nobility and Church-men. Howbeit her Days are ill-spoken of, by reason of the barbarous Cruelty of the Bishops, who (which was a sad Spectacle to behold) polluted England in all Parts thereof by burning the Protestants alive.[66]

Nonetheless, as Camden himself admits, the tide was turning decisively against Mary's reputation, and during the early seventeenth century she came to be personally identified with the burnings, becoming branded – at least implicitly – as Bloody Mary. Theresa Grant deals with some of these works in Chapter 4, but it is worth ending here with Christopher Lever's *The history of the defendors of the Catholic faith,* printed in 1627. In one of the vignettes on the title-page, Mary holds a banner depicting the burnings. Although beneath her are the words '*non natura sed pontificorum arte ferox*' (ferocious not by nature, but by the wiles of priests), in the text itself Lever explained that Mary was indeed directly responsible for the 'bloodie and horrible deeds to the great displeasure of God, and dishonour of her princely place'. Certainly she had listened to bad counsel, but so had Rehoboam and Catherine de' Medici. Mary was no longer portrayed as 'abused' by her clergy; instead she was 'monstrous in her evill'; her 'rare excellencies of nature' had to be dismissed as worthless in the face of her ungodliness.[67]

Foxe, Fleming and Lever's view did much to fashion the negative reputation of Mary that has dominated modern historiography. After all, the *Acts and Monuments* and Holinshed's *Chronicle* were long used as important sources for the reign. So, despite rejecting their providential paradigm, post-Enlightenment historians did not stray far from their path, continuing their emphasis on the 'disastrous' marriage, the bloody burnings, Mary's unhappiness and unpopularity. Only now is the story being retold.

Acknowledgement

I owe Thomas S. Freeman great thanks for his helpful comments and excellent suggestions.

2

Her Majesty, who is Now in Heaven: Mary Tudor and the Elizabethan Catholics

Victor Houliston

It would have been very impolitic, at best, during Elizabeth's reign to express a preference for her deceased royal sister Mary Tudor or to lament her passing too pointedly. Elizabeth's reign was by so much the longer that comparisons between the two queens, especially in retrospect, must have appeared imbalanced or disproportionate. Thus it requires an effort of the imagination to reconstruct, from the relatively meagre evidence, just how deeply Elizabeth's Catholic-minded subjects felt the loss of Queen Mary. Yet the queen who was gone had been recognizably the legitimate heir, where Elizabeth's birthright was open to question; Mary was chaste and wifely where Elizabeth's reputation needed some repair work; and whatever one felt about the burning of heretics there was never any doubt that Mary's faith was genuine and her concern for the spiritual health of her people passionate, where Elizabeth was ever the politician. There were strong grounds for loyalty to Mary and attachment to her memory. In reviewing the references to Mary Tudor in Elizabethan Catholic writings, we can detect several broad lines of development: the initial grief and pious affirmation of her virtue, the replacement of the residual Marian clergy with the missionary priests, the assessment of her policies in the context of the uncertainty about the successor to Elizabeth (which raised hopes of a second attempt at restoration under a new Catholic monarch), and the legacy of her programme of reform. To

be Catholic in Elizabeth's reign entailed some tough decisions, and
although it usually involved some nostalgia for the days of good
Queen Mary, such sentiment was overshadowed by the more urgent
questions of recusancy, loyalism and the role of the Jesuits. Still, Mary
Tudor was not forgotten.

Catholic Responses 1558–85

Mary's funeral, decently supported by the new queen, took place on
14 December 1558. John White, bishop of Winchester, delivered the
sermon and found himself under house arrest for praising Mary too
extravagantly. This was felt, records John Strype, to imply that 'he
too much depreciated her present Majesty'.[1] Apart from commenda-
tions of Mary's piety, clemency and care for her subjects, the most
striking element in Strype's summary of the sermon stresses her modesty and compliance in that she refused to be called the Head of the
Church like her father. She was a learned woman, but this she would
not take upon herself. White thus signalled the important constraint
on Elizabethan Catholics in their honouring of Mary's memory: the
Church was greater than the queen, so that although attachment to
the Catholic religion might be presumed to entail loyalty to Mary, the
latter was normally muted or even cursory.[2]

Funeral orations conventionally affirm that the deceased was too
good for this world, or, as White was reported to have said, 'That the
World was not worthy of her, and that she was too good to tarry any
longer here.' But the deaths of Queen Mary and Cardinal Pole on the
same day exercised the minds of those who struggled to discern the
hand of God in the Elizabethan religious settlement. Nicholas Sander,
writing to the Cardinal Protector of England, Giovanni Morone, in
mid-1561, found comfort in the steadfastness of the bishops, declaring
that 'it pleased God to try the faith of the good, and to make manifest
the evil designs of the wicked'.[3] According to his account of White's
sermon, the bishop had strongly warned of the danger of the 'rabid
wolves' approaching from Geneva. It was thus entirely the responsibility of the politicians if they 'cast themselves into the infernal pit'.[4]

For White, Mary's death represented the temporary triumph of evil
despite the best efforts of the faithful, according to the permissive will
of God: such an interpretation placed her history in a providential
framework elevated above commonplace eventualities. Sander's more
extended narrative is found in his *Rise and growth of the Anglican
schism*.[5] As the title implies, Sander's theme is the English Church's

breach of faith, a betrayal that had brought down the wrath of God:
he might well have appropriated a phrase from the Book of Common
Prayer, 'provoking most justly thy wrath and indignation against us'.
In this context, Mary's untimely death was all that the faithless people of England could expect; England was abandoned to her fate; this
was the hour of Satan and the power of darkness.[6] The Judas motif
surfaces again in a passage describing an encounter between Thomas,
duke of Norfolk, and a Catholic woman in a London street:

> 'When your grace,' she said, 'gave your vote – formerly given, and as you were
> bound to give it, for the defence of the Church and the Catholic faith – unto
> heretics and for the ruin of religion, you had probably forgotten that you and
> your family, brought to the very brink of ruin by the heretics, had been, by queen
> Mary of most blessed memory, saved and raised to its present rank: well! because
> you have done this, loving the praise of man more than the glory of God, God
> will punish you, and the rest of the old nobility who have had a share in this sin,
> by means of these very heretics and upstarts.'[7]

Even the premier Catholic nobleman of the kingdom, who was to
lose his life in 1572 as a consequence of the Ridolfi plot, failed to resist
the prevailing forces of apostasy when Elizabeth succeeded. Sander
renders the story of Mary's reign, as the last chance of redeeming the
country from error, even more poignant by his account of her accession. Drawing attention to her status as princess of Wales, he explains
the origin of the term 'Wales' as 'non-German', applied to Britons by
the Anglo-Saxons. 'The government or direction of this province', he
notes, 'is given only to him who is the heir of the reigning sovereign.'[8]
The intention is not only to stress Mary's legitimacy but to assert
the fully British nature of her Church, contradicting John Foxe's
attempt to differentiate between the true British Church, which was
proto-Protestant, and the Saxon Church, which was an alien Roman
planting.[9] In 1567, indeed, Sander had affirmed, in a preface clearly
directed at Foxe, 'concerning which is the true Church', that Mary
had reconciled the English Church to the true Church by submit-
ting to the papacy.[10] Without her, England was left desolate. Sander
offered up another earlier work, *The supper of our Lord* (1566), in the
hopes that 'thou wilt not suffer ... the truthe of thy gospel to be long
unrestored in the desolate Ile of pitifull England'.[11] Although Mary's
name is not mentioned, Sander evokes an image of bereavement that
was to become a staple of recusant writing. As late as 1599 the figure
of weeping Anglia dominated a short play composed for the Jesuit
school at St Omer.[12]

Sander died in the ill-fated papal expedition to Ireland in 1579–81. The simultaneous Jesuit English mission consolidated an important shift in Elizabethan Catholic mentality from clinging to the residual Marian Church to expecting renewal from the seminary priests. In this regard it was symbolic that Thomas Goldwell, last of the surviving Marian bishops, accompanied Campion and Persons towards England, but turned back at Rheims.[13] The plan had been that he should be reinstated as episcopal leader of the Catholic Church in England. Sander had written of him with admiration, but it has been suggested that William Allen, the genius of the Catholic Church in exile, distrusted him and was therefore relieved that he did not complete the journey.[14] This view is based on a 'Memorial on the English hospice, Rome', written around 1568, possibly by Allen, where an unnamed prelate, conceivably Goldwell, is presented as an exception to the rule of the Marian prelates' standing up boldly for the faith.[15] If the memorialist was indeed Allen – and there is no certainty – his assessment of Goldwell's behaviour at the time of Elizabeth's accession is unfair, and J. H. Pollen argues that Allen entertained hopes of Goldwell's contribution to a revived Catholic community in England. If the task proved too much even for Campion and Persons, it is not surprising, observed Pollen, that the aged Goldwell succumbed.[16]

Politics and Persecution

Goldwell's death in 1585 effectively marked the end of the Marian survival. Wisbeach castle, the mild prison for other Marian clergy, later became the site of conflict between Jesuits and seculars. Persecution began in earnest. Mary Queen of Scots became for a while the focus of Catholic hopes, and it is telling that little connection was made between her and Mary Tudor, despite the fact that (for example) the rising of the northern earls combined 'chivalric feelings of fealty' for Mary Queen of Scots with nostalgia for the ancient faith revived under Mary Tudor.[17] The weakness of association between the two Marys may have been a function of the transfer of English Catholic attention from Spain to France. After Mary Tudor's death, Philip II showed little interest in exercising his influence, as the former royal consort, to challenge the Elizabethan religious settlement, even if he did feel a responsibility to the Catholics in exile. In fact, he was more interested in keeping England out of the clutches of the French.[18] His ambassador to England, Gómez Suárez de Figueroa, first duke of Feria, ritually referred to the deceased queen as 'Her Majesty, who is

now in heaven', but reassured Philip that the popular opinion that she
had died of sorrow for his absence was a base calumny spread abroad
by 'this scurvy Lord Chamberlain Hastings'. His description of Mary's
death, tactful as it is, suggests that he had very little more respect for
her than her turncoat subjects:

> She had been unconscious most of the time since I arrived, but always in the fear
> of God and love of Christianity, indeed the nation soon sees what a good Christian
> she was, for since it was known that she was dying they have begun to treat the
> images and religious persons disrespectfully.[19]

The impression is given that Philip was well rid of the burden of the
English queen. There may be a sardonic touch in the term 'good
Christian', the evidence for which is not entirely flattering. In the
event, Philip, after half-hearted offering to marry Queen Elizabeth
in January 1559, was rapidly pursuing a new alliance: he proposed an
alliance with Elizabeth Valois of France in April. He did not, however,
join forces with Henry II (who died in July that year) or his successor,
Francis II, to intervene in England or Scotland at this crucial juncture,
so with the papacy inactive and preoccupied with the Council of
Trent, Elizabeth I was the more emboldened to pursue a religious
policy that was hard to reconcile with the assurances she had given
before her accession.[20]

Politically, the most promising development for English Catholics
thereafter was the proposed French match of 1579–81, but the break-
down of negotiations with Anjou (Alençon) embarrassed the Catholic
party at court, which then went into exile in France. The Lords
Paget and Arundel (as it appears) then directed their antagonism
towards Leicester, the queen's favourite, whom they accounted chiefly
responsible for their discomfiture. One of the charges made against
him in the notorious 'libel' they published in 1584, popularly entitled *Leicester's commonwealth*,[21] was that he had been instrumental in
Norfolk's execution for treason. Among the papers of Norfolk's son,
Philip Howard, is a manuscript, apparently one of the sources for
Leicester's commonwealth, which intensifies the accusation by noting
how the Catholic duke had successfully entreated Mary Tudor for
Leicester's life:

> [Robert Dudley, after treason to Mary, obtains mercy] ... by that thrice noble
> duke, the duke of Norfolke, too whome in most base manner the wreach
> came ... crep[ing] prostrate on the ground, beseching his grace to be a meane,
> if it were possible for the preservation [of his] life. Whose wreached case this noble

duke pitying, as one always preste to helpe the distressed, in fine [he] so labored with [the Queen] that, that which these leaste lookte for, he [obtains] a pardon for [his] treacherous life, which [he] full well requited, proving the [cause] of the duk[ke's] confutation.[22]

Political manoeuvres on behalf of English Catholicism thus made only subdued use of the memory of Mary Tudor. She was not a particularly strong card to play. In the propaganda wars surrounding the execution of Mary Queen of Scots in 1587 and the Spanish Armada in 1588 it was persecution that was stressed as a justification for military action, rather than (for example) Philip II's right to the throne. Given the subsequent reputation of 'Bloody Mary' and 'Good Queen Bess', however, it is notable how often Mary Tudor's policy was favourably compared with Elizabeth's. The most forthright defence of the Smithfield fires was given by Edward Jones before his own execution in 1590:

'And after the reign of Queen Mary (quoth he) there were great speeches and outcries for the burning of heretics, which was not done by any peculiar law made by herself, but by a law made and received & put in execution by all Princes Christian whatsoever, & when any heretics were taken they were brought to the Bishop, who with his Chaplains in all charitable sort sought by often conference to reduce them to their mother Catholic Church. But what may be said after in the reign of Queen Elizabeth when so many Priests & Catholics are butchered by a peculiar law made by herself & never heard of before, without all charity, except it be charity to carry them to Bridewell or to the Tower to be racked, or hanged against a wall by the arms, or some other torture, & that without any conference of religion, except it be religion to examine where he hath said Mass, who gave him any maintenance, who relieved him, or what money he hath in his purse, as you, Mr Topclif, did by me.'[23]

The martyr thus praises Mary's programme as charitable and religious, pursued always with the greater good of souls in mind, whereas Elizabeth's is purely a matter of policy. He also emphasizes the legality and antiquity of the proceedings by contrast with Elizabeth's innovation. This is zeal governed by precedent and good order. The implication that Mary's treatment of dissent was a matter of prosecution rather than persecution chimes with her own attitude, as recorded in her 'Directions . . . to the Counsell touching the reforminge of the Church to the romaine religion': 'me thinketh it ought to be done without rashness not lacking in the meane while to doe justice to such as by learning would seme to deceive the simple'.

The fact that there is a copy of this document in a seventeenth-century collection of materials relating to the reigns of Henry, Mary, Elizabeth and James suggests that this interpretation of the Marian policy as one of legitimate and restrained legal proceeding was alive alongside the more widely publicized version of John Foxe.[24] Foxe saw to it that Bishop Edmund Bonner was remembered as a bogey-man, but the nineteenth-century historians T. E. Bridgett and T. F. Knox attempt to refute the 'imaginative historians' who claim that Bonner was so unpopular that he had to be kept in prison for his own safety. They point out that in fact he was at liberty for almost a year before his deprivation in May 1559.[25] Indeed, he was only imprisoned on 20 April 1560.[26]

There was an uneasiness, nevertheless, among Catholics about the severity of the prosecution of heretics under Mary Tudor. Nicholas Sander found it necessary to defend Bonner by describing him as the victim of persecution:

> a man endowed with such greatness of mind that he has suffered infinite perse-cutions. For even some Catholics, assuming an air of pity, often found fault with him in persecuting heretics, having himself alone expelled from the Church and delivered to the secular arm more than all the other Bishops. To such this learned man was accustomed to answer that one death, by which many lives would be saved, was full of mercy.[27]

The reputation of Mary's inquisitors was therefore tied up with the status of the men and women they handed over to be put to death. Elizabethan Catholics' respect for Mary's memory depended largely on the pseudo-martyr debate. The argument to disqualify Foxe's martyrs, based on the Augustinian dictum '*non poena sed causa facit mar-tyrum*', was vigorously advanced first by Nicholas Harpsfield, then by Thomas Stapleton, and finally, and most comprehensively, by Robert Persons. In 1565 Stapleton published his *Fortress of the faith* to ques-tion the credentials of those who died for a faith other than that inherited from their forefathers.[28] Harpsfield devoted the sixth and longest of his *Dialogi sex* to a refutation of Foxe's account of the Marian martyrs.[29] When first Sir Francis Hastings and then Matthew Sutcliffe questioned the loyalty of English Catholics, Persons retaliated by composing his three-volume *Treatise of three conversions of England*, which sought to demonstrate that Catholics were faithful to the true ancient religion of England. The second and third volumes of the treatise comprised a month-by-month examination of the claims to

martyrdom of those commemorated in a mock calendar of mainly
non-Catholic saints prefixed to the 1570 and later editions of Foxe's
Acts and Monuments.[30]

Persons incorporates many of the arguments of Harpsfield and
Stapleton in his sustained critique. His emphasis is on the generosity
and compassion of the bishops, contrasted with the unlearned
stubbornness of the pseudo-martyrs. He satirizes as facile the tendency to 'jest, scoffe, doubt or deny. Which are points that are easily
learned, & pleasing to the corrupt humor of mans sinfull state and
condition.'[31] He relies on the exposure of the spirit of Protestant
dissent to affirm the validity of the inquisition: there is an implicit
defence of Catholic learning and tradition as something assembled
with care and courtesy over many centuries. The Marian hierarchy,
therefore, is presented as acting reasonably and in a crucial sense conventionally, that is, pursuing the ordinary procedures of the universal
Church. Such a view of Mary's treatment of heretics emerges in strong
contrast with the transgressive, disorderly, excessive and outrageous
operations of the Protestants, as Harpsfield, Stapleton and Persons
present them.

The Succession

With the failure of various schemes for military intervention in the
1580s – and the more dubious and murky assassination attempts –
the next succession came to represent the best hope for toleration
or restoration of the Catholic faith. This prompted serious consideration of the programme to be followed should a Catholic monarch
succeed Elizabeth. Mary Tudor's uncompleted restoration thus came
under scrutiny, especially by Allen and Persons. Persons's fundamental
position is outlined in two of his unpublished memoirs, 'A storie of
domesticall difficulties in the Englishe Catholike cause' and 'The first
entrance of the Fathers of the Society into England'.[32] He pays tribute to Mary's 'zeal and sincerity' but blames political complications
for her failure to establish an effective re-education programme; there
were just too many distractions. As a man of great organizing powers himself, he could empathize but was chiefly concerned with the
lessons learnt: the need for Church unity and the crucial role of the
Jesuits. Ironically, these priorities were to cause even greater friction
at the turn of the century, during the archpriest controversy.[33]

The notorious *Conference about the next succession*, which addressed
the question of God's approval of good and evil princes, made little

reference to Mary Tudor, but it did uphold the rights of women and foreigners to wear the crown. This was partly to secure the interest of the Spanish Infanta Isabella Clara Eugenia, against the powerful claims of James VI of Scotland. Whatever the motivation, it tended to counteract the image of Mary Tudor as an alien, associated with the 'monstrous regiment of women', a Protestant notion used by John Knox against Mary Tudor but studiously excluded from any discussion of Queen Elizabeth.[34]

Allen and Persons were both involved in the conception of the *Conference*, which finally appeared in 1595, after Allen's death.[35] Persons then undertook the design of a potential restoration for consideration by the infanta. In a letter dated 10 June 1601 he described to her how Mary Tudor's 'excellent intentions as to the rights and good of the Church before her accession [were] not carried out' (as the nineteenth-century index puts it). Persons wanted to cast the infanta in the role of a new and better Mary, sharing her high ideals and fervent devotion but better able, through his guidance, to plan her strategy. Human and divine providence might combine in the new reign: 'I put my trust in our Lord to whose divine providence this glorious enterprise has been entrusted.'[36]

Persons was ready, then, to play a shrewd Cardinal Pole to Isabella Clara Eugenia's more accomplished Mary. His blueprint for the restoration after Elizabeth's demise was laid out in *A memorial for the intended reformation of England*.[37] The most telling aspect of the *Memorial* for the light it throws on Mary's reputation is the proposed treatment of heresy. Persons defended the legitimacy of the heresy burnings but questioned the wisdom of renewing such a policy half a century later. Protestantism was too well established in the land for it to be treated under the old protocols according to which heresy was represented as a social threat by its outrageous contravention of all that bound the community together.[38] Instead, Persons proposed a series of public disputations that would discredit the Protestant heresy so convincingly and comprehensively as to require little more than a mopping-up operation thereafter.

Mary's Piety

Whatever Elizabethan Catholics thought of Mary's methods of coercion, they were united in paying tribute to the genuineness of her piety. Of Elizabeth's personal religion, as of William Cecil's, they were deeply sceptical: perhaps the most trenchant attack on the alleged hypocrisy of Elizabeth's religious policy is to be found in Persons's *Philopater*, published in 1592 in defence of the seminary priests accused of treachery in the aftermath of the Spanish Armada. Persons questioned whether Elizabeth and her counsellors spent much time in genuflexion, beating the breast or moving the lips in prayer.[39] Historians are now turning their attention to Mary's more positive programme of reform: church reconstruction, catechesis, devotional practice and the re-establishment of the religious orders.[40] It is noteworthy how Mary's pious intentions extended, in an attenuated and ghostly form, into Elizabeth's reign. Her entourage of Spanish theologians, headed by Bartholomé Carranza, left soon after her death,[41] but their legacy can be detected in the steady stream of works of Spanish devotion, especially by Luis de Granada, that reached England in translations printed in the Netherlands.[42]

There are bibliographical traces of the Marian reformation in such publications as the edition of Richard Whitford's translation of the *Imitatio Christi* printed by William Carter in about 1575. This was falsely dated 1556 so that it could innocently include the Fourth Book, 'Concerning the sacrament', mostly omitted in Protestant versions.[43] Antonio de Guevara's *Dial of princes*, translated by Sir Thomas North, was first published, with a dedication to Mary Tudor, in 1557.[44] Anthony Munday had this reprinted in 1568 and 1582, retaining the dedication, and the book accompanied Stephen Vallenger to prison in 1582 when he lost both his ears for possessing a manuscript copy of *A true report of the death and martyrdom of M. Campion Jesuit*. Given Munday's opposition to Campion, there was a certain irony in this, but it indicates how Spanish literature connected with Mary continued to circulate despite the divisions within Elizabethan Catholicism.[45]

Mary's restitution of the Benedictine house at Westminster Abbey was short-lived, but the memory was kept alive by Abbot John Feckenham, who was held in custody by Robert Horne, the Elizabethan bishop of Winchester. The two engaged in a well-publicized quarrel over the oath of supremacy, taken up by Thomas Stapleton in his *Counterblast*.[46] The best known of the English Benedictines of this period, Augustine Baker, acknowledged Mary's part in the preservation of the Benedictine tradition, but without dwelling on it.[47] There is a further association of Mary with the promotion of religious life in Robert Persons's preface to the *History of the wanderings of Syon*, relating to the fortunes of the Bridgettine nuns. A small party of nuns returned to the country briefly from 1578 to 1581, thus intersecting with the Jesuit English mission. Persons looked back with satisfaction to the restoration of the order under Pole and Mary, and saw the hand of providence even in their fortunes under Elizabeth, when the few who returned were dispersed and persecuted. However grievous it was that the community was split up during this time, they were given the opportunity, through persecution, to make 'a most constant and glorious confession of their religion'.[48]

Persons's desire to connect the English mission with the piety associated with Mary Tudor can also be seen in his resistance to Jasper Heywood's attempt to relax the severity of the fasts introduced in Mary's reign.[49] He recalled with pride his own vigorous determination to enforce the Lenten fast at Balliol College in 1574,[50] and the later conflict at Wisbeach castle when the Jesuit William Weston tried to enforce a more austere regimen among the captive Catholic priests.[51] These continuities may qualify our sense of the conflict between the secular priests, often associated with Marian survival, and the Jesuits at the turn of the century.

Amongst lay people the tradition of Catholic piety passed down from generation to generation included relics of Queen Mary's devotion. The 'Sydenham prayer-book', which dates back to the 1590s, contains a long prayer in English, headed 'GOOD QUEENE MARYES PRAYER: which she used everye mornynge all her lyfe tyme'.[52] The prayer is marked by strong personal feeling and moral rigour, and would certainly have reinforced the image of the late queen's deep commitment and zeal. Richard Smith, later to become leader of the English Catholics as the bishop of Chalcedon, recalled Mary's court in glowing terms in his *Life of Lady Montague*, composed as a funeral oration for the aristocratic Catholic lady who had spent her youth attending on Mary Tudor:

> For at that tyme the Court of England was a schoole of vertue, a nursery of purity, a mansion of piety. The Queene her selfe did shine as the Moone in all kind of vertue, whose prayses all histories doe record. Her Ladyes and women did glitter as the starres; and what shining starres they were, the Reader may conjecture by what I will relate of one of them from the mouth of the La. Magdalen. . . . O happy Court with such Courtyers! and happy England with such a Court! which for vertuous lyfe, gave not place to many Cloysters, & whence, as from a fountain-head, examples of piety did flow into all Provinces of England! Would to God this purity had continued in our Virgin Courtiers, and the Mother therof, the Catholike Religion, had still flourished; then had not the Court of England byn spotted with the notorious infamy of lasciviousness, as soone after it was.[53]

Here is a portrait of Mary's court that is as unfamiliar to the popular
English imagination as the curious description of Mary as a young
woman, fashioned in the sonneteering tradition by John Heywood:

> Shee maye bee well compared
> 	unto the Phenix kinde,
> Whose like hath not byn harde,
> 	that anye nowe can finde,
> In lyfe a dyane chaste,
> 	in truth Penelopye,
> In worde and deede steedfaste,
> 	what neede I more to seye...[54]

If Queen Elizabeth's figure stands in the background of the love son-
nets of her reign, and her famed learning is remembered in Ascham's
The schoolmaster, we do well to recognize that there was an alternative,
suppressed icon of the beloved wronged princess who reflected the
glory of Catholic Europe.

3

The Exclusion Crisis of 1553 and the Elizabethan Succession

Paulina Kewes

The reign of Mary Tudor has traditionally been viewed through the prism of persecution. Yet, from the moment of her death, the Marian regime was examined in the light of numerous issues, of which its harassment of reformers was only one. Towards the end of the sixteenth century, moreover, the interpretations of Mary's rule were becoming less negative, even her religious policy being occasionally judged no more harshly than that of her father and siblings.[1] Alongside confessional matters and relations with Spain, the chief concern that drove the reassessment of Mary's rule under Elizabeth was the question of the succession.[2]

Modern scholars have understandably focused on Mary as the principal target of the abortive coup designed to place Lady Jane Grey on the throne. But of course had the coup succeeded, Elizabeth too would have been a loser. The story of Edward VI's and the duke of Northumberland's attempt to divert the succession enjoyed a rich afterlife in historiography, public argument and imaginative literature. To trace how the 1553 Exclusion Crisis was recounted, represented, and reassessed during the reign of Elizabeth, as I do in this chapter, is not only to gauge the changing polemical uses of one particularly sensitive episode from the recent past but also to take measure of developments in political thought. Throughout the period, constitutional implications of the attempted exclusion of Mary Tudor were being variously reinterpreted by both Protestants and Catholics wishing to address, however obliquely, the succession to Elizabeth. My aim is to show how in dealing with the country's dynastic future, Elizabethan controversialists and imaginative writers sought to reconcile confessional concerns and the claims of blood and statute law, and what they made of ideas of exclusion and election.

The Marian Aftermath

David Loades, Diarmaid MacCulloch and most recently Dale Hoak have demonstrated that the plan to prevent Mary Tudor's accession and make Jane Grey queen was Edward's own idea rather than a nefarious plot hatched by Northumberland.[3] Contemporaries, however, either thought otherwise or found it convenient to say they did.

Why Edward was determined to bypass Mary is self-evident. He feared that as a Catholic she would wreck his religious settlement and return England to the papal fold. To explain his decision to exclude the Protestant Elizabeth is more difficult. The official reason given by Edward and publicized in print and from the pulpit was the alleged illegitimacy of both his half-sisters.

The exclusion of Mary and Elizabeth and enthronement of Lady Jane Grey would have effectively spelled out the end of the Tudor line. What were the constitutional ramifications of the scheme? As Mortimer Levine and other modern commentators have pointed out, Edward's 'Devise' was illegal.[4] Mary Tudor was the next in line as well as being designated heir in Henry VIII's third Succession Act (1544) and his will (1546). Jane was fairly distant in dynastic terms; not only Mary and Elizabeth Tudor but also Mary Stuart and Jane's own mother Frances Brandon had priority over her.[5] Moreover, Edward was a minor and could not draft a valid will. Nor did he have the right to alter his father's legislation and will by his letters patent even if he were an adult. The exclusion project thus violated both common law and statute law, though whether royal succession ought to obey these was not clear and would become subject of fierce debate under Elizabeth. One thing, however, is certain: statutory arrangements were taken more seriously than common law. The only legitimate way forward would have been for Edward's letters patent to have been ratified by parliament, which is what the king and Northumberland had hoped to secure.[6] Their bid was only prevented by Edward's premature death.

The proclamation of Jane as queen elicited little enthusiasm in the City of London.[7] Tellingly, the only man punished during her

nine-day reign was one Gilbert Potter who had his ears cropped
for asserting the rightfulness of Mary's claim.[8] In the immediate
aftermath of Mary's resounding victory, we find, predictably, dozens
of triumphalist Catholic poems, sermons, and pamphlets celebrating Mary's accession as nothing short of miraculous and denouncing
Northumberland as a rebel and traitor.[9] With the duke cast as the
chief culprit, Edward was not so much being exculpated as shown
to have been misled and manipulated, perhaps even poisoned by
him.[10] Protestants too affirmed the legitimacy of Mary's title, though
their professions of loyalty were implicitly conditional on the queen's
preservation and continuation of the Edwardine reforms.[11] They also
vilified the apostate Northumberland. The duke was a convenient
target for both Catholics and Protestants. The former exploited to
the full his ignominious recantation. The latter did not wish to be
tarnished by Northumberland's treasonable doings; and they were
thoroughly disgusted by his 11th-hour apostasy.

What of the evangelical exiles? There are relatively few references
to the failed plot to set up Lady Jane Grey in Marian resistance
writings. From Thomas Becon's *A humble supplication* in 1554 to
Christopher Goodman's *How superior powers ought to be obeyed* (1558)
and John Knox's *First blast* (1558), the emphasis is on the illegitimacy
of female rule. Goodman drew a contrast between the idolatrous
Mary and the pious Elizabeth; but rather than suggesting that
Elizabeth should have acceded to the throne instead of Mary, he
insisted that on Edward's death the 'meetest' man ought to have been
elected king.[12] Knox also called for election, though neither man
specified how the process would work in practice.[13] The exiles rarely
if ever referred to Jane and when they did, it was as a Protestant martyr, not a would-be-queen. John Ponet's *A short treatise of politic power*
(1556) is an exception. Ponet acknowledged the illegality of Edward's
will and the wrongfulness of the attempt to disinherit both Mary and
Elizabeth.[14]

The Elizabethan Exclusion Crisis

Unlike Mary's five years earlier, her younger sister's accession in
November 1558 went smoothly. For all the persecution of the godly
and subversion of the 'true' religion by the Catholic queen, to have
then described the attempted exclusion of Mary as in any way justified or legitimate would have been tactless given that had the plan
succeeded, Elizabeth too would have been cut out of the succession.

Moreover, the expedient of blaming Northumberland for concocting the plan and perhaps poisoning Edward was no longer available, given the rapid rise to favour of his son Robert Dudley (the future earl of Leicester), who had been extensively involved in the events in East Anglia in July 1553.[15] It is thus instructive to consider the earliest historical depiction of the abortive coup, which appeared in Robert Crowley's continuation of Thomas Lanquet's *Chronicle*, printed in April 1559. Divine, publisher, poet and formidable polemicist, Crowley, freshly back from Continental exile, was hardly in a position to endorse the scheme that would have meant the exclusion of Elizabeth. He nonetheless sought to exonerate the Protestant martyr Lady Jane Grey as well as painting in the darkest colours the atrocities of Mary Tudor's reign. Crowley's was not merely a forerunner of Foxe's more substantial martyrology; much of it was incorporated into the latter word for word. Like Ponet before him, Crowley conceded the illegitimacy of Edward's plan designed to prevent Mary's accession. Yet he emphasized that what the king had feared did indeed come to pass. Mary, the rightful heir according to statute, was used by God as a scourge.[16] Crowley established the basic contours of how the Marian succession crisis would be described in Elizabethan historiography, even if the stresses would be slightly differently distributed in abridgements by Grafton, Cooper and Stow and major projects such as Holinshed's *Chronicles*.[17] Stow, for one, avoided Crowley's providentialism. By contrast, Foxe in the *Acts and Monuments* de-emphasized the illegitimacy of Edward's plan and instead highlighted its potential benefits.

At the start of Elizabeth's reign, the relevance of the 1553 Exclusion Crisis to the nation's collective concerns appeared slight. Elizabeth was widely expected (and urged) to marry and procreate, and in the meantime, to regulate the order of succession by statute. But by 1561–2 the situation changed radically in the aftermath of three events: the return to Scotland of the principal dynastic claimant Mary Stuart; the revelation of the Suffolk claimant Katherine Grey's marriage to the earl of Hertford and her resultant pregnancy (both in August 1561); and Elizabeth's nearly fatal brush with smallpox in October 1562. The outcome was what Patrick Collinson has dubbed the Elizabethan Exclusion Crisis: the recurrent attempts to secure the Protestant religion by barring, through statute, the Catholic Mary Stuart from the succession, and the corresponding attempts made early in the reign to persuade Elizabeth to recognize as heir the Protestant Katherine Grey.[18]

Militant Protestant opponents of Mary Stuart repeatedly stressed that her advent would spell a return to popish tyranny akin to that perpetrated by her Tudor namesake. Yet the advocates of exclusion were careful not to draw parallels between the measures they were proposing and the illegal bid to exclude Mary (and Elizabeth) Tudor that Edward and Northumberland had sought to effect back in 1553. While maintaining resolute silence about that earlier Exclusion Crisis, they justified their opposition to the Stuart title on the grounds of the Scottish queen's foreign birth and Henry VIII's will, which privileged the Suffolk line over the Stuarts.[19] John Hales's tract calling for recognition of Katherine Grey as the rightful heir (1563) studiously avoided any reference to her elder sister's abortive seizure of the throne.[20]

Unlike Hales, whom Elizabeth incarcerated for speaking out of turn, John Foxe ostensibly stayed aloof from the unfolding succession debate. However, his handling of the 1553 crisis provides telling clues about his position. We would not turn to the 'Book of Martyrs' to learn about the rules of succession. On reading it, however, we might well conclude that primogeniture does not always work to the country's advantage, and that in such circumstances altering the normal course of succession might not be amiss. For all Foxe's protestations of the inscrutability of divine decrees, his account of how 'our young Josiah' Edward VI attempted to divert the succession from Princess Mary in favour of Lady Jane Grey suggests that in this instance the martyrologist might have welcomed a violation of the hereditary principle. 'Albeit he in his will had excluded his sister Mary from the succession of the crown, because of her corrupt religion', writes Foxe, 'yet the plague which God had destined unto this sinful Realm, could not so be voided, but that she being the elder and daughter to king Henry, succeeded in possession of the crown'.[21] Foxe's readers must have come away from his book with an abiding sense that there are more important things to look for in a king than the strongest lineal claim. For Foxe religion comes first; and he would have readily agreed with the Jesuit Robert Persons that to exclude a claimant of a contrary faith is not only desirable but strictly necessary.[22]

If the advocates of excluding Mary Stuart refrained from drawing parallels between their plans and the Edward–Northumberland abortive exclusion of Mary Tudor, their Catholic opponents were quick to exploit the similarity. Chief among them was John Leslie, bishop of Ross, one of Mary Stuart's staunchest supporters. By castigating Mary's deposition from her Scottish throne as illegal and her son's coronation as 'unnatural', and by making the vindication of the Scottish queen's hereditary title to the English crown the centre-piece of his *Defence of the honour of the right high, mighty and noble princess Mary queen of Scotland and dowager of France* (1569), Leslie effectively exposed the exclusionists as proponents of both election and resistance. His strategy is rather clever. '[T]he noblemen of this our realm', he says disingenuously, 'acknowledge and accept her, for the very true and right heir apparent of this realm of Englande'.[23] Anyone who does not is by default no better than Knox and the Scottish insurgents.

There is every hope, writes Leslie, that Elizabeth will have issue of her own body. In the meantime, however, it is imperative to reaffirm Mary Stuart's right to succeed her 'by the nearest proximity of the royal blood'.[24] Leslie disposes of the common law objection to the Scottish queen's title on the ground of her foreign birth, and questions both the authenticity and validity of Henry VIII's will. Imperceptibly sliding from a denial that the will was genuine to a supposition that Henry did in fact frame it, Leslie draws a parallel between the current attempts to exclude Mary Stuart and the abortive exclusion of Mary and – Elizabeth – Tudor in 1553 which Henry's tampering with the succession had set in train: 'And did not, I pray you this drift & device fall out even so, tending to the utter exclusion of the late Queen Marie, and our gracious sovereign Elizabeth' (fol. 92r). In a passage which would not be out of place in John Aylmer's *A harbour for faithful and true subjects* (1559), and which targets parliamentary speeches such as Sir Ralph Sadler's[25] as much as Knox's *First blast*, Leslie inveighs against those who wilfully ignore the constitutional difference between elective and hereditary regimes and credit the people with the right of choice which properly belongs to God. Denouncing the exclusionists as upholders of 'free and voluntary election and choice of a king', Leslie insists on the prevalence in England of 'birth & succession, wherein we have none interest: but God, who is the only judge and umpire, and has by his divine providence made to our hand his choice already, which if we would undo and reverse, we might seem to be very saucy and malapert with him' (fol. 136r). To oppose Mary Stuart's claim, he argues, is tantamount to opposing divine will.

Neither the attempts to persuade Elizabeth to allow for the succession to be determined by parliament in her lifetime nor William Cecil's plans for an interregnum in the event of her childless and heirless death succeeded.[26] The Treasons Act of 1571 prohibited debate about succession and made publication and dissemination of writings dealing with the issue an offence punishable in the first instance by a year's imprisonment and forfeiture of half of one's goods.[27] Implicit in the opening clause of the Act was the idea that the ultimate assessment of the various titles to the crown would take place in parliament. The queen's resolute refusal to countenance any such public airing of the matter made the prospect of a parliamentary settlement in her lifetime remote.

Such debate as there was became perforce confined to surreptitious pamphlets, mostly by Catholics. In them, references to the attempted exclusion of Mary Tudor sometimes function as a means of libelling the pillars of the Elizabethan regime: the earl of Leicester and William Cecil, Lord Burghley. Catholic pamphleteers excoriated Leicester as a corrupt favourite; and they gleefully recalled the unsavoury past of Leicester's father, the duke of Northumberland. One of the most poisonous of the libels, *Leicester's commonwealth* (1584) which, like Leslie's *Defence*, sought to defend the Stuart title, predictably trotted out the plot to set up Lady Jane Grey in place of Mary Tudor so as to impugn Leicester's supposed attempt to advance the House of Huntingdon to the crown. The pamphlet also charged him with conniving to become king himself.[28] Overall, however, *Leicester's commonwealth* had little new to contribute to the succession debate.[29]

The years 1584–5 mark a shift in the thinking about the succession on both sides of the confessional divide. Until then Catholics had been by and large legitimists. Conversely, Protestants had seemed to favour a quasi-elective solution predicated on the disabling of the Catholic Mary Stuart and a subsequent parliamentary determination of the succession. That was the thinking behind the Bond of Association and the Act for the Queen's Surety, as well as the plans for an interregnum prepared by William Cecil and Thomas Digges.[30] From the mid-1580s onward, some Catholics, notably the expatriate Jesuits, concluded that to stand by the Stuart title might not be politic given that the Scottish queen's son had been brought up as a Protestant. Like their counterparts in France, thenceforth they began to entertain quasi-elective solutions not far removed from those once advocated by Knox and Goodman, in which religion was the chief criterion of the suitability of the candidate for the throne. At the same time some Protestants started seriously contemplating a Stuart succession after Mary.

The Late Elizabethan Succession Crisis

The decisive turning point was, of course, Mary Stuart's execution in February 1587, although we find a fascinating premonition of later developments in the second edition of Holinshed's *Chronicles* which was only released for publication after Mary's death. The *Chronicles* registered the concluding stages of the Elizabethan Exclusion Crisis. The book also anticipated the onset of a new national emergency: with Mary gone, English Catholics might well turn to the House of Spain, instigating a pamphlet campaign in support of their favoured candidate (an English or a foreign Catholic) and bringing upon England a foreign invasion backed by the pope.[31] We find hints of that sort of settlement of the succession in Cardinal William Allen's *Admonition to the nobility and people of England and Ireland*, which was timed to coincide with the Spanish Armada of 1588.[32] The fullest statement of the Catholic theory of election (and resistance) in the aftermath of Mary Stuart's beheading was the Jesuit Robert Persons's *A conference about the next succession to the crown of England* (1594/1595).[33]

Neither Persons's argument in favour of combining heredity with election, nor his contention that religion is a legitimate ground for exclusion of a lineal heir, needs rehearsal here. Less well known is Persons's astute if opportunistic manipulation of the Edward/Northumberland plan to secure a Protestant succession in his bid to secure a Catholic succession to Elizabeth. First deployed in the English context by the Marian exiles in the late 1550s and now revived by Catholics such as Allen and Persons, the language of election became pervasive in the clandestine writings produced during the late Elizabethan succession crisis. The prominence of election in turn-of-the-century political discourse is attested, we shall see, by two literary treatments of the 1553 coup.

Persons's *News from Spain and Holland* (1593), an important forerunner of the *Conference*, invoked the events of 1553 in order to vilify Burghley (and rile James VI of Scotland) in a manner similar to the attack on Leicester in *Leicester's commonwealth*. The piece is written partly in the form of a dialogue. One of Persons's mouthpieces charges Burghley with a plot to engineer the succession so as to safeguard his own monopoly of power. Like Suffolk and Northumberland, who 'when all men looked for a Mary Queen ... came forth with a Queen Jane, and so may this man ... with some Arbella Queene or the like, when least it is expected'. Fanning James VI's anxieties about his title, and preying on the king's aversion to Burghley as the instigator of his mother's death, Persons hints that 'the lot shall fall upon some woman or child' – Arbella Stuart was 17 at the time – 'whom he may govern as he has done hitherto, for under any male prince of age, he will never willingly live'. Given the uncertainty of the dynastic claims of the various pretenders, and given his near-absolute sway over the queen, Burghley, Persons alleges, will be in an unequalled position to make his own 'choice' of successor.[34] Beyond the obvious aim of lambasting Burghley, however, the reference to the machinations designed to prevent the accession of Mary Tudor in the *News* does not carry any substantive ideological weight.

Conversely, in the slightly later *Conference about the next succession*, Persons used the memory of that earlier crisis to score points against his hypothetical Protestant detractors. Like Leslie before him, Persons here placed on a par Henry VIII's will and Edward VI's 'Devise' for excluding Mary (and Elizabeth). But whereas Leslie had argued that both these schemes were equally invalid and potentially harmful, Persons credited them with equal constitutional legitimacy. And he mounted a defence of exclusion by statute which would have appealed to militant Protestants, who after Mary's execution tried to persuade Elizabeth to allow parliament to determine the succession in what would effectively amount to a form of election. The threat posed by the popish queen removed, Protestant Englishmen were hopeful that Elizabeth would at long last name her preferred heir or else allow parliament to attend to the succession. The obvious candidate was James VI of Scotland. His accession, however, could entail a new settlement of religion as well as raising the thorny issue of Anglo-Scottish relations. So there might be a case for placing some conditions on the Stuart succession, perhaps even limiting James's royal power. Yet before any such matters could be fielded in the forum of parliament, on Elizabeth's orders the privy council clamped down severely on those who sought to broach them, notably the Puritan MP Peter Wentworth.[35]

Persons's promotion of religion as a legitimate ground for excluding a hereditary heir and a crucial criterion for electing a new monarch, no less than his open endorsement of resistance, sent shockwaves through the political world. The Jesuit brought out into the open the contest between confessional allegiance and constitutional principle which had remained under-articulated during the Protestant campaign for exclusion. In doing so, he undertook a wholesale revaluation of England's constitutional make-up. At the heart of his case were arguments drawn from history, notably the country's recent past, such as the 1553 conspiracy to block the accession of Mary Tudor, which his opponents now had to confront. Although Persons's *Conference* elicited numerous refutations from both Protestants of various confessional stripes (Peter Wentworth, Sir John Harington,

John Hayward, Sir Thomas Craig) and an equally varied assortment of Catholics (Englishmen and Scots, Jesuits and secular priests), their hostile responses were hardly free from the language of election.

In conclusion I turn briefly to two late Elizabethan literary works, one a poem predating the release of the *Conference*, the other a play which postdates it, both of which depict the 1553 exclusion crisis and Mary Tudor's successful ascent to the throne. William Warner's *Albion's England* is a verse history which, starting with the first edition of 1586, was progressively expanded and updated. In the 1592 edition, Warner tackled the late Tudor past. Like Crowley and Foxe before him, Warner found it hard to reconcile his admiration for the Protestant Jane with the need to condemn the plan to bypass the Catholic Mary in her favour. Even as he conceded the illegality of the scheme and acknowledged Mary (and Elizabeth's) better title, Warner presented Jane, the 'queen elect', as worthy of the throne because of her virtue and piety. In portraying the nobility, dignity, and fortitude in death of Jane and her husband Guildford Dudley, Warner was adamant that they were the innocent victims of others' machinations.

For all his castigation of Mary Tudor's reign as 'a tragedy to England meant from Rome',[36] Warner was not harsh or unsympathetic towards the Catholic queen, whose uncommon courage he freely acknowledged. The 'seduced Mary' was neither '[b]lamelesse' nor 'all to blame'. She experienced, moreover, a fair share of personal misfortune which, though Warner does not say so explicitly, might have been a punishment for her 'moste tyrannous Raigne' and 'triftles Mariage with the trustles king of Spaine'.[37] Philip II was a known philanderer, and like many a hapless royal consort before her, Mary had to endure his infidelities. Rather than dwelling on her persecution of the Protestants, Warner invented an imaginary exchange between her and an unnamed attendant, in which the latter related at length Queen Eleanor's murder of her husband Henry II's paramour Rosamund. Here is an object lesson for Mary on how not to behave: as the following exemplum of a long-suffering wife demonstrates, her best course is patience and submission. Mary, it seems, died of a broken heart. Even though 'Her death did many a good mans life from Tyranny redeeme',[38] the reader cannot but feel compassion for the popish queen's pathetic end.

Finally, I turn to a play conceived in the aftermath of the furore created by Persons's pamphlet. Taking as its theme the accession of Mary Tudor and the suppression of Wyatt's rebellion, *Sir Thomas Wyatt* by Thomas Dekker, John Webster, and others was produced in 1602, in the wake of the Essex rebellion and only a year before Elizabeth's death.[39] Drawing on Foxe's 'Book of Martyrs' and Holinshed's *Chronicles*, the play reassessed Edward VI's and Northumberland's manoeuvres.

In the play, the architects of the coup insist on figuring it as 'Lady Jane's election'; and they cite Edward's will in support of it. 'You are by the king's will, and the consent / Of all the lords, chosen for our queen', Arundel tells Jane.[40] She is repeatedly referred to by her champions as 'the queen elected' even if her husband Guildford and Jane herself acknowledge her to be a usurper.[41] Wyatt, who stands up for heredity, stresses that there is no historical precedent for election when a legitimate, lineally descended heir is alive. To enthrone Jane would be wrongfully to bypass both Tudor sisters. 'In actions roving from the bent of truth', he says, 'We have no precedent thus to persist / But the bare name of worldly policy'.[42] Contrary to the historical record, the stage Wyatt defies the plotters and proves instrumental in ensuring Mary's triumphant accession. We are, it seems, led to condemn the coup as a failed usurpation instigated by a pair of overweening noblemen on behalf of their reluctant and essentially innocent children. Yet as the action unfolds, and the now securely installed Mary decides to pursue a Spanish match as well as breaking her promise of religious toleration to the Protestants, the spectators are invited to revise their original view of what the play intermittently calls election. The once strongly legitimist Wyatt now rises against the queen; and although his rebellion is hardly condoned, the play goes out of its way to paint in the darkest colours the despotism of the popish regime.

Like Persons's *Conference*, *Sir Thomas Wyatt* pits confessional concerns against the claims of blood and statute law. Foxe ultimately eschewed endorsing Edward VI's unconstitutional remedy designed to prevent the accession of his Catholic sister. Warner tied himself in knots trying to avoid offending Elizabeth even as he made plain that Jane would have been a better ruler than Mary. *Sir Thomas Wyatt's* graphic depiction of the bigotry and brutality of the Marian regime, epitomized by Jane and Guildford's trial and execution, heightens the pathos and makes for a strongly emotional audience response. At the play's end, the intimation that the need to safeguard Protestantism might justify the exclusion of a legitimate heir is all but inescapable.

In his early political writings, *The true law of free monarchies* (1598) and *Basilikon Doron* (1599), and in the letters to Sir Robert Cecil and others at the English court written in the aftermath of the Essex rebellion, James VI of Scotland persistently invoked the rhetoric of divine-right hereditary kingship. Cecil echoed that rhetoric in what was technically a treasonable correspondence in which he engaged with James following Essex's fall. Cecil employed natural metaphors – 'cutting', 'grafting', 'the natural branch', 'wild stock' – to signal his acceptance of James's lineal claim. 'God hath instituted [your majesty]', he acknowledged, 'to sit (in his due time) in the chair of state.' Cecil also spoke of election even as he drastically redefined the term. In order to dissuade the king from seeking public designation as heir or indeed doing anything that might savour of too great a regard for popularity, he cautioned that 'although it be a common rule with many rising princes to refuse no address, yet you will find it in your case that a choice election of a few in the present, will be of more use than any general acclamation of many'.

Here election stands neither for the formal choice made in and by parliament nor for a popular vote. Rather, it denotes the secret pledge of support by the powerful few. Cecil is not using the word 'election' innocently or unadvisedly. He expects that James will be alive to the gulf between the meaning he attributes to it and the definition current in the writings of Persons and other pamphleteers. Cecil's counsel, moreover, contains a submerged warning. Should James attempt to exploit the promises made to him by 'the extraordinary persons (though small in number)' in order to 'increase a publicke party', their backing might well be withdrawn. For James to do so would be pointless anyway, 'it being ordinary for the vulgar to follow better example, without any such precedent insinuation'.[43]

The polemicists engaged in the late Elizabethan succession debate invoked history first to assess the viability of a range of constitutional solutions, and second to probe the claims of the various pretenders. The use of history by contemporary playwrights and poets was remarkably similar to that of the prose pamphleteers. History plays and poems as much as the succession tracts provide parallel assessments of the benefits and drawbacks of both election and heredity. In imaginative literature as in public polemic, the contest between Mary Tudor and Lady Jane Grey was the key exemplum from the country's recent past. The accession of James VI of Scotland in 1603 ostensibly marked the triumph of indefeasible hereditary right. Yet my reconstruction of the turn-of-the-century reinterpretations of the Exclusion Crisis of 1553 by both polemicists and imaginative writers demonstrates that in late Elizabethan England the idea of electing a monarch was seriously considered as a potential alternative to lineal succession.

To recognize that from the 1590s onward Lady Jane Grey's ascendancy was figured by both Catholics and Protestants as a form of election is to realise not only how contemporaries rationalized the past but also what ideas and expectations they might have had of the future. It is perhaps also to recognize that James's accession to the English throne was not, as the authors of both his proclamation as king and the parliamentary act of recognition claimed it was, a natural outcome of his lineal and indubitable right, but rather, a tacit decision to disregard legal impediments to the Stuart title – Henry VIII's will, the bar against foreigners inheriting in England – and thus a *de facto* election of the best candidate for the job. One way or another, the succession debate which had rumbled on throughout Elizabeth's reign, and which gathered momentum in the last decade of her life, provides a salutary reminder that Mary Tudor and the events of her reign were being continually reappraised in the light of contemporary political concerns and objectives.

Acknowledgements

The work on this chapter was made possible by the generosity of several institutions: the British Academy and the Huntington Library which awarded me a Visiting Fellowship at the Huntington; the Arts and Humanities Research Council which granted me a term's leave; and Jesus College and the English Faculty at Oxford, both of which provided much-needed travel grants. I am grateful to Dr Thomas S. Freeman, Professor Dale Hoak, Professor Diarmaid MacCulloch, and Professor Blair Worden for valuable comments on earlier drafts.

4

'Thus Like a Nun, Not Like a Princess Born': Dramatic Representations of Mary Tudor in the Early Years of the Seventeenth Century

Teresa Grant

In 1624, at the height of the political crisis engendered by Prince Charles's 'Spanish Match', a wisely anonymous writer penned *Vox coeli*, or *News from heaven*, a pamphlet in which Henry VIII, Edward VI, Mary I, Elizabeth I, Anne of Denmark and Prince Henry debate the motives of the Spanish and the desirability of the marriage from a British perspective.[1] When the rest of the company is assembled they are suddenly seized with doubt as to whether they should also admit Mary into their council, finally deciding that she will be more useful than not:

> at last ... considering that she knew many secrets of Spaine, wherof peradventure they were ignorant; as also from her innate and inveterate malice to England, she might (either in jest or earnest) bewray somthing that might turne and redound to the good of England, they all consented that she should be advertised hereof, and so admitted.[2]

The caricature of Mary Tudor which follows does indeed present her as being blindly partisan to the Spanish cause, a cause which the pamphleteer reveals to be intimately tied to her Catholicism. Mary defends any assault by Spain – military, diplomatic or romantic – on the country on the grounds that Protestant England comprises 'an heretike King and People, who refuse to enter into the bosom of the Church' and, in such circumstances, the Pope will encourage any attempt at 'the displanting and rooting out of Heretikes, and the establishing and preservation of the Romane Catholikes in England'.[3] Hispanophobia had reached fever pitch by the end of James I's reign and because of her Spanish marriage Mary Tudor provided an obvious stick with which to beat those pushing for another Spanish match. The anti-Spanish feeling of 1623–4, as has been amply demonstrated by Jerzy Limon and others, prompted a direct response from playwrights and playing companies, most famously in Thomas Middleton's *A game at chess*.[4] Mary Tudor's representation in *Vox coeli* shows how useful she was in 1624, and how straightforwardly she was perceived by those of the anti-Spanish party, but it was not for this unflattering portrait of her that the author John Reynolds was jailed but for expressing his disapprobation of royal policy. Mary's supposed views had become useful shorthand for exposing the evils of the Spanish and the Catholics, and it is notable that the persecution of Protestants during her reign is not a major feature of Reynolds's attack.

Twenty-five years earlier things were not quite as black and white: this chapter will show that Mary's representation in the dramatic writings of the early years of the century just before and after James acceded to the English throne demanded careful negotiation of contemporary political issues. In this transitional period for the English monarchy, Mary appears in two plays – Thomas Heywood's *If you know not me you know nobody, Part 1* (1605) and Dekker and Webster's (et al.) *Sir Thomas Wyatt* (1607). In Samuel Rowley's 1605 *When you see me you know me*, she also writes a letter, some of which is read out to the audience by her brother, Prince Edward. *Sir Thomas Wyatt* shows how playwrights sought to position the Stuarts in relation to their predecessors, but that they did differentiate between these Tudor predecessors with polemical purpose, using Mary Tudor to underline the playwrights' support for the rightful monarch while reminding the monarch that with rights go responsibilities.[5]

Sir Thomas Wyatt is a curious play; the only texts we have are the corrupt versions, possibly pirated, printed in 1607 and 1612, some years after it was originally composed in 1602.[6] There is a further complication: Arthur Melville Clark suggested in 1931 that both

Sir Thomas Wyatt and *If you know not me you know nobody, Part 1* (and three scenes in *Part 2*) were originally part of the two-part *Lady Jane*.[7] Indeed, the contributions we believe Heywood to have made to *Sir Thomas Wyatt* and his handling of the same material in *If you know not me, Part 1* are remarkably similar, but this is better explained, as Mary Forster Martin does, as Heywood recycling ideas from his sources and his previous work rather than reusing actual chunks of text.[8] Clark also refuses to believe that *The overthrow of rebels* and *Lady Jane* are the same play, suggesting that the former dramatizes the 1569 uprising against Elizabeth. In fact, all we really know about the 1602 plays are their titles, and we cannot even say for sure whether *The overthrow of rebels* is a subtitle for *Lady Jane* (Part 2?) or a play in its own right.

However, Julia Gasper is almost certainly correct in assuming, even if only from these titles, that the earlier plays were written as a response to the Essex rebellion. From what we know about the practice of the playwrights concerned with regard to their source material in other cases, Gasper's hypothesis holds water – the subtle changes made to the source material for Wyatt's rebellion do draw direct and deliberate comparisons with Essex's attempt to take London in 1601.[9] However, it is very difficult to ascertain with any real certainty how the scenes in *Sir Thomas Wyatt* featuring Mary would have played in 1602, or even if these scenes as we have them were included in the *Lady Jane* plays. Indeed, one argument would be that impersonating the monarch's sister on stage was a risk better not taken, no matter how flattering this portrayal would be (and, in the text we have, it is not that favourable). Because we cannot say for sure that these scenes were even included in 1602, this chapter mostly investigates the intervention that this act of publication made into the public political debate in 1607, though it also touches in passing on its possible intervention into the cultural politics of 1602. The most important questions, perhaps, are why pirate the play and what might be the reasons for and repercussions of the portrayal of Mary that it contained? Obviously, a first stage in this investigation has to be a detailed consideration of this portrayal.

The Representation of Mary in *Sir Thomas Wyatt*

There are only two scenes – I.iii and III.i – in the extant play in which Mary actually features.[10] This is significant in two ways: it is a small number of scenes, and the fact that Mary's appearance does not open the play indicates that she is not one of the major characters, a fact we could already have gleaned from either title (*Sir Thomas Wyatt* or *Lady Jane*). Indeed, the sequence of scenes at the start of *Wyatt* shows the narrative and dialectic method used throughout. The nature of the problem – a dying king and a succession struggle – is set out in I.i by introducing the fathers of one set of claimants to the throne (the Protestants Jane Grey and Guildford Dudley) and then Sir Thomas Wyatt as a spokesman for the true succession in the persons of the daughters of Henry VIII.

It is worth noting that even at this stage in the play, in Northumberland's first long speech, Mary cannot claim a starring role: she is part of a package, 'the King hath left behinde, / Two sisters, lawfull and immediate heires, / To succeed him in his Throane.' (ll. 14–16). Even Mary's major supporter, Wyatt, speaks of the wrong done to 'those Princely Maides' (l. 30), his fury at the diverting of the succession being based not on a fondness for Mary but on his sense that heredity is paramount. As becomes apparent later, the play (as were many of the same era, such as *Richard II* which was also used during the Essex rebellion) is much concerned with the problems that occur when the monarch's body natural so distorts the body politic as to threaten the stability of the kingdom – particularly, in this case, in matters of religion. This is a issue that the playwrights probably took from John Foxe, who notes right at the start of his narrative of Mary's reign not only that Edward VI's will 'did appoynt . . . Ladye Jane . . . to be inheretrice unto the crowne . . . passing over his two sisters Mary and Elizabeth', but also that the charges laid against Mary that cut her out of the succession were that she would marry a stranger and alter the religious settlement.[11] There is an insistence in *Wyatt* on Sir Thomas's argument that the proclaiming of Queen Jane may have been done with the right motives – 'for religions love his simple act' (I.iv.81) – by the dying king and his councillors, but that it is illegal:

> We have no president [precedent] thus to persist
> But the bare name of worldly pollicie.
> If others have ground from Justice, and the law,
> As well divine as politicke agreeing,
> They are for no cause to be disinherited. (I.vi.67–71)

The play deliberately foregrounds the hereditary right of both princesses – Mary and Elizabeth – as a way of making clear that it does not support Mary's religious or marital policies. Wyatt's justification of his rebellion to Winchester (Bishop Stephen Gardiner) is

simple: 'here's the end of Wyats rising up, / I to keepe Spaniards
from the Land was sworne, / Right willingly I yeelde my selfe to
death . . ./But now King Phillip enters through my blood' (V.ii.32–4,
37). On the other hand, in III.i Wyatt does not react to Mary's revo-
cation of her oath to preserve the Edwardine religious settlement in
return for the aid of the men of Suffolk in defeating the usurpation
of her throne. In the corrupt text we have, rather than being played
out as it is in *If you know not me Part 1*, this is simply an allusion that
the readers of the 1607 quarto were clearly expected to understand
(probably from having seen Heywood's play recently): 'Your sacred
Highnesse will no doubt be mindefull / Of the late Oath you tooke
at Framingham' (III.i.22–3).

Wyatt and Norfolk do protest at the lack of mercy shown to Jane
and Guildford Dudley – 'your next of blood . . . deserves some pit-
tie' (49–50); 'They were misled by their ambitious Fathers' (52). It is
notable that this lack of mercy might seem to have offered the playwrights an opportunity to adumbrate the Marian persecutions, but it
is not a hint they follow up, preferring to concentrate on Mary's religious error rather than her persecution of those who disagree with
her. So, it is not until the Spanish marriage is offered as a *fait accompli*,
and Wyatt's arguments that it is contrary to Henry VIII's will, ratified
by an act of parliament (crucially, unlike Edward's will, which Wyatt
has just rejected as illegal) are summarily dismissed by Winchester and
Mary, that Wyatt feels he has no option but to rebel. These ideas about
the right hereditary claim to the throne would be appealing to both
the monarchs of 1602 and 1607, and a rejection of the primacy of the
Suffolk line equally welcome (though, of course, to spare James's feelings the playwrights do have to gloss over the fact that Henry VIII's
'legal' will famously privileged the Suffolks, putting them next in line
after his own children, to the detriment of the Stuarts).

As far as Elizabeth's sentiments over the succession could be ascer-
tained, she seems to have privileged the claim of the Stuarts over
the Suffolks.[12] For James, of course, a play that supports the notion
of direct heredity as the only guiding principle of succession – and
which specifically rejects as 'worldly pollicie' even the terms of a
king's will – keys directly into his own conviction that his claim to the
English throne is undoubted and by inherited right.[13] Furthermore,
the coincidence of names with which Mary Tudor may remind an
audience of James's mother, Mary Queen of Scots, avoids offending
in the play's treatment of Mary Tudor's peccadilloes. Though they
were both Catholic, critical treatment of that religion is safe ground

for a play being examined by a Calvinist king; and the anti-Spanish sentiment cannot be said to be a coded criticism of Mary Stuart, as she famously depended upon the 'auld alliance' with France, a nation conspicuously absent from *Wyatt*. Finally, the insistence upon hereditary right bolsters rather than demeans Mary Stuart. Though James might publicly deplore the forced abdication of a rightful monarch, hers had done him no end of private good, and he could always protest that it was none of his doing (since he had been so young when it happened). Indeed, he could in some ways claim to be the restitutor of her right.

Throughout the play, Mary's presentation continues to be dependent upon viewing her either in tandem with Elizabeth's right, or in opposition to Lady Jane Grey's superior character. I.ii, the scene in which we are introduced to Jane and Guildford, comes immediately before Mary's first appearance and pointedly offers an alternative to her in ways that cannot be considered to be in Mary's favour. Jane's meekness and her grasp of her 'proper' role as a woman are shown in her description of her marriage to Dudley as 'I doe injoy a Kingedom having thee' (I.ii.15). This metaphorical parallel between marriage and monarchy speaks to Mary's later choice of bridegroom, where she entangles the realm in a threesome by choosing badly. By 1607, of course, the idea that Elizabeth had married her realm instead of a husband was a commonplace, and Jane's mental rejection of the crown in *Wyatt* in favour of matrimony – the flip-side of Elizabeth's choice – should be read as a further suggestion that queens, particularly, must prioritize their bodies politic over the natural in the interests of the realm. Of course, this is advice that playwrights also encouraged kings to take, but at least the gender politics of marriage in the seventeenth century permitted a king to be head of his family as well as his realm.

Jane also manages to tick many other 'ideal woman' boxes in this scene: she is convinced, in Dudley's words, that as queen she 'wouldst prove but an Usurper' (I.ii.24), indicating her own rectitude and her rejection of what she calls 'thoughts so ranke, so growne to head, / As are our Fathers pride' (ll. 13–4). She also shows a disinclination for the pomp of the world, as any good Protestant should: she would as soon be housed in a 'Sheep-cote' as a 'fairest roofe of honour' (ll. 17–8) and rejects the 'fetters' of monarchy, 'though they were all of golde' (25).[14] The meeker Jane is, the more we notice the facets of Mary's character in the next scene which contrast with her cousin's behaviour. The scene-change between I.ii and I.iii physically juxtaposes the princesses: as Jane exits, her parting words a prophecy of her doom, Mary enters for her first appearance in the play 'with a Prayer booke in her hand, like a Nun' (I.iii.1SD). This description indicates that there was capital to be made by the physical contrast of the two women, as well as in their words.

I have noted elsewhere that Heywood (who is the most likely candidate for this scene's authorship) reuses many of the tropes from Mary's first speech in *Wyatt* I.iii in Elizabeth's speech praising the English Bible in *If you know not me Part 1* (1578–98), indicating an expedient oppositional method of characterizing the queens and their religious doctrine.[15] Playgoers of the time were used to reading meaning across as well as within plays, and as the responsive titles of Heywood's *If you know not me* (for Queen Anne's Players) and Rowley's *When you see me you know me* (for the Prince's Company) indicate, this was not confined to plays by the same playwrights or even for the same company. Perhaps especially in these plays which drew so heavily on Foxe too, audiences could be expected to recognize the stories and the characterizations of the main characters from a kind of shorthand which depended on their knowledge of ballads and chronicles that treated the same material, a good example being Mary's oath at Framlingham, discussed above.[16]

It is this oppositional method that makes the treatment of Mary less straightforward than it might be; cheek-by-jowl with Jane's meekness and unworldliness, Mary's first speech has an ambiguity which might otherwise be lacking. Of course, the stage direction dressing her as a nun identifies her as Catholic, and an audience would draw the correct critical conclusion from that in itself. But Mary's first speech identifies her as an unhappy Nun, 'ruinat[ing]' (I.iii.5), as she complains, while her brother 'Edward lives in pompe and state' (4). In direct comparison to Jane's lack of worldliness in the previous scene, Mary's immediate drawing of attention to the status she should enjoy – 'a Princesse borne / Descended from Royall Henries loynes' (1–2) – reveals the playwright playing a clever double game. Mary's decision to forsake courtly 'pleasures . . . pride and honour' (7) for 'a rich prayer book' (8) might seem laudable, were it not for the wrong-headed doctrine of the prayer book she has chosen and for the way in which the speech seems to protest too much that the prayer book is richer than empire.

In the light of Jane's rejection of the throne and the trappings of worldly glory, Mary's 'pride and ambition' (terms associated with the fathers of Jane and Guildford Dudley in the previous scene) are shortly revealed when it turns out that the prayers she has been so fervently making with the aid of her missal are that she become queen: 'I see my God, at length hath heard my prayer' (22). Though the formal structure of her argument is similar to Jane's, in that it ostensibly rejects worldly wealth, her very Catholicism sets her up as a hypocrite and gives her claims that Edward's court enjoys 'rich attire' and 'delicious banquetting' (6) more than an overtone of envy. In the early seventeenth century, Protestant playwrights had a mental habit of considering the Catholic Church to be irredeemably hypocritical and worldly.[17] Furthermore, in the case of our first glimpse of Mary in *Wyatt*, this kind of prioritizing of wealth over spiritual well-being is prophetic of things to come. In III.i she states her intention to bribe the nation to accept a return to Catholicism:

> Wee heere release unto our faithfull people,
> One intire Subsidie, due unto the Crowne
> In our dead Brothers daies. The Commonaltie
> Shal not be ore-burdned in our reigne,
> Let them be liberall in Religion,
> And wee will spare their treasure to themselves (28–33)[18]

This shows a political expediency directly in contradiction to her claim in I.iii that the 'rich prayer Booke' is 'the joy, and comfort of the poore' (8; 11). In the speech that marks her triumphant entry in state as queen at the start of Act III, Mary continues to show her obsession with worldly grandeur, promising not only to restore the 'ancient honours due unto the Church' (7), but to do so in an ostentatious way, clearly contrasting with Protestant religious practice, and also with the styles of dress adopted by Protestant noblewomen (see note 14):

> Zeale shall be deckt in golde, Religion
> Not like a virgin robd of all her pompe,
> But briefly shining in her Jemmes of state,
> Like a faire bride be offerd to the Lord. (11–14)

Again, at the end of this speech, Mary equates the material riches of religion with the spiritual, offering as justification for physically redecking the Church 'better a poore Queene, then the Subjects poore' (17). An audience, of course, would recognize the irony that was intended here, with the wrong-headed queen choosing physical riches and spiritual poverty – made even clearer, as we have seen, in her intentions of bribing her realm to accept Catholicism.

The imagery of this first speech in III.i also draws attention to the marriage question, severally relevant to Mary's own subsequent decision to wed Philip of Spain, to the juxtaposition of Jane and Mary in *Wyatt*, and in the passing nod the play would have given in 1602 to Elizabeth's decision not to marry. If we accept that the material would have been intended in 1602 to celebrate the cult of Elizabeth's virginity rather than criticize it (which would have been foolhardy), then we have to read Mary's comments here as revealing her to be misguided.[19] The adumbration in metaphor of what the playwrights present as her rushed and ill-advised marriage to Philip draws attention to the greater wisdom of her younger sister in retaining a virginal Church and a virginal self.[20]

We have seen also the purposeful contrast the playwrights offered in the first act between Jane's happy marriage and Mary's sterile and unhappy life in the 'Cloyster' (I.iii.33), and this theme is continued in the third act. At first thought, the prospect of marriage would seem to offer the playwrights an opportunity to allow Mary an escape from the overtones of sterility and Catholicism with which they tarred her in the first act, but it is clearly not one they wished to exploit. Instead, in comparison with the (historically inaccurate) love match between Jane and Guildford presented in I.ii and continued even more forcefully at the start of III.ii, Mary's match to Philip is shown to be a result of Spanish plotting and Mary's desperation to love and be loved.[21] The same dramatic method used to such good effect in the first act – where a scene containing one queen supplants one featuring the other, pointing up the parallels – is repeated but the order reversed this time to reflect the ascendancy of Mary.

Whereas Jane and Guildford follow the Spanish marriage 'negotiations' in III.i with protestations of their interdependent love – 'my lovely Dudley' (III.ii.2), for instance, insisting that 'In my Janes joy, I doe not care for care' (8) – the previous scene demonstrates nothing so much as Mary's credulity, susceptibility to flattery and the poor advice she receives. While the physical nearness on stage of Jane to Guildford (they always appear together) is intended to underline the genuine affection they have, poor Mary is forced to fall in love with an image: 'lovely Princely Philip, / Whose person wee have shrined in our heart / At first sight of his delightfull picture' (III.i.62–4). Of course, this icon reflects Catholic idolatry and what has been shown already as her tendency to privilege outward show over inner worth. But this 'love' of Philip also contrasts strangely with her cloistered existence in I.iii, where she would have had us believe her to have actively forsaken the court and the world for her religious devotion. The quick change from using the idolatrous missal as a focus of her religious fervour to meditating in worship on her suitor's image undercuts the value of both her religion and her betrothal.

One of Wyatt's objections, that Spain's seeking her hand '[is] policie deare Queene, no love at all' (III.i.136), is cynically reversed by Winchester, who finally recognizes Mary's vulnerability to the notion that she is sought as a women as much as a queen. In fact, Wyatt has already argued that Mary's beauty should be a rich enough prize for any suitor, and that Winchester's notion that Philip is doing Mary and England a favour is scandalous (84–92). Wyatt pedantically uses the word order of Winchester's 'this iland and our Queene' (100) to try to demonstrate to Mary the true nature of the marriage proposal: 'Pardon me Madam, hee respect your Iland / More then your person? thinke of that' (101–2). Wyatt, and the playwrights, set forth important legal barriers to the match (such as Henry VIII's ban on all Spaniards in England) and point out that, as a result of Mary's marrying Philip, there would be very real disadvantages to the nation, particularly a Spanish control of English wealth tantamount to slavery.

A theme that *Wyatt* and *If you know not me* share is an exploration of the sovereign's ability to judge the true value of counsel and her (and, by extension to James, his) responsibility to accept the good and reject the bad. Mary in both plays is shown to be too easily swayed by counsel which accords with her own wishes. In her first scene with Wyatt, when he urges her to leave the cloister and fight for her crown, she admits that 'Your Counsel, good sir Thomas, is so pithy / That I am woon to like it' (I.iii.41–2), but an audience recognizes that this advice is what she wants to hear. However, the scene also shows Mary to be too dependent on Wyatt – he rather than she formulates the plan that takes her to Framlingham to raise troops – and she is somehow un-regal in her too-accepting attitude to advice (though in this case it happens to be correct). In III.i, having substituted Winchester for Wyatt as her main counsellor, the flaw in her method becomes much clearer since, by choosing a Catholic prelate over a valiant Englishman, Mary lays the country open to the sorts of unsuitable influences that threaten national sovereignty by privileging her religion and her fancy (in the case of her 'love' of Philip) over the needs of the nation.

In III.i, as we have seen, Mary rejects Wyatt's advice three times when she goes back on her oath to retain the religious settlement, takes the harder line urged by Winchester over Jane and Guildford, and uses his support to suit herself in the matter of marriage. Mary's

way of dealing with dissent is to threaten to execute Wyatt if he does
not shut up. Her next line shows a callous disregard for the truth of the
situation when she asks the gathered lords if 'With one consent . . . you
like this match?' (150), knowing full well that at least one of them
has been prevented from fully expressing his objections, and also that
anyone else of that opinion is hardly likely to protest if their 'over-
boldness should bee payde with death' (148). The poor counsel Mary
receives is also a theme in *If you know not me Part 1*, where she is said to
be 'much besotted' with the prelates who are her main advisors.[22] In
Heywood's play this is deliberately set against Elizabeth's recognition
of the commonalty both as her responsibility and her rightful advisors,
a theme that Elizabeth exploited in real life too.

In *Wyatt*, Jane's response to counsel is also used to throw Mary's into
relief: although Jane is forced by her father and father-in-law to usurp
the throne, she does so with a reluctance and a vocal resistance, which
retains her moral integrity. Mary's behaviour in both plays contradicts
the realizations of Jane in *Wyatt* and of Elizabeth in *If you know not
me* that there is a divinely-ordained pattern for English rulers (which
fits with the playwrights' own perceptions, of course) which relies
upon precedent, tradition and a legally based negotiation with the
commonalty enshrined in parliament. Mary's riding roughshod over
the law reveals her weakness, relying on the promptings of her prelates
and the authority of the pope when she should be supreme governor
of her own Church and country.[23]

Mary's refusal to consult properly, and particularly her lack of
respect for the House of Commons, was something to which
Reynolds' pamphlet also harked back in 1624, when Elizabeth accuses
her sister thus: 'you onely proposed [the match with King Philip] [to
the parliament] but for forme, and had secretly concluded it before
hand your selfe'.[24] When Mary protests that she 'had reason to follow
her own Judgement, not [parliament's] Passions', her father retorts:
'you contrariwise followed your own passion, not their Judgements'.[25]
This notion of Mary as ruled by feminine passion and lacking in real
judgement, which we have seen in her scenes in *Wyatt*, had become
commonplace by the end of James's reign.

The Political Context: 1602

Playwrights did try to suit their thematic treatment of Mary to their
understanding of the reigning monarch's expectations of what was
acceptable, though this was not always clear. Because the memory of

her reign was comparatively fresher and her kinship to Elizabeth much nearer, Mary would have been a much more sensitive subject before the Stuart accession. Playwrights and authors had got themselves into real trouble with the authorities when writing 'history' plays which mapped too closely onto contemporary events, and no one would risk a wholly unflattering portrait of the queen's sister, however Catholic she had been.[26]

Early in the century the exact royal policy of Elizabeth towards Spanish aggression was not easy to fathom. In the popular mind, of course, it was clear – because she defeated the Armada in 1588 – that Elizabeth was robustly anti-Spanish but not all of her subsequent actions actually demonstrated this. Her dithering about sending relief to Calais in 1596 lost the port to the Spanish, and the earl of Essex's spectacular but ultimately fruitless Cadiz expedition of the same year suffered from the queen's lack of enthusiasm and strong leadership, and provoked another Spanish armada.[27] But the anti-Spanish polemic in *Sir Thomas Wyatt* would have received public approval at all the key moments of the play's dissemination.

In 1602, the probable year of its first composition in some form, the ongoing war between England and Spain had been given added piquancy by the notion, put about in the 1590s by such Catholics as Robert Persons, that the infanta was Elizabeth's rightful heir. The fall and execution of Essex also meant that the anti-Spanish cause has lost its main spokesman, and a restatement of Spain's calumnies was overdue, especially in a play which uses Wyatt's rebellion as a cipher for Essex's. In the play, for Wyatt the final straw is Mary's refusal to listen to sensible counsel in the matter of Spain's menace; for the playwrights, and for posterity tracing the spiritual Protestant militaristic link from Sidney to Essex to Prince Henry, Elizabeth's ignoring Essex's just insistence on the importance of military action against the Spanish is another explanation for what he claimed was an attempt to remove her bad counsellors.

But the play is also careful to ensure that enough ambiguity exists in the portrayal of Mary to exculpate its authors in the event of royal disapproval, and does make a real attempt to play to Elizabeth's inter- ests. The insistence on Mary's right is, as we have seen, presented as intimately bound up with Elizabeth's own. The criticism of Mary's Catholicism and her hispanophilia are unexceptional, especially when one possible reading – it could at least be argued by a playwright in a tight spot – of her inability to take good counsel is that it is so difficult to find good counsel from Catholic advisers and she has been led astray by her religion. I would argue that in these scenes there is, in fact, a coded warning to Elizabeth that she needs to look again at her councillors, but it is a reading that could be as easily denied by playwrights as proved by the Star Chamber.

The Political Context: 1604/5

James's foreign policy – largely successful until 1619 – depended upon his balancing diplomatic relationships with European Protestant and Catholic powers against each other, and avoiding war with one side and direct aid to the other. One of James's first diplomatic acts on his arrival in his new kingdom was to seek peace with Spain, successfully concluded in the Treaty of London of 1604. Early in his reign, two plays featuring Mary respond to this peace-making: Rowley's *When you see me you know me* and Thomas Heywood's *If you know not me you know nobody, Part 1* (both plays were printed in 1605 but it is hard to determine which was written first).

In the first, the generous welcome afforded to Emperor Charles V (a Spanish Habsburg) by Henry VIII and his son argues forcefully for an 'un-Elizabethan' attitude to Spaniards in concert with James's peace manoeuvres. Princess Mary, however, is not celebrated in this forgiving spirit: Prince Edward is so disgusted by the Catholic nonsense of her letter to him that he abandons reading it halfway through. This reflects the subtlety of James's foreign policy, where he was prepared to come to terms with foreign powers as long as the settlement allowed him to maintain that the pope had no earthly jurisdiction.[28] James Ellison has also argued that many plays of 1604/5 respond to what some Protestants saw as too much royal toleration of the Catholics, and urge James to return to the more repressive policies of his predecessor.[29] Certainly, the dismissal of the Catholic Mary's letter in a matter of nine lines (2397–405) and a celebration of the right doctrine, as espoused by Elizabeth and Prince Edward himself, shows us a playwright recalling for James the errors of Catholicism.[30] Even though he may be prepared to accept, and even support, the peace with Spain, Rowley wishes to remind the king that domestic policy is another matter.

The portrayal of Mary through her letter depends, as it does in *Wyatt*, upon an unfavourable contrast with Elizabeth, as representatives respectively of Catholic and Protestant doctrine. Mary starts her missive 'The blessed Mother of thy redeemer, with all the Angels and holy Saints to preserve thee of Idolatrie, to invocate the Saints for helpe' (2399–401), a direct contradiction of Elizabeth's epistolary advice some ten lines later: 'let thy prayers / Be dedicate to God onely.../And give thee grace to shun Idolatrie' (2411–12; 2416). Edward's assessment of the reason for Mary's errors is also familiar when it puts the blame on those bad counsellors who lead her astray: 'These are thy blinded Tutors, Bonner, Gardner, / That wrong thy thoughts with foolish heresies' (2403–4). The oppositional method from Wyatt is also apparent in Edward's backing of Mary's suggestion that Cranmer and Bonner go head-to-head in a religious disputation (2382–3), pitting, as it does, his advisers against his Catholic sister's. Since this is the only part Mary plays in *When you see me*, we have to conclude that Rowley introduces her purely as a means of representing the religious divide, underscoring that, even as early as 1605, she is a stock character 'Catholic'.

The first part of *If you know not me* actually stages Mary as queen. As in *Wyatt*, the playwright's method is oppositional, and concentrates on showing, almost scene by scene, how superior Elizabeth is to Mary.[31] The play also stages Mary's Spanish husband who, rather surprisingly, comes off better than she, showing a regard for Elizabeth and good sense that the queen manifestly lacks. This might also be part of the differentiation playwrights in 1604/5 seemed to make between foreigners, who could not help being Catholics, and the English (especially the monarch) who should know better. James's 1604 rapprochement with the Spanish may be the underlying cause of this representation of Philip, but it is a trick Heywood is unable to repeat in the second part of the play (1606), which stages the Spanish Armada of 1588, a historical event which any English playwright would really struggle to spin in favour of the Spaniards (and indeed, after the Gunpowder plot, none would want to).

The Political Context: 1606–7

Wyatt was probably printed in 1607 to feed the post-Gunpowder Plot appetite for drama that showed the Spaniards in a bad light. The years 1606–7 saw a flurry of plays which critics have noted respond to the Plot. In the case of Dekker's own *The whore of Babylon* or Part 2 of Heywood's *If you know not me* this is done by restaging the defeat of the Armada to remind the audience of the threat from Spain.[32] Although the official line was that the Spanish had nothing to do with the plot at all, many Protestants of the time, and for many years to come, thought otherwise.[33] It is in this context that the 1607 edition of *Wyatt* was printed, possibly pirated but almost certainly not quite as it had been in 1602. There might have been a revival performance in 1606/7, which could explain why the play was printed in bad quarto, perhaps as a memorial reconstruction. We could speculate about the changes that might have been made, suspecting the playwrights of cutting and pasting so as to draw attention to Spanish iniquity and to the errors into which Catholicism leads even the great.

As we have seen, the play (as we have it) appropriately keys into James's interests in hereditary right and in the heinous crime of rebellion, while also tactfully suggesting that perhaps peace with Spain was not such a good idea after all. In 1612, when the play was reprinted, it responded to the idea of a Spanish match for Prince Henry, an idea which reared its ugly head once more (it had also done so in 1604–5) in diplomatic balance to the Palatine marriage that had been arranged for Princess Elizabeth. In contrast to the plays of 1604/5, no attempt is made in the 1607 *Wyatt* to temper criticism of the Spanish or to encourage a rapprochement. This is also a contrast noticeable between the two parts of *If you know not me*, the second part clearly being a response to the events of November 1605, in its portrayal not only of the Armada but also of domestic attempts on Elizabeth's life.

Why Use Mary?

The period 1604–7 marks a particular political moment where a negotiation of the issues raised by the change of government took place, and where the repertory system of the London theatres allowed this discussion to take place in the public domain, if in coded terms. The three plays in which she appears show Mary to be primarily useful as shorthand for Catholic or for hispanophile, and that in her portrayal as representative of these things playwrights were able to stage the political and religious negotiations of these years, conveniently mapped onto those of Mary's reign. However, playwrights also took the opportunities offered by other facets of Mary's reign, most notable in *Wyatt*'s treatment of her right to the throne, which flattered or bolstered the king by association.

There is a real difference – complicated by the fact that we have no extant 1602 text of *Wyatt* – between those plays written and printed before the Gunpowder Plot of 1605 and those that were printed or written as a response to it. This pertains particularly to their treatment of the Spanish: in *When you see me* and *If you know not me, Part 1*, James's peace policy is given a chance and the Spaniards are

not such bad sorts after all. In the 1607 *Wyatt*, though, the major
threat to England and right religion is Mary's unwise decision to ally
herself with Spain, a reflection of public opinion which saw the Gunpowder Plot as renewed evidence of Spanish untrustworthiness. But
Mary's Catholicism is never forgiven and forgotten in any of the plays;
it prevents her again and again from doing her duty as an English-
woman and as a monarch because the advice she receives is tainted
with papal self-interest. However, the Marian persecution of Protestants is not a strong feature of the plays, perhaps because this would
force too critical a reading of a former monarch's behaviour for either
of the later incumbents to stomach, or possibly because, in a climate
where playwrights were trying to encourage James to crack down
on Catholics, a mixed message would be sent by plays that criticized
religious persecution, albeit of another flavour.[34]

If the use of Mary in these three plays shows anything, it demonstrates that Protestant playwrights were more consistently concerned
with domestic Catholicism at the start of James's reign than with
Spanish interference in English affairs. *Wyatt*, the only dramatic
response to the Gunpowder Plot that actually includes Mary, is
notably the one that was written well before the plot took place, and
concentrates on the dangers of hispanophilia as one of the results of
bad Catholic advice rather than as something to be criticized in itself.
Most importantly perhaps, there is a very real sense in all of the plays
that it is not possible, as some English Catholics claimed, to be a loyal
English subject and a Catholic.

5

Inventing Bloody Mary: Perceptions of Mary Tudor from the Restoration to the Twentieth Century

Thomas S. Freeman

The myth of 'Bloody Mary' is like a shadow: dark, without substance and apparently destined to follow its subject, England's first sovereign queen, forever. The myth was not created in the sixteenth century and it was not an immediate response to the events of her reign. Instead of being forged in the dying embers of Smithfield, the myth originated in the constitutional turmoil of the late seventeenth century. It grew and intensified throughout the eighteenth century, as Mary came to be perceived as the epitome of the qualities that historians of the period thought most undesirable in a monarch. The myth was modified significantly in the nineteenth century, in response to changes in the ranks of those who wrote history and those who read it. The form that the myth took in the nineteenth century was given definite and enduring shape by A. F. Pollard, whose portrait of Mary remained essentially unquestioned throughout most of the twentieth century. The historiography of Mary Tudor reveals surprisingly little about the actual queen, although it reveals a great deal about the historians of her reign. But an examination of the myth of 'Bloody Mary' does provide an essential starting point for an accurate assessment of Mary Tudor, by showing that many of the commonly accepted views of the queen rest on nothing more than the crystallized prejudices of bygone eras.

By the time of the Restoration, the passions aroused by Mary Tudor's reign had begun to subside. Although, as events would demonstrate, the fear of Catholicism remained potent among English Protestants, the example of Mary Tudor no longer seemed particularly relevant. Oliver Cromwell could be – and was – accused of many failings, but that of harbouring a secret desire to impose popery on the three kingdoms was not among them. Nor, at least at the beginning of Charles II's reign, were there widespread fears that the king would return the realm to Roman rule. This lack of relevance fostered a certain detachment, and in the twilight of the Protectorate and the dawn of the Restoration, historians, while hardly admiring, were so restrained in their assessments of Mary that, in effect, they praised her with faint damnation.

Thomas Fuller, in his *Church history*, printed in 1655, was surprisingly lenient in his depiction of the queen. Fuller followed Foxe's interpretation in that he characterized Mary as melancholy and unsuccessful, and of course, he denounced the persecution of Protestants. Nevertheless Fuller also praised Mary's piety, honesty and generosity, and he went to declare that 'she had been a worthy princess, had as little cruelty been done under her as was done by her'.[1] Peter Heylyn, in a work printed six years later, was scathing about Mary's reign, which he declared was 'only commendable in the brevity or shortnesse of it'. Yet he also conceded Mary's personal virtues and he further praised her, albeit somewhat grudgingly, for her benefactions to the clergy and the universities.[2]

This qualified appreciation of Mary was shattered by the conversion of James, the duke of York, and heir to the throne, to Catholicism, which was made public in 1673. Charles II's own sympathies for Catholicism had already become apparent, and confidence in his commitment to the 'true religion' was further undermined by the fact that one of the king's chief ministers, Lord Clifford, was a Catholic and another, the earl of Arlington, had Catholic leanings. Of even greater concern than influential Catholic men were influential Catholic women: two of the king's most prominent mistresses, Barbara Villiers and Louise de Kérouaille, were Catholics. Nevertheless, this situation, while disquieting, was hardly unprecedented: each of the Stuart monarchs had had Catholic wives, favourites and confidants.

Having a professed Catholic as a potential monarch was more novel (the situation had not arisen since the execution of Mary Stuart in 1587) and far more dangerous. The situation grew more acute as it became increasingly apparent that Charles II would not sire any legitimate children and that the duke of York would indeed become king. James's Catholicism dominated political life; it destroyed a ministry, created a determined parliamentary opposition and nurtured an atmosphere of persistent fear and unease. However, it was the accusations of Titus Oates, made in the late summer of 1678, of a Popish Plot to assassinate Charles II, place James on the throne and restore Catholicism in England, that led to what has come to be known as the Exclusion Crisis. Three consecutive sessions of parliament – in March 1679, October 1680 and March 1681 – were dominated by unsuccessful attempts to enact legislation excluding the duke of York from the succession.

In these circumstances, the life and reign of Mary became strikingly, and to many horrifyingly, relevant. The efforts to prevent the duke of York from becoming king were based less on anything that James had actually done, than on widespread, shared fears of what he would do.[3] And these fears arose from the expectation that a future James II would be, in the words of an anonymous pamphleteer in 1681, 'Queen Mary in breeches'.[4] In particular, this meant that, as the Whig propagandist Elkanah Settle warned, should the duke of York ascend the throne, a persecution 'as Bloody or Bloodier' than the one in Mary's reign would follow.[5] Another polemicist luridly elaborated on this theme:

> If we consider how much protestants suffered, what numbers of them were burnt at the stake, as well as murdered in gaols . . . and what endeavours of all kinds were used for the extirpation of our religion under Queen Mary, we may gather and learn from thence what is to be dreaded from James II, who is the next popish prince to her, that, since the Reformation, hath sat on the throne of England.[6]

Graphic, indeed melodramatic, accounts of Mary and the horrors of her reign were central to the arguments for abandoning the hereditary principle and barring James from the throne.[7] This propaganda was disseminated in media that would maximize its popular impact: tracts, broadsides and even drama. In 1680 one play, *The coronation of Queen Elizabeth*, was performed at the Bartholomew and Southwark fairs before being printed.[8] This work emphasized the horrors of the Marian persecution and its victimization of ordinary people. And there are numerous indications that these messages took hold within the

popular imagination. In 1683, for example, Robert Homes, a yeoman from Stepney, told his neighbour's wife that 'Popery is coming
into the kingdom and if the duke of York should succeed his brother,
he would be a worse popish tyrant than ever Queen Mary was.'[9] The
anonymous author of a treatise arguing against Exclusion was forced
to admit that the 'severe persecution of Queen Mary' was 'sufficient
to have begot an eternal hatred in the nation of any future popish
successor'.[10]

 This hatred also manifested itself in an increasing vilification of
England's first queen regnant. Some writers of the period maintained
that Mary was fundamentally decent – a lingering vestige of the older
tradition of Fuller – but that Catholicism itself made her cruel. As
one writer put it, Mary, 'though she was not of a bloody, or of an ill
disposition in her self, yet her religion obliged her to those cruelties,
which have at once left an indelible stain upon her memory'.[11] However, even this very qualified approbation became increasingly rare.
Earlier writers, as we have seen, tended to place the blame for the
persecution on the Marian bishops; now the responsibility was shift-
ing to the queen. For example, in *The coronation of Queen Elizabeth*,
the usual villains, Edmund Bonner and Stephen Gardiner, are not so
much as mentioned. Yet there is a scene where the pope and his cardinals meet together and praise Mary as the 'scourge of heresie'. They
also propose that she be canonized for her persecution of heretics and
for bringing England under the sway of Rome.[12] It was at about this
time that the epithet 'Bloody Mary' began to come into circulation.
The first appearance of the term in print that I have found occurs in
1658, in a poem by Nicholas Billingsley, a Presbyterian minister.[13] But
it was in the reigns of Charles II and James II that the sobriquet began
to crop up in scattered works. For example, an anonymous ballad,
added in 1674 to a collection of Thomas Deloney's ballads, declared
that after Edward VI died:

 Then bloody Mary did begin
 In England for to tyrannize.[14]

Although the epithet 'Bloody Mary' did not yet become a commonplace, the image of Mary as cruel became increasingly familiar.
In Benjamin Harris's *The Protestant tutor*, a frequently reprinted text
which taught religious bigotry along with basic literacy, Mary the
'cruel Queen', who was 'imitating Jezebel', persecuted her Protestant
subjects until

this too cruel Pope defending Queen
(The bloodiest princess that this land hath seen)
she did decease and persecution ceast.[15]

But Mary now was being accused of more than simple brutality, she was also accused of reigning tyrannically. This new complaint grew out of the most basic fears of the whigs.[16] Proponents of excluding Catholics from the succession could rely on parliamentary support; opponents rested their hopes on the king. In these circumstances, the whigs perceived – and dreaded – a conspiracy to introduce both popery and arbitrary government, in which a tyrannical monarchy would impose Catholicism on a Protestant Britain while a Catholic or crypto-Catholic clergy would collaborate in arbitrary rule.[17] These fears were not unprecedented; they had arisen on the eve of the Civil War and been articulated in John Pym's opening speech to the Long Parliament.[18] But on that occasion the fears of popery and tyranny, while intense, were not enduring; in fact, the ensuing war and the martyrdom of Charles I identified the monarchy with the Church of England, not with Catholicism.

During the Exclusion Crisis, however, these fears revived so strongly that the terms 'popery' and 'arbitrary government' became interchangeable.[19] The concept of a powerful conspiracy to impose both on the British was given powerful expression in Andrew Marvell's *The growth of popery and arbitrary government in England* (1678), which one scholar has described as 'one of the most influential pamphlets of the decade'.[20] Although Marvell barely mentioned Mary, the conspiracy theories that he outlined had a powerful effect on the queen's reputation. Other writers saw in Mary an example of a monarch who sought to impose both arbitrary rule and Catholicism on England. In this political climate, wild assumptions and suspicions spread and clung to Mary's reputation like ivy to a wall. An instructive example of this occurs in the notes a contemporary, Roger Morrice, compiled for a history of the puritans. Morrice wrote that during Mary's reign, 'Parliaments were packed, and members corrupted and bribed . . . and tyranny like to be established.'[21] Morrice apparently based this charge – according to his citations – on passages in Gilbert Burnet's history of the English Reformation, but if so, he exaggerated what he had read. Burnet had declared that violence or threats of violence, and false returns, were used by the Marian authorities to return certain MPs to the 1553 Parliament, but he did not claim that these practices were used systematically or perennially by either the queen or her councillors.[22] Morrice may not have been a moderate voice, but his was hardly an isolated one: in 1681, an anonymous pamphleteer, apparently drawing on the same passage in Burnet, claimed that Mary routinely packed her parliaments and bribed MPs to get her legislation enacted.[23]

During the reigns of the later Stuarts, whig writers created a hostile portrait of Mary that went far beyond anything written under Elizabeth or the early Stuarts. Not only did the whigs place a much greater emphasis on her alleged cruelty, they also depicted her as the archetypal English tyrant. The fear of absolutism kept the whigs implacably hostile to Mary's memory, as she had been – in this version of history – not only a threat to Protestantism, but to parliament and the ancient English constitution as well. Little good could be said, and little good would be said, about such a fundamentally misguided ruler. The polemical red meat of innumerable late-seventeenth-century broadsides and pamphlets was served up piping hot at the high table of Gilbert Burnet, a cleric, whig propagandist, and historian, whose services to William III would be rewarded with the bishopric of Salisbury. Few writers tried as hard to blacken Mary Tudor's reputation, and with the possible exception of John Foxe, none had Burnet's success in doing so. Given the circumstances in which Burnet's portrait of Mary Tudor was penned, this is hardly surprising. Although the second volume of Burnet's *History of the Reformation* was written during the spring and summer of 1680, and licensed on 10 September, the book was not printed until parliament met at Oxford in March 1681. Burnet declared that the delay was due to the printer, who hoped that issuing the book with the meeting of parliament would increase sales, but it may also have stemmed from Burnet's hopes that the work would influence MPs debating whether or not to exclude the duke of York from the succession.[24]

Burnet maintained that the extirpation of heresy was Mary's overriding priority during her reign, but he also made a novel, unfounded, charge, which was destined to be widely repeated: that Mary's zeal to restore Catholicism was not motivated by religious fervour but rather from a desire to avenge the wrongs she had suffered during the reigns of her father and brother.[25]

In 1713, as Protestant nerves jangled on the eve of the Hanoverian accession, Burnet wrote an introduction to a third part of his history, in which he modified his portrayal of Mary. With the current threat of Catholic restoration stemming from foreign invasion, Burnet now placed much of the onus of the burnings on the Spaniards.

Having read the records of Mary's privy council, Burnet also blamed the privy councillors for the persecution. Yet Mary still remained monstrously cruel, although this time it was Catholicism, rather than bitterness that 'so carried her to an indecencie of barbarity that it appears that Bonner himself was not cruel enough for her'.[26] In Burnet's history, the boiling animus against Mary that had flowed like lava during the later seventeenth century cooled into a flinty conviction – hard, sharp and enduring – that Mary's implacable cruelty had manifested itself in persecution.

Burnet's assessment of Mary was not unchallenged. The nonjuring historian Jeremy Collier perceptively noted that Burnet supplied no evidence for charges which went beyond anything that any previous historian, even Foxe, had alleged. Collier proceeded to contradict Burnet flatly, declaring that Mary 'was not of a vindictive implacable spirit'. Instead, Collier argued that the persecution was the policy of Gardiner and Bonner. Collier also credited Mary with 'resolution' and 'martial vigor' in facing the challenge of Wyatt's rebellion. And Collier deftly turned a traditional charge made against the queen on its head, by observing that Mary's grief at the loss of Calais demonstrated that she placed the interests of England above those of Spain.[27]

Although Collier's evaluation of Mary would be influential in a later period, in its own time it did little to alter the current consensus on the queen. Partly this was because Collier shared the suspicions of Mary's Catholic piety, and although he did not see it as making her vicious, he did feel that it contributed to making her a failure. 'It must be said that religion had the over-balance; the other world was uppermost with her and she valued her conscience above her crown'.[28] This made Collier's assessment rather contradictory and to that extent, unconvincing; Mary was somehow at once resolute and vigorous but also impractical and unworldly. Collier's representation of Mary was more nuanced and more accurate than Burnet's but it was also less dramatic and consistent.

A larger problem was that Collier's interpretation of Mary was swimming upstream against powerful social and political currents. Although the Revolution of 1688 had placed a Protestant on the throne and the Act of Union of 1707 permanently and completely excluded Catholics from the succession, Jacobite invasions, and rumours of Jacobite invasions, whetted fears of a Catholic prince mounting the throne throughout much of the century.[29] And myriad preachers, propagandists and pamphleteers continued to proclaim that persecution would be the inevitable consequence of a Catholic monarch. As one Protestant declared in the aftermath of the '45, had the Jacobites succeeded, 'soon should we have seen our rivers redden with Protestant blood and the flames of martyrdom blaze in our streets'.[30]

The corrosive effects of anti-Jacobite sentiment on perceptions of Mary can be seen in a 1746 publication, *A select history of the principal English Protestant martyrs*. In a pointed reference to the '45, the anonymous editor of the book declared that a history of the Protestant martyrs was particularly relevant in a time 'when the enemies of our happy Constitution and established religion have made such a bold and daring attempt, to ruin the one and abolish the other'.[31] Moreover, by Protestant martyrs, the editor really meant Marian martyrs, as title page makes clear by proclaiming that the work is an account 'chiefly of those executed in the bloody reign of Queen Mary'.[32]

Fears of the Jacobites helped to brand an image of Mary's cruelty onto the English imagination; tellingly, one collection of debates in the Commons on Exclusion, printed just after the fateful year of 1715, referred to Henry VIII's eldest daughter as 'Bloody Mary'.[33] Yet the legend of the bloody queen was also fixed in the popular imagination by the abridgements of Foxe's martyrology, which proliferated in the eighteenth century. These works varied greatly in size and in their fidelity to Foxe's text, but for the most part, they shared several important features. The first was their visceral anti-Catholicism.[34] The second was their marked tendency to focus on Mary's reign and to ignore or downplay earlier persecutions.[35] The third was their popularity: thanks to the growing literacy rate, the expansion of provincial presses and the practice of printing works in cheap instalments, the eighteenth-century editions of Foxe reached far more people than their sixteenth and seventeenth-century predecessors had.

These eighteenth-century versions of Foxe were not only more popular than his original texts, they were far more strident in their denunciations of Mary. One fairly typical example maintained that Mary 'joined a cruel and vindictive temper' to 'excessive bigotry' and called her the 'bloody Queen'.[36] Henry Southwell, the rector of Asterby, Lincs, depicted Mary in terms that made her barely recognizable as a historical figure, or indeed as a human being. After claiming that Mary was 'destitute of human compassion', Southwell continued:

> The whole progress of her reign does not furnish us with a single instance of merit in her, either as woman or a sovereign. On the contrary, all her actions were of

the most horrid and gloomy cast, and the barbarities she committed during her sovereignty, were so great as to exceed description.[37]

Moreover, the two most popular abridgements of Foxe each contributed to demonizing Mary. The first of these was *The Book of Martyrs containing an account of the sufferings and death of the Protestants of the reign of Queen Mary the First*, which was edited anonymously and printed in 1732 by two London publishers, John Lewis and John Hart. This work was reprinted by various publishers in 1741, 1746, 1760, 1761, 1776 and 1784. Apart from material on the French wars of religion, the Spanish Armada, the Gunpowder plot, and the massacre of Waldensians in the Valtelline – all drawn from the 1684 unabridged edition of the *Acts and Monuments* – the contents of the massive volume, which totalled nearly one million words, covered Mary's reign exclusively. Although this work added nothing to Foxe's already negative portrayal of Mary, its detailed coverage of the martyrs of her reign did her reputation no favours.

Far worse was to come with *Fox's original and complete Book of Martyrs or, an universal history of martyrdom*, edited by Paul Wright and first printed in 1782. Although this book was even larger than the Lewis and Hart *Book of Martyrs*, it enjoyed instant and startling success, being reprinted in 1784, 1785, 1790, 1795, 1807 and twice in 1810. Wright's edition of Foxe cast unblinking eyes on the Marian persecution; 725 of the book's 951 pages were devoted to it. It also consistently denigrated Mary, calling her 'Bloody Mary' on its title page and throughout the text. Indeed, probably more than any other single work, Wright's immensely popular abridged edition of Foxe made the epithet 'Bloody Mary' a historical commonplace by the beginning of the nineteenth century.

Vilification of Mary, however, was not confined to the popular literature of anti-Catholicism; it was also found in the magisterial tomes of the leading historians of the eighteenth century. One particularly influential work was the history of England written by Laurence Echard. Begun in 1707 and completed in 1718, it went through seven editions by 1729. Echard, the archdeacon of Stow, was a Tory, whose hostility to Catholics and Jacobites gave him some common ground with the whig historians. As a result, although he admitted Mary's virtuous character, Echard followed the trail blazed by Burnet, and claimed that hardships she suffered made her 'sower and splenetick', faults aggravated by her 'Spanish Moroseness'. And Echard also echoed Burnet in claiming that Mary's 'barbarous cruelties' were 'her revenge, though she coloured it with zeal against heresie'.[38]

Yet Echard was almost sympathetic to Mary, at least in comparison to the whigs who dominated historical writing in the first half of the eighteenth century. These writers turned the negative portraits of Mary into caricatures. Paul de Rapin de Thoyras, the author of a very popular history of England, was a Huguenot who had fled his homeland when the Edict of Nantes was revoked. He served as a soldier in the army that landed with William of Orange in 1688 and he went on to fight for the Protestant cause at the battles of Carrickfergus and the Boyne.[39] Predictably, his verdict on Mary was an intensification of Burnet's:

> The excessive bigotry of Queen Mary is evident from the history of her reign. To this she joined a temper fierce and vindictive, which she cloaked with a pretended zeal for religion, for when it was not possible to reconcile her temper with her religion, she made it manifest that natural cruelty had the predominancy over her zeal.[40]

Another influential whig historian, John Oldmixon, was if anything even more hostile. After asserting that Mary 'had not one valuable or agreeable quality of soul', Oldmixon shifted into high gear:

> The Papists say she was pious and zealous. If there can be true piety in idolatry, hatred, revenge and cruelty, she must be allowed to be pious, and if true zeal is to be met with in bigotry and blind-devotion, she was zealous. As to any other virtues, Christian or royal, the Papists do not insist upon them in her character. She was sullen, proud and obstinate and had her father's bad qualities, without his good ones: inveterate in her hatred, and merciless and bloody in her revenge.[41]

What is perhaps surprising is that these adverse views of Mary came to be shared by those who were completely free of any suspicions of whig (much less Whig) sympathies. Thomas Carte, for example, was a nonjuror and enthusiastic Jacobite whose outspoken Tory sympathies have led Linda Colley to describe his history as a 'four-volume partisan extravaganza'.[42] Yet Carte's description of Mary merely added lurid colours to whig portraits of Henry VIII's eldest daughter:

> Mary was not formed to please, she had nothing of the woman in either her history or her behaviour; she was stiff, formal, reserved, sour, haughty and arrogant, her face plain and coarse, without any soft features to smooth its roughness or any

insinuating graces to shade its defects. Everything in her looks, her air, her carriage and manner, was forbidding . . . scarce ever was there a person so utterly void of all the agreeable qualities. . . . She pretended, and perhaps fancied herself, to have a great deal of religion. . . . But it was a religion of a low kind, that of a bigot and choked with superstition. . . . Her fundamental defects were the same as her father's: an unmeasurable pride, a furious impetuosity, the effect of her violent and ill-natured passions, a willfulness to which she would have sacrificed the world and an insatiable avarice. She equalled him in at least all those respects, but wanted his judgement on the exercise of them and far outdid him in arbitrariness and cruelty.[43]

In 1757, Tobias Smollett tersely epitomized the general consensus on Mary: 'We have already observed that the characteristics of Mary were bigotry and revenge; we shall only add that she was proud, imperious, froward, avartious [sic], and wholly destitute of every agreeable qualification'.[44] Burnet had planted the suggestions that Mary was motivated by viciousness and spite rather than religious zeal, and in the favourable soil of the eighteenth century, a dense underbrush of calumny and misrepresentation had sprung up from the seeds Burnet had sowed, one which almost completely concealed the historical Mary Tudor.

Unfortunately the myth of Mary as a cruel and arbitrary tyrant was enhanced in the pages of David Hume's *History of England*, the most authoritative and influential survey of English history written under the Hanoverians. Hume differed from the whig historians in fundamental respects, and, in fact, his work was an unacknowledged, but thorough and effective, demolition of Rapin's history.[45] In contrast to the whigs, Hume did not believe in an ancient English constitution that had be defended against monarchical absolutism. And while the major whig historians of the eighteenth century were almost all Anglican clerics who equated Protestantism with progress, Hume, like one of H. G. Wells's Martians observing humankind, contemplated all forms of organized religion with a vast, cool and unsympathetic intellect.

Nevertheless, although Hume was suspicious of all forms of Christianity, he had a particular distaste for Roman Catholicism. In Hume's view, the authority of civil magistrates over the clergy was necessary for political and social stability. He regarded Catholicism, with its claims to universal authority and its clerical hierarchy, as inherently inimical to secular control. Only a foolish and bigoted monarch would attempt to undermine royal authority by imposing

Catholicism, and only a violent bigot would attempt to do so by force. Thus Hume reached similar conclusions about Mary as the whigs had done, although he came to them by different roads. Mary

> possessed few qualities either estimable or amiable and her person was as little engaging as her behaviour and address. Obstinacy, bigotry, violence, cruelty, malignity, revenge, tyranny; every circumstance of her character took a tincture from her bad temper and narrow understanding. And amidst that complication of vices which entered into her composition, we shall scarcely find any virtue but sincerity.[46]

Hume not only repeated the verdicts of his eighteenth-century predecessors on Mary, he perpetuated them well into the nineteenth century. Hume's history was a best-seller for over a hundred years. Five editions of the history were printed between its completion in 1762 and Hume's death in 1776. A further 62 editions appeared between 1776 and 1864, with another six editions being published between 1864 and 1900.[47]

Furthermore Hume felt that women played a crucial role in the moral reformation of society and was concerned that both genders learn the lessons of history. As a result he took pains to make his work accessible to women, by orienting the coverage of his history away from politics towards family, gender and social history.[48] As a result Hume's history influenced broader audiences than most conventional histories, not only women, but also, since the writers of history books for juveniles were often women, their children as well. Through Hume, the 'Bloody Mary' of the eighteenth century became familiar to the young readers of the nineteenth century.

The influence of Hume can be seen in Elizabeth Penrose's *History of England*. Penrose (who wrote under the pseudonym of Mrs Markham) declared that she wrote the book when her eldest son experienced difficulty in reading Hume's history, out of a desire to make Hume's work accessible to her own and other children.[49] She succeeded, perhaps beyond her expectations; in the years 1826–75 her *History of England* went through 14 editions. In doing so, Penrose made Hume's depiction of Mary, as well as his general history, accessible to generations of children. Penrose asserted that 'I have in general avoided saying the worst of a character, because few people are, in reality, so bad as they are made to appear.'[50] Mary was apparently an exceptional case. Although Penrose did give Mary credit for being 'sincere in her unfortunate bigotry', she also declared that the persecution of

Protestants filled her 'with horror at the wickedness of Mary'.[51] As earlier writers had done, Penrose explained Mary's 'wickedness' by emphasizing the queen's character and personality flaws: 'Her person is described as having been very homely and her manner unengaging. Her education had probably been much neglected, and she inherited her mother's gravity with her father's violence and obstinate temper.'[52]

Penrose's history was popular, but its popularity was dwarfed by that of Maria Collcott's *Little Arthur's history of England,* which went through 70 editions between its first appearance in 1835 and the end of the nineteenth century. The tone of Collcott's account of Mary was struck in its opening sentence: 'Mary, the daughter of Henry VIII, and of Catherine of Aragon, was so cruel that she is always called Bloody Mary.' Later, Collcott described the queen's religious policies 'as the most cruel and wicked things I ever read about'.[53] So reluctant was Collcott to praise Mary for any achievements whatsoever, that she gave the duke of Norfolk credit for defeating Wyatt's rebels.[54] (In actual fact, the octogenarian duke was humiliatingly defeated by the rebels and it was Mary's decisive leadership that saved her throne.)

The works of Penrose and Collcott were only the most popular of numerous early nineteenth-century children's textbooks that castigated Mary as bigoted, cruel, vengeful, bad-tempered and generally unpleasant, and also damned her as 'Bloody Mary'.[55] Yet even as the textbooks of Penrose and Collcott were reaching the heights of their popularity, shifts were taking place in Victorian history writing – not to mention Victorian society itself – which would permanently alter views of Mary. She had been vilified in the long eighteenth century because she was seen as the epitome of forces that most English historians feared and despised: Catholicism, absolutism and reaction. But two new groups, hitherto marginalized, were beginning to elbow their way into the mainstream of British historical writing. Both groups had a stake in rehabilitating Mary's reputation, and both would have some success in doing so.

Catholics had an obvious interest in trying to discredit the myth of 'Bloody Mary', since it had been wielded so relentlessly against them. Hugh Tottell, a priest writing under the name of Charles Dodd, wrote the most important English ecclesiastical history, from a Catholic viewpoint, penned in the eighteenth century. In it Dodd made a thorough defence of Mary's character, maintaining that 'she was a princess in all respects worthy of that high station in which providence had placed her'.[56] Dodd emphasized Mary's virtues in a manner that implicitly contrasted the queen with Elizabeth, her successor.

He pointedly praised Mary for not concealing her religious beliefs, for not aiding foreign rebels, for not having favourites at court and for not despoiling the Church. Dodd displayed the same partisanship in his analysis of the loss of Calais, which he suggested had been betrayed to the French by English Protestants, and which he maintained that Elizabeth should have retaken.[57] This partisanship, along with Dodd's failure to provide evidence to support his assertions, and even more importantly, the fact that he was advocating an unpopular view, ensured that Dodd's reappraisal of Mary had little popular impact.

However about 80 years later another priest and historian, John Lingard, penned a sweeping re-evaluation of Mary. Like Dodd, Lingard emphasized Mary's personal virtues. Apart, from her prosecution of heresy, Lingard declared, Mary

> has been ranked, by the more moderate of the reformed writers, among the best, though not the greatest, of our princes. They have borne honourable testimony to her virtues: [they] have allotted to her the praise of piety and clemency, of compassion for the poor and liberality to the distressed.... It is acknowledged that her moral character was beyond reproach.[58]

Lingard also extolled Mary's education, eloquence and intelligence. Lingard was outspoken in his disapproval of the burnings of Protestants, but he also pointed out that Mary was hardly unique among early-modern monarchs in resorting to persecution, and that the capital punishment of heretics was almost universally approved of in the sixteenth century. 'It was her misfortune, rather than her fault, that she was not more enlightened than the wisest of her contemporaries.'[59]

In contrast to previous sympathetic depictions of Mary advanced by Collier and Dodd, Lingard's portrait of the queen gained wide acceptance. In part, this was due to the moderate, unpolemical tone of Lingard's prose. More fundamentally, Lingard was the first historian of the English Reformation, since Burnet, to undertake significant new research on Mary and her reign. Lingard's account of the queen was based on a number of sources – such as reports from the Venetian ambassadors in the Barberini archives in Rome, the papers of the Imperial ambassador Simon Renard, at Besançon, and the letters of Cardinal Pole in the Vatican archives – which had not been previously used by British historians.[60] This new material not only enhanced Lingard's credibility, it also made it virtually impossible to rebut his account of Mary simply by repeating traditional narratives. And perhaps most importantly, Lingard's history was written on the eve of Catholic Emancipation; although anti-Popery remained potent, England had changed since the days of Rapin, Oldmixon and even Hume.

Women, as well as Catholics, were increasingly active as historical writers in the nineteenth century, and they tended to specialize in biography and social history.[61] Two of the most successful female historians in nineteenth-century England were the sisters Agnes and Elizabeth Strickland. Their immensely popular *Lives of the queens of England* contained a biography of Mary, written by Elizabeth Strickland, which permanently altered perceptions of the queen and influenced accounts of her throughout the twentieth century.[62] Strickland based her revisionary assessment of Mary on what may appear to be unlikely sources: Frederic Madden's *Privy purse expenses of the Princess Mary* (1831) and Patrick Fraser Tytler's *England under the reigns of Edward VI and Mary* (1839), a work which contained numerous hitherto unpublished letters of Mary Tudor.[63] The documents in these works did not conform to the vengeful, cruel queen of popular legend. Instead, in Strickland's opinion, 'These records speak only of charity, affection to her little sister, kindness to her dependants, feminine accomplishments, delicate health, generosity to her godchildren, many of whom were orphans dependent on her alms, very little hunting or hawking is mentioned, and no bear-baiting'.[64] As this quotation suggests, having found evidence in letters and household expenses that Mary was educated, refined, and gave generously to charity, Elizabeth Strickland came to view, and portray, the Tudor princess and queen as a proper Victorian gentlewomen. In her biography, Strickland not only emphasized Mary's charitable largesse, but also her fondness for embroidery, her skill at needlework and her love of music.[65] With considerably less justification, Strickland depicted Mary, in actuality an enthusiastic hunter, as averse to blood sports. And she carefully said little or nothing about other aspects of Mary, revealed in her household accounts and letters: a love of cards and gambling as well as a passion for jewellery and expensive apparel. Strickland also reassured her readers that Mary 'never swore, either on paper or by utterance'.[66]

Both Agnes and Elizabeth Strickland were apparently aware that Elizabeth's demolition of a national myth would be criticized, but it is doubtful if they anticipated the storm that broke around them. After the fifth volume of their series, which contained the life of Mary, was published in 1842, clergymen denounced the work from the pulpit, and demanded that it be kept away from children. Other members of the Strickland family, as well as Agnes (whom the public assumed to be the author of the biography of Mary), came under considerable social pressure. (Agnes increased her attendance at church and also increased her teaching at Sunday school, in an effort to dispel rumours that she was a Catholic.) For a while, sales for the entire series of lives of the queens – hitherto a considerable success – dried up.[67] Both sisters declined to apologize for, or retract, the offending biography, and eventually the storm blew over, although Elizabeth Strickland's account of Mary provoked moral outrage for some time to come. Although he did not mention his targets by name, a decade later Charles Dickens took direct aim at the Stricklands (and probably Lingard as well), in his *A child's history of England*:

As BLOODY QUEEN MARY, this woman has become famous, and as BLOODY QUEEN MARY she will ever be justly remembered with horror and detestation in Great Britain. Her memory has been held in such abhorrence that some writers have arisen in later years to take her part and show that she was, upon the whole, quite an amiable and cheerful sovereign! 'By their fruits ye shall know them', said OUR SAVIOUR. The stake and the fire were the fruits of this reign, and you shall judge this Queen by nothing else.[68]

Yet despite his huffing and puffing, Dickens expressed what was coming to be a minority view. Revisionist though it was, Elizabeth Strickland's interpretation of Mary gained rapid popular acceptance. Nowhere was this change more apparent than in children's textbooks. As early as 1844, one history book for juvenile readers praised Mary's character and referred the reader to Strickland's biography of Mary.[69] Although William Legge did not cite Strickland in his successful textbook of English history, her influence is clear in his assessment of Mary: 'In every thing excepting religion, Mary seems to have been amiable and gentle.'[70] The even more influential *Outlines of English history* was even more beholden to Elizabeth Strickland. It denounced the persecution of Protestants, but conceded that Mary thought that the punishment of heresy was her duty. The authors of the textbook also extolled Mary's intellect, courage and impeccable conduct. But the textbook most closely conformed to Strickland in emphasizing Mary's personal charity, and describing her visiting the sick and poor.[71] The influence of Elizabeth Strickland, however, extended far beyond school textbooks. For example, Hilda Prescott,

Mary's first modern biographer, echoed Strickland – without ever citing her work, even in her bibliography – in describing Mary's personal virtues, her charitable largesse, and her clemency.[72]

Why was the rehabilitation of Mary's reputation so successful? Once again, part of the reason was that Elizabeth Strickland, like Lingard, had new documentary evidence to support her interpretations. The timing of both Lingard and Strickland was also fortuitous. The reputation of Hume's history, whose weighty authority had all but crushed Mary's reputation underneath it, was in sharp decline by the mid-nineteenth century. Hume's overt irreligion, his distaste for martial adventures and his scepticism about the antiquity of the British constitution, made his work increasingly unattractive to the Victorians. Thomas Macaulay's neo-whig history appeared at exactly the right time (between 1849 and 1861) to further eclipse Hume, and fortunately for Mary's reputation, Macaulay did not write about her reign. Even more importantly, Strickland's portrayal of Mary conformed much more closely with Victorian preconceptions about gender and human character. Mary's charity, love of music and embroidery, skill at needlework, even her fragile health, fitted prevailing ideas of upper-class female gentility. And both Strickland and her readers found it difficult to believe that a well-bred lady could be the monster of revenge and cruelty that tradition painted.

Yet attempts by Lingard and Strickland to restore Mary's good name inevitably ran into an almost insuperable obstacle: the burnings conducted during her reign. Strickland was all too aware that a defence of Mary could easily be perceived as a justification of persecution. As she observed, penning a sympathetic account of Mary was 'dangerous ... because the desire of recording truth may be mistaken for a wish to extenuate cruelty in religious and civil government'.[73] And Strickland made no attempt to downplay the cruelty of the Marian persecution, in fact, she maintained that contemplating it 'curdles the blood with horror'.[74] Strickland was able to reconcile her admiration for Mary with her detestation of the persecution by insisting that it was instigated, planned and executed by the bishops and the privy councillors and that Mary often tried to intercede on behalf of condemned Protestants.[75] The problem with this explanation was that it was less than credible that the burnings could have taken place without the queen's knowledge and approval.

Catholic writers faced a similar dilemma in an even more acute form. They had ample reason for wanting to discredit the legend of Bloody Mary, but at the same time they had compelling reasons to avoid giving even the merest hint of approval for the burnings. As we have seen, Strickland was concerned about the dangers of appearing to condone the burnings, but this was a far greater anxiety for Catholics. Any attempt to exculpate Mary ran the risk of fanning paranoid, yet still widely held, fantasies that the Catholics schemed to extirpate English Protestantism, if not English Protestants. In 1827, the historian Henry Hallam, who favoured tolerance for Catholics, warned Catholic writers that they would:

> do better by avoiding for the future either such panegyrics on Mary and her advisors, or such insidious extenuations of her persecution as we have lately read, and which do not raise a favourable impression of their sincerity in the principles of toleration to which they profess to have been converted.[76]

Many Catholic writers had already grasped this point. Around the turn of the nineteenth century John Milner, a leading Catholic controversialist, insisted that 'if Mary was a persecutor, it was not in virtue of any tenet of her religion that she became so'.[77] Having made this point, Milner went on to argue that Mary was provoked into persecuting the Protestants by Wyatt's rebellion and by the seditious works printed by Protestants. He further observed that early-modern Protestants, as well as Catholics, persecuted those they regarded as heretics.[78] Milner's arguments were quite influential, at least within Catholic circles. An indication of their popularity and wide dissemination can be discerned in the following exchange in a catechism on English history prepared by Father Thomas Flanagan, a professor at St Mary's College, Oscott:

Q. But for all that, Mary was very cruel, was she not?
A. If she were as cruel as people sometimes say, she must have forgotten the teachings of her religion.
Q. But was she so very cruel?
A. No, not near so cruel as people sometimes say; and it was not until she had been provoked by repeated disturbances and rebellions that she became at all severe.[79]

However, since Mary's defenders were nearly as vociferous in denouncing the burnings as in praising the queen, the basic problem remained: how to reconcile the image of a virtuous, kindly women with the enormity of religious persecution?

The solution lay in emphasizing both Mary's misfortunes and the effect that they had putatively had on her character and judgement. Writers began insisting that Mary's misfortunes, ranging from her conflicts with her father to her 'abandonment' by her husband, corrupted her gentle nature and corroded her judgement. This interpretation had several strengths. Traditional accounts of Mary had already described her as morose and melancholy, although they tended to subordinate these qualities to her supposed cruelty and fanatical zeal. At the same time, the new sources deployed by Lingard and the Stricklands contained numerous references to Mary's general ill health and her 'hysteria'. The interpretation of Mary as hysterical was completely compatible with Victorian preconceptions about gender, and was further reinforced by Mary's false pregnancies.[80]

The characterization of Mary as hysterical, and the claim that her policies were rooted in this hysteria, was made forcefully by James Anthony Froude, one of the pre-eminent nineteenth-century historians of Tudor England. Although militantly pro-Protestant in his interpretation of the English Reformation, Froude was sufficiently influenced by Lingard and Strickland to admit of Mary that 'from the passions which in general tempt sovereigns into crime, she was entirely free: to the time of her accession she lived a blameless, and, in many respects, a noble life'.[81] Froude bridged the gulf between Mary's virtuous character and her 'cruel' acts by describing the latter as arising from hysteria and derangement, of which her false pregnancies were both symptoms and exacerbations. He linked the renewal of the Marian persecution in 1555 to Mary's uncontrollable passions, and a desperate desire to appease God, both of which were triggered by her discovery that she was not with child.[82] He went further and declared that Philip's 'abandonment' of Mary and the repeated collapse of her hopes of being a mother 'affected her sanity'. In Froude's opinion, Mary suffered from 'hysterical derangement' and was, indeed, by the end of her reign, 'insane'. (It should be pointed out that Froude's standards for assessing insanity were less than clinical: he regarded Mary's participation in Corpus Christi processions as *prima facie* evidence of dementia.[83])

Although Froude's history was admired, it was also controversial, yet his assessment of Mary was readily accepted as it accorded with both the available evidence and existing preconceptions. In the last three decades of the nineteenth century, juvenile textbooks were portraying Mary as a pitiable and tragic figure, rather than a cruel and bloodthirsty one. William Collier's verdict on Mary, in an 1870 textbook, provides an interesting example of how newer views of Mary were soldered onto earlier traditions about her. After asserting that Mary died in sorrow, Collier continued portentously:

> Sorrow is sent for our good, but Mary's heart was hardened in her disposition and soured by the events of her early life. Her strongest passion was hatred of the Protestant faith. Instead, however, of branding her with the name of Bloody Mary, we should rather pity the Queen who, in her fierce religious zeal forgot the mercy natural to women, and who saw, before she died, every hope of her life baffled and broken.[84]

By the end of the century, an even softer portrait of Mary emerged. The judgement of a popular school text is typical:

> Mary's private character was stainless, her court pure. She was liberal to the poor and distressed.... She might have been a great queen, for, Spanish as she was in her bigotry, her heart was English. But the interests of the nation were sacrificed to those of the church and, as 'Bloody Mary', she left behind her a hateful and abiding memory. Had she been less sincere she probably would have succeeded in her grand design. She failed, and utterly, from the very intensity of her purpose.[85]

Lingard and Strickland had succeeded in relegating the legend of cruel Mary to the dust heap of historiography. But they toppled one misconception only to replace it with another: that of Mary as a tragic figure, not only because she endured tremendous misfortunes, but also because these misfortunes warped her character and her judgement. This nineteenth-century conception of Mary was carried into the twentieth century by one of the greatest historians of his day, A. F. Pollard. He was brought up in a Methodist family, but he really worshipped the British empire and its parliamentary system, which he believed attained something like political perfection. Pollard regarded Henry VIII as a great statesman, with the foresight to anticipate England's imperial destiny and the insight to understand the national will of his subjects. It was during the king's reign, and due to Henry's leadership that both empire and parliamentary democracy were born. Mary's reign, by contrast, did nothing to further England's progress towards these objectives. As a result, Pollard dismissed the queen as a 'palpable failure', and, in an often quoted passage, he wrote that 'Sterility was the conclusive note of her reign.'[86]

Yet Pollard was considerably more sympathetic to Mary as a person:

> The most honest of Tudor rulers, she never consciously did what she thought to be wrong. So far as she could, she kept her court and her government uncorrupt, and she tried to help the poor. In spite of her cruel treatment in youth, she was compassionate except when her creed was concerned.[87]

Having followed the lead of the Victorians in emphasizing Mary's virtues and fundamentally gentle nature, Pollard also followed their lead in emphasizing her misery. When Philip left England, Mary was, according to Pollard, forsaken by her husband and estranged from her people'.[88] As a result, Pollard claimed in a wild and uncharacteristic burst of hyperbole, even the agonies of the Marian martyrs 'were slight compared with the long-drawn agony inflicted on Mary by the consciousness of failure and her husband's conduct'.[89] In fact, Pollard felt that Mary's hysteria, induced by grief and exacerbated by illness, was the cause of the notorious persecution: 'In vain she strove to satisfy by burnt-offerings the cravings of a mind diseased in a disordered frame.'[90]

Due in part to Pollard's pre-eminence in the field of Tudor history, his depiction of Mary became authoritative. As Robert Tittler observes, 'the popular image of Mary and her government tends even now to resemble the negative judgements passed by A. F. Pollard'.[91] Certainly Hilda Prescott, the first major biographer of Mary in the twentieth century, followed in Pollard's footsteps by continually insisting on Mary's ill fortune and personal misery. Prescott saw Philip's departure as a crucial, disastrous, turning point in Mary's life, 'the end of her happiness'. She describes Mary, during Philip's absence, in passages worthy of a historical romance:

> torn between anger and pain, Mary spent the days; and in the long sleepless nights, turning over the past in her mind while the owls swooped and hooted outside, she would decide sometimes, and tell her women, that she regreted her marriage, and would not, had she again the chance, choose as she had done. Yet she could never shake herself free for long from the uncontrollable desire for Philip's return.[92]

Prescott did not cite any source for these detailed descriptions of Mary's intimate thoughts and feelings, which almost certainly reveal more about Prescott's preconceptions of Mary Tudor than they do about the queen herself. Nevertheless the Victorian image of Mary as a doomed, woeful figure has flourished right up to the present; one recent biography of Mary is subtitled 'The Tragical history of the first Queen of England', while another, even more recent, biography declares that Mary'failed as a woman' although she 'triumphed' as a queen'.[93]

What evidence is there to support the widely held belief that Mary was both exceptionally unhappy and exceptionally unfortunate? We actually know little concerning her feelings for and about Philip at the various stages of their relationship. It was, of course, a misfortune for her that she died at a relatively young age, but then so did Henry V, and yet few historians have considered him a tragic figure. Every monarch, indeed every person, experiences loss, grief and personal tragedy, and Mary was no exception, but this hardly makes her experiences exceptionally dire. Her 'tragical' reputation is partly based on her false pregnancies, just as the idea that grief undermined her judgement or even her sanity is partly based on contemporary descriptions of them as instances of 'hysteria'. As Judith M. Richards demonstrates in her chapter in this volume, both the false pregnancies and the claims of 'hysteria' need to be understood within the framework of sixteenth-century medical ideas, and with the knowledge that the meaning of the word 'hysteria' has changed between the sixteenth and the twenty-first centuries.

In any case, the idea of Mary as warped by grief was really not adopted because of the false pregnancies and reports of hysteria; they simply provided justification for believing it. The idea was readily accepted because it explained how a gentle person (such as Victorians considered Mary to be) could execute hundreds of religious dissenters. This idea validated, and at the same time was supported by, two series of assumptions. The first set of assumptions concerned gender. Believing that Mary became bitter and hysterical through grief not only provided an explanation for the persecutions, it also conformed to nineteenth-century ideas of female character: women were more gentle and inherently virtuous than men, but they were also more passionate and their intellect was governed by their emotions. The second set of assumptions was that the restoration of Catholicism was doomed to failure and was, in any case, highly undesirable, thus reinforcing the idea that Mary's policies were ultimately irrational and arose from her emotions, not her reason. The way that these concepts came together, buttressing each other, can be seen in the conclusion of Prescott's biography, where Mary is depicted as a Mary Magdalene figure, needing to repent, not her personal sins, but her wrongheaded policies: 'For mistaken often, almost always misguided in her public office, with much blindness, some rancour, some jealousy, some stupid cruelty to answer for, she had yet trodden, long and manfully, the way that other sinners know.'[94]

The vicissitudes of Mary's reputation provide a humbling, yet valuable, lesson for writers and readers of history. They provide an object lesson in the dangers of allowing prejudice and preconception to shape interpretations of the past. Mary has continually been judged by the standards of the eighteenth, nineteenth and twentieth centuries, and not surprisingly, has been found wanting. Even when new evidence has been uncovered, it has been interpreted in the light of fixed assumptions. There is no reason to expect that this will change; after all, what has made the recent revisionist work on Mary possible has not only been new research, but more fundamentally, the decline of old attitudes towards both women and Catholicism. No one is able to overcome his or her biases, but we can at least try to keep them in check.

Mary and the events of her reign still provoke powerful emotions and excite twenty-first century prejudgements, if not prejudices. Yet understanding relevant biases and preconceptions is only the first step in recovering the historical Mary. We must also understand how earlier prejudices have shaped conceptions of Mary and then, like art restorers, carefully remove the layers of overpainting to reveal as much as possible of the original portrait that lies beneath.

Part II

NEW PERSPECTIVES

6

'*Ad Omne Virtutum Genus*'? Mary between Piety, Pedagogy and Praise in Early Tudor Humanism

Andrew W. Taylor

Evaluations of Mary's humanistic accomplishments have been caught up in the religious politics of Tudor historiography. The thin, rather intermittent evidence has tended to render their representation vulnerable to manipulation. Some, like Elton, forcefully perpetuated the equation of Mary's religious disposition with a profound, almost pathological, closed-mindedness:

> arrogant, assertive, bigoted, stubborn, suspicious, and (not to put too fine a point upon it) rather stupid.... Humanism had passed her by as much as had Protestantism. If it is not clear whether she leant towards the new rigour of the rising Counter-Reformation or a pre-Lutheran conventional piety, this is mainly because she never gave any sign of a genuinely intelligent interest in the issues that confronted her; she depended on the mass because it gave her emotional satisfaction.[1]

More recent assessments of Mary's learning have tended the other way, in an inflationary spiral involving both Katherine of Aragon and Katherine Parr. Mary's mother, Katherine of Aragon certainly received a Latinate literary education unusual for her time, and sought to build on this for her daughter. She therefore differs from an earlier powerful patroness of humanistic learning, Mary's paternal great-grandmother, Lady Margaret Beaufort, whose pious translations were from French.[2] The ability of Mary's and Elizabeth's step-mother, Katherine Parr, has been equated with that of the learned ladies of Thomas More's household, with claims that she was fluent in French, Latin and Italian, learning Spanish as an adult.[3] As holographic specimens of Katherine's Latin epistles do not survive, the degree of secretarial assistance in the official correspondence that attracted praise remains unclear. Moreover, Mary has been more plausibly presented as Katherine's tutor during the mid-1540s.[4] Yet questions also arise about Mary's linguistic competence. Warm official reports sent home from Henry's court by visiting diplomats interested in ingratiation or fostering alliances through marriage fail to provide credible coherence in their praise for her. Mary's grounding in Greek, for example, is remarked on only once, which throws doubt on that claim, while other diplomatic comments convey as much surprise at any level of linguistic competence as particular excellence. Beyond these, there is little direct evidence that she spoke Spanish fluently or Italian at all.[5]

Humanists, of course, promoted themselves through pedagogical writings and activities to far wider audiences and for service quite different from that of the classroom. Thus interests other than Mary's were often involved in much of their well-worked testimony about her knowledge of the classics. Humanists looked to antiquity, both pagan and Christian, for wisdom to authorize reforms which ranged from the canons of literary style to political practice and social provision. Courtiers increasingly saw the display of eloquence and learning as attracting patronage from those who valued this learning. Humanists dreamed of philosopher-kings and composed treatises on the education for princes and magistrates, those with the power to exercise enlightened authority – wisdom in action. In 1516 Desiderius Erasmus, in his *Institutio principis christiani* (*The education of a Christian prince*), counselled that 'the main hope of getting a good prince hangs on his proper education, which should be managed all the more attentively, so that what has been lost with the right to vote is made up for by the care given to his upbringing'.[6] And just as the people had not chosen Henry VIII for their king, he had not chosen a daughter to be his only surviving legitimate issue by Katherine. Mary's exposure to the *studia humanitatis* is therefore related to a consideration of her education as a preparation for rule.[7]

Humanists imposed certain limits on their reform of female learning, which tended to reinforce a woman's primarily domestic, nonpolitical role.[8] Women were prescribed edifying distractions from idleness through studying only certain areas of the broad humanistic field, which included philosophy (predominantly moral), political thought, jurisprudence, medicine, theology, mathematics and the creative arts.[9] Nonetheless, Judith M. Richards has countered the prevailing scholarly tendency to read sixteenth-century monarchical ideology as 'extreme political and patriarchal misogyny'.[10] Uncertainties, then, seem to have surrounded the status of a female monarch in mid-Tudor discourse, especially one destined to marry a foreign prince: the higher the status of the woman, the more ambiguous the transfer of authority to a husband might be.

This chapter first offers an interpretation of Mary's formal education in this context, before exploring more broadly aspects of the literary representation of her learning, to suggest how her religious and political commitments seem to have both informed and limited her engagement with humanism.

Mary's Formal Education

On 18 March 1523, when the Spanish humanist Juan Luis Vives sailed for England from the Low Countries, his writings had already met with the approval of Erasmus and Thomas More. His influence as spiritual counsellor to Katherine of Aragon led to her commissioning a brief manual on Princess Mary's educational provision, which he delivered as an extended letter dedicated to Katherine from Oxford, in October 1523. Vives added a second epistolary treatise for Charles Blount, son of William Blount, Lord Mountjoy, the queen's chamberlain and influential patron of Erasmus. Together, as the *De ratione studii puerilis* (*On the plan of study for children*), they express Vives's attitudes towards male and female education. His more extensive *De institutione feminae christianae* (*The instruction of the Christian woman*) appeared in print in 1524, bearing a dedication to Katherine of 5 April 1523. The *De institutione*, as we shall see, reasserted chastity as a woman's defining virtue, even in praising female eloquence.[11] Nevertheless, the political reading for Mary in the *De ratione studii puerilis* may be seen as having gently accommodated the possibility that she might rule.[12]

To the *De ratione studii* Vives soon added the *Satellitium animi* (*Escort of the soul*), a collection of gnomic mottoes or devices, dedicated to Mary from Bruges in 1524, and the *Introductio ad sapientiam* (*Introduction to wisdom*), an introductory synthesis of Stoic and Christian morality.[13] Meanwhile Thomas Linacre, in the Latin dedication to Mary of his English work, the *Rudimenta grammatices*, flatteringly noted 'a certain disposition towards every one of the virtues [*ad omne virtutum genus*] which can be remarked upon in a woman and the noble impulse of your own most abundant ability towards the study of literature';[14] more anticipatory than confirmatory for the seven-year-old Mary. Linacre possibly acted briefly as tutor before his death in 1524. George Buchanan sufficiently rated Linacre's grammar to translate it into Latin, and it regularly appeared in print with Vives's *De ratione studii*.[15] However, in 1525, soon after this bundle of treatises arrived, Henry Fitzroy, the king's bastard by Elizabeth Blount, was ominously raised to the dukedoms of Richmond and Somerset. Henry ordered Mary, aged nine, to Ludlow Castle and the Welsh marches much as Prince Arthur had been, separating her from her mother, the overseer of her studies. Fitzroy was sent to the north of England with a grander household which included his new tutor, the prominent humanist and first reader in Greek at Cambridge, Richard Croke. His appointment suggests the desire for a more prestigious tutor for the boy as well as anxiety over the succession.[16]

Margaret Pole, countess of Salisbury (1473–1541), close ally of Katherine of Aragon, was Mary's governess between 1525 and 1533. In the Welsh marches, Mary was expected 'to pass her tyme most seasons at her virginals or other instruments musical, so that the same be not too much and without fatigation or weariness. To intend to her learning of latin tongue or French. At other seasons to drawe'.[17] Margaret may have influenced the appointment of Katherine's chaplain, Richard Fetherston (BA Cambridge c.1500, MA Oxford 1505), probably the figure approved as 'learned and honest' by Vives in the dedication to his *De ratione*.[18] Vives mingled approval with apology for having provided only an outline: 'I was content to indicate the matter, as it were, with a finger.' Fetherston's handling of Mary's Latin from 1525 was probably subject to his absences defending Katherine during the growing troubles over her marriage to Henry. Richard Wolman, the king's almoner, was employed as tutor in 1532, possibly deputizing.[19]

Giles Duwes (Du Wés), who like Linacre had tutored Prince Arthur, produced at this time for Mary an *Introductory for French*, a language spoken at the Henrician court.[20] Unlike Linacre,

Duwes, although the librarian of the king's books at Richmond, was no professional teacher of humanistic bent, more a courtly educator-cum-entertainer from the pre-Erasmian period.[21] In 1527, when Margaret brought Mary to court during marriage negotiations, a French envoy commented favourably on Mary's mental endowments as well as her French and lute playing.[22] Although she seems to have lacked formal instruction in Spanish, she could understand her mother's letters in that language, even if she had no oral fluency. Far later, in 1557, Giovanni Michieli, the Venetian ambassador, gave possibly the most enthusiastic report, praising the quickness of her understanding, her ability to speak English, Latin, French and Spanish, and to comprehend Italian, adding, 'but the replies she gives in Latin, and her very intelligent remarks made in that tongue surprise everybody'.[23] However, there is little firm evidence of Mary's early fulfilling of the 'princely' scope of either Vives's or Erasmus' prescriptions.

As Mary approached her tenth birthday, Katherine remarked, 'As for your writing in Lattine, I am glad that ye shall chaunge from me to Maister Federston, for that shall doo you moche good to lerne by him to write right'.[24] Katherine requested written Latin exercises from Mary, prepared for (and with) Fetherston, similar perhaps to the extant letters later composed by Edward and Elizabeth. Although Fetherston was versed in humanistic Latin, his Greek learning is as uncertain as his adherence to Vives's prescriptions.[25] Like Wolman, he was no scholarly rival to Croke (formerly servant-pupil to Hellenist William Grocyn), or to the younger Roger Ascham, John Cheke or Anthony Cooke, the royal tutors of the 1540s. If Mary performed such exercises, they sadly do not survive. Thus we can only surmise how she was taught Latin and whether she ever graduated to works like Linacre's enduring *De emendata structura Latini sermonis* (*On the correct structure of Latin prose*), Erasmus' *De ratione studii* and *De copia* (*On abundance*), the slightly older *Rudimenta grammatices* of Perrotus, or Vives's *Linguae Latinae exercitatio* (*The practice of the Latin language*) of 1539. Moreover, these works are properly seen as springboards to intensive reading in, and emulation of, the Roman authors of the *studia humanitatis*.[26]

By mid-May 1528, Mary had been recalled and was at Greenwich. Vives returned to London by October, when Katherine's situation was rapidly deteriorating, but she seems not to have replaced Fetherston.[27] Although the presence of such a teacher would have been less important to the nine-year-old Mary of 1525, her education by Fetherston and others over the following seven or eight years seems not to have produced conspicuous and illuminating achievements. We are finally left with very little on which to base an appraisal of her humanistic accomplishments and early disposition towards learning.[28] According to those original instructions, Mary was to receive 'an honourable education and training in virtuous demeanour; that is to say, to serve God, from whom all grace and goodness proceedeth'. Duwes's French dialogues, composed for use with Mary in the Welsh marches between 1525 and 1527, included St Augustine on peace and St Isidore on the nature of the soul, mingled with such topics as love, the meaning of the mass, and the speaking of French. It is not known whether analogous Latin dialogues were composed to develop vocabulary around everyday life as prescribed in the *De ratione studii*.[29] Her sole surviving translation from Latin during her education is that, made aged 11, of a prayer of St Thomas Aquinas, 'the scholastic most acceptable to the pious humanist circle'.[30] We have contemporary comment drawing attention to lost writings by Margaret Roper (b. 1505), whose translation of Erasmus' *Precatio Dominica in septem portiones distributa* (*The Lord's Prayer divided into seven parts*) of 1523 was printed in 1524, as well as letters from her father which chart her growing literary abilities.[31] In contrast, Mary's musical skills and other courtly accomplishments draw comment, while any sense of a sustained programme of reading and composition or translation is almost entirely absent or lost.

Henry Parker, Lord Morley, recalled Mary's translation in the dedication of 'The Angelical Salutacion set forthe by Thomas Alquine', one of the eight surviving manuscripts he gave to her as New Year's gifts between the later 1530s and his death in 1556. Mary's version was 'so well done, so neare to the Laten that when I loke upon yt, I have not only marvell at the doinge of yt, but farther, for the well doynge'; the text survives only in a lavish, contemporary *Book of Hours*.[32] Mary was at least 20 by the time Morley complimented her ability to 'perfectly rede, wright and constrewe Laten, but farthermore translate eny harde thinge of the Latin'.[33] But if the 12-year-old Mary had 'a good command of both classical Latin and French', she seems not to have been encouraged to showcase widely or memorably her juvenile abilities.[34] Moreover, Morley's indifferent competence as translator from Latin creates further uncertainty: in another preface he confesses, 'the wordes of Cicero ar so wonderfull, and the sense in many places so diffuse, that it passeth my learnynge or capacyte to put it in oure speache'.[35]

Flattery of Mary's education was, however, used by Erasmus to encourage Charles Blount's further study of Latin and Greek in his enlarged edition of his *Adagia* in 1528:

> first your father provides an example, next that most noble girl, almost equal to you in age, Princess Mary, born of a learned king and a queen no less learned than pious, who already writes letters well in Latin and has a nature worthy of such lineage. Then the several girls of More's household, so very like a chorus of the Muses.[36]

Erasmus, who no doubt relied on reports of Mary's skill in writing letters, looks beyond Mary to Henry and Katherine in associating his old patron's son (and potential future benefactor) with not merely noble, but royal, endeavour. Equally, the association of Mary with the conspicuously superior achievements of her seniors indicates the conventionality of this praise. Moreover, even reading alleged compositions could deceive: where Blount's father had revealed corrected drafts to convince Erasmus of Henry VIII's youthful epistolary accomplishments, Erasmus, having praised Charles's eloquence in the dedication to his Livy, found that his tutor Petrus Vulcanius had applied the final polish.[37] But this aside, the boy Blount, rather than Mary, was prescribed a thorough grounding in *bonae litterae* and had his letters circulated for approval.

Unstudied for Action: Did Mary Ever Read Livy?

It is telling that Mary's part of *De ratione studii puerilis* promotes Livy only as a source of the story of Lucretia, who, alongside Griselda and others found in the likes of Valerius and Sabellicus provide figures for the straightforward commendation of virtue or the averting of vice.[38] This conforms to the list of *autores* (authors) with which the epistle ends, including Cicero, Seneca and Plutarch, whose role is to cultivate correct language and behaviour equally in their readers.[39] The recommendation of those of Plato's dialogues on statecraft (already widely available in print in Latin translation), and More's *Utopia*, an equally demanding text for the novice, register Vives's desire to reflect Erasmian interests.[40] For Mary, however, history should be easy reading (*non anxie*) from the digests and epitomes of Justinus, Florus and Valerius.

Charles Blount's reading is organized differently, under *Historiae, Scriptores agricolationum, Poetae, Grammatici,* and *Interpretes* (histories,

writers on agriculture, poets, philologists and translators). Conversa-
tional eloquence and concomitant oratorial skills should be developed
through eclectic reading in *historiae*: the most delightful fluency of
Livy; the terseness of Suetonius, more sinews than flesh; Caesar,
the faultless model of Roman eloquence; the inimitable Sallust –
read by Margaret Roper, as we learn from Thomas More's letters
to his daughter, and suitable for the more advanced reader, as Tacitus
recommends.[41] Besides style, historians teach the budding statesman.
Charles, as dedicatee of Erasmus' translation of Livy, was publicly
exhorted to emulate his father:

> no reading is more suitable for great men (*magnatibus viris*)...when your father
> was the schoolmate of this King, even as a young man, they pored over histories
> in detail, and, what is more, with the greatest encouragement of his father, Henry
> VII, a prudent King of especially good judgement.[42]

Erasmus had recently dedicated his *Apophthegmata* (1531), his translation and interpretation of mainly Plutarchan aphorisms and anecdotes,
to the young William, duke of Cleves, stating that 'history, which,
because it presents achievements, admirable or otherwise, to be
viewed as if in a painting, and not without enjoyment, would seem to
be more suited than philosophy for great men (*magnatibus viris*)'.[43]
Mary's treatises do not encourage such encounters with classical
historians for their political and rhetorical lessons. The cultivation
of personal devotion points instead towards a contemplative, passive
virtue instead of active and eloquently persuasive *virtù*.[44]

Vives's discussion of pious and moral reading in his *De institutione* similarly marginalizes history, and generally narrows that of
the *De ratione studii*. He draws on Jerome's advice to Laeta on the
instruction of her daughter, Paula: ' "Let her not hear anything nor
speak anything except what pertains to the fear of God." '[45] Doubt-
less he [Jerome] would give the same advice with regard to reading.'
Vives's discussion of Greek literature confirms the difference between
Mary's and Charles's horizons of expectation. Charles's reading list
includes some of Lucian's dialogues, the short orations of Isocrates
and Aesop's fables, then the orators (more Isocrates, Demosthenes,
Lysias, Aeschines, Aristides and further Lucian), philosophers (Plato,
Aristotle, Xenophon, Theophrastus), followed by Thucydides and
Plutarch.[46] The poets (Aristophanes, then Homer, then Euripides and
Sophocles), tackled only after study of Attic grammar through Apol-
lonius and Johannes Grammaticus, complete the provision in terms

similar to those of Erasmus' *De ratione studii*, which concludes that 'almost all knowledge of things is to be sought in the Greek authors', a call echoed by English humanists from Pace to Ascham.[47]

But Greek aside, the *De institutione* persistently delimits the relevance to women of the arts of eloquence and their political context, just as the *De ratione studii* exhorts Charles more forcefully than Mary. Her prescriptions stress the private context of the moral discourse for defending virtue or chastity. Thomas More, indeed, considered the cultivation of virtue in his learned daughters primarily a preparation for intellectual equality in the domestic sphere, to be 'more truly and steadfastly chaste', as Vives put it.[48] For Vives, female education should foster 'the study of wisdom, which forms morals in the way of virtue, the study of wisdom which teaches the best and holiest way of life. I am not at all concerned with eloquence. A woman has no need of that; she needs rectitude and wisdom.' He equivocated in stating that:

> in the art of speaking I put no limit either on male or female, save that it is reasonable that a man may be equipped with the knowledge of many and varied subjects, which will be of profit to himself and to the state, and that he is endowed with experience and learning, which will be diffused and transmitted to others.[49]

Then he reasserted that

> it is not shameful for a woman to be silent [...] in a woman no one requires eloquence or talent or wisdom or skills or administration of the republic or justice or generosity; no one asks anything of her but chastity. If that one thing is missing, it is as if all were lacking to a man. In a woman chastity is the equivalent of all virtues.[50]

Loades's account of Mary's education stays close to these prescriptions: 'Piety, chastity and humane letters were the objectives of those who guided her lessons from the very first, and the prospect of marriage dominated the classroom as much as it did her role in the political life of her father's court'.[51] Marillac, the French ambassador, conveyed to François I in 1541 the report of an alleged lady-in-waiting who stated that Mary consoled herself with '*litterae humaniores*'.[52] If 'humane letters' implies *litterae humaniores* – that is, the curriculum of the *studia humanitatis* – neither prescriptions nor evidence suggest a full liberal programme. Back in June 1530, a Milanese envoy, Augustino Scarpinello reported from London – on an earlier marriage negotiation, this time to the duke of Milan, Francesco Sforza – that 'the princess occupies herself with her very becoming studies in her usual residence'.[53] Although music was among these frequently mentioned decorous accomplishments (Mary's passion for hunting aside), as Loades states, by the mid-1530s 'there are remarkably few references to either instruments or books'.[54] If her literary education was supposed to stress morality in support of chastity and her potential future role as royal wife, the emphasis was on Christian devotional rather than ancient philosophical or historical works.

The End of Mary's Formal Education

In March 1531 while Charles was warmed by Erasmus' dedication of his Livy, Mary's studies cannot have insulated her from the disintegration of her family. She fell ill in early April: what Chapuys described as her stomach pains, Scarpinello, following the physicians, termed 'hysteria'.[55] Relations between Katherine and Henry finally collapsed in May; in July, Henry dismissed Katherine from court and forbade her further contact with Mary. After an ambiguous interim during which Henry seems not to have actively mistreated Mary, in the summer of 1533, Henry told Cromwell to have Lord John Hussey, Mary's lord chamberlain, take into his possession Mary's princely jewels, a task hindered temporarily by Margaret Pole. On 7 September, following Elizabeth's birth, Mary was informed that she was no longer a princess and her household was dissolved.

At this point Mary's formal education probably finished.[56] Fetherston refused the Oath of Supremacy in 1534, and was executed on 30 July 1540 after six years in the Tower.[57] Hussey and Margaret Pole fell similarly on the wrong side of Henry's policy. How intensively humanistic Mary's 'very becoming studies' had been in these last few years is questionable, given the disruptions to health, and the unavoidable distractions of her mother's plight. However, a significant glimpse is caught in one of Katherine's last letters from Buckden Place in April 1534, shortly after Archbishop Cranmer had nullified her marriage. Here she counselled Mary to preserve her virtue and to find 'good things' in the accompanying pious Latin works: Lodolphus of Saxony's *Vita Christi* (*Life of Christ*), popular throughout the fourteenth and fifteenth centuries, with a 'declaration of the Gospels', and also the consolatory epistles of Jerome to Paula and Eustochium.[58] The late-teenage Mary thus appears inclined to read, or was at least encouraged to study, specific, short patristic epistles and traditional devotional works. Yet despite her later encounter with

Erasmus' biblical paraphrases, Katherine seems not to have sent
to Mary her copy of his recent *De praeparatione ad mortem* (*On
the preparation for death*), printed 1534 and dedicated to Thomas
Boleyn.[59]
 Looking back at what Bernard André recorded on his tutoring of
the hapless Prince Arthur shows the considerable gap between his
'modish' education and that of the niece he would never know:

> before he had reached his sixteenth birthday, he had either committed in part to
> memory or had at least handled and read, at one time or another, with his own
> hands and eyes, all of the following: in grammar, Guarino, Perotti, Pomponio Leto,
> Sulpizio, Aulus Gellius, and Valla; in poetry, Homer, Vergil, Lucan, Ovid, Silius
> Italicus, Plautus, and Terence; in oratory, the *De officiis* (*On duties*), the *Letters*, and
> the *Paradoxa stoicorum* (*The paradoxes of the Stoics*) of Cicero, and Quintilian; and in
> history Thucydides, Livy, Caesar's *Commentaries*, Suetonius, Tacitus, Pliny, Valerius
> Maximus, Sallust, and Eusebius.[60]

No doubt the Greeks were read in Latin translations since in late
fifteenth-century England the texts of most Greek authors were
only available in Latin although a few were available in the original
language. In comparison, very little is known about Mary's reading habits over the eight years following the dissolution of her
household. In the dedication of one manuscript, Morley invited
Mary to compare his translation of part of Athanasius's 'Letter to
Marcellinus' on reading the Psalms with the Latin original, which
appeared in sundry small-format Latin paraphrases of the Psalms during this period. His modesty at thinking Poliziano's style 'exselent'
but difficult again indicates Morley's problems as translator from
Latin rather than Poliziano's from Greek, while the donor emphasizes, instead of *exegesis* of the Psalms, the pious 'saynge with your
Chapleyn the seruice of the daye'.[61] Until Mary became involved
in Katherine Parr's proposal for the translation of Erasmus' *Paraphrases on the New Testament*, the topic of Aysha Pollnitz's chapter in
this volume, we have little to suggest Mary's earlier interest in the
philosophia Christi and its literary expression, let alone broad classical
reading.

Praise and Piety

The sundry epigrams of the Henrician antiquarian and humanist scholar John Leland provide a different perspective on Mary's
learning. Leland's sustained celebration of Henrician humanism is

expressed in the cosmopolitan epideictic of poems such as *Instauratio bonarum literarum* (*The revival of literature*)[62] and *Commigratio bonarum literarum in Britanniam* (*The coming of literature into Britain*).[63] These occasional poems circulated in manuscript, making many frustratingly difficult to date. However, those addressing learned English ladies, with adjustments advisably made for the excesses of flattery, suggest limits on how Leland wished, or felt able, to represent Mary. One poem concerns the gift, possibly Leland's, of the *De re uxoria* (*On wifely duties*) by Francesco Barbaro, 'not inappropriate for your responsibilities', first composed in Florence by the visiting early Venetian humanist for Lorenzo de' Medici's marriage to Ginevra Cavalcanti in 1416.[64] Beyond Mary's duty, another possibly epigraphic poem (*Clarum virgineae decus cohortis*) hints at her reading:

> Brilliant glory of the virginal throng, who brightens your nation's glowering storm clouds with the lights of your virtue, behold, I have brought flowers concealed in Seneca's blooming garden, sweeter than those the rose-gardens of purple Paestum bears. For these caress the twin openings of the nose with a scent destined for a few hours. But those caress the mind's sacred recesses with an ambrosial scent for a very long time.[65]

Were these 'flowers' excerpts copied into a manuscript, or a printed book, large or small? Did Seneca appear in his original Latin, or in French or English (first printed version 1547)? Latin dedications sometimes introduced vernacular works. This interest in Seneca, one of the best-known Latin authors with a medieval tradition, is rendered more likely by the translation of Seneca's 'moral epistle' 91 fused with a portion of letter 120 presented by Morley to Mary on one New Year between 1537 and 1547.[66]

We can compare this poem to Leland's poems to More's daughters, the Moriades – Margaret, Elizabeth and Cecily. In one, he sings of his astonishment at the 'Graces' of More's household.[67] In another the three outstrip the learned daughters of Hortensius, Cicero's friend and rival orator:

> Not for them is the carding of Milesian wool, nor, with a ready hand, to spin thread. To meditate often upon the monuments of Latin eloquence and to adorn its words with their learned annotations is their delight. Nor less to read Greek authors, Homer, and him who holds greatest glory in speaking [Demosthenes]. Nor will I mention the passion with which they study Aristotle's books, mystic

gifts of the goddess of wisdom. It will henceforth be shameful for men to be ignorant of the arts of Minerva, as a bevy of women so adores them.[68]

It is her half-sister Elizabeth rather than Mary who received applause similar to that bestowed on More's daughters: for example, Leland recalls the 11-year-old at Ampthill, when John Cheke, the royal tutor, 'arranged for you to greet me in Latin, so that I might learn how much grace was in your mouth. I had conceived every great notion of you, but, fair lady, you surpassed all my judgement'.[69] Leland addresses Charles Blount in another poem, mentioning the gift of a Greek work in translation, perhaps the *Batrachomyomachia* (*Battle of the frogs and mice*): 'Nor should you scorn a man playing Greek Homer's sweeter songs on the strings of a Latin lyre'.[70] Elsewhere, Leland praises Blount's eloquence, 'the enduring grace of the Attic tongue, and the pure delights of the Latin one'.[71] His former tutee Thomas Howard and Henry Fitzroy, duke of Richmond, are addressed in similar terms in other poems. Where these *encomia* press towards Greek, rhetorically or otherwise, those for Mary fall short of its association with true eloquence, just as in Vives's *De ratione*. No one like William Gonnell, John Clement or Richard Hyrde, the resident humanist servant-scholars in More's household, seems to have been involved in Mary's education.[72]

In the mid-1530s, Mary's reading is best suggested by her mother's books. At the time of Katherine's death on 8 January 1536, her goods included 'a primer, written in vellom, covered withe clothe of golde, having two claspis of silver and gilte'; 'three bookes covered withe golde foyle, and tyed with grene reabande'; and 'seevyntene other bookys, smalle and greate, lockid in a cheste'.[73] Carley considers the first four books most probably devotional, the remaining 17 most likely reflecting Katherine's 'musically sophisticated and pious' tastes. Sallust in Spanish or Latin, a Dante and Petrarch's *De remediis utriusque fortunae* (*On remedies for good and bad fortune*) in Castilian translation perhaps account for a few. Birrell finds many items with poignant personal associations for Mary among the surprisingly large number of her books surviving in the Royal Library, while Carley, instead, suggests that Morley's gifts provide the most coherent picture of her reading.[74] The black covers of her books of 'devout humanism', scuffed probably through use, contrast with the more formal finely bound folios of Augustine and presentation copies of later apologetic works of Catholic ecclesiastics like Stephen Gardiner, Cuthbert Tunstall and Alban Langdale. Pedro de Soto's

Assertio Catholicae Fidei (*Defence of the Catholic faith*) and Alfonso de Castro's *De iusta haereticorum punitione* (*On the just punishment of heretics*) register more sombre doctrinal concerns.[75]

In 1553, the Queen's Printer, John Cawood printed Joannes Genesius Sepulveda's treatise on the *magna questio* (great question) of her parents' divorce, *De ritu nuptiarum et dispensatione* (*Concerning the rites of marriage and dispensation*). Although Birrell terms this a 'futile republication' by royal command, it does seem to suggest an ongoing preoccupation with legitimacy which returned Mary to a traumatic and disrupted past.[76] Her possession of *Le livre...faisant mention des sept parolles que...Jesuchrist dit en larbre de la croix* (The book mentioning the seven words that Jesus said on the cross, 1545) by Jean Gagnay (Gagnaeus) again expresses a conservative piety.[77] On the other hand, John Hopton, Marian bishop of Norwich and energetic restorer of the 'old faith', left instructions in his will that certain books familiar to the queen be returned to her: a Bible, a Greek New Testament, and a de luxe (perhaps finely bound) copy of Aristophanes, the last a particular distraction from his 'gruelling programme of work'.[78] But how familiar Mary was with the Greek texts remains frustratingly unclear. Had Hopton become attached to them while Mary's former trusted private chaplain under Edward, and had Mary had any interest in them before Hopton's departure for Norwich? Lamentably, they seem not to have found their way back to the Royal Library to reveal their use.

For Elizabeth, as David Starkey states, 'style was everything'.[79] Yet Mary was far from negligent in projecting forcefully a traditional, pious image for public consumption. Lacking the exemplary austerity of her maternal grandmother Isabella, her devotional habits derived instead from both her father's paternal grandmother, Lady Margaret Beaufort, and her mother.[80] Vives suggested in his *Linguae Latinae exercitatio* that Katherine's suffering was comparable to the patient Griselda's; William Forrest's *History of Grisild the second* made this equation unmissable under Mary.[81] There is a sense in which Mary's understandable resistance to the attacks on traditional religious practices and loyalty to memory and the past positioned her between the emergent and receding cultures. In 1555, Miles Hogarde was far from alone in articulating in print his relief at Queen Mary's restoration of Catholicism, 'when hope was almost past, as al men do knowe'.[82] Mary's earlier involvement with Erasmus' *Paraphrases* signals their flexible compatibility with late-Henrician religious policy, which was far from doctrinally evangelical. McConica's conclusion endures: 'In Udall's mind Henry's work was a wholly Erasmian achievement'.[83] Mary was perhaps not sympathetic to the view of Gardiner, who not only found the partiality of the translation objectionable, but thought Erasmus' original was written 'when his penne was wanton'.[84] Yet if they provided the pretext for Mary's participation in Katherine Parr's pious coterie of devotional translation, that itself can be seen partly as a continuation of Lady Margaret's interests.

However, Mary lacked Elizabeth's and Katherine's desire to explore through translation that intensely inward, penitential voice to express a human impotence towards salvation which could seem Lutheran in tendency. Thus Mary's tastes and books have more in common with the literary culture of that late-fifteenth-century confessor to both Lady Margaret and Henry VII, Christopher of Urswick, which J. B. Trapp termed 'sub-humanist'.[85] Hussey, for example, whose painful duty it was to relieve Mary of her princely jewels, gave her an early-fifteenth-century manuscript containing Augustine's *Soliloquia*, a work which furnished some of the extracts on the priesthood written for Urswick by Pieter Meghen in 1504–5.[86] Significantly, Hussey, who was executed on 29 June 1537 following his involvement in the Lincolnshire uprisings, received the dedication of *The mirror or glass of Christ's Passion* in 1534 from John Fewterer, the confessor-general of the Brigettines of Syon Abbey, Middlesex. That Hussey's wife was sent to the Tower in 1536 for persisting to call the queen dowager's daughter 'princess' suggests the defiant support Mary received, how such literary networks operated, and how gifts could become painful memorials of costly loyalty.[87]

Many of Morley's gifts to Mary suggest a quietistic, conservative devotional solidarity in the face of the Henrician Reformation: Turrecremata on Psalm 36 from the *Expositio super toto Psalterio* (*The explanation of the whole psalter*), may be added to Athanasius on the Psalms, Aquinas on the *Ave Maria*, and Anselm on 'The stature and form and life of our blessed lady and of our saviour Christ Jesus'.[88] Morley's Erasmus is more the younger, conventional writer of the *Paean Virgini matri dicendus*: the *Laud and praise to be said unto the Virgin Mary mother of Christ Jesus*, the translation of which gave Morley the opportunity, in its dedication to the living Mary, to lament the decline in the worshipping of the Virgin, and more broadly the traditional cult of the saints.[89] Morley, a 'backwoodsman' and ingratiating political survivor who seems to have become associated with Mary around the time of Hussey's death, owed much of his religious outlook to early service in Lady Margaret's household.[90] Like Hussey, he gave Mary 'an olde boke' in manuscript, Richard Rolle's *Latin Psalter*.[91] These works were far less pertinent to Katherine Parr and her reforming circle, despite a shared interest in the Psalms. Carley suggests how devotional rather than antiquarian attachment to such works would flow into the recusant preservation of 'old' religious culture in the early Elizabethan years.[92] We may see this anticipated in Morley's last gift to Mary, a quasi-hagiography of Lady Margaret, the *Miracles of the Sacrament*, donated in 1556, the year of his death.[93] Here Morley presents to Mary, as Claudian did to Theodosius, 'an exemplar of public and private virtue, an ordered regime embracing both pomp and charity'.[94] His account, he apologizes, stands in for John Fisher's, who 'shewyd me not long before his death that he had writen her life', invoking his martyrdom on 22 June 1535. Warmer recollections of Lady Margaret's exemplary habits nevertheless dominate:

> the myddes of her dynner either her amner [almoner] or I redde some vertuous tale unto her of the life of Chryst or such like, the latter ende of her dinner agayne she was disposed to talk with the bishop or with her chauncelour, which satt at her bordis ende, of some godly matter.[95]

The historical procession which constitutes the *Miracles of the Sacrament* ends with Lady Margaret, coming full circle not so much to the present but to the era before the internecine and schismatic politics of the Reformation. Mary as 'Defendoresse of the Faithe', the title granted to her Catholic father in 1521 by Pope Leo X, is called upon to correct the late 'barbarous estate' which 'denyed the head of the Church, the popes holynes'.[96] The example to which Mary's virtue is directed is, once again, the era immediately preceding the royal divorce, the Act of Supremacy, the humiliating dissolution of her household, dignity and independence, and the death of her saintly mother.

Morley's recognition of papal authority should probably be taken more as reflecting the recipient's position in 1556, rather than advising a shift in policy; any earlier ambiguity in Mary's attitude to the Supremacy was resolved in Rome's favour by Cardinal Pole's return to England. Thus if Erasmus' *Paraphrases* provided comfortable biblical material which could be shared around the Parr circle, the added polemical prefaces would have caused Mary increasing concern during her reign. Neither would the vehement expressions of anti-Roman sentiment in these long dedicatory addresses to the monumental folio by the editor-in-chief, Nicholas Udall, have won Erasmus' approval. Moreover, while the Edwardian Injunctions of 1547 demanded a copy of the *Paraphrases* in every church, opinion is divided over whether or not the *Paraphrases*, like the Great Bible, was left in Marian churches, and if it was left, whether this was because it presented only a slight threat to the restoration of Catholicism, or because its popularity rendered removal too problematic.[97]

The *Paraphrases* certainly had some influence on how Mary was perceived. Although dedications of the 1550s dwell mostly on her piety and virtue, with the latter tending to be absorbed into the former, John Standish borrowed significantly from Udall's prefatory dedication to the *Paraphrase on John* for the part of the preface to his *Discourse* (1554) which praises Mary:

> an example of all vertue, devotion and prayer, a spectacle to al realmes? And suerly the common voice is that her grace is not onely moste noble, moste vertuous, most wittie, and most studious, but also moste excellent in learning, farre passinge eyther the Romaines, Cornelia & Hortensia, or the godly learned women of whom S. Hierome writeth Eustochium Paula and Blesilla.[98]

But Standish's second-hand praise finally subsumes Mary into her mother's reputation: 'I wyl say no more but only this, yt the doughter may welbe knowen by the mother, and that as we fell from all goodnes at the most uniust fall of her Mother Queene Catheryn: So do we nowe rise agayne'.[99] Similarly, Robert Wingfield's *Vita Mariae Angliae Reginae* (*Life of Mary, Queen of England*), an account of Mary's 'coup d'etat and first regnal year', states that on her accession Mary 'turned her whole attention to religion and godliness [*pietatem*], the excellence of which she had learnt from her early childhood under the guidance of that most sacred [*pientissimae*] princess her mother'.[100] As in most other celebrations of Mary, piety and religiosity predominate.[101] Wingfield declines the opportunity to mention Mary's learning – perhaps it did not suit the political purpose of his *Vita* – yet does record that William Cecil and Nicholas Bacon 'married two sisters of remarkable education [*duas sorores perquam doctas*], daughters of Sir Anthony Cooke', Mildred and Anne respectively.[102]

Under Edward, Mary emerged as a conservative magnate, whose 'household became ever more explicitly founded on the dictates of the princess's personal piety and defined by the confessional affiliation of her servants. ... Catholic allegiance and personal loyalty to Mary became inextricably linked'.[103] Although reform-minded learned ladies like Anne Cooke were household familiars, Mary's religion became the heart of her personal rule, and it is this which dominated dedications to her. The translator of St Vincent of Lerins's *Pro catholicae fidei antiquitate libellus* (*A short book defending the antiquity of the Catholic faith*), John Proctor, for example, praised Mary as 'a lady of heauenly simplicitie . . . so noble a Quene, soo godly a Mary, so heavenlye a uirgin'. The emphasis, here as elsewhere, is on 'the olde religion, newlye recouered and set furthe by our heauenlye and vertuous maiden Quene'.[104] For John Aungel, her chaplain, she was 'garnished with so many excellent giftes of grace, vertue, nature, and fortune' and 'whollye geven to the study of vertue & godlines'.[105] But if this is the general tenor of sundry dedicatory addresses, accompanying remarks about Mary's learning are either fleeting courtesies or altogether absent. As Wizeman concludes, dedications to Mary generally marked the authors' regard and gratitude for her devotion to Catholicism and their desire to show their own support for its revival.[106]

In contrast, Elizabeth's letters conspicuously showcased her learning and advertised her tutors.[107] Although schoolroom exercises, they convey more than the bald prescriptions of Vives's *De ratione studii puerilis*. Elizabeth's locating, weighing and manipulation of classical maxims or biblical quotations for her compositions here testify to her advancement in the *studia humanitatis*, learning and independent judgement combining with growing eloquence.[108] Display was perhaps as significant as their production. In his posthumous, unfinished *The Schoolmaster* (1570), Ascham keenly rehearsed his epistolary account of Elizabeth's assiduous reading of Greek orators of 1555 in describing her exemplary daily practice of double translation, a Latin-English exercise undertaken by More's daughters decades before.[109] Political interests undoubtedly influenced the shaping and promotion of Elizabeth's learned image, with Ascham taking a lead in the exchange and circulation of laudatory letters.[110] In 1550, Ascham had attempted to persuade Johann Sturm to dedicate his work on Aeschines and Demosthenes to Lady Jane Grey.[111] That year, he succeeded in eliciting very public dedicatory compliments for Elizabeth from Sturm in his *De periodis* (*On sentences*). The presentation copy at Trinity College, Cambridge, bound in blue silk, bears Sturm's autograph Greek verses to Edward VI, which he was expected to comprehend.[112] Ascham manages Elizabeth's further praise by Sturm in a letter soon printed in 1551 as half of *Epistolae duae de nobilitate Anglicana* (*Two letters concerning the English nobility*):

Since she can unravel the most artful speech and the most complex webs, she can also judge this little work … it is most fitting that I have sent her this little book. For when it comes to the publication of books, it is foolish to address them to those who know nothing about what is dealt with, or who do not really love the same things.[113]

For all the political and personal interests entailed in such textual exchanges, contrasts between the representation of Elizabeth's and Mary's learning are less easily reduced to merely rhetorical effects. The burden of evidence still lies with those wishing to close the gap between Mary and Elizabeth. After all, there was no want either of Catholic learned ladies at court or praise for them.

Under Mary, the pragmatic Ascham sought patronage in 1554 from Mary Clarke (Bassett), the daughter of Margaret and William Roper, granddaughter of Thomas More, and resolutely Catholic lady-in-waiting to the queen. Her abilities fulfilled her genealogy: fluency in Greek and Latin are well represented in her Latin translation of the first book, and Englishing of the first five books (dedicated to Mary), of Eusebius's *Ecclesiastical History*, and the English translation of More's *De tristitia Christi* (*On the sadness of Christ*).[114] In his petition to Mary Clarke, Ascham implicitly registered the difference between her abilities and the queen's when he stated that 'From this our ruler you have obtained your commitment to virtue, from your grandfather your genius for learning, and from both your great excellence in both areas'.[115] Mary's virtue, as we have come to expect, signifies exemplary piety and devotion more than humanistic accomplishments.

Nevertheless, she enjoyed the company of learned women, embracing both the religiously conservative Mary Clarke and the reformist Anne Cooke, already a translator of Ochino's Calvinist sermons on election and predestination. Mary Clarke's scholarly competence allowed criticism of the recent Greek edition of Eusebius, and provided Catholic humanists like John Morwen, a member of the conservative humanist circle at Oxford, with a conduit for patronage. In the Edwardian Latin translation of a Greek Menology he dedicated to Mary, Morwen records his inspiration by Mary Clarke's handling of patristic works.[116] Princess Mary also attracted the dedication of her chaplain confessor and accomplished Hellenist, John Christopherson's *De futili loquacitate* (*On the futility of talkativeness*), his Latin version of Plutarch's essay on talkativeness (*De garrulitate*), which matched Cheke's translation of the *De superstitione* for her father.[117] Christopherson would succeed to the Mastership of Trinity College,

Cambridge in 1553, would become dean of Norwich the following year (Hopton, another of Mary's chaplains, was his bishop within
months), and bishop of Chichester in 1557. Both ambitious works
displayed their scholarship to those learned scholar-courtiers around
Mary who advised her on patronage and advancement.

The limits of Mary's humanistic education and its fruits thus remain
difficult to define. There are too many lacunae, a paucity of firm
evidence offered by the books she owned or was known to have
read. She was certainly not completely untouched by humanism.
Jane Stevenson recently concluded that where Elizabeth, 'one of the
most scholarly members of her court', was given 'a full humanist
education in Latin, Greek, and modern languages', Mary 'was very
carefully educated, but she does not seem to have had any personal
taste for humanism'.[118] Against this, and Elton's harsher view, the pattern of female education Katherine of Aragon successfully offered
through her daughter should be thought of as having provided the
basis for Elizabeth's, whose 'princely' education was later developed
and displayed alongside Edward's, when it became paramount that
she, like Jane Grey, exhibit a consummate humanistic grasp of 'good
literature' in the service of monarchical and religious authority. Mary's
predominant role was instead latterly shaped in defending the 'old
religion'. Her later supporters seem to have either lacked a glitter-
ing image of learning to reflect consistently in their dedications and
eulogies – she had no former or current tutors to benefit from such
displays – or felt it unnecessary to exploit what she offered. Instead
Mary was represented through her intense devotion to the mass and
the pious traditional fulfilment of daily religious offices, a politicized
private preoccupation which substituted for much of the humanistic
potential she may have possessed.

7

Religion and Translation at the Court of Henry VIII: Princess Mary, Katherine Parr and the *Paraphrases* of Erasmus

Aysha Pollnitz

In July 1547 Edward VI's council ordered every parish church in England to equip itself with a copy of the English Bible, and within 12 months the 'Paraphrasis of Erasmus also in English upon the Gospels'. This work was printed on 31 January 1548, edited by the evangelical schoolmaster and playwright Nicholas Udall.[1] By the terms of Edward's proclamation, it was to be chained 'in some convenient place, within the said church' so that 'parishioners may most commodiously resort unto the same, and read the same'.[2] In 1549 a second volume comprising Erasmus' paraphrases on the epistles and Leo Jud's commentary on Revelation was printed. Both tomes were revised in 1551–52 to reflect the stridently evangelical second prayer book.[3]

The Edwardian printing and injunction set the tone for the reception of English *Paraphrases*. John Craig has pointed out that they were purchased by and used in at least 162 parishes in the period between 1548 and 1666. During Mary I's reign, Archdeacon Nicholas Harpsfield ordered nine parishes to remove copies of the English Bible and *Paraphrases* but the Elizabethan injunctions of 1559 returned the work to churches.[4] Thomas Cromwell had been an early patron of Leonard Cox's translation of the *Paraphrase on Titus*. Stephen Gardiner despised both the Latin original and the 1548 translation, which was championed by Archbishop Thomas Cranmer.[5] Katherine Parr was its patron. The 1549 tome was sponsored by Anne Seymour, duchess of Somerset. In short, Erasmus' *Paraphrases* have been described as a barometer which indicated the progress of the English Reformation.[6]

It is surprising then to open a copy of Erasmus' *Paraphrase on John* and discover that one of its translators was Princess Mary, a woman whose subsequent reign was dedicated to returning the English Church to Rome. Udall explained to Parr that the princess had taken 'great studie, peine and travaill, in translatyng this paraphrase of the said Erasmus ... at your hyghnesse speciall contemplacion'. Her attempt was a 'plaine declaracio[n] of [Mary's] most constaunt purpose to promote Goddes worde, and the free grace of his gospell'. The princess, however, had made herself ill 'with over peynfull studie' and had had to commit 'the same weorke to Maister Frauncisce Malet ... to be finished and made complete'.[7] In his dedication to the *Paraphrase on Acts*, Udall denied having done anything more than 'placed the texte, and divided the paraphrase' since it would have been a 'cryme of great arrogancie and presumpcion ... to entremedle' with Mary and Francis Mallett's translation.[8] Without a manuscript, however, it is difficult to ascertain how much of the translation was the princess's work and how much her chaplain contributed. The corroborating evidence of the princess's involvement, a letter from Katherine Parr to Mary in Princess Elizabeth's hand, was probably written on 20 September 1547. The letter confirms that Mary's translation was halted on account of illness and that Parr urged the princess to give her text to Mallett 'for correcting' (*in corrigendo*) and to be 'corrected' or 'repaired' (*emendatum*). Again it is not clear how much remained to be done.[9]

Mary's Catholicism and the ambiguous nature of this evidence have encouraged scholars to minimize her involvement in the *Paraphrases*. It has been suggested, for instance, that Parr pressured the princess to translate the *Paraphrase on John* to convert her stepdaughter and that Mary left it unfinished by way of protest.[10] As David Loades has said in another context: 'Mary was a Catholic' and this is 'the one thing that is, and always has been, clear' about her.[11] In this chapter I revisit the *Paraphrase on John* and argue that Mary's involvement should be viewed in other contexts. Firstly the English *Paraphrases* need to be considered in light of Henry VIII's religious policy, not Edward VI's. Secondly a strain of aristocratic female piety which flourished in the English court may help explain why Mary would have wanted to perform this 'royall exercise ... of virginly educacion'.[12] Ultimately

I suggest that the translation provides the best surviving evidence for the princess's intellectual life in the 1540s.

Mary, the *Paraphrases* and Religion under Henry VIII

In understanding how Princess Mary came to contribute to the translation, the timing is all. The *Paraphrases* were printed in 1548 but Udall's epistle dedicatory to Luke, dated 30 September 1545, shows that Parr's scheme was alive by the autumn of that year.[13] That Mary was invited to contribute to a Henrician project, not an Edwardine one, is important. As Loades has pointed out, once Mary had accepted the royal supremacy in June 1536 she made no overt protest about religious worship in England until Edward's council struck against the mass. She may have had reservations about aspects of Henry's Church but she was a consenting member of it.[14] The question, then, is how the princess may have viewed Erasmus and his *Paraphrases* in the final years of her father's reign.

Erasmus composed paraphrases on the New Testament (apart from Revelation) between the summer of 1517 and 1524. His work on the Gospel of John was printed in February 1523. Erasmus intended the *Paraphrases* to be 'in place of a commentary', clarifying interpretations of his New Testament (1516, 1519 and 1522) and *Annotationes* upon them.[15] Unlike medieval biblical commentaries, however, the *Paraphrases* provided a simple narrative for the uniform understanding of scripture. Erasmus recommended them for 'bridging gaps, smoothing rough passages, bringing order out of confusion and simplicity out of complication' in the New Testament.[16] They were meant to promote the personal imitation of Christ instead of learned disputation. Erasmus dedicated his gospel paraphrases to princes: Charles V got Matthew; the Archduke Ferdinand got John; Francis I got Mark; and Henry VIII received Luke in August 1523. Naturally, Erasmus was seeking patronage, but he was also encouraging lay readership of the *Paraphrases* and emphasizing the spiritual responsibilities of civil magistrates.[17]

The *Paraphrases* were immediately and enduringly popular. Johann Froben published complete editions in folio and octavo in 1524 and another complete version, revised by Erasmus, in 1532 (Epistles) and 1534 and 1535 (Gospels and Acts, octavo and folio editions respectively), prior to the posthumous *Opera omnia* (1540).[18] The *Paraphrases* were translated into German by 1530 and French in 1543, despite their condemnation by the Parisian theologian Noël Béda in 1526.

Béda had argued that Erasmus' descriptions of the importance of faith in Christ (on John 3.17–18, for instance) smacked of *sola fideism* and denied the importance of works and the sacraments.[19] It was certainly true that the vernacular *Paraphrases* found their readiest continental audiences among Reformers.

During Henry's reign, however, the Sorbonne's criticisms did not sound with great force in England, even among religious conservatives. The humanist Juan Luis Vives, who remained loyal to Rome and Katherine of Aragon during the divorce, recommended the *Paraphrases* to the young Princess Mary in his *De ratione studii puerilis* (1523).[20] Even after 1534 they were not regarded with particular suspicion by traditionalists other than Gardiner. In 1546 Richard Smith's and William Peryn's high-profile defences of the 'blessed sacrament of the aulter' attacked Martin Luther, John Frith, John Bale's paraphrase on Revelation and Philip Melanchthon, but they left Erasmus well alone. This is less surprising when one remembers that both clerics were drawing on *De veritate corporis et sanguinis Christi in eucharistia* (1527), the work of Erasmus' former student and patron, John Fisher. In short, an Erasmus who believed in free will, the real presence and the unity of Christ's Church was alive and well in late Henrician England.[21]

Mary was undoubtedly familiar with this Erasmus. Between 1537 and 1546 Henry Parker, Lord Morley, a humanist and religious conservative, presented the princess with an English version of Erasmus' *Paean Virgini matri dicendus* (*Praise to be said to the Virgin Mother*, 1503). In his preface Morley lamented the decline of the veneration of saints in England. Particularly at fault were those clerics who 'fallynge frome one hereticall opynyone to another, at last deny the honour due to God hymsellf in the moste holy and dyvyne Sacrament of the Aulter'.[22] For Morley, however, Erasmus was on the side of Mary and the angels.

In the 1530s, however, Erasmus' *Paraphrases* had been translated into English to support a cause which Fisher, and initially Mary and Morley, could not stomach. The preface to Cox's 1534 translation of Erasmus' *Paraphrase on Titus* extended the humanist's arguments for the religious role of civil magistrates to justify the royal supremacy.[23] Indeed stridently reformist appropriations of Erasmus typically had to push his temperate claims further. When Udall was revising the English *Paraphrases* in 1551 and 1552, he thought it necessary to add marginal notes to give Erasmus' topology teeth against the 'tirannie of the Romishe Babilon'.[24] He even apologized to radical Edwardine readers for Erasmus' doctrinal moderation. The humanist 'wrote in

suche a daungerous season, as he was of force constreined either to
kepe silence, or els to speake within such limites & compace as the
world might than beare'. By 1552 the 'reformed' Erasmus who advocated the 'word of God' royal supremacy, vernacular scripture and 'the
true doctrine of our religion', was an important figure in England.[25]
Yet his status as an evangelical was not uncontested.

In explaining how Erasmus' composite reputation evolved,
Henrician religious policy is significant. After Thomas Cromwell's
fall in 1540, official doctrine grew more conservative regarding
the eucharist. *The King's Book* (1543) took a firm line against
sola fideism and emphasized the real presence in the mass.[26] In an
apparent about-face, the 1543 'Act for the advancement of true
religion' also prohibited the common sort from reading vernacular scripture. Yet Henry and Cranmer had not retreated from
the propagation of the *verbum Dei*; they simply filtered God's
word through authorized, interpretive guides. In 1544, for instance,
the royal printer issued vernacular prayers and an English primer
which included select scriptural readings that set out English subjects' 'dutye towardes God, [and] their prince'.[27] As Richard Rex
has argued, the word of God was too useful an idea to abandon; it justified obedience to royally sanctioned prescriptions for
worship.[28]

Erasmus' *Paraphrases* were well suited to this religious climate. As
Udall pointed out in his 1545 letter to Parr, the vernacular *Paraphrases* provided just this sort of digestible para-scriptural instruction
for 'the grosse, rude & greene stomaked englishmen'.[29] He expressed
his hope that the translators had 'dooen a thyng to your moste
regal spouse the kynges Maiestie so acceptable' that it would be
authorized.[30] The editor punctuated Erasmus' *Paraphrases* with the
text of the Great Bible to stress its orthodoxy. Thomas Caius was persuaded to translate Mark by the king's physician George Owen; he
had reason to think that Henry would support the translation. Indeed
the prospect of the king's approval is likely to have been important
to all the known contributors to the 1548 tome, none of whom
were hot gospellers.[31] Even Udall gave up proclaiming the reformed
faith under Mary to become her 'welbeloved' court playwright.[32]
From their inception, the English *Paraphrases* were intended to
further Henry's commitment to spreading the carefully mediated
verbum Dei.

The Henrician *Paraphrases* did not come about, possibly because
the project commenced at the moment when the king's energies
were starting to move in other directions. Yet the idea that Henry

would support the printing of English *Paraphrases* was not unrealistic in 1545. The contributors to the translation may have been aware that the king had read with approval parts of the Latin *Paraphrases* in the Froben folio of 1524.[33] When it came to marginalia, Henry VIII was no Gabriel Harvey. His annotations on Erasmus' *Paraphrasis in . . . Joannem* were graphical with the occasional '*nota*'. Nevertheless the king was attentive to passages that related to questions of faith and the sacraments. Henry placed lines, stylized trefoils and a manicule beside several discussions (on John 3:16–19, 3:31–34, 14:5–6) which emphasized the necessity of faith in Christ's divinity. Indeed, he included passages which had struck Béda as *sola fideist*.[34] Yet Henry VIII also marked with stylized trefoils, a bird's beak and a '*nota*', places on John (14.12–21) where Erasmus confirmed that Christians should subsequently demonstrate charity, imitate Christ's words and deeds and follow God's commands.[35] Additionally Henry drew a manicule (with a long index finger) to indicate Erasmus' insistence that John 6:51–56 confirmed Christ's real presence in the bread and wine. Erasmus would subsequently appeal to this verse and his paraphrase upon it to demonstrate his eucharistic orthodoxy.[36]

Without over-interpreting this evidence, Henry's ethical pointers direct us to a further, textual reason for the *Paraphrases*' acceptability to some English traditionalists in the 1540s. At a time when the efficacy of the sacraments was being questioned, Erasmus's *Paraphrase on John* marshalled scriptural evidence to support the conservative position of *The King's Book*. While modern commentators have doubted Erasmus' sincerity on this point, sixteenth-century readers could interpret the *Paraphrases* as defending the eucharist and mass as both sacrament and sacrifice. This was the view to which Mary would cling throughout her life.[37]

In 1545, then, neither Erasmus nor the *Paraphrases* were inevitably linked to Lutheranism in England. Mary probably saw the *Paraphrases* as congruent to Henry's late religious policy: they emphasized the *verbum Dei*, albeit para-scripturally, and offered an orthodox view of the sacraments. Indeed after Mary had accepted the royal supremacy, she may even have found the doctrine of Erasmus' *Paraphrases* comforting. They were commentaries that Vives had instructed her to read when she was still parsing her Latin for her mother.[38] Moreover, the idea of translating para-scriptural works for the benefit of 'grosse, rude & greene stomaked englishme[n]' would have had an intrinsic appeal to the princess.

Aristocratic Female Piety and the Act of Translation

Mary's positive reasons for contributing to the last great translation project of her father's reign may have sprung from a tradition of learning among English noblewomen. When Udall praised Mary's grammatical efforts in 1548 he emphasized that she was one of:

> the great noumbre of noble weomen in this our time and countrey of Englande, not onelye geven to the studie of humaine sciences and of straunge tongues, but also so throughlye experte in holy scriptures, that they are hable to compare with the beste wryters as well in endictynge and pennyng of godlye and fruitfull treatises to the enstruccion and edifiynge of whole realmes in the knowlege of god, as also in translating good bokes out of Latine or Greke into Englishe for the use and commoditie of suche as are rude and ignoraunte of the sayd tounges.[39]

Scholars have attributed this fashion for female religious translation to the Reformation. Certainly the evangelical emphasis on scripture reading and the scarcity of outlets for women's literary expression encouraged its development.[40] Yet its origin lay elsewhere.

Before the Reformation, Countess Margaret Beaufort, mother to Henry VII, translated two devotional treatises from French to English, for the edification of her son's subjects. Beaufort's rendering of the fourth book of Thomas à Kempis's *De imitatione Christi* (1441) was printed in 1504. *De imitatione Christi* was originally a dialogue between the Lord and a monk, but Beaufort's penitent generally speaks as a layman in order to emphasize the importance of the mass for all. The text also drew on Paul's first letter to the Corinthians to show its relevance to the unlearned. The Lord did not require men 'to be to[o] curious' regarding the nature of the sacrament. It was enough, indeed preferable, that they meekly submitted their 'reason & felyng to the holy feyth'.[41] The first chapter of Beaufort's second translation, *Mirror of gold for the sinful soul* (1506), similarly explained that the zenith of earthly wisdom was the realization of man's wretched condition. Using the combined authority of Church fathers and Biblical passages, the *Mirror* offered laymen and women a daily guide for penance for sinful souls.[42]

With these contemplative works Beaufort made an active contribution to the spiritual welfare of her son's subjects. As John Fisher explained, the countess's works were conceived 'for the proufyte of other[s]' and they appealed to a growing market of literate laity: both were reissued three times by rival printers.[43] As well as patronizing the scholars of Cambridge University, Beaufort provided for the edification of subjects who could read or understand English alone. By her own admission Beaufort worked from French versions of her texts. Yet the devout Latin translations subsequently performed by royal women were considered in the light of her efforts. In 1527 Princess Mary produced an English translation of a Latin prayer of Thomas Aquinas. Like Beaufort's works, Mary's prayer was an intimate expression of devotion and psalm-like in tone.[44] On a small scale it was also used for the edification of the unlearned. Lord Morley insisted that having marvelled at Mary's translation himself, he had set it 'in my pore wyfes [book] . . . and [those of] my chyldern'.[45] Morley was well placed to recognize Mary as Beaufort's successor in piety and learning. His last New Year's gift to Queen Mary in 1556 included remembrances of Morley's own upbringing in the countess's household. Morley praised both royal women for their piety, especially for their devotion to the 'blissyd sacrament'.[46]

Beaufort's example survived Henry's break with Rome. We can see her legacy in Katherine Parr's decision to draw from chapters 4 and 16–54 of the third book of *De imitatione Christi*, in her *Prayers and meditations* (1545). *Prayers and meditations* was not strictly a translation; the queen had come to Latin late in life.[47] Instead Parr had adapted the text of a 1531 English version of à Kempis's work, ascribed to Richard Whitford.[48] In order that the text should speak to a lay readership, Parr refigured it even more strenuously than Beaufort had. She replaced the dialogue with a single, generic voice who addresses a prayer to Christ. As with Beaufort's translation, *Prayers and meditations* modelled the fervour Englishmen and women were exhorted to experience during an act of religious worship. Here the act was prayer rather than the mass, though the work made no prejudicial comment regarding the real presence.[49] Janel Mueller has argued that Parr's treatise was intended as a companion piece to Cranmer's *Litany* (1544), making it part of the late-Henrician project of printing vernacular para-scriptural works.[50] Like Beaufort's translations, Parr's *Prayers and meditations* went forth under her own name and appealed to a relatively popular market: 24 editions were in circulation by 1613, including one printed in Mary's reign. Parr regarded it as her duty to provide for the spiritual amelioration of her husband's subjects.

Typically, northern humanist advocates of female learning, like Juan Luis Vives, had described its passive benefits for the commonwealth. An educated woman was less likely to commit lewd acts, annoy her husband or corrupt her children.[51] According to Erasmus it was the

Christian prince who took responsibility for the common good (*publica utilita*). Yet in sixteenth-century England, Tudor princes' female relations took up this mantle enthusiastically. Through translating pious texts aristocratic English women actively contributed to the welfare of the king's subjects and were praised for doing so.

As queen, Parr established a circle of learned ladies who were involved in producing pious treatises for the English multitude. In addition to the Princess Elizabeth, they included Katherine Brandon, duchess of Suffolk, who encouraged Parr to commit her *Lamentations of a sinner* to print in 1547; Anne Herbert, the queen's sister and a Latin correspondent of Roger Ascham; and Anne Seymour, countess of Hertford, who sponsored the second tome of the English *Paraphrases*.[52] These noblewomen became supporters of Edward VI's Church militant but during Henry's reign Mary was part of Parr's circle too.

The bond between Parr and Mary developed socially and politically. Following Mary's 1536 submission to the royal supremacy the princess gradually returned to court and Henry's favour. By 1542 places in Mary's chamber were widely sought and Parr was one of her appointments. Indeed Mary probably introduced Henry to her future stepmother, and along with her half-siblings, the princess was a guest at their wedding on 12 July 1543.[53] After Parr's marriage she and Mary remained friends and frequently lodged together. They exchanged gifts, shared servants and even wrote courtesy letters on the same sheet of paper.[54] Eustace Chapuys, the Imperial ambassador, claimed that the queen was a strong voice in favour of Mary's restoration to the succession in 1544.[55] Through Parr, Mary became socially intimate with other learned ladies of the court. Alongside the duchess of Suffolk, for instance, she acted as godmother at the christening of Katherine Dudley, daughter of Jane Dudley, Lady Lisle, on 26 November 1545. When Prince Edward wrote to his half-sister on 20 May 1546, he asked her to pass his salutations on to ladies Tyrwhit, Herbert and Lane. These were the very women whom John Foxe claimed Stephen Gardiner had planned to interrogate to prove that Parr possessed heretical books.[56]

Yet the bond between Mary and Parr was actually strengthened by faith. They shared a spiritual counsellor: Francis Mallett, who went on to complete the *Paraphrase on John*, was Parr's chaplain in 1545.[57] Rather than see Mallett's transfer to Mary's household, and indeed the women's relationship, as the queen's attempt to reform her stepdaughter, we should remember that Parr's own beliefs were evolving between 1543 and 1547. She was increasingly influenced by Cranmer but her almoner remained the relatively conservative Bishop George Day. Their common ground was Erasmus: she sent Day copies of *Enchiridion militis Christiani (Handbook for a Christian soldier)* and *De praeparatione ad mortem*.[58] Both queen and princess sat somewhere on the religious spectrum between Gardiner's grudging acceptance of the royal supremacy and Cranmer's blossoming evangelicalism. As long as they both believed in the real presence, Parr and Mary could regard each other as heirs to Beaufort's legacy.

It was in this spirit that Mary and Parr probably embarked on the English *Paraphrases*. They played to their strengths: Parr was the natural patron; Mary, who had repaired to the study of classical authors *(litterae humaniores)* for consolation in the 1530s, was the stronger grammarian.[59] Mary's scholarship has been called 'passive rather than active',[60] but by attempting this translation she put her learning to use for the commonwealth. Not only were Erasmus' *Paraphrases* congruent with the doctrine of the late Henrician Church, but para-scriptural translations for the 'enstruccion and edifiynge of whole realms in the knowleage of god'[61] were the prerogative and duty of Tudor royal women. Parr and Princess Elizabeth asked Mary to allow the 'most beautiful and useful work', which she had undertaken 'for the greatest good of the commonwealth', to go forward under her name.[62] Little wonder that Mary said yes. The translation was a celebration of her return to the succession and to Beaufort's elite tradition of pious royal women.

Mary's Translation

When considered in the light of this tradition, late Henrician religious policy and her friendship with Parr, Mary's involvement in the English *Paraphrases* no longer seems improbable or even surprising. Rather than imagining that she feigned illness, we might now allow Parr and Udall's corroborated evidence that Mary made a serious attempt at the translation over a period of two years. If we accept (though we cannot know) that Mallett acted as an editor rather than a ghost writer, the translation offers us the most substantial evidence for the princess's intellectual life in the 1540s. It provides insights into her grammatical and rhetorical skills, her wider reading and her personal religion. In this space I can do little more than sketch an outline in the hope that Marian scholars will begin to give the *Paraphrase on John* the attention it deserves.

Admittedly those seeking Mary's authorial voice may be disappointed initially. Her translation was rigorously literal, yet this is revealing in itself. Mary cleaved so closely to Erasmus' Latin that it is possible to determine that of the many editions of the *Paraphrases* in existence, she worked from Froben's 1534 octavo. This choice may have related to the substantive changes that Erasmus introduced in 1534 in response to Béda's allegations. In chapter eight, for instance, Mary accurately translated *sola credulitas via et aditus est ad immortalitatem* as 'onely belefe is the way and entrie to immortalitie'.[63] Had she been working from an earlier edition, the suggestion carried by *et aditus* that belief preceded, rather than excluded, good works would have been absent. It is less obvious why Mary did not translate the 1535 folio edition, which incorporated Erasmus' final revisions.[64] Udall certainly used it for his *Paraphrase on Luke*.[65] Perhaps Mary, who travelled regularly between 1545 and 1547, preferred the portability of the 1534 octavo.

The literalism of Mary's translation is instructive on a stylistic level too. Scholars have suggested that early-modern women's sense of female subservience and their lack of rhetorical training rendered them slavish translators.[66] This is not the case here. The male translators of the *Paraphrases* also strove for verisimilitude, occasionally at the expense of clarity in their renderings.[67] Perhaps all contributors were following Erasmus' advice that in translations, the author's voice should remain audible.[68] Close renderings were especially important when dealing with scripture. The Word, after all, was God's.

Mary seemed to respect this; she translated Erasmus' philological nuances sensitively as well as literally. In parsing his famous explication of John 1, *In principio erat sermo* (in the beginning there was the Word) Mary used, 'word' and 'speache' as appropriate substitutes for Erasmus' *sermo* and *oratio*.[69] She was also familiar with Erasmus' insistence in his *Annotationes* that John 1:8 stressed the definite article in its comment on John the Baptist, 'He was not the light.' As Mary explained, the Baptist 'was a certaine light . . . nevertheles he was not the lighte whiche should bring life to the whole worlde'.[70] She seems to have been acquainted with Erasmian biblical scholarship beyond the *Paraphrases* and with Henry VIII's Great Bible. She inserted English equivalents for Jewish rites: for instance, Easter for Passover.[71] Indeed Mary managed technical and rare words well throughout. She translated *aculei*, literally 'stings' but colloquially torture instruments, as 'broddes to pricke with'.[72] She also accurately parsed *collybistae*, an unusual Latinized version of the Greek word for 'bankers'.[73] The princess was philologically curious.

Despite her inquiring mind, Mary was also an inexperienced or hasty grammarian. She missed an entire sentence in chapter nine and often lost the subject of a subordinate clause.[74] She also had something of a blind spot for possessive pronouns which could alter the meaning of entire passages. In translating *sibi magnam conflasset inuidiam apud suos* (Jesus inflamed much envy among his people), for instance, the *suos* indicated the nation of the Jews, but Mary offered 'He gat himself muche envie amo[n]gst his own disciples'.[75] Béda would have been horrified by the doctrinal implications! Yet these regular minor errors hint that Mallett's and Udall's editorial pens had indeed scored lightly.

Occasionally Mary's translation also suggests lacunae in her wider reading. When describing the wedding in Cana, Mary translated *conuiuium incaluisset* as the 'feast was at the hottest'. This was correct but if the princess had been familiar with Livy or Tacitus she would have recognized that the verb *incalesco, -ere* was used by Roman historians to describe drunkenness.[76] As Andrew Taylor notes in his chapter for this volume, Vives had not prescribed the *artes historicae* for Mary's education.

Vives had also been anxious about recommending the study of rhetoric for Christian women; yet Mary's rendering of a number of phrases suggests her knowledge of figures and tropes. Erasmus had adopted a phrase from Cicero's rhetorical treatise *De inventione* to mark the beginning of Nicodemus' speech to Christ (John 3:2), *capat benevolentiam Iesu*. Mary recognized that this indicated that Nicodemus was embarking upon a formal appeal to Jesus, and parsed it appropriately as Nicodemus 'maketh suite to gette his [Christ's] good will with this preface'.[77] The princess's translation also showed her facility in modest rhetorical amplification, which she may have studied by reading Erasmus' own *De copia* (1512). When translating, Erasmus explained, one could create interest and even enhance the meaning of the original text through varying speech.[78] If lightly done, this practice was consistent with his emphasis on preserving the authorial voice. Her favourite technique was *synonymia*. In other words, she often used two English nouns or adjectives to express the nuances of Erasmus' Latin: *simplicissimus* was rendered as 'most sincere and pure'; *spiritus* meant 'a spirite or wynde'; *subtiliore* was 'right subtile and fyne'; *in peccatis natus* became 'borne wicked and ungracious'.[79] Mary's translation increased the emotional force of Erasmus' discussion of John's metaphors. While the princess sometimes rushed her grammar she had some flair for decorous amplification.

In examining what this translation reveals of Mary's religious thought, small variations from the Latin are critical. For instance, Mary actually intensified some of Erasmus' latent clerical criticisms. Her translation of his discussion of the Pharisees' treatment of the paralyzed man at the pool of Bethesda, *Adoriuntur igitur eum* ... *& obiurga[n]t perverse religiosi* (So the clerics perversely attacked and chided the man), became 'Therefore these, like perverters of true religion, fall in hand and chide with him'.[80] Erasmus had emphasized an irony: those who claimed to keep God's law reckoned that saving men was not fit work for God's day. By introducing a simile, 'like perverters of true religion', however, Mary aimed squarely at contemporary clergy who failed to minister to their flock. Subsequently clerical diligence in preaching and ministering became a fundamental concern of her regime.[81]

Indeed the princess's translation of the *Paraphrase on John* endorsed ideas which may once have seemed discordant with Marian Church doctrine, but which scholars now argue struck key notes in her reign.[82] These included the importance of faith and charity, the power of grace, the word of God, and the sacrament and sacrifice embodied in the mass which bound the faithful in an eternal 'covenaunte'. Such were the beliefs of 'an evangelicall minde'.[83] These elements were also central to two authoritative statements of Marian Church doctrine: Bishop Edmund Bonner's *Profitable and necessary doctrine* (1555) and Bishop Thomas Watson's *Wholesome and Catholic doctrine* (1558).[84]

Further, these doctrinal continuities paralleled Marian attitudes towards Erasmus and the *Paraphrases*. Apart from Harpsfield's 1557 visitations, there were some unauthorized and localized instances of the *Paraphrases* being removed from, sold, burned or possibly concealed in parishes during Mary's reign. Yet John Craig has found no evidence that the queen took official action against the tome herself.[85] Indeed Udall, as editor of the *Paraphrases*, rose higher in Mary's service than he had under Edward. The queen evidently had no wish to distance herself from her translation or from Udall's account of her 'most constaunt purpose to promote Goddes worde, and the free grace of his gospell'.[86] Not only were Erasmus' works absent from the list of books prohibited by the royal proclamation of June 1555, as Lucy Wooding has pointed out, Erasmus himself was actually reclaimed for the Marian Church. A letter in which Erasmus had defended his belief in the real presence by referencing John 6 was printed in English in

1554.[87] Mary happy to be involved in the last great religious translation begun in Henry's reign and she remained affiliated to its doctrine throughout her life.

Such continuities encourage us to view her religious thought as fundamentally unified, and to look to political circumstances to explain the sharp divergence in its expression during her lifetime. Erasmus' warnings against religious persecution (on John 16:2–3, for instance) probably struck her as pertaining to Cranmer's 'pretense of godlinesse' and his accusations against her in Edward's reign, rather than her own government's treatment of 'ungodly persons & malefactours'.[88]

Conclusions

The English *Paraphrases* of Erasmus, then, were not the sole preserve of Protestants. Mary's attempt to translate John reveals their significance as para-scriptural guides to the centre ground of an increasingly diffracted confessional spectrum. The *Paraphrases* spoke equally to Henry VIII, a defender of his first wife, the sensibilities of his last queen and all three children who succeeded him. Rather than attributing Mary's involvement in their translation to a plan to convert the princess, we should perhaps reform our own understanding of the broad allegiance to Erasmian ideas, such as the *verbum dei* and the critical importance of faith and clerical diligence, in sixteenth-century England.

Mary's translation and Parr's patronage of the *Paraphrases* also point us to a neglected, civic aspect of female religious translation in this period. Far from being a Protestant creation, the tradition sprang from Margaret Beaufort's aristocratic desire to promote the spiritual welfare of her son's unlearned subjects. This active justification for female learning galvanized a circle of noblewomen in the court of Henry VIII. Parr and Mary were at its centre until Edwardine attacks on the real presence and the mass drove a wedge between them. Their friendship was one of the factors that encouraged Mary to attempt to translate the *Paraphrase on John*. The work reveals that the princess was a careful Bible reader, an enthusiastic if inexperienced grammarian, and in possession of greater rhetorical sophistication and a more nuanced and consistent religious ideology than some scholars have supposed. Mary, like Parr, was proud to have provided for the 'enstruccion and edifiynge of whole realms' through her contribution to the English *Paraphrases* of Erasmus.

Acknowledgements

The author would like to thank Thomas S. Freeman, Susan Doran, Patrick Collinson, John Craig and Deirdre Serjeantson for their instructive comments on this chapter, and Trinity College, Cambridge for its generosity in supporting this research.

8

Maids and Wives: Representing Female Rule during the Reign of Mary Tudor

Thomas Betteridge

Mary I's gender has played a significant but under-explored role in historical accounts of the sixteenth century and the English Reformation. Admittedly it has been consistently used as an explanatory metaphor for Mary's reign. This is particularly so in the field of religious studies where both sides in the debate have used Mary's status as a woman to explain the success or failure of the restoration of Catholicism. Yet Mary's gender is at once a problem and a solution. It has served to provide the coordinates for a whole set of historical tropes, metaphors and explanations. At the same time there has been little work on how writers represented Mary's gender during her reign. In this chapter I look briefly at the gendered ways in which historians have discussed Mary Tudor. I then examine a number of early representations of Mary before moving to discuss in detail the way in which William Forrest depicts her in his poem, *The history of Grisild the second*.

Mary, History and Gender

In Holinshed's *Chronicle* it was above all Mary's gender that determined the meaning of her reign. The opening description of her coronation hints at something amiss, with the suggestion that Mary found the crown so heavy that she was 'faine to beare up hir head with hir hand'.[1] Even in this short quotation the possibilities and dangers for the authors of Holinshed of using Mary's gender to explain what they regarded as the failure of her realm are clear. The image of a ruler unable to carry the weight of her crown is clearly intended to suggest a more general degree of incapacity. In particular, it works to imply that a physical weakness, perhaps gender specific, indicates a more general political and symbolic one. But of course the one thing that the authors of Holinshed wanted to avoid was any suggestion that it was Mary's gender alone that made her a bad ruler. In this context the false pregnancies that Mary appears to have suffered played a crucial role.[2] This is reflected by their status in the summing up of Mary's realm in Holinshed:

> Hitherto the affaires of queene Marie have had no great success, as you have heard. But never was worse success had any woman, than she in her childbirth. For seeing one of these two must be granted, that either she was with child or not with child, if she were with child and did travel, why was it not seen? If she was not, how was all the realm deluded? And in the meane while where were all the prayers, the solemn processions, the devout masses of the catholike clergy? ... If their masses *Ex opera operato* be able to fetch Christ from heaven, [and] to reach downe to purgatory, how chanced then they could not reach to the queen's chamber, to helpe her in her travel, if she had been with child in deed? If not, how came it to passe, that all the catholike church of England did so err, and was so deeply deceived?[3]

This passage is a typical piece of Protestant historiography in the way that it suggests, but does no more than this, that there is a relationship between Mary's failure as a woman marked in her failed pregnancies and a more general and pervasive failure of the restoration of Catholicism during her realm. In particular, this passage deploys a voyeuristic logic in which the reader is invited to speculate upon the intimate details of what happened in Mary's chamber and at the same time incited to draw a comparison between the alleged secrecy over the results or rather non-results of the pregnancies and the status of the Catholic Church. The readers of Holinshed are meant to draw a parallel between the apparent promise of fertility marked by Mary's ostensible pregnancy and the resulting disturbing barrenness and the Catholic Church's teaching, which on the surface looks fruitful but is ultimately revealed to be sterile. Mary claimed to be pregnant but all that was actually produced was confusion and error, just like, from a

Protestant perspective, the difference between the surface finery and spectacle of Catholicism and its fundamental emptiness.

The basic coordinates of the construction of Mary's reign as portrayed in Holinshed have been dominant until very recently within its historiography. G. R. Elton in *England under the Tudors* quoted with approval Pollard's suggestions that the reign's conclusive note was sterility.[4] In the process Elton was aligning himself with the version of Mary's reign articulated in Holinshed and even more forcibly in John Foxe's *Acts and Monuments* and Robert Crowley's *Epitome of chronicles*. Yet there were other more positive contemporary English views of both Mary's pregnancy and the impact of her gender upon her suitability to be a monarch. For example, Foxe printed a number of poems by William Forrest celebrating Mary's pregnancy, one of which was based upon the *Pater Noster*. Forrest concluded this work by making a general plea for the protection of the queen:

And lette us not to be overcome
By fowle temptacion,
Our queen thou graunt (of thy wisdom)
To honour thee alone.
But us deliver by they might
From every kinde of ill.
Quene Mary keepe both daye and night,
And prosper to thy will.[5]

In this work Forrest adapts the words of the *Pater Noster* so that they became the framework of his prayer for Mary's protection. It is noticeable, however, that in many ways there was nothing inherently 'Catholic' about Forrest's work. And in these terms it is typical of many representations of Mary during her reign. Writers like Forrest and John Heywood used Mary's gender in order to construct her not so much as a Catholic figure as a non-confessional one, rising above the squabbles of her errant subjects in order to restore them to the true path. This deployment of Mary did, however, put considerable pressure on traditional assumptions about the gendered nature of the division between private and public. Despite this, Forrest and Heywood found ways of turning Mary's gender into a positive asset that could be deployed to support and sustain the Marian Reformation.

Marian polemical works consistently deployed gender-specific imagery. In particular, there was a consistent emphasis, and in places a celebration, of the feminine as an antidote to the masculine arrogance of heresy and heretics. At the same time Marian writers were not slow to argue that Protestants subverted gender norms. Miles Hogarde, for example, argued that it was the overriding sexual desires of the Protestant women that led them to exploit the feminine weakness of their husbands. He claimed that Protestant women encouraged their husbands to become martyrs in order to satisfy their desires for new and better husbands.[6] In a more positive sense, a number of Marian writers made a virtue of Mary's gender. John Christopherson, in his *An exhortation to all men to beware rebellion*, used a number of images of Mary to condemn Wyatt's rebellion, and in particular stressed Mary's virginity:

> But alas what harde hartes have those, that if she were but a private woman, being so gentle of nature, so vertuouse and so merciful, coulde drawe their sworde against her. . . . For albeit that all bloudeshedde is cruel and horrible in the sight of god, yet the shedding of so a pure virgins bloude, is of all other moste cruell and detestable.[7]

It is important to note, as this quotation suggests, that not only were writers like Christopherson well aware of the political and symbolic implications of Mary's gender, they were prepared to embrace them as potentially positive aspects of her queenship. In effect Marian apologists argued that yes, Mary's gender does lead to a collapse of the public and private, and this is why she is such an improvement on Henry and Edward, since it means that with Mary there is no secret heretical agenda hidden behind a public face of orthodoxy and good government – with Mary what you see is what you get. Although it was clearly potentially problematic to depict a ruling queen as in some ways a simple, even naïve, loving daughter or mother, Marian writers consistently did so. And this move was no more conservative or less successful then the polemical approach adopted by Protestant writers when they used Mary's gender to attack her rule.

Supporters of Mary's religious policies also used gender-specific imagery to argue that the feminine Church, and by association Mary herself, were the proper guardians of a religious truth that was beyond man's reason. James Brooks, in his *A sermon very notable, fruitful and godly*, argued that the Catholic Church was the mother of the Scripture, 'Whose pappes are the two Testamentes: Whose milke is the true sence of the word of God: Out of those her pappes onelye to be sucked, of al christian suckinges.'[8] Brooks went on to develop this analogy, arguing that 'Even as all women have given unto them by nature, sense to discerne the good temperature of their owne pappes, from the distemperature of the same, so hath the Church given her by God, authoritie to discerne the true Scriptures from the forged.'[9]

John Proctor used similar imagery, in his prologue to *The way home to Christ and truth leading from Antichrist and errour*, when recommending to his fellow countrymen that they renounce the malicious harlot, heresy, and 'Come home to this swete nurse [the loving mother Church], that you maye sucke from her brestes the holsome foode of your soules healthe and comforte: and leave the stinkinge carren wherwith this whore feedeth you.'[10]

This use of maternal imagery reflects an important gender-specific aspect of the self-understanding of the Marian Reformation. Eamon Duffy in his work, *The stripping of the altars: Traditional religion in England 1400–1580*, argues that what has been regarded by some as the failure of the Marian regime to exploit the possibilities of print and engage in a full-scale pamphlet war with its Protestant opponents was instead a deliberate policy based upon a 'considered distrust of the social and religious effects' of aggressively polemical publications similar to those produced in such abundance by writers like John Bale during the proceeding reign.[11] The use of maternal imagery, obviously drawing on that associated with the Virgin Mary, by writers like Brooks and Proctor can also be related to the regime's rejection of the kind of polemics produced by supporters of the Edwardine Reformation in favour of instruction. There is, however, a clear tension between the use of maternal imagery and the policy of persecuting Protestants, and it is the case in that in relation to writers like John Heywood and Nicholas Udall, the emphasis on Mary's gender was coupled with the advocacy of moderation in terms of the treatment of Protestants.

The spider and the fly is an extended allegory upon the Edwardine Reformation. It tells the story of how a fly, 'the best and most luckiest of flies', is caught in a spider's web and his attempts to escape. In Heywood's poem the spider and fly try to resolve their differences through debate, law and finally battle, but not surprisingly given that one wants to live and the other wants to have supper, in the end there can be no resolution that does not mean complete victory for one and failure for the other. At the end of the poem, however, the maid of the house suddenly appears, sweeps the cobwebs and kills the chief spider. The maid is clearly at one level a figure for Mary, who by her actions effectively makes the chief spider Northumberland.[12]

Having restored order to the world of the window, the maid goes on to instruct the spiders and the flies on how to lead their lives.

> As God orderly created creatures all,
> So were they created, orderly to intent,
> To Use themselves, each creature in his call.
> Of which created sort the creator meant
> Spiders and flies twain, to order to relent.[13]

Having restored order, the Maid departs. In these terms the message of Heywood's poem is that the Henrician and Edwardine Reformations were aberrations, mistakes, without long-term or permanent results; despite the violence and conflict, the debates and disputations, nothing has really changed.

Heywood concludes the poem by making an explicit plea for moderation. He writes:

> This merciful maiden took in hand to sweep
> Her window, this realm, not to kill but to keep
> All in quiet, on her bringing us thereto,
> As that maid all spiders and flies showeth to do.
> And as under that maid spider died but one,
> So under this maid, save one, (in effect) none.
> And as that one under that one maid did die
> Repentant, so this other repentantly,
> Under this other maid, the death meekly took.[14]

The two maids that Heywood refers to here are the one in the poem and Mary, although the term 'maiden' here also has other associations, including the Virgin Mary. These lines clearly suggests that the only person who should die, and indeed needs to die, for order to be restored is the chief spider, Northumberland. The implication of these lines is that Heywood did not see a complete separation between Protestants or Catholics. Or perhaps more accurately he felt that in the struggles and conflicts of the previous 30 years, both sides had behaved in ways that were more conducive to strife then harmony. The image of Mary as a maid clearly feeds into Heywood's moderate agenda since, while lauding Mary's role as the sweeper away of the source of conflict, its homely nature suggests a restricted and limited model for the scope of the Marian Reformation.

The image of Mary as maid was, however, at one level potentially problematic. This is partly because the pun on maid/virgin had a limited life-span given Mary's desire to marry. It was, however, also potentially problematic to depict the monarch engaged in such lowly activity as sweeping away cobwebs. What Heywood's poem reflects is the extent to which Marian writers were prepared to deploy carnivalesque and inversion tropes, central to Christianity and perhaps particularly to aspects of Erasmian reform, to undermine Protestantism and celebrate Mary's rule. Mary is simply a maid, and it is this simplicity that allows her to work as a real servant of Christ sweeping away the world of the spiders and flies: or rather restoring it to order so that a fly is simply a fly and a spider a spider. In these terms Mary as maid is a potentially radical figure, rejecting not only the norms of Tudor politics but also assumptions concerning the nature of good rule.

In Nicholas Udall's play *Respublica* Mary was also cast in the role of the restorer of harmony and order.[15] The play is a morality drama which stages the Edwardine Reformation through four vice figures, the leading vice Avarice, Insolence, Oppression and Adulation. The vices take over the country by disguising themselves as Authority, Reformation, Policy and Honesty. Having reduced the country to a state of ruin, and the central character Respublica and the commonality to complete destitution, the vices are confronted by a figure called Misericordia (Mercy) who ushers unto the stage three other virtues, Veritas (Truth), Justice and Pax (Peace), who go on to defeat the vices. At the end of the play the figure of Nemesis enters and restores order. It is important to note that it is this figure, and not the virtues, who creates the harmonious ending of the play. In particular, while the virtues adopt a simplistic oppositional stance towards all the vices, the approach of Nemesis is more measured. She effectively pardons Adulation provided he promises to be henceforth honest. Avarice is sentenced to 'bee pressed, as men doo presse a sponge / that he maie droope ought teverye man hys lotte, / to the vtmoste farthing that he hath falslie gotte'.[16] It is only Oppression and Insolence that Nemesis leaves to the none too tender mercies of Justice.

> Nemesis: Now Justice for these two that do here remain
> Because the faulte of Insolence is heinous and greate
> Lucifer's owne faulte to aspire to the highest seat
> And because Oppression hath wronged men so sore
> That he spoiled innocents of all they had and more,
> People shall deliver them unto safe custody
> Where they may no further annoy any body
> Whan the time may serve / to examine and try their cause
> Can them bother before you, and Judge them by the lawes.[17]

Nemesis' treatment of these two vices is significant since it suggests that the causes of the distress created by the Edwardine Reformation are less religious then simply human sinfulness.[18] Insolence is a real danger to the commonwealth, as is Oppression, but the leading vice, Avarice, while being dangerous, is less so. The priority is not to imprison and try him so much as to squeeze him like a cheese so that he gives all his ill-gotten goods. Greg Walker comments that:

> Like Heywood's *The Spider and the Fly*, a work of genuine catholic celebration at Mary's succession, Udall [in *Respublica*] lauds the queen as a new broom who will sweep away the abuses and divisions of the recent past in favour of a virtuous and harmonious new order. Like Heywood, Udall also calls for moderation in the punishment of those responsible for the previous regime.[19]

Nemesis is a specifically female ruler who rejects the possibility, embodied on stage in the figure of Justice, of harsh and retributive punishment of all those responsible for the state of the commonwealth. Instead her restoration of order is marked by proportion and discrimination. Not all vices (heretics) are the same, and like a wise mother Nemesis knows that not all are equally dangerous to her children. Heywood and Udall both use the possibilities created by Mary's gender to argue for a moderate approach to the religious reform and correction.

William Forrest's *The history of Grisild the second* adopts a similar set of strategies, but in a very different context from that in which Heywood and Udall wrote. *Respublica* and *The spider and the fly* were written to celebrate Mary's succession and rule, *The history of Grisild the second* to address the experience of defeat.

The History of Grisild the Second

Very little is known about William Forrest. He was made royal chaplain soon after Mary's succession, and it was in this capacity that he wrote the poems celebrating Mary's putative pregnancy. *The history* is an extended poetic celebration of Katherine of Aragon. It is not an allegory. In a move identical to Heywood's at the end of *The spider and the fly* Forrest states plainly that:

> So clokedlye under darke coverture
> We have not walked in this Historye
> But that readers may understande sure
> The meane of oure mentioned memorye,

Not figures as by Alligorye,
But this sayde Grysilde, plainly to define,
Is plainly ment the goode Queene Catheryne.[20]

Grisild is explicitly Katherine, and not merely as an allegory. Ursula Potter has recently commented that the 'Catholic Forrest's strong feelings at the mistreatment of Katherine leave no place for hidden meanings and ambiguity or even personal discretion'.[21] It is, however, noticeable to what extent Forrest frames his poem entirely in gender-specific terms, and in particular that he completely ignores religion. Protestantism and heresy are simply products of Katherine's fall, not the cause. Forrest also constructs the relationship between Mary and Katherine as a self-enclosed drama and as one that defines the nature of Mary's rule. In *Grisild* Mary rules as Katherine's daughter. There is no mention in the poem of Mary's husband, despite the fact that the poem was presented to Mary in June 1558 and contains numerous references to the Marian period. One wonders if there is a slippage between Henry as Walter, Grisild's tyrannical husband, and Philip. Certainly it is noticeable to what extent the Mary of the poem is a daughter and maid. There is no sense of her as a wife (and of course none of her as a mother).

In his Prologue to *Grisild* Forrest told Mary, the addressee of the poem, that:

Her [Katherine] I heere liken to Grysilde the goode,
As well I so maye, for her great patience:
Considering althinges with her howe it stoode.
Her giving that name theare is none offence;
Your noble Father workinge in like pretence
As Walter to Gyrsidle, by much wickedness,
By name of Walter I dooe expresse.[22]

Forrest's adaptation of the well-known story of patient Griselda to the events of the Henrician Reformation served a number of purposes. It worked to place the story of Katherine within a European context. It also allowed Forrest's text to participate in the deliberate return to pre-Reformation literary norms that was a feature of writing under Mary, since probably the most well-known version of Grisild's story to mid-Tudor readers would have been the version told by the Clerk in Chaucer's *Canterbury tales*. Indeed it is possible that Chaucer's tale seemed particularly apposite to Forrest given its gender-specific staging of tyranny and resistance. Lynn Staley has recently commented that in Chaucer's work, Griselda's ' "femininity" defines Walter's 'masculinity' . . . it is bombast, the noise of power'.[23] Katherine as Griselda is a saint in the making, and Forrest consistently stresses her refusal to engage in the kind of political games that he depicts as the norm of Tudor political life.

The problem with using the story of Griselda for Forrest is that, as the *Clerk's tale* consistently emphasizes, Walter's behaviour is entirely irrational and unexplained. Forrest does grasp this nettle, or rather he gives his readers a range of possible explanations for Walter's/Henry's behaviour:

> Which noble Father, I cannot but saye,
> Was leaded in some parte by mens of the light [light person]
> Perhaps for sin, that reigned at that daye
> God suffered this Royalme so to alter quite
> Or that He wolde shewe His divine might
> Hable terecte by the weake and frayle sex
> Howe ever Sathan His Church did heere vex.
>
> Or, peraduenture, Hee wolde it bee so
> To try (in meekenes) her stabilitee
> In higher merit to have her to go.[24]

Forrest places the story of Katherine's tribulations within a specifically gendered morality tale, and in the process creates a history of the Henrician Reformation that focuses almost entirely on the personal. Mary's role in this story is to become an actor in her mother's trials. This has the effect of making the Marian Reformation the end of a morality tale in which good order is restored through narrative closure. The end of *Grisild*, unlike Chaucer's text, ends with the restoration of Katherine in the person of her daughter.

Forrest's text constructs the Henrician Reformation as a product of Walter's tyranny, which in turn is a product of his infatuation with Anne Boleyn. Forrest writes that after Oxford University had consented to the divorce:

> Then florished Flatery triumphantly,
> Then Falsehood beeare rule,
> Then weare the goode maligned throughe envy
> Then was true Meekenes overcome with Pride,
> Then to perdition all Goodenes faste hide,

Then was Self will chief Ruler over all
Then might, in right, none for Advocat call
Then of the Churche began thaffliction
Then entred Heresies cursed and nought

...

Theis myscheifes, with hundredefolde moe, began
At the incoming of this newe Queene Anne [25]

Forrest's version of the Henrician Reformation, like that found in
much revisionist history, has the advantage of giving a clear explanation of why it happened. It was all because of the that beastly
woman Anne Boleyn – without her England would have remained
a happy contented Catholic country. This may be a veiled attack on
the woman likely to succeed Mary, Anne Boleyn's daughter Elizabeth.
Grisild, however, illustrates the problems with this approach, since its
implication is that with the advent of Mary all should be well, and yet
this was clearly not the case. Marian England was still a place where
falsehood and might ruled over truth and right. Forrest's account
of the Henrician Reformation deploys a set of generic conventions
and gives them a specific gender inflection in order to celebrate
Katherine and Mary and sidestep entirely the question of historical
causation. Ironically what Forrest ends up creating is an image of
Mary as, in A. G. Dickens's words, the 'prisoner of a sorrowful
past'.[26]

At the same time *Grisild* engages in a persistent rewriting of the
past. It seeks to subvert the norms of Tudor history writing by placing at its centre a number of highly charged encounters between
Katherine and Mary. The fact that many of these are fictional, and
acknowledged as such by Forrest, only adds to their interest. It
is, however, problematic to describe these passages as based upon
encounters between Mary and Katherine since invariably they relate
to meetings that did not take place. For example, Forrest prints
Katherine's dying prayer to her daughter, during which she tells
Mary to be obedient to Henry in the hope that he will show her
benevolence. Forrest also writes the speech that Mary would have
made at her mother's funeral had she been allowed to attend:

She [Mary] was chief Mooarner, it maye well bee saide,
All other to her weare but as countrefettes;
She, heearynge her Mother under booarde laide
In to her closet demurelye shee gettes

Her cheeks all withe tears she ruthefully wettes,
Kneealynge a downe in contemplation,
Lamentynge her Mother under this fashion.

'O heauynly Father and Kinge celestiall,
lorde of all Lordys, They title is so
To Whome specyall obeisance dothe fall,
Thy ordinance divine no man may parte fro
All one to convince, in feawe as in mo
My Mother hense rapte from this worldys vision
To wheare Thowe pleasiste to have her go,
Thowe graunte her, (Lorde), Thy heavenly fruition.'[27]

In *Grisild* Mary is the chief mourner at her mother's funeral, even though she was not actually there. Forrest here again deploys gender, the link between mother and daughter, to suggest that his work can expose the private truths behind the counterfeit public displays of Tudor history. It is in Mary's closet that one can hear the truth of Katherine's death in her daughter's grief.

We might wonder, however, how Mary, if she read *Grisild*, felt about Forrest writing a fictional account of her reaction to Katherine's death. Indeed there is something slightly disturbing about Forrest's insistence on Mary's presence in her closet. At one level the incitement of this kind of voyeuristic penetration of private spaces is a norm of the Tudor court poetry in *Tottel's miscellany* which, as is too often forgotten, is a Marian text published in 1557. We could also speculate that perhaps as a royal chaplain Forrest had a sufficiently close relationship to Mary to allow him to safely write a fictional account of the queen's private words to her mother. If this were the case it is interesting that the Mary of Forrest's speech consistently suggests that she desires a life of religious observance:

Thowe parted this life, O meeke Mother of mine!
The lovingiste that ever to chylde might bee,
What shall I dooe but this worldys joyes resigne,
And daily praye to God to fetche mee to thee?[28]

Forrest depicts Mary as in some ways the junior partner, not surprisingly, in the relationship with her mother. In the context of 1557–8, however, when the poem was written, this is a loaded decision. It suggests a desire to relocate the meaning of Mary's queenship away from the public sphere, and therefore may indicate an attempt by Forrest to

protect the reputation of Mary from the disappointments and compromises of the Marian regime. After all, by 1557 Mary had been on
the throne for a number of years, and was a married woman who
had faced down one serious rebellion and was at war with France.
Forrest's decision to look back to Chaucer is also significant. 1557
saw the publication of *The complete English works of Thomas More*.
Eamon Duffy has argued that this publication, far from being simply
a More/Roper family effort, was part of Cardinal Pole's reform campaign. Duffy comments on the way that Pole, in his St Andrew's Day
sermon 1557, deployed the historical example of More to sustain a
particular version of the Marian restoration.[29] Forrest's leapfrogging of
recent history in his search for a model for his account of the divorce
may represent a deliberate turning away from more immediate and
polemical potential models.[30]

Grisild ends with an address to Mary. In this, despite the fact that it
is explicitly not part of the history of Griselda's/Katherine's tribulations, Forrest persists in placing Mary within the narrative of the tale.
In particular, there is a transference of her relation with Katherine
to God, so that there is an almost seamless progression in terms of
the key person in Mary's life as depicted by *Grisild*. Forrest creates an
extended parallel between God, Mary and her subjects, writing:

Hee [God] above everlastingly reigning,
Thowe [Mary] heere alowe, passible and mortall;
Hee in Hym selfe althinges containing,
Those at His will to fit or to fall;
Hee omnipotent, Thowe but as His thrall,
Hee to commaunde, Thowe meekely to obeye;
Such Hee, suche Thowe, thowe canniste not saye naye.
Hee God, That althinges created of nought,
And sendethe the fruits tencrease to and sprynge;
Thowe His Creature, upp traded and bought
Over His People to have the governing;[31]

It is interesting to note the acknowledgement in these lines of not only
Mary's mortality but also God's rule in sending fruits to increase and
spring. Forrest's poem in some ways is a lament and is sufficed with a
sense of melancholy quite lacking from, for example, John Heywood's
The spider and the fly. *Grisild* is a lamentation for Katherine's suffering,
and although it is anachronistic to suggest this, a lament for the failure
of the Marian Reformation. In the same way that late Edwardine

literature reflects world-weary recognition of the failure of the high
hopes that greeted Edward's succession, Forrest's work reflects a realization of the failure of the promises of social and religious restoration
that marked the opening years of Mary's reign.[32] Indeed it is impossible to imagine Katherine's daughter as depicted in *Grisild* being able,
or indeed wanting, to rule. Forrest's Mary shares many characteristics
with Heywood's maid but there is one fundamental difference: while
the former sweeps away all the past and restores order, there is a sense
in which Forrest's Mary is being sucked back into the past. John Guy
has argued that the 'greatest irony of [Mary's] reign is that her interests
as queen of England were sacrificed to those of her husband and the
papacy when events in Europe required it'.[33] The Mary of Forrest's
poem is located firmly within a morality tale set in England without
any reference to husbands. It can therefore be read as a piece of poetic
counsel to Mary. arguing that she should focus on events at home and
not embark on foreign adventures.

Conclusion

Given the use by writers of gender-specific imagery to support the
Marian Reformation and celebrate Mary's rule, it is disappointing
that little work has been done on this aspect of her reign. This relative lack of interest is particularly noticeable in comparison with the
considerable number of studies on Elizabeth I and gender. This is
particularly problematic since it is clear that for Marian writers like
Heywood and Udall, Mary's gender was potentially a positive quality that would enable her to avoid the prideful mistakes of her father
and brother. The Marian regime's understanding of Protestantism as
arrogant and self-centred created a space for images of female rule
and power which, in their femininity and lack of masculine bombast,
could in themselves be regarded as part of the solution to the problems
caused by the Henrician and Edwardine Reformations.

It is important to note, however, that there were a number of Marian writers, perhaps particularly Miles Hogarde, who seem to have
had little interest in deploying gender-specific imagery. In particular, Hogarde's work tends to use gender simply as a tool to attach
to feminine Protestant men and masculine Protestant women. This
can be related to Hogarde's commitment to a wide sweeping reform
of the realm, and more specifically his commitment to a rigorous
prosecution of the aims of the Marian Reformation, going beyond
simply repairing the damage caused by the Henrician and Edwardine

reformations. There is a class and ideology division marked in the use and non-use of gender-specific image to support the Marian Reformation, which relates to larger tensions within the regime and the country more generally. Devout writers like Hogarde were not interested in a moderate, meek, caring maid, daughter or queen sweeping away trouble and strife; they embraced struggle and violence in the pursuit of reform and reformation.

Finally we should note the extent to which gender is still an important element in our understandings of Mary's reign. For Forrest and Heywood, focusing on gender allowed them to explain the Henrician and Edwardine reformations – it at once restricted the scope of historical explanation and provided a clear reason for the religious changes that they rejected. We should notice, however, that focusing on gender was a deliberate polemical strategy designed to avoid addressing other potentially far more difficult explanations for the Henrician and Edwardine reformations. We of course have moved well beyond this. No one would now blame the English Reformation simply on Henry's infatuation with Anne Boleyn and his desire for a divorce, would they?

9

The Religious Policy of Mary I

William Wizeman, SJ

Like most of Mary I's policies as queen, her strategies for religion in England have traditionally been seen by historians as wrongheaded, if not disastrous. Her desire to restore Catholicism in England after 20 years in which many tenets of the Protestant Reformation were implemented has often been viewed as reactionary and impolitic. Religious persecution during her reign was the key in forming her image as a bloodthirsty tyrant.

However, another interpretation of Mary's strategies for Roman Catholic renewal in England may also be presented. As Judith M. Richards has stated, 'there are good grounds for thinking of Mary as a political realist, who like other contemporary monarchs, conflated her realm's interests with her own'.[1] There is no question that Mary was a devout Catholic, and that she intended and was generally successful in imposing her religion on England. Yet rather than merely thinking her nation's past was her nation's future, Mary followed religious policies that were in the vanguard of the Counter Reformation that was beginning to transform the worship, theology and spirituality of much of Catholic Europe and its spheres of influence in the Americas and Asia. This chapter will consider the Counter-Reformation *avant la lettre* (before the term existed) in Marian England.

Mary's overt involvement in the religious affairs of her kingdom is best seen in her proclamation to the realm on 18 August, 1553, her injunctions to her bishops on 4 March 1554, and the legislation of her early parliaments in those years. In the injunctions she put an end to the usage and power of the title 'Supreme Head of the Church'; the governance of the Church from that point resided once more in

153

the hands of the Church hierarchy, especially the bishops, and from thence forward Mary's influence upon ecclesiastical affairs became more discreet or was largely exercised through personal patronage and example. She had also hoped that her personal example would lead her subjects to return to Catholicism very early in her reign. The 1553 proclamation states that 'she, her father, grandfather and all progenitors kings of this realm', along with the people of the near and long past had adhered to 'Christ's true religion', and she hopes all will return to it, in contrast to the 'diversity of opinions in religion' that had caused tumult in England for the past 20 years.

How she considered her father to have been a member of the true faith remains controversial, unless Mary was making a circumspect distinction between her father's reign before and after 1534; even if Mary deemed her father to be merely in schism with the Church, he could hardly be called a practitioner of true religion. Mary's unclear views of her father may have been due to political reasons of legitimizing her succession, and perhaps even more to the 'legality' of Henry's reforms, in contrast to the religious changes during the minority of Edward, which were swiftly repealed by her first parliament.[2] It is noteworthy that in her will she stipulates prayers for the soul of her mother, but not for her father or brother.[3] In any case the proclamation appears less ambiguous when we note that her half-brother, Edward VI, is not listed among the followers of the faith of her fathers. Nevertheless it is not ironic that Mary's first religious action as England's first queen regnant was offering a requiem mass for her brother, a central element of Catholic worship that would have been utterly repugnant to him and his regime. The queen also states that 'she will not compel [the people] to break laws of this realm in force concerning church service, but will permit all that will to use the same laws until further order'.[4] Yet here Mary's example during Edward's reign of resolutely maintaining the mass in her household despite its abolition in 1549, and the evident desire of most of her subjects, led to the swift restoration of Catholic liturgy through most of the realm in the first months of her rule.[5] In fact all those laws concerning religion enacted since 1546, the last year of Henry's reign, would be repealed in parliament in a few months, although remarkably no penalties were enacted for the continued usage of the Edwardine liturgy.[6]

The relative indistinctness of Mary's policy regarding religion, as to whether she would maintain Henry's post-1534 polity or seek reconciliation with Rome, for example, evaporated in her injunctions to the episcopate in March 1554.[7] In fact, signs of her intent to reunite

England with the Catholic Church may be discerned as early as her first parliament in October 1553.[8] She had already signed one of the first bills presented, which nullified the Henrician treason legislation, so that it was no longer a crime to deny Henry's supreme headship over the Church; there were further signs of her desire for reunion in September 1553, though these actions on her part may also be seen as politic negotiating with the Empire and Rome.[9] She restored canon law as it stood in 1529, before the break with Rome, and thus effectively brought the royal supremacy to an end. The bishops were no longer dependent upon royal authority for enforcing ecclesiastical laws, and were now at liberty to renew Catholic life and doctrine in their dioceses.

This included the deprivation of the married clergy of Edward's reign from parishes and other offices, and the ordination of those men made ministers of the Church according to the Edwardine ordinal, which was deemed heretical. Schoolmasters who were also reckoned to sympathize with Protestantism were to be dismissed and replaced by men who would instruct children in Catholic belief and practice. Most importantly, the hierarchy was to ensure the restoration of the mass, the other sacraments, the entire liturgy of the Catholic Church, the traditional observance of holy days and fast days, and the restoration of sacramentals and other forms of devotion. To this end Protestant literature was to be destroyed, and Protestant belief suppressed and replaced not only with the renewed forms of Catholic worship, but also with the composition and distribution of collections of sermons that would inform priests and people of the merits of Catholicism and of their obligations to the faith for their salvation.[10] In her command for books of catechetical homilies, the queen appears to be directly copying one of Archbishop Thomas Cranmer's strategies for Protestant reform in the reign of Edward, though Cardinal Reginald Pole, as Cranmer's successor, would claim other, more ancient precedents for such an endeavour.[11] The bishops would make her demands their own in Cardinal Pole's Legatine Synod, 1555–6, not least the publication of Catholic homilies and the regulation of religious print, the second being an important element of Counter-Reform in the rest of Europe after the Council of Trent.[12]

Needless to say Mary was presenting her bishops, let alone the clergy and laity of each parish, with an enormous task. The deprivation of married priests alone caused havoc in many dioceses. Yet it is amazing how many elements of Mary's injunctions had been successfully carried out by the time of her death less than five years later; and many of these changes occurred with active popular support.[13] Even in London, with a substantial population of committed Protestants and committed non-Catholics, the Marian regime appears to have met considerable success. Indeed, only recently have historians begun to acknowledge that 'Mary knew her own culture well enough to use symbols and rituals', including religious ones: 'not only to communicate with her subjects but also to help establish a political base.'[14]

Mary's parliament in late 1554 saw the completion of her obvious role in recalling Catholic England back to life. Her involvement in the negotiations between Cardinal Pole and parliament for the Church's reunion with Rome was far-reaching. The culmination of her efforts was Pole granting absolution to the realm for the sins of heresy and schism and reconciling England with the Roman Catholic Church on 30 November 1554, which she personally witnessed beside Philip. However because of her fidelity in past years, she was not in need of absolution. This was only the beginning of a close working relationship between the queen and the cardinal and papal legate, who in less than two years would also be archbishop of Canterbury and primate of all England.[15]

Pole, a scion of the royal house of Plantagenet, had fled England at the time of Henry VIII's schism. A man of great breadth and depth of humanistic learning, he became the doyen of Catholic renewal while living in exile in Italy in the 1540s. Created cardinal by Pope Paul III, he became one of the three cardinals who oversaw the first series of sessions of the General Council of Trent, the institutional Church's chief form of response to the challenge of nascent Protestantism. Especially in the absence of her consort, King Philip, Mary seems to have relied a great deal on Pole's advice regarding national and international, as well as ecclesiastical affairs. For example, in 1558 Pole appointed special preachers for the Salisbury diocese, which was *sede vacante* (without a bishop) from October 1557, and Mary commanded the local justices of the peace to aid them in their work. Pole also directly interceded with the queen in having Bishop Tunstall's London residence restored to him for use during parliament and convocation.[16] In his own assessment, Pole took on the role of trusted councillor and even *confidant*, to the point that he was accused by some of not showing sufficient pastoral care for his own archdiocese or even the London parishes under his jurisdiction.[17]

The most important way in which queen and primate cooperated in renewing the Church was in their selection of bishops. Here Mary anticipated the Counter-Reformation in the rest of the world by seeing the need for pastors and theologians to govern the Church; the Council of Trent too would seek to transform bishops 'from exploiters of benefices into ministers'.[18] It also seems quite likely that the office of bishop would not have survived had the Edwardine religious revolution been able to continue; in this sense one of Mary's lasting legacies to her nation is the continued existence of the episcopate in the Church of England. The clerics that they raised to the episcopate were men with known pastoral skills and theological acumen. Even Edmund Bonner, made infamous by John Foxe as a vengeful persecutor of non-Catholics, revealed immense creativity in the catechetical works that were produced for his diocese of London, works that were deemed effective enough by Mary and Pole to become official and standard religious texts for the rest of the English Church.[19] Gardiner, Tunstall, Watson, White, Pate, Goldwell, Scott, Oglethorpe, Brooks, Hopton, Christopherson and Glynn were all men of keen intellect, organizational skill and pastoral vigour.[20]

For example, Anthony Browne, Viscount Montague, wrote to the queen that Bishop Christopherson had advised him to enlist Alban Langdale, the archdeacon of Chichester and controversialist, to preach to congregations while he fulfilled Mary's commission to tour Sussex.[21] Montague wrote that he himself also encouraged local gentry and the people to maintain the faith; both Montague and Langdale became noted recusants in Elizabeth's reign. Thomas Mayer has shown how highly competent were the men Pole appointed to lower positions in the hierarchy.[22] Mary herself stepped in to present the Fellows of Magdalen College, Oxford, where Pole himself had been a member, with a *terna* (a list of three names submitted to the pope as recommendations to fill a vacant benefice) of three distinguished clerics from which to choose their new president.[23] One of Mary's own chaplains, the controversialist Richard Smith, would flee into exile under Elizabeth I to become the first professor of sacred scripture at the new University of Douai, a city where he was instrumental in attracting his fellow countrymen such that it would soon become the centre of English Catholic exiles, and continued to be prolific in his published arguments against Protestant theologies.[24]

Mary's relations with the papacy were more complex than is often realized. On the one hand she showed all reverence to that institution and the individual holders of the Chair of St Peter, but she was not blind to the frailties of those individual bishops of Rome and especially to the needs of her Church and people. It remains unclear whether she was thwarted in swift reunion with Rome by the dire warnings of privy councillors, the emperor and a fractious parliament, or was politic in taking almost a year and a half before reconciliation with the rest of the Catholic world, allowing her subjects to become used to the notion of ecclesiastical unity under the pope after 20 years of violent denigration of that unity.[25] She also was not averse to ignoring the demands of Pope Paul IV for the return of Cardinal Pole to Rome, to undergo investigation for heresy. Pole's friend, Bishop Pate of Worcester, strongly advised her not to let Pole go, for her sake as well as the nation's.[26] She may have realized that the charges were weak and that Paul was unbalanced, but she certainly realized how much she and her Church were dependent upon Pole for advice and support while King Philip was out of the country.[27] Nevertheless, in insisting on England's reconciliation with Rome and her Church's overall obedience to papal authority, she showed her subjects and the rest of Europe the premium she placed on ecclesial unity, the doctrine which, along with the Roman Catholic mass, her hierarchy saw as most important for salvation and the most denigrated in England in the recent past.[28]

Beyond her explicit endeavours on behalf of the renewal of the Catholic Church in England, especially in terms of royal decrees, parliamentary legislation and their enforcement (including laws requiring the arrest of Protestants and others who rejected the Catholic Church and the execution of those who would not recant their contrary views, episcopal appointments and placing the Church and nation once more under papal obedience), Mary also took on the role of exemplar to her subjects in embracing Catholicism and actively supporting its works of charity and devotion. Once the elements of normal ecclesiastical governance were restored, such as papal jurisdiction and ecclesiastical freedom in seeing to the Catholic worship of God and the needs of the faithful, Mary retired to the usual role of the sovereign as benefactor of the Church. Perhaps with her grandfather, Henry VII, and even the revered Henry VI in mind, she gave generously to the Church in both monies and deeds, personally undertaking the spiritual and corporal works of mercy, that were a key element of the Catholic understanding of the Christian's duty to God and their fellow Christians, both before and during the Counter-Reformation. This may have been Mary's way of 'Renaissance self-fashioning'; she was certainly conscious of her religious activities as Queen of England, but it remains unclear to what extent, if any, the presentation did or did not match her interior self. Perhaps now is the time for a study of Mary akin to Thomas Mayer's exhaustive work on the self-fashioning of Mary's cousin Reginald Pole.[29] Still, in these endeavours she also took on another traditional role of the monarch: the chief layperson of the realm, exemplifying what it meant to be a devout member of the Church after 20 years of religious furore and bitter attacks on Catholicism.

As benefactor of the Church she moved against the advice of her councillors, and restored lands to the Church that were still in crown hands from the time of the suppression of most non-parochial religious institutions during the previous two reigns. She forfeited the crown's right to receive most fees from the Church, which she knew to be impoverished both from dire economic conditions and forced alienation of Church property, land and movables, since 1529. For example, she surrendered her patronage of numerous parish livings to the bishops of dioceses where these churches were situated; this would also allow the bishops themselves to select their parochial clergy.[30] Such actions caused the crown to lose considerable revenue, and to give the hierarchy greater power in the pastoral care of their sees, a key element of the Counter-Reformation. In fact the great historian of the Council of Trent, Hubert Jedin, maintained that concern for episcopal duties was 'the vision underlying Trent's many decrees on reform'.[31] Moreover, in restoring ecclesiastical property to the Church, she acted as an exemplar; 'more pressure than is sometimes realized was put on individuals to return their ecclesiastical property'.[32]

Mary also personally aided the restoration of religious life in her kingdom, especially in re-establishing those orders renowned for the strict observance of their respective rules and their taking the call to Catholic reform throughout the early-modern period to heart, both before and after Trent.[33] 'Mary in fact founded or reestablished more religious communities than any other English monarch in history', a fact which puts paid to the notion that her regime was too conservative to embrace the nascent Society of Jesus.[34] The Carthusians, who claim never to have been deformed, Observant Franciscans and Brigettine nuns and priests, all of whom had suffered under Henry and had their share of martyrs and exiles, restored at least one house each, including the foundations near the royal palace of Richmond. Other orders with an ancient history in England, such as the Benedictines, Dominican friars and nuns and the Hospitallers, reopened communities with the support of the queen. John Feckenham, the abbot of the restored community of the royal foundation of St Peter's, Westminster Abbey, was renowned for his devotion to his Church and his order, and died untried in an Elizabethan prison decades later for his dedication.[35] These communities had been important centres of prayer for the Church and nation, as well as providing religious writing, publications and education, especially among the Dominican friars, and sources of charitable giving to the poor. Mary and Philip also resurrected the Savoy Hospital, London, founded by Henry VII, as a place of aid for pilgrims, travellers, the poor, the sick and the dead, the last in terms of its refoundation as a royal chantry.[36] Mary intended to grant further munificent bene-factions to these religious communities and to the Savoy, to establish a new hospital in London for poor, ill and elderly soldiers, and that the huge sum of £1000 be distributed to the poor upon her death.[37] All her desires for the poor and for these institutions were in keep-ing both with the medieval and Counter-Reformation emphases on doing deeds of charity and undertaking Christ's and the Church's command to fulfil the corporal and spiritual works of mercy.

It was at one of these religious houses that Mary also personally supported the renewal of the shrine and cult of the saints: in the person of her predecessor on the throne, St Edward the Confessor in his own foundation of St Peter's Abbey, Westminster. She also restored St George, England's patron saint, to his role as patron of the Order of the Garter, after he had been ignominiously thrust out by Edward VI himself.[38] Even in her brother's reign, she and her large entourage of knights, ladies and gentleman had entered London on horseback, all bearing large rosary beads, at that time an outlawed sign of devotion to the Virgin Mary.[39]

Besides the episcopate, Mary's other great and lasting religious and cultural contributions to the variety of the Counter-Reformation in England were education, music and the renewal of cathedrals as centres of worship. She restored Manchester College in 1556 'that God might be more diligently served and the town better furnished with priests and men meet for that service'.[40] Higher learning for her clergy was pivotal in Mary's plans for Catholic renewal, and she moved rapidly to reform Oxford and Cambridge universities.[41] Here she once again preceded her bishops by stressing clerical education for the sake of Catholic reform; they in turn preceded Trent in its determination to establish diocesan seminaries to that end.[42] Both universities had become seriously impoverished in the previous two reigns. For example, under Henry, all the colleges and halls of the universities belonging to the religious orders were suppressed along with the monasteries and friaries. During Edward's reign, Oxford's library had much of its collection destroyed, and colleges at both universities, even such royal foundations as King's, lost their ancient choral foundations. Mary reversed this trend by giving generously to Oxford and Cambridge. She re-endowed her father's foundation of Trinity College, Cambridge, not only giving it funds for the regular singing of mass and the liturgical offices, but also building its chapel. At Oxford she was imitated by Sir Thomas White and Sir Thomas Pope, who in 1554 created St John's and Trinity Colleges, and in Cambridge by John Caius who reinstituted Gonville Hall as Gonville and Caius College.[43] All four institutions were to serve as chantries for the founders (or re-founders) and their families and for the education of men in reformed Catholic life and doctrine so that they would serve the Church as ordained clergy.[44]

Both universities received official visitations from the queen and representatives bearing Cardinal Pole's legatine authority. These visitations, like those under Edward, were disruptive. Books were again burnt; the Marian visitors also commanded the exhumation of the remains of reformers such as Martin Bucer, for the burial of heretics in consecrated ground was seen as sacrilege.[45] Protestant heads of colleges, fellows and students fled into exile; many would return to become leaders of the Elizabethan Church. The Marian visitors stipulated that collegiate statutes were to be restored to fulfil the intentions of their founders, which usually emphasized the education of clergy in Catholic doctrine and masses and prayers for deceased benefactors.[46] In her will Mary intended to give enormous legacies to both universities, in terms of scholarships for poor men who intended to become priests and religious; she also requested prayers for her soul and the souls of her loved ones from the Dominicans at Oxford.[47]

Instruction in canon law and scholastic theology was restored, though the latter hardly challenged the strength of humanist education, since Mary herself and most of her bishops and leading clerics had been trained in that mode themselves and looked for its continuance. For example, the humanistic program for education at St John's College, Cambridge, created by Erasmus' friend, Bishop John Fisher, was renewed in Mary's reign. Some of its fundamental Catholic elements had been eviscerated by Thomas Cromwell as university chancellor. Learned men of national and international reputations taught or served as leaders of the colleges and universities, as many members of the Marian hierarchy had done before their consecration.[48] With the imposition of the Elizabethan religious settlement, however, many of the men trained in the Catholic

humanism of the Marian universities, especially Oxford, became leaders of English Catholics in exile, and many returned secretly to serve
the Recusant Church, as secular priests or religious, especially as
members of the most significant order of the Counter-Reformation,
the Society of Jesus. The survival of Catholicism in England owes
much to Mary I and her fundamental role in establishing, albeit
briefly but nevertheless with incredible potency, the rigorous Catholic
education at Oxford and Cambridge in the latter 1550s.[49]

Mary also seems to have taken a particular interest in the printing of
religious books as sources of catechesis, polemic and devotion, beyond
the homilies she had called for in her injunctions of 1554. Mary's
own personal tastes regarding religious books are enlightening. Her
'personal choice of devotional books is in the mainstream of devout
humanism'.[50] All these texts were used frequently by the queen;
one in particular would later be made popular by Peter Canisius in
Counter-Reformation Germany and by Cardinal Bérulle in Counter-
Reformation France. This volume was the *Margarita Evangelica*, a
late-medieval Dutch work circulated by the reform-minded Carthusians and translated into Latin by Nicholas Van Ess, an author who
was at that time under the influence of the Jesuits; he would adapt and
publish Ignatius Loyola's great work of Counter-Reformation spirituality, *The Spiritual Exercises*. This 1548 work in turn would be adapted
and translated into English by William Peryn, prior of the Marian
Dominican community in London.[51]

Numerous works published in her reign were dedicated to the
queen, and it is doubtful that these texts would have been proffered
without her previous consent. She certainly possessed presentation
copies, printed or in manuscript, of works by Gardiner, Bonner,
Tunstall and Miles Hogarde.[52] Printers of these texts were granted
royal licences, which, along with their dedications to Mary, implied
royal favour and protection from unscrupulous printers who would
market the work without paying the author and licensed printer.
For example, the best-selling devotional work of the period was the
primer, or collection of prayers, to be used at mass and throughout
each day. This compendium of psalms, communion devotions, prayers
asking for the intercession of the saints and prayers for the dead
appeared in numerous editions; the *Wayland primer* was among the
most popular, and a 1555 royal proclamation gave the printer, John
Wayland, a monopoly on all such works approved by the Church.[53]

Clerical (usually of considerable standing) and lay authors brought
out books old and new, of prose and verse, in English, Latin

and translations from the Latin, and overtly offered them to the queen in recognition of her piety and to help further her Counter-Reformation. The most significant work printed with a dedication to Mary was the enormous 1557 edition of the English *Works of Thomas More*, including his works of devotion and his polemics against early Protestantism in England.[54] The most prolific Marian author was also a layman, Miles Hogarde, who described himself in his books as servant to the queen; in fact her hosier. This remarkable London artisan with no university education produced numerous expositions of late-medieval and early-modern Catholic spirituality, most of which were dedicated to Mary and mostly written in poor verse, which invariably included numerous attacks on Protestant belief throughout each book. His one extent prose volume, *The displaying of the Protestants*, is a remarkable text just in relation to its dedication to the queen. An original edition appeared early in 1556, and later that year an enlarged edition, complete with index, was printed with a royal dedication and an allusion to the aid of friends in high places. In it he produced one of the most comprehensive attacks on underground, exiled and martyred Protestants and their contradictory beliefs.[55] Only the anonymous *Plain and godly treatise, concerning the mass*, offered a similar all-encompassing delineation and denunciation of Protestantism in the 1550s. This book was also specially favoured, for it is often found bound together with the *Wayland primer*.[56]

A key work initiated by Mary's bishops for the Counter-Reformation in England which would have a profound impact on the Counter-Reformation in the rest of the world was the catechism of Bartholomé Carranza, a Spanish Dominican friar who had been a theologian of humanist inclinations at the Council of Trent and had accompanied Philip to England in 1554, and remained for some years as confidant to both Mary and Pole. He dedicated his *Comentarios sobre el catechismo Christiano* to the king, but the dedicatory letters possessed words of high praise for the queen's work of Counter-Reformation in England. Originally written and published in Spanish, it was being translated into English under Pole's auspices for the use of the clergy in catechizing the laity in England. The Spanish edition would be the foundation for the Roman catechism of 1566, an important source of Catholic doctrine for seminary professors and students and parochial clergy into the twentieth century.[57]

Besides dedications, a sermon by James Brooks, later Marian bishop of Gloucester, was published twice early in the reign with royal authority. Even copies of an earlier work by Stephen Gardiner, an attack on Cranmer's eucharistic theology, were stipulated as possessing the approval of Mary's privy council, and also re-appeared early in her reign. Both the Marian regime and the Marian ecclesiastical hierarchy also worked to censor heretical texts. The Legatine Synod called for the inspection of religious books, and several texts state their approval by Bishop Bonner of London, the location of England's small printing industry.[58] Mary and Philip also granted a royal charter for the incorporation of the Company of Stationers in 1557; among the duties of this guild was 'to search and seize' heretical books.[59]

One of the glories of Counter-Reformation Catholicism and the Anglican tradition of Christianity is sung worship. Rooted in the medieval past, the latter still thrives while choral and instrumental accompaniment of the liturgy in the rest of Europe has largely evaporated. However, England's tradition was under serious threat in the Edwardine religious revolution. While some religious music for the Prayer Book was composed, many cathedrals, collegiate churches, college chapels and even the Chapel Royal had been stripped of the funds, and sometimes even of the church organs, to perform even what little was deemed appropriate for a reformed Church. Queen Mary, however, loved religious music and appreciated its importance in drawing her people back to the Catholic liturgy and Catholic belief; once again Mary showed prescience in perceiving the didactic role of the liturgy, and music that displayed 'orthodoxy', 'intelligibility' and 'uniformity' could serve this end.[60]

The bishops of the Council of Trent and their successors who patronized such geniuses as Palestrina, Victoria and Lasso were like the queen in utilizing church music to advance Catholic reform.[61] She lavished funds on musical foundations under royal patronage, most especially her own Chapel Royal, an institution of singing men, boys, instrumentalists and servants who saw to their needs that usually accompanied the monarch on her or his peregrinations, rather than an actual building.[62] The leading composers of England, many of them also among the most significant musicians in English history, served in her chapel: Thomas Tallis, Christopher Tye, John Shepherd and a young William Byrd among others. Their music is still sung in Catholic and Anglican liturgies throughout the English-speaking world. These men arranged and performed sophisticated and exquisite religious music for the worship of God, but also to attract people to the truths of the Catholic faith by the beauty of its communal prayer, especially the mass and sacrament of the eucharist.[63] Several Marian festal masses are still largely, if not completely, extant, as is the one completely surviving elevation motet by an English composer.[64] Such compositions were sung at the raising of the consecrated host and chalice for the adoration of the congregation throughout the Catholic world, especially in the medieval and Counter-Reformation periods. Motets such as these would have no place whatsoever in reformed services, and that probably explains why none survive in England, with the exception of Robert Parson's Marian composition and a heavily reconstructed work by Robert Fayrfax, who died in 1521.[65] Moreover, Marian musicians worked not only for the queen's chapel, but also for St Paul's and other English cathedrals, Westminster Abbey, London parishes and Oxbridge colleges. Musicians from these other institutions also shared musical ideas; a young Robert Whyte at Mary's Trinity College, Cambridge, is just one example.[66]

This was also the first time when there was large-scale cross-fertilization of musical ideas among living artists from England and other Catholic nations, with the coming of the Spanish royal chapel's musicians with Philip for his marriage. After two decades of artistic isolation, English, Welsh, Spanish and Flemish musicians, as well as other musicians of other nationalities attached to Philip's and the Imperial court, not only heard each other perform, such as at a Spanish Corpus Christi procession in Kingston-upon-Thames in 1555, but also performed with each other, as at the nuptial mass of Queen Mary and King Philip at Winchester Cathedral on July 25 1554.[67] The great composer of Counter-Reformation Germany, Orlando Lasso, composed a motet for Cardinal Pole's return to England.[68] Certainly the fruitful musical interchange, decades later, between the renowned composers, Philippe De Monte and William Byrd, had its roots in this collaboration of musicians from throughout Europe at the service of the Marian Church.[69] In this way the Marian Church, and the recusant English community which succeeded it, kept in stride with the flowering of beautiful and doctrinally sound Catholic religious music of the sixteenth and seventeenth centuries.

Mary's personal devotion to religious music, which caused her to be munificent to her Chapel Royal, in turn aided the liturgical music and liturgy of England's cathedrals. Worship at the mother church of each diocese served as a model for the parishes and other religious institutions in which the mass and the divine offices were held. While their role as models of communal prayer disintegrated with the accession of Elizabeth – parochial music was limited to the metrical psalter, for example – nevertheless England's cathedral choirs continued to sing works composed for Protestant usage by Tallis, Byrd and other Marian musicians to the present day. Indeed, for many Anglicans, the only worship they attend is evensong, and it was the cathedrals that maintained that tradition until it could be handed on to parishes when interest in sung worship waxed in the nineteenth and twentieth centuries, beginning with the Oxford Movement. Having been almost annihilated during Edward's reformation, England's ancient musical heritage rose from the ashes during Mary's Counter-Reformation, to be preserved under Elizabeth I and after; though Marian music's *raison d'être*, the Catholic Counter-Reformation, had been extinguished.[70]

Besides displaying interest and especially concrete support for religious orders, clerical education in the universities, the printing of religious texts of various kinds, particularly works of catechesis and devotion, and beautiful worship such as that produced with the assistance of exceptional liturgical music, Mary also displayed personal devotion for her subjects to see or to hear of. Although she used, as her half-sister would do later, clothing, jewels, speeches in times of crisis, royal processions and progresses to order to fill her people with awe of her, the Lord's anointed who had come to the throne against all odds and who had maintained her position despite the challenge of being England's first queen regnant, with seeming devotion and without undue ostentation she also practised elements characteristic of Catholic life and doctrine for all to see and to imitate, according to their station.[71] She, like her half-brother, heard sermons preached before her but on very different subjects, some of which she insisted on having printed; like Brooks's call to England to awake from Protestant heresy, and Watson's sermons on Christ's corporeal presence in the eucharist and the sacrificial nature of the mass.[72] Her initial royal act of having a requiem mass sung for her half-brother is most telling of her views on one of the most controversial of religious subjects, prayers for the dead.[73]

Her personal concern for the restoration of the intercession of the saints in the life of the nation, in the case of St George, England's patron saint, and St Edward the Confessor, its only canonized monarch, speak of her devotion to the saints and her desire for renewal of their veneration. In taking a personal concern for the refurbishment of St Edward's shrine in Westminster Abbey, she did more than practise mere familial *pietas*.[74] She was renewing an element of Catholicism deeply loathed and excoriated by evangelical reformers since her father's day: a pilgrimage shrine.[75] In her evident concern for prayer to the saints and for the dead in her kingdom, the queen once again revealed how she prefigured the concern for the same doctrines at Trent, and their importance in Counter-Reformation spirituality.[76] Why she did not restore the two other great shrines of England, that of Thomas Becket at Canterbury Cathedral and Our Lady of Walsingham, is probably because the focal points of both were lost. The relics of the martyred archbishop and the Holy House and statue of Mary had been utterly destroyed; the relics of St Edward the Confessor had remained untouched. Also, while later monarchs would follow her revival of touching those afflicted with 'the king's evil' (scrofula) with prayers for healing, Mary was the last to pray over 'cramp' rings, sacramentals blessed by God's viceroy in England for those seeking relief from epilepsy; not surprisingly both of these rites were attributed to St Edward the Confessor. She also had political reasons for reviving the good works of her saintly predecessor on the throne: they underlined the sacred character of anointed monarchs which she claimed to possess despite her gender and her former illegitimate status.[77]

The eucharist and the mass were of the utmost importance to Mary as devout ruler. Her refusal to give up having mass offered in her household once it was outlawed in 1549 and throughout the Edwardine reformation, despite intense pressure, was notorious. Now, as queen, she made her devotion to the key element of Roman Catholicism public in various gestures. She did not keep her eyes off the host during her nuptial mass in Winchester Cathedral. Even on her deathbed she had mass offered in her chamber, and it was reported that she died with eyes yet again fixed on the host during the chanting of the *Agnus Dei* towards the end of the liturgy.[78] She was present at the ostentatious Corpus Christi procession organized by the king's Spanish clergy, musicians, retainers and Spanish residents in London. Throughout the religious turmoil of her half-brother's rule and her own reign, she remained a steadfast witness to Christ's corporeal presence in the eucharist and the sacrificial nature of the mass, two of the most contested doctrines in the Reformation period, and with the exception of the papacy, the most vilified by English Protestants and the most strenuously maintained in the Counter-Reformation world.[79]

Thus, Queen Mary viewed her relationship to the English Church as that of chief model of the faithful and devout layperson. Lay piety and spirituality had been growing in Catholicism through the Middle Ages, especially through the growth of confraternities or guilds that were controlled by the laity, and would be transformed further into the 'active, virile, exacting religious outlook of counter-reforming Catholicism' that was 'given to thousands of devout laity. . . in the sixteenth and seventeenth centuries'.[80] She utterly rejected the role which her father created and which Edward VI and Elizabeth I embraced: that of Supreme Head or Governor or ruler of the Church in England. Once traditional, and for her, divinely ordained, ecclesiastical governance of the bishops in union with the pope and the rest of the Catholic Church had been restored, she consciously imitated her ancestors on the throne as models of beneficence to God's Church: her grandfather and founder of the Tudor dynasty, Henry VII; and also perhaps St Edward the Confessor in her concrete concern for his shrine and monastic foundation and undertaking the prerogative of the Lord's Anointed by healing illness, and the saintly Henry VI in her concrete concern for clerical education at the universities and schools, as a means of sustaining the Christian life and doctrine of the Catholic Church, and as remedy for heresy.

Henry Parker, Lord Morley, also recommended to her the example of Lady Margaret Beaufort, her great-grandmother, in his manuscript gift to her. Lady Margaret was equally devoted to the eucharist and according to sources she too died while gazing upon the host. She also restored an ancient shrine and centre of pilgrimage, St Winefride's Well in Holy Well, North Wales. Both women were noted for their generosity to the poor. Lady Margaret displayed keen interest in learning at both universities by endowing professorships in divinity, and in the founding of Christ's and St John's Colleges, Cambridge.[81] Ultimately, however, it may have been the example of her own mother, Katherine of Aragon, who was noted for her Catholic piety and making of pilgrimages, love of learning, and generosity to the poor and to scholars, that shaped Mary's religious policies the most. This doughty woman, child of the Catholic monarchs of Spain and their worldwide empire, dutiful to her husband as far as her conscience allowed, deeply religious, learned in the humanist mode and courageous in the practice of her faith and maintenance of her personal and royal dignity, even in the face of overwhelming opposition, and finally utter isolation, towered in her daughter's mind as the exemplar *par excellence* of how Catholicism should be maintained and reinvigorated.[82] Thus the movement for Catholic Counter-Reformation had a claim on her kingdom, for which, in Mary's eyes, her mother had suffered unto death.[83]

Much of the information about the Marian Church's renewal has been buried in the triumphalistic historiography of Protestant

England that began with John Foxe's *Acts and Monuments*. Now much of that data has been recovered or reinterpreted, but with more detailed information comes the concomitant problem of assessing that increased knowledge. What now can be said of the Mary I's religious policy? Given the increased historical knowledge that scholars now possess about the Marian Church, coupled with perspectives less bound to confessional divisions, it seems that a new assessment is in order.

In the long term, Mary's attempt to return England to Catholicism failed. Now more and more historians are placing the blame not on the queen, but on her death and therefore the brevity of her reign.[84] Catholic doctrines of salvation, the Church and its unity, the interconnection between scripture and ecclesial tradition, the eucharist and the other sacraments of Catholicism, the intercession of the saints, even religious art and music, were lost to the majority of the English people; and only in the nineteenth century were large numbers of people introduced to these Catholic doctrines and spirituality, beginning with the Oxford Movement. Prayers for the dead, forbidden for so long, found a place in the failed 1928 revision of the Book of Common Prayer; but it was not until 2002 in the funeral of Queen Elizabeth, the Queen Mother, that such prayers were uttered at a royal funeral in England for the first time since the death of Mary herself. Moreover, the Protestant Reformation was a success, at least in a negative sense; not only was Catholicism almost forgotten in England, it came to be deeply hated by most of the nation from the seventeenth to the first half of the twentieth century as a corrupt religion barely worthy of the name of Christian. When John Henry Newman left the established Church in 1845, it was seen as a perversion of one of the greatest minds of the contemporary Church of England to something little better than paganism. While Newman himself did much to make Catholicism understandable to his countrymen through such writings as his *Apologia pro vita sua* and 'A letter to the duke of Norfolk', it was only the dramatic changes the Catholic Church underwent in the Second Vatican Council and the secularization of post–Second World War British society that made Catholicism in England non-threatening, if not acceptable.[85]

Mary's Counter-Reformation, which included so many elements that would be embraced by the Catholic Church at large after the Council of Trent, and including those actions on behalf of Catholicism which were peculiarly her own as queen and as a devout layperson, met with amazing success, given the shortness of her rule and the obstacles over which she had little or no control, such as the crop failures, famine and epidemic which plagued the second half of her reign. Had she lived longer and produced or found an heir who was attached to the Catholic Church, the Church in England would have maintained its majority status. There was certainly no threat of religious war in England, with all possible Protestant leaders (aristocratic or gentry) of rebellion having compromised themselves in their conformity to the Church. Even in the midst of famine and a devastating influenza epidemic during most of her reign, most of the nation had conformed, if not embraced Catholicism, and the hierarchy's initial attempts to re-educate people in Catholic life and doctrine through the liturgy and the spoken and written word had made remarkable headway in such a short period. Historians have also shown that while it was relatively easy to cut the legal ties to the papacy and the rest of the Catholic world and place the remnants of the leaders of the Marian Church under house arrest or in prison without trial, expunging Catholicism from the national psyche took decades of determined effort on the part of Elizabeth, her privy council and her bishops. Even while it is in general much easier to destroy rather than to build, the eradication of English Catholicism was a slow and painstaking task; and an ultimately unsuccessful one.

For at least another generation after 1558, Catholicism maintained some impact on the faith and religious imagination of most of the people. For those who were most attached to the Counter-Reformation Catholic Church of Mary, the lessons of the Church of Edward VI were too recent to be forgotten. Catholic recusancy began early after the Elizabethan settlement became legally binding, and many, especially religious, clergy and students of divinity, fled to create, among other communities, a veritable Marian Oxford abroad, with all its faith in Roman Catholicism intact. Despite the necessary discontinuities in terms of structure and much of its spirituality between the Catholic Church under Mary and the Catholic Church under Elizabeth, the people who kept Catholicism alive in the 1560s had been among its leaders in the 1550s, such as Richard Smith, William Allen and Thomas Harding. The Counter-Reformation Catholic life and doctrine as known in Marian England continued and even flowered anew in Elizabethan England. For the English Catholicism that endured the penal years from Elizabeth I to George IV, in the beginning was not the Church of England.[86] In the beginning was the Catholic Church of Mary I, with all its Counter-Reformation vigour, 'variety and vitality'.[87]

10

Burning Zeal: Mary Tudor and the Marian Persecution

Thomas S. Freeman

Any assessment of Mary Tudor's reign must inevitably include a discussion of her regime's burnings of convicted heretics. This is not because these burnings were a priority of Mary's government. The restoration of Catholicism was the central feature of Marian policy, and the burnings were simply one of a number of measures intended to effect this. The burnings, however, are significant in any analysis of Mary's success and abilities, and they shaped how she was perceived in subsequent centuries. Above all, the burnings decisively influenced the history of the British Isles. The 1707 Act of Union – an unprecedented subordination of dynastic succession to legislative fiat – was the culmination of Protestant efforts to ensure that the fires of Smithfield were never rekindled.

Until very recently, the historiography on the burnings was uncomplicated. With only a handful of dissenting opinions, the consensus has been that the policy of burning heretics was a brutal, short-sighted and ill-considered programme that undermined the regime.[1] In his revisionist study, *Fires of faith*, Eamon Duffy has challenged this consensus, arguing that the burnings were part of an overall strategy which was well-planned and realistic in its objectives, that they were well organized and, most importantly of all, they were succeeding in their objectives up until Mary's death.[2] Given this stark difference of opinion as to its effectiveness and consequences, it is worth providing a re-examination of the Marian persecution.

Broadly speaking, I agree with Duffy's analysis of the burnings, particularly his crucial point that they were successful, at least until Mary died. In this chapter, however, I will examine some aspects of the burnings not discussed by Duffy in detail: Mary's responsibility for the persecution, and the reasons for the intensity of the persecution as well as the consequences, for Mary's regime, of its unexpected spread and ferocity. In doing so, I will be trying to qualify and complement Duffy's seminal study.

Mary and the Burnings

The first point to be considered is the responsibility of Mary herself for the burnings. Did she instigate or simply consent to them? Did she exercise any control over the process of persecution? One of the queen's modern biographers has sought to distance her from the burnings by observing that they were the results of enforcing the laws and that this enforcement was carried out by local officials, under the oversight of the privy council.[3] This is not entirely convincing. The laws mandating burning as a penalty for heresy had been repealed in Edward VI's reign and had to be revived under Mary. The crown did not simply enforce existing laws against heretics; it made a determined effort to re-enact these laws. After parliament failed to revive the heresy statutes in the spring of 1554, they had to be reintroduced in the next session, and only then became law.

Although much of the Marian persecution was indeed carried out by local officials, it does not follow that the queen was not involved. In fact, a series of documents demonstrates Mary's acute interest in, and oversight of, the burnings. On 24 March 1555, Mary and Philip complained to Edmund Bonner, the bishop of London, that local magistrates were handing suspected heretics over to the ecclesiastical authorities, only for the clergy not to pursue these cases. The monarchs admonished Bonner to try all suspected heretics brought to him, if they refused to recant.[4] The next day Mary and Philip ordered the Norfolk JPs to give special attention to the arrest of teachers of heresy and those who held heretical conventicles. The justices were also ordered to recruit informers in each parish and to urge the local constables to vigilance.[5] In 1555, Mary also ordered that sermons be preached at the burnings and that privy councillors attend those burnings that took place in London.[6] It may well be that, in issuing these orders, she was following the advice of Reginald Pole.[7] But her readiness to follow this advice, and to establish guidelines for local officials on the arrest and execution of heretics, speaks volumes about the importance she attached to these activities. The burning of heretics was a policy zealously implemented and enforced by Mary, and as sovereign ruler, she bears the greatest responsibility for it.

The burning of 284 religious dissidents is morally unjustifiable from a twenty-first-century perspective. It is important to remember, however, that the values of the twenty-first century are not the values of the sixteenth century, and that in the sixteenth century, the execution of obstinate heretics was almost universally regarded as a necessary duty of a Christian ruler.[8] Whether that duty, however, was conducted with rigour or relative leniency was left to the discretion of the individual ruler.

Was the Marian Persecution a Policy Failure?

Even accepting that, in sixteenth-century Catholic perceptions, the burning of the Marian martyrs was justified and even commendable, was it nevertheless a mistake? In the long run, it certainly was. For at least three centuries, the blood of the Marian martyrs was seed for harvests of anti-Catholic bigotry throughout the English-speaking world. However the fact that it was a mistake, let alone one of such magnitude, was owing to two almost entirely unforeseeable factors. The first was the sudden death of Mary a few years after the persecution had been initiated. The second was the memorialization of the Marian martyrs in John Foxe's *Acts and Monuments*. It was inevitable that during Elizabeth's reign there would be celebration of the victims of the Marian persecution. It was not inevitable that this celebration would take the form of a massive, painstakingly researched book which wielded remarkable influence. The *Acts and Monuments* profoundly altered the ways in which the Marian persecution was perceived. This was not only due to factors such as the book's graphic illustrations and its abundance of vivid anecdotes; it was also because of its comprehensiveness. The majority of Mary's subjects would not have witnessed a burning. Almost all of the remainder – unless they lived in or near London, Lewes, Colchester or Canterbury – might have had the opportunity to witness, at most, a handful of burnings. Generations of Foxe's readers, however, knew of almost all these executions, some of them in excruciating detail. Had Mary lived longer, Foxe would still have published an account of her persecution; he was preparing one in Basel during the final years of her reign. But it would necessarily have been shorter and less detailed, and, since it was written in Latin, it would not have had the impact in England that his Elizabethan martyrology enjoyed.

Was the persecution succeeding in its objectives when Mary died? And, if so, was this success worth the price that had to be paid? The second question is as important as the first. A policy, programme or campaign might attain its specific objectives, but create problems which lead to it being judged a failure. The objective of the persecution was simple: the eradication of determined and visible opponents of the restoration of Catholicism. Duffy rests most of his argument, that this objective was being attained, on the basic fact that the numbers of those burned declined dramatically during the year 1558.[9] Forty-three convicted heretics were burned in the period from January to November 1558, in contrast to 82 heretics burned in 1557 and 85 in 1556 (see Figure 10.1). The traditional explanation for this decline is that by 1558 doubts had set in among the magistrates and religious authorities – whether arising from popular antipathy to the burnings, the consequences of famine and pandemic, the ill health of the queen, a perception that the burnings were ineffectual, or a combination of all of these factors – as to the wisdom of continuing (in an uncomfortably literal sense) a scorched earth policy.[10]

There are, indeed, some examples of magistrates and local authorities hesitating to burn people. On 28 July 1557, the privy council wrote to the sheriffs of Kent, Essex, Suffolk and Staffordshire,

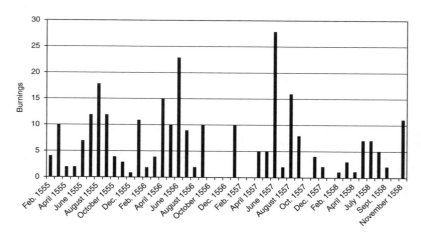

Figure 10.1 Executions by burning 1555–8

the mayor of Rochester and the bailiffs of Colchester, demanding that they explain why they had stayed the burning of condemned heretics.[11] Some scholars have cited these letters as proof that local authorities had lost their enthusiasm for the burnings and were, by the end of Mary's reign, reluctant to consign convicted heretics to the flames.[12] Upon closer examination, however, a more complicated picture emerges. The letter to the sheriff of Staffordshire must have been in regards to Joyce Lewes, burned at Lichfield on 10 September 1557. (The sheriff had flatly refused to burn Lewes and the privy council was forced to wait until he left office in September 1557, for his successor – who did not share his scruples – to execute her.[13]) Joyce Lewes was a gentlewoman, and her social status may well explain the sheriff's reluctance. The letter to the sheriff of Suffolk almost certainly concerned Thomas Spurdance, the only martyr executed in the county between July 1557 and May 1558. He had been condemned in May 1556, but he was not executed until November 1557.[14] Spurdance was a royal servant and, as with Lewes, the local authorities' hesitation to execute him may well have been due to his having influential connections. These cases probably demonstrate the authorities' reluctance to burn the well-connected rather than any doubts about the penalty for heresy or a reluctance to enforce it.

In all probability, the bailiffs of Colchester and the sheriff of Essex were being admonished over Agnes Bongeor, who was scheduled for burning on 2 August. Her name was incorrectly rendered in the writ authorizing her execution and the Colchester bailiffs refused to execute Bongeor until they received a correct writ.[15] Unquestionably feelings against the burnings were running high in Colchester (as will be discussed further on) and, for their own protection, local officials were careful to observe the legalities. In any case, Bongeor's reprieve was ephemeral; she was executed on 17 September 1557.[16] The letter sent to the mayor of Rochester and the sheriff of Kent would have been about the martyrs who were burned in the city in August 1557.[17] Unfortunately, we do not know enough about them to state why their executions had been delayed, if indeed they had been delayed. However, in this case, the local authorities seem to have responded to the wishes of the privy council with alacrity.

Tensions with the authorities in Bristol may also have arisen over the burnings. Martha Skeeters has observed that the mayor and aldermen of the city refused to worship at Bristol Cathedral, thereby incurring a reprimand from the privy council, who also ordered them to resume attending services. 'The reprimand came on 26 August 1557, the eve of the death of Thomas Banion, the last of some four to eight Bristol inhabitants to be burned as heretics during Mary's reign.' Skeeters speculates that the civic authorities refused to attend church in protest at the burning of Banion (or Benion).[18] But if there was some disenchantment with the burnings among Bristol's civic elite, this epiphany must have been sudden, as David Harris, an alderman, had been instrumental in the arrest of Thomas Hale in the spring of 1557. Hale was burned, along with one Richard Sharp, just outside the city walls on 7 May 1557.[19] Benion, moreover, had been arrested by a constable, which suggests some degree of civic involvement in his detection and apprehension.[20] However, the civic authorities might well have been offended with the haste in which Benion was condemned and burned, especially if corners were thought to have been cut. First arrested on 13 August 1557, he was burned only a fortnight later. It is perhaps significant that Benion was the last Marian martyr to be burned in Bristol.

There is, moreover, one case where the local officials stalled the execution of heretics long enough to save their lives. Some time in 1557, the JP Henry Clifford urged his father-in-law, Sir Anthony Hungerford, then sheriff of Wiltshire, not to execute John Hunt and Richard White. Hungerford then refused to burn the pair, maintaining that the writ authorizing their execution was invalid. On 4 June 1558 Hunt and White were re-examined, and a correct writ was presented in late August to the under-sheriff, who burned it and then denied ever having received it.[21] Mary died before the matter was resolved, and Hunt and White survived her reign.[22] The motives of Hungerford and Clifford for non-cooperation can only be guessed at, but it might well be that the under-sheriff was influenced by news of the queen's ill-health. He was almost certainly emboldened by the death of William Geffrie, the chancellor of the diocese of Salisbury, on 28 August 1558. Geffrie's passing not only removed a vigorous persecutor (he had tried and condemned Hunt and White), it deprived the diocese, which had already lost its bishop, of leadership for the remainder of the reign.[23]

Against these rather isolated examples stands solid evidence that the machinery for the repression of heresy rolled on with uninterrupted effectiveness throughout the final year of Mary's reign. In late April 1558 a group was arrested attending a clandestine Protestant service in Islington. Seven of them were examined on 14–17 June, condemned on 17 June and executed on 27 June. Another six were examined on 20–23 June, condemned on 12 July and burned on 14 July.[24] At no period in Mary's reign did the process of trying a large group of heretics operate with greater efficiency.

On 28 March 1558, Cardinal Pole established a new commission to hunt down heretics in the diocese of Canterbury, and it detected the last heretics to be burned in Mary's reign.[25] In April, Bishop Bonner issued a commission to William Chedsey, archdeacon of Middlesex, Thomas Mowrton, his chaplain, and John Boswell, his clerk, ordering them to search for heretics in Harwich and Colchester. On 20 April, Chedsey wrote to Bonner, complaining that he had been summoned to London by the privy council and protesting that his departure would encourage the heretics in Colchester and would also impede his investigation of 'iii most obstinate and cumbrous heretics'. The commissioners soldiered on, and the three heretics, William Harris, Richard Day and Christian George, were burned in Colchester on 26 May.[26]

Clearly, there was no lack of determination to eradicate heresy on the part of Chedsey and his colleagues, yet only three heretics were burned in Colchester in all of 1558. In contrast, six people were burned in the city in 1556 and twelve in 1557. The system for detecting, apprehending and executing heretics was in place, and it was being administered by zealous officials, but the number of victims was still declining.

Some scholars have maintained that the prosecution of heresy finally unravelled in the summer of 1558. According to Alexandra Walsham:

> As the reign of Mary progressed, officials began to find that the fires of Smithfield were not healing the social ruptures wrought by heresy but rather serving to inflame and exacerbate them. As a mechanism for enforcing and restoring concord, they had become counter-productive.... After June 1558, public burnings were halted altogether.[27]

In actual fact, 25 people – over half of the heretics burned in 1558 – were publicly executed in the period from July to November. Furthermore, in contradiction to those who insist that that fears of Mary's imminent death were responsible for the precipitous decline in the number of burnings in 1558, 11 of the 43 burnings of the final year of her reign – just over one quarter of the total – took place in November, when it was readily apparent that the queen's health was precarious.

Although the number of those burned declined in 1558, in some respects the persecution was more severe towards the end of the reign than it had been previously. Of 30 people arrested at a conventicle in the churchyard of St Mary le Bow in January 1555, two were ultimately burned.[28] When 22 conventiclers were arrested in Essex in 1556, they were all released after signing a loosely worded recantation.[29] In contrast, of the 22 people arrested attending the clandestine service in Islington in 1558, no fewer than 13 were burned.[30]

There were several reasons for this escalating rigour, but the most fundamental was that the earlier policy of releasing heretics after they had formally recanted was not working. Of the 22 Essex heretics who were released after recanting, seven – Margaret Hide, William Bongeor, Helen Ewring, William Munt, Alice Munt, Rose Allin and Richard Roth – were burned within a year of their release. An eighth, Richard George, was in prison awaiting execution when Mary's reign ended.[31] In most of these cases, we do not know the specific offences that led to their rearrest, but the Munt family not only refused to attend mass, but stood outside their parish church reviling the parishioners and mocking the Host.[32] Ralph Allerton, a fellow-villager of the Munts, had himself publicly recanted at Paul's Cross on 10 January 1557, and returned home to preach illegally and lead conventicles. Within three months he was back before Bonner, and he was burned on 17 September 1557.[33] In a number of cases, the martyrs did not wait for the authorities to discover that they had relapsed, but renounced their recantations publicly. Three of them did so during mass.[34]

The Marian authorities, both clerical and lay, were fully aware of the difficulties caused by those who recanted and then relapsed. As early as 15 July 1555, Pole wrote to the bishop of Salisbury ordering him to deal with sacramentarians who had been received back into the Church but were continuing in their wicked ways.[35] On 7 August 1557, the privy council fined Sir John Butler, the sheriff of Essex, £10, because his deputy had reprieved Margaret Thurston when she recanted.[36] But the privy council's unwillingness to relent, even for those who repented, was made fully manifest in the case of Thomas Bembridge, a gentleman of Hampshire. During his burning, Bembridge cried out that he recanted. Sir Richard Pecksall, the sheriff of Hampshire, then called off the execution. On 1 August, the privy council wrote to Pecksall, 'signifying that the Queenes Majestie cannot but fynde it very straunge that he hath stayed one Bembridge from execution, being condempned for heresye, and therfore he is straightly commaunded to cause him to be executed out of hande'. If Bembridge continued in his recantation, 'as he outwardly pretendeth', he was to be allowed spiritual counsel 'for the better ayding of him to dye Goddes servaunte', but God's servant or not, he was to be burned without delay. Bembridge was executed on 5 August. Pecksall was summoned before the privy council, fined £100 and, according to Foxe, imprisoned in the Fleet, for having stopped the burning.[37]

Occasionally the execution of individual heretics encountered delays, resistance or even obstruction from local officials. As has already been seen, reluctance could stem from the status and influential connections of the condemned or from a desire that correct legal procedure be followed meticulously. In Bristol and Salisbury it is possible that there was also resentment at what were perceived as high-handed, even unjust, prosecutions by over-zealous clerics. Yet it is important not to overstate the nature and significance of this local non-cooperation. With the exception of Colchester, these delays and obstructions owed nothing to popular feeling or a general revulsion against the burnings. And only in Salisbury was anything more than a temporary reprieve won for the condemned. In general, during the last year of Mary's life the campaign against heresy proceeded with unbroken vigour, and increased rigour, particularly in the confessional battlegrounds of Kent, Suffolk, Essex and Middlesex.

The decline in the numbers of those burned in this period cannot therefore be explained by a supposed demoralization among the persecutors nor by the claim that the machinery of ecclesiastical justice broke down; as the Islington conventiclers discovered, it worked with grim efficiency. The decline in the number of burnings was because the persecution was succeeding in its overall objective: the elimination of incorrigible dissenters, who insisted on displaying their recalcitrance publicly. The number of those prepared to die in agony for any cause is always limited, and the burnings had critically reduced this very finite number by 1558. The execution of such die-hards was a not insignificant achievement. It meant that the restoration of Catholicism could continue without open defiance and that the leaders and most active agents of any religious opposition were being increasingly eliminated.

The Intensity of the Marian Persecution

But the elimination of hard-core religious dissidents was only achieved through a persecution of remarkable intensity. There was no precedent in England for heresy executions on this scale. By my count the 37 years of Henry VIII's reign saw 76 people burned for heresy.[38] Even when compared with continental heresy executions, the Marian burnings seem particularly fierce. Only two persecutions in western and central Europe during the sixteenth century rival the Marian persecution in lethal intensity, and both of these followed tremendous social upheavals. In the wake of the Peasants' War, nearly 250 Anabaptists were executed as heretics in the Tyrol during the years 1528–33,[39] and at least 400 Anabaptists were executed between the years 1534 and 1540 in Holland and Frisia following the tumults in Münster.[40] If William Monter is correct in his estimate that over 3,000 Protestants were executed for heresy throughout Reformation Europe by 1565, the four years of the Marian persecution contributed approximately 10 per cent of this total.[41] Moreover Mary's persecution was by far and away the largest persecution of magisterial, mainstream Protestants. In contrast to the Anabaptists, who in the sixteenth century did not have access to major presses and who lacked supporters from clerical and lay elites, the Marian martyrs could at least broadcast news of their sufferings.

There were a number of factors, beyond the determination of Mary and her officials, that made the Marian persecution so lethal. First of all, arrests for heresy were generally made on the basis of personal behaviour, especially a suspect's display of irreverence towards the Host or refusal to participate in religious rites. Although there was nothing unprecedented about this, the importance of such behaviours as a cause for arrest loomed much larger in Mary's reign than ever before. Of the 312 people who were burned for heresy or who died in prison after being charged with heresy during her reign, the reasons for the initial arrest of 108 of them are known. Twenty of these were arrested for failing to attend church services, nine for refusing to participate in the sacraments of baptism or confession, or for attending church but refusing to receive the eucharist, while a further six were arrested for obstructing the celebration of the mass in some manner.[42] If this percentage is extrapolated to all of those who died at the stake or in prison under Mary, about one-third were arrested for offences that took place at a parish level. This inevitably increased the number of martyrs. Many people were not in a position to read or write a heretical book or preach a heretical sermon, but they all had the choice of conforming to or defying the Marian Church.

A further reason why this emphasis on prosecuting deviant religious behaviour at the parish level produced so many victims was that it was accompanied by unprecedented local supervision of religious conduct. Archdeacon Nicholas Harpsfield's 1557 visitation of the diocese of Canterbury inquired into whether people were working or going to taverns instead of church on Sundays, whether those with good voices were singing in the choir and whether rosary beads were being used.[43] In four Wealden parishes – Sandhurst, Hawkhurst, Benenden and Cranbrook – where heresy was rife, Harpsfield ordered that all adults must confess once in the first half of Lent and again in the second half. A rota was drawn up to see that each household complied. A member of each household was compelled to attend the processions on Wednesdays and Fridays. Easter communion was to be withheld from those who did not venerate the Cross on Good Friday.[44]

Harpsfield was a tireless administrator with a gimlet eye for religious deviance, but his unblinking supervision of parish life was matched by a number of his colleagues. On 2 April 1557, the heresy commission for the diocese of London issued orders to all its ministers, curates and churchwardens to search out those who did not go to church, make confession or receive the sacrament. That same month, churchwardens in the diocese had to answer questions about heretical behaviour among the parishioners, whether any of the clergy were married or living with former wives, the conduct of midwives, the spread of seditious rumours or slanders within a parish, the maintenance of church fabric and whether patrons of ecclesiastical livings were abusing their power.[45] Justice Drainer of Smarden, a centre of religious dissidence, went so far as to drill holes in the roodloft in order to see if anyone averted his or her gaze when the Host was elevated or otherwise failed to display the proper reverence.[46] Others, further down the social ladder, were equally vigilant. Foxe recounts that, in Rochester, an innkeeper and his wife took it upon themselves to denounce those who did not display reverence during mass, and also went door to door in their parish, checking that everyone in each household attended church.[47] If the ranks of the Marian martyrs swelled because of the range of behaviours that could cause someone to be suspected of heresy, they also swelled because these were more likely to be reported to the authorities than at any previous period in English history.

Parish Clergy and the Persecution

The level of supervision (not to say spying) at the parish level was further increased by a Marian policy which profoundly, if unintentionally affected the persecution of heresy: the deprivation of clergy for marriage. On 4 March 1554, Mary ordered that all married clergy be deprived of their benefices. Those clerics who left their wives and publicly promised to remain abstinent were allowed to resume their vocation but in different parishes.[48] Since many married priests were understandably sympathetic, if not necessarily committed, to Protestantism, the effect of the new law was to remove parish clergy who would almost certainly have turned a blind eye to religious deviance from their livings. In the new political and religious environment, the replacements for the deprived ministers were almost invariably religious conservatives. Significantly, if predictably, the level of deprivations for marriage was greater in the south-east, where Protestantism had strongest influence.[49] And, of course, the south-east was the epicentre of the persecution.

The effects of these deprivations on the persecution were significant. Most obviously, five of the martyrs – Rowland Taylor, Robert Samuel, Robert Drakes, Thomas Whittle and Richard Yeoman – were parish priests who had been deprived of their livings because they were married.[50] But the most important consequence of this shuffling of clerical personnel was that it placed religious conservatives in a position where they could closely observe unorthodox activity. Often this was the first effective oversight the authorities had in areas whose inhabitants had displayed a tendency towards evangelical or Protestant beliefs. The imposition of staunchly orthodox clergy on less orthodox parishes helped to fuel the persecution.

This can be seen in what Eamon Duffy has referred to as the heretical badlands of Essex. In Thundersley, Robert Drakes, who would be burned at the stake on 24 April 1556, had been instituted as rector in January 1550, by Lord Rich (in his capacity as lord chancellor), at the behest of Thomas Causton, a local gentleman, and Nathaniel Traheron, a noted evangelical minister. In June 1554, Stephen Gardiner, now lord chancellor, presented the living to one John Hollyman (not to be confused with the Marian bishop of the same name).[51] This lethal succession of first a Protestant, then a Catholic, rector is probably a major reason why Causton and Thomas Higbed, another gentleman of the parish, were among the first victims of the Marian persecution.

Thorpe-le-Soken was home to no less than four people who were burned at the stake.[52] Here John Blank had been presented at the behest of Thomas Lord Darcy in 1553, only to be deprived a year later for being married. Darcy, suddenly a pillar of Catholic orthodoxy after Mary's accession, appointed a staunchly orthodox successor, and this change almost certainly contributed to Thorpe-le-Soken becoming a cradle of martyrs.[53] Similarly in the parish of Great Burstead (which contained the independent chapel and township of Billericay), Lord Rich appointed the orthodox Thomas Holland to replace Hugo Gibson, who had been deprived in 1554 for being married. During Holland's ministry, four people from his parish were sent to Bonner, at least one for non-attendance at church. Three were burned, and the fourth died in prison awaiting execution.[54]

In Leigh, William Aston had been made rector at the personal presentation of Lord Rich. Deprived in 1554 for being married, Aston was subsequently imprisoned in the Tower for circulating 'a slanderouse bill' denouncing Philip and Mary.[55] Under Aston's successor Hugo Hall, Agnes Stanley was denounced to Lord Rich for failure to attend church, a denunciation that sent her to the stake.[56] In Great Bentley, Thomas Tye was formally appointed vicar on 11 December 1557, some time after John Shearman's deprivation for marriage.[57] Tye had previously acted as de facto vicar of the parish, and established a reputation there as an ardent opponent of heresy. At the end of 1556, he wrote to Bonner's commissary protesting that the Munt family, after having recanted, were harassing his parishioners and leading a conventicle. Tye also spearheaded a petition, signed by leading parishioners of Great Bentley and sent to Lord Darcy, demanding that action be taken against the Munts. The Munt house was raided at two o'clock in the morning, when William and Alice Munt and their daughter Rose Allin were arrested, and also John and Margaret Thurston.[58] The Munts and Margaret were burned at Colchester, while John died awaiting trial.[59] Learning that one of his parishioners was being instructed in heretical doctrines, Tye tracked down the teacher, Ralph Allerton, and denounced him to Lord Darcy. Allerton would be burned at Islington.[60] Tye provides a striking example of the important role that a parish priest could play in the suppression of heresy.

That the Marian authorities understood this point is demonstrated by their strenuous efforts to hound Gregory Doddes from his parish of Smarden. The living's patron was Sir John Baker, one of the most militant heresy hunters in Kent.[61] Doddes had been instituted when Cranmer's influence was strong enough to override Baker's entrenched opposition. As Doddes was not married, removing him from office took some effort. A JP of Smarden named Drainer (the same magistrate who would later drill holes in the roodloft at the parish church of Smarden in order to spy on the congregation) tried to entrap Doddes into making seditious remarks during a 'private' conversation held in a room in Drainer's house in which a scribe was placed, out of sight but within earshot, to record any incriminating remarks. Although this ploy failed, Drainer accumulated enough evidence to have Doddes brought before another JP, who bound the rector over to appear at the next sessions in Canterbury. Prudently, Doddes fled the area. He is recorded as having 'resigned' his living by 16 May 1556. His successor was George Heydon, one of Sir John Baker's chaplains.[62]

Generally, however, such machinations were unnecessary in Kent, where the number of married clergy was high. Here too the sudden transformation of the parish clergy ensured a fresh infusion of zeal and oversight into the pursuit of heresy. As just one example, Richard Beesley, the rector of Staplehurst, was deprived for being married, and in May 1557 he was replaced by Thomas Hendon, the candidate of Sir John Baker, the patron of this living as well. Although two residents of Staplehurst, Alice Potkins and Alice Benden, had already been arrested for heresy, Hendon denounced a Protestant couple from the nearby parish of Frittenden to Baker.[63]

The Gentry and the Persecution

The revolution in the ranks of the parish clergy was accompanied by changes in the relative power of religious conservatives among the gentry in Suffolk, Essex and Kent, which were to prove no less deadly for zealous Protestants. During her brother's reign, Mary had assumed the role of leader of the Catholic gentry in East Anglia, where her estates and influence were concentrated. When Mary challenged Jane Grey for the throne, these gentleman rallied to her cause.[64] Once she ascended the throne, her supporters assumed a degree of local power that they had never previously enjoyed. The new political realities were most clearly demonstrated in the 'systematic remodelling' (to quote Diarmaid MacCulloch) of the judicial bench in Suffolk, as Edwardine appointees were replaced with Marian loyalists and reliable Catholics.[65] Many of those swept into local power by the Marian tide waged war on heresy with remarkable zeal.

Foxe gives a vivid description of Francis Nunn, a Suffolk JP, who had joined Mary's supporters in July 1553, riding out with a javelin in his hand to pursue two heretics. Nunn, on his own initiative, hunted down three of the Marian martyrs.[66] Sir Henry Doyle, along with his two sons, also joined Mary in mid-July. Appointed the sheriff of Norfolk and Suffolk, his severity towards heretics was remarked on several times by Foxe.[67] But probably the most zealous heresy hunters in East Anglia were Sir John Tyrell and his cousin Edmund. Both men had been in Mary's service and supported her conspicuously in the 1553 accession crisis. (Sir John, in particular, played a key role in persuading Thomas Lord Wentworth to back Mary).[68] Mary's triumph left the Tyrells free to burn their way into the pages of Foxe.

Edmund's frenzied heresy hunting has been related in colourful detail by both John Foxe and Eamon Duffy, so there is no need to narrate these episodes here.[69] Foxe was unsure whether Edmund Tyrell's actions were motivated 'of a blind zeale, or of a parasiticall flattery'.[70] Both elements may well have been at play. Tyrell, a member of an old and respected family, was blessed with splendid connections: Sir William Petre, the consummate Tudor courtier and bureaucrat, was a kinsman by marriage and also a close friend, while William Parr, marquis of Northampton and the dominant figure in Essex, was his patron. Yet Tyrell's religious conservatism had blocked his rise under Edward VI, and he neither sat in parliament nor held county office.[71] Now under Mary, he was rewarded for his zeal with a seat on the bench, a seat in parliament and local offices and lands.

The desire to settle scores, or to put it more charitably restore order, after years of powerlessness, seems to have lain behind Sir John Tyrell's rigorous campaign against heresy in Winston and Mendlesham, in central Suffolk. Both villages, but especially Mendlesham, had a history of religious dissent going back to the 1530s. The landlords of Mendlesham, the Knyvets, were absentees, and Sir Edmund Knyvet tried to enforce orthodoxy from a distance, without conspicuous success. In June 1537, Sir Thomas Tyrell, the father of Sir John, denounced the vicar of Mendlesham for having moved his companion and his children into the vicarage and openly declaring that he was married.[72] Nothing was done and the Tyrells were forced to endure the burgeoning heresy on their doorstep, until Mary's accession let slip the dogs of war. In 1555, the vicar of Mendlesham was deprived and replaced by John Brodish, who, according to Foxe, was of significant assistance to Sir John in his campaign against heresy.[73] Then during 1557 Tyrell relentlessly purged both villages of heresy. Thirteen Protestants were driven from their homes in Winston and 23 in Mendlesham. In addition, Tyrell ordered the arrests of Adam Foster and William Seaman of Mendlesham, Thomas Spicer of Winston and Robert Lawson of Bedfield (a village five miles west of Mendlesham) for heresy. They were burned in May and June of 1557. (William Seaman's wife and his 66-year-old mother were among those driven from their homes, while Robert Lawson's mother Elizabeth was also arrested and spent nearly three years in prison).[74]

The new regime's favour towards Catholic loyalists was so marked that people of relatively humble backgrounds sometimes attained positions of local influence. Their new-found power could be used to chastize heretics. A striking example is Philip Williams, an Ipswich resident of Welsh descent, who prospered as a merchant and innkeeper and who became the town's chamberlain in 1550. In July 1553, he did valuable service to Mary.[75] This adherence to Mary sealed Williams's influence in Ipswich. He became its treasurer in 1557 and, startlingly for someone of relatively humble background, whose family was not entrenched in Ipswich, he became MP for the town in the 1558 Parliament. He also became a leading persecutor of the town's Protestant population. In 1556, along with two others he drew up a complaint listing the town's Protestants and their sympathizers, and sent it to a royal heresy commission sitting at Beccles.[76]

As a heresy hunter, however, Williams was outshone by a fellow townsman, a lawyer named William Foster. Foster was made a JP as a reward for rallying early to Mary's cause.[77] In cooperation with Walter Clerke, the bailiff of Hadleigh, he provoked a confrontation with Rowland Taylor, the town's rector, who was also the archdeacon of Bury St Edmunds and the leading Protestant cleric in Suffolk. This set in train Taylor's arrest in March 1554, and ultimately his execution on 9 February 1555.[78] Clerke, Foster's ally in this affair, was a clothier whose loyalty to Mary and his connections with other Marian loyalists led to his appointment as JP, one of only two people of non-gentry background to be promoted to the bench in Suffolk in the entire sixteenth century.[79] Clerke died in 1554, but Foster went to claim another head when he had Robert Samuel, the deprived former curate of East Bergholt, secretly followed on the (accurate) suspicion that he was the leader of an underground Protestant congregation in Ipswich. Samuel was arrested when he secretly visited his former wife, and was burned on 31 August 1555.[80] Williams, Foster and Clerke were all examples of individuals who, despite relatively low social status, rose to positions of local power and influence through their loyalty to Mary and to Catholicism. They wielded this new-found power energetically to suppress those who defied both the queen and true religion.

There were other magistrates, who were perhaps even more dangerous to heretics. Some grandees who had not originally supported Mary or her Church became zealous persecutors to show their loyalty to the new order. Lords Darcy and Rich and the sixteenth earl of Oxford are good examples. Because of his support for Jane Grey, Thomas Lord Darcy lost his court offices and his seat on the privy council. He retained his position in Essex, however, and sat on several heresy commissions.[81] Darcy seems to have been particularly active in cracking down on heresy in Great Bentley: he initially arrested Ralph Allerton and seems to have been behind Edmund Tyrell's arrest of the Munt and Thurston families.[82] Along with the earl of Oxford (who had also formerly embraced Edwardine Protestantism), Darcy captured 23 Protestants (presumably attending a conventicle) and sent 22 of them (one was pregnant) to London, as has already been related.[83] This mass arrest in the summer of 1556 was the climax of Oxford's war against heresy, which began when he sent Thomas Haukes, a gentleman of his own household, to Bonner because Haukes refused to let his son be baptized according to Catholic rites. Haukes was burned at Coggeshall on 11 June 1555. That same year, Oxford sent six prisoners from Coggeshall to Bonner, because they refused to receive the sacrament at Easter; half of them recanted, but three were burned in different Essex locations on 15 June 1555.[84]

But Rich's change of loyalties was the most violent (in all senses). Initially a supporter of Jane Grey, he moved with lightening speed in July 1553 to declare for Mary. With equal readiness, he went from being a patron of Essex Protestants to being their greatest lay persecutor. In eight, or perhaps nine, of nearly 30 instances (about a third of the total), where lay people in Essex either arrested suspected heretics who would be burned or denounced them to the ecclesiastical authorities, Rich was the responsible party.[85] On one occasion, he was thanked by the privy council for his zeal in apprehending those attending heretical assemblies in Harwich.[86] Rich also presided over numerous heresy executions in Essex. One of these was the burning of Thomas Wats, a linen draper of Billericay, the first of the people to be burned whom Rich denounced. From the stake, Wats called out to Rich, chillingly invoking the peer's evangelical past, by warning him to 'beware, beware, for you doe against your owne conscience herein, and without you repent, the Lord will revenge it: For you are the cause of this my death.'[87]

Mary's triumph in 1553, therefore, helped to kindle what Duffy has called the fires of faith in Suffolk and Essex, by putting

Catholic loyalists in these counties into local office, in place of many Edwardine officeholders. Grandees such as the earl of Oxford and lords Darcy and Rich, who could not easily be shunted aside, also felt obliged to prove their loyalty through the vigorous suppression of heresy. A similar situation existed in Kent, although the turning point there was not Mary's coup in the summer of 1553 but the collapse of Wyatt's rebellion in 1554. During Henry VIII's reign there emerged a coterie of conservative Kentish gentry united in opposition, first to Thomas Cromwell, and then to Archbishop Thomas Cranmer.[88] In alliance with Bishop Stephen Gardiner and with the conservative clergy in the diocese of Canterbury, they initiated an attempt to discredit Cranmer as a sponsor of heresy, in what has come to be known as the 'prebendaries plot'.[89] It did not succeed and Cranmer remained the predominant political figure in Kent until Mary's accession, even though the conservatives retained control over the county administration. However, after Wyatt's rebellion was crushed, the government revolutionized the Kentish bench by excluding those involved, along with known Protestants. By the end of 1554, 'Power had shifted decisively to the old group of conservative leaders . . . . The stage was set for a full-blooded Catholic reaction.'[90]

The role of the conservatives in the Marian persecution was epitomized in the ordeals of John Bland. Bland had been one of the radical preachers that the prebendary plotters had denounced in their attempt to incriminate Cranmer. After attempting to stop the mass as it was being celebrated (by a priest brought in for the occasion) in his church at Adisham, Bland was arrested, but subsequently released on bond. The matter might have ended here, but in late February 1554, Sir Thomas Moyle ordered that Bland's bail be revoked. Moyle had been one of the leaders of the prebendaries plot.[91] Now Moyle seized the opportunity to finish what he had started. Bland could not, however, be tried for heresy, as the statute making it illegal had been repealed under Edward VI and would not be restored until late in 1554. During the following year, an elaborate cat and mouse game unfolded, as Bland was released on bail, then arraigned in an ecclesiastical court, then transferred to the county sessions, and finally sent back to the spiritual courts. The purpose of this manoeuvring was to keep Bland detained so that he could be charged with heresy the moment that the law permitted. In the meantime (and this demonstrates the extent to which Bland was a marked man), he was examined in the chapter house of Canterbury Cathedral a year before he was formally tried for heresy. Remarkably, a number of Kentish gentry participated in this examination, including Moyle himself. Another participant was Cyriac Petit, a key player in the prebendaries plot.[92] Also instrumental in arranging Bland's prolonged imprisonment was Sir John Baker, who, in February 1555 personally examined Bland again.[93] Baker was also a Marian loyalist whose ties to the queen went back to the 1520s, and like Moyle, he had been a leader of the prebendaries plot.[94] Bland's burning on 12 July 1555 was therefore both the final act of the prebendaries plot and the end of a long vendetta.

These gentlemen did not confine their attention to Bland. Moyle arrested two suspected heretics, William Foster and Richard Yeoman, on separate occasions; both died in prison.[95] Baker personally arrested Edmund and Katherine Allin on charges of heresy. When Katherine persuaded her husband to withstand pressure on him to attend mass, Baker beat her on the head with his staff. The Allins would escape from Baker's custody, be rearrested, examined by Baker, and die together in the flames on 18 June 1557.[96] In his zeal, Baker also ordered his bailiffs to search for those who smuggled heretical literature into Kent.[97]

But Moyle and Baker were hardly alone among Kentish magistrates in hunting out heresy.[98] The magistrates in Kent had particular power to suppress heresy for a profoundly ironic reason: these devout Catholics – especially Baker and Moyle – had been exceptionally aggressive purchasers of ex-monastic lands.[99] With these lands often came patronage over clerical livings. In this manner Baker became patron of the livings of Frittenden, Smarden and Staplehurst.[100] As Kentish clergy were deprived, transferred or died, their replacements were chosen by some of the most hard-line Catholics in the kingdom. When the clerical patronage of the archbishop is added to this, there was considerable potential – only cut off by Mary's death – for total reordering of the clergy in Kent.

The conservative clergy and the conservative gentry were like the blades of a pair of scissors, seeming to move separately but actually linked together, as they attacked heresy from different directions. A number of events – notably Mary's coup in 1553, the failure of Wyatt's rebellion and the deprivations of married clergy – had the unintended consequences of bringing some particularly fierce persecutors into positions of local power and influence. Their zeal helped to ensure that the Marian persecution was the most intense persecution of Christians in English history. But it was the victims, as

well as the persecutors, who helped to transform the Marian suppression of heresy into a relentless persecution. The overt defiance
by a surprisingly (given that such defiance put them in deadly peril)
large number of rank and file Protestants was without precedent in
England. Previously Lollards and evangelicals had, with some notable
exceptions, recanted when necessary and lived to proselytise another
day.[101] Under Mary, however, demonstrations of heretical attitudes
and opinions were being made in the most public circumstances, and
recantations, when made, were ostentatiously retracted. At the most
extreme, figures such as Simon Miller, who marched into Norwich
and demanded to know where Protestant communion was being celebrated, and Thomas Hudson, who walked through the town of
Aylsham, crying out against the mass, suggest not so much lambs,
as lemmings, going to the slaughter.[102]

This is not to deprecate the courage or sincerity of those who
died for heresy during Mary's reign or to imply that in any way they
deserved their agonizing deaths. Rather it is to point to a sea-change
in attitudes towards resistance and conformity that had taken place
among English Protestants late in the reign of Henry VIII. There is
not space in this chapter to discuss the reasons for this sea-change,
which have never been fully analysed. The attacks on outward conformity with Catholicism made by leading reformers such as Calvin
and Bullinger may have played a part, although it is doubtful that vil-
lagers in Suffolk and the Weald were scanning continental writings
for guidance on the life and death decisions they would have to make.
The sudden and drastic changes in official religious policy during the
reigns of Edward VI and Mary also probably played a part; the perception that religious policy, like a pendulum, was not only moving
in opposite directions, but was also swinging between further and
further extremes, convinced many of the magnitude of what was at
stake and eroded any disposition towards compromise. Whatever the
reasons behind this new-found refusal to conform, it spread widely
enough among Marian Protestants to keep the fires of persecution
burning.

The Costs of the Persecution

The Marian persecution was a perfect storm in which a number
of disparate factors came together to increase its ferocity. The scale
of the persecution, which was unforeseen and, in fairness, largely
unpredictable, created significant problems for the Marian regime.

Examples of disruption and hostility towards the authorities arising from Marian burnings are numerous. When John Noyes was burned in his native village of Laxfield in Suffolk in September 1556, all but one of the households in the town extinguished their fires in a vain attempt to prevent the authorities from using the already lit coals to ignite Noyes's pyre.[103] The execution of Edward Horne in Newent, Gloucestershire, was so violently unpopular that after Mary's death, the village's inhabitants reportedly drove the vicar out of the parish in retaliation.[104] Burnings also provided a very public site for expressions of sympathy for the martyrs. Richard Carman and Cecily Ormes both began their own journeys to the stake with public demonstrations of support for other martyrs at their executions.[105] When Alice Driver and Alexander Gouch were executed in Ipswich in 1558, sympathizers rushed forward to comfort and encourage them. The sheriff ordered the arrest of these supporters, but when others ran out to join them, he decided to abandon the effort.[106] Such incidents should not be too lightly dismissed; the Marian authorities themselves were quite concerned about sympathy building up for the martyrs. They commissioned an extensive literature to make the arguments that those who were burned at the stake were criminals and heretics, not martyrs for the gospel.[107]

Nevertheless these examples of ill-feeling should not be given more importance than they deserve. They were expressions of sympathy for particular victims rather than indications of a general disapproval of the Marian persecution itself. Noyes and Hornes, for example, were burned in the villages where they lived, and communal solidarity was probably responsible for the outrage their executions provoked. In any case these episodes were isolated, and any acrimony they stirred up was generally ephemeral and invariably parochial. More serious was the anger created by the burnings in Colchester and London, where the numbers of heretics condemned were far greater and where burnings took place throughout the reign.

Three urban areas – London with 44 burnings, Canterbury with 41 and Colchester with 23 – were the sites of just over a third of the burnings.[108] Despite the large number of burnings that took place within Canterbury, there is no indication, either in the pages of Foxe or elsewhere, of any popular unease there over the burnings. This may have been partly due to the city's religious conservatism and the strong influence (under Pole's leadership) of the staunchly Catholic cathedral chapter and personnel. Another probable factor was that – in marked contrast to Colchester and London – only one of the people burned at Canterbury was actually a resident of the city.[109]

The situation in Colchester was far more problematic. The town contained a substantial Protestant minority, and at least 12 of the 23 people burned there were residents. The first burning in Colchester took place on 29 March 1555. As the victim, a priest named John Laurence, was consumed in the flames, 'young children came about the fire, and cryed, (as wel as young children could speake) saying: Lorde strengthen thy servaunt and keepe thy promise, Lord strengthen they servaunt, and keepe thy promise'.[110] In May 1555, possibly as a consequence of this spectacle, the privy council summoned Thomas Dibney, one of Colchester's aldermen before them, 'having byn complained upon for his evill behaviour in matters of religion'. He was forced to promise to confess his offences publicly in two parish churches in Colchester and to have this penance certified by 'some of the chiefest and most honest of that towne'.[111] A few months later Sir Anthony Browne launched an investigation into heresy at Colchester, assisted by the ubiquitous Edmund Tyrell, Richard Cosen, an innkeeper and fervent Catholic, and Jerome Gilbert, the recorder for the town. Those identified by Tyrell, Cosen or Gilbert as religiously suspect were interrogated and released on recognisance.[112]

The participation of Gilbert in Browne's heresy hunt is indicative of how the persecution was conducted in Colchester. Heresy in Colchester was repressed through royal commissions, but the commissioners' work was made possible by the active cooperation of at a sizeable number of the town's civic officials. William Chedsey, the archdeacon of Middlesex, who was in effect the overseer of the persecution in Colchester, boasted that 'officers of the town be very diligent with us'.[113] Even a cursory examination of Foxe bears out Chedsey's claim. Elizabeth Pepper, who was sent from Colchester to London to be burned, stated that she was arrested in Colchester by two constables, led by an alderman.[114] One alderman, Robert Maynard, was cited by no less than three martyrs as the person responsible for their arrest.[115] Bonner's commissary commended another alderman, Robert Browne, to the bishop as 'the doer of all things'. Foxe, on the other hand, characterized Browne as a 'hoate and hasty Iustice in persecuting gods people'.[116] Foxe also castigated Benjamin Clere, another alderman, as 'a cruell en[e]my' to the godly, in particular damning his determined pursuit of the itinerant preacher George Eagles and his callous treatment of six Colchester martyrs.[117]

Thanks to the close cooperation of civic officials, the persecution in Colchester escalated. On 28 April 1556, six people were burned together. Five of them were residents of the town, and one, John Mace, was the brother-in-law of Alderman Dibney. Despite his public disgrace, Dibney had enough influence to retain his office, but the execution of his kinsman must have enraged him and his allies. After this group burning, tensions which were just below the surface became manifest. In late August 1556, Bonner's commissary asked the bailiffs to supply him with armed guards as he went through Colchester 'in greate preasse and daunger'. He also asked that the town clerk accompany him and record the names of those who harassed him.[118] In the following December, Thomas Tye reported to Bonner that:

> The rebels are stout in the Towne of Colchester. The ministers of the church are hemd at in the open street and called knaves. The blessed Sacrament of the aultar is blasphemed and rayled upon in every Alehouse and Taverne. Prayer and fasting is not regarded. Seditious talkes and newes are rife, both in towne and in countrey.[119]

Colchester was becoming a town sharply divided, with the divisions extending into daily life. The White Hart inn, owned by Richard Cosen (Sir Anthony Browne's informant), was a gathering place for Catholics where the heresy commissioners and Bonner's agents met when they were in town; the heresy trial of Elizabeth Folkes was actually held there. Protestants, on the other hand, congregated in the King's Head, which was a meeting place for clandestine preachers and their flocks; the woman who ran it was carted off to London and imprisoned by Bonner.[120] Meanwhile the tensions continued to rise. When ten martyrs were burned in Colchester on 2 August 1557, the spectators chanted: 'The Lord strengthen them, the Lord comfort them, the Lord pour his mercies upon them.'[121]

In a letter of 20 April 1558, Chedsey protested against a summons the privy council had sent, ordering him to report to them. Chedsey warned that if he went to London it would be assumed that he and the other heresy commissioners did not really possess royal commissions (and authority). He also warned that this would bring the investigation of heresy in Colchester to a halt.[122] There could be no more telling indication of how greatly the burnings had upset the town. Ultimately the persecution only succeeded there because of the naked exercise of royal authority.

Another indication of the bitterness and polarization in Marian Colchester was the fate of the town's leading Catholics under Elizabeth. Robert Maynard was ousted from his post as alderman in 1560 and Robert Browne left office in 1561. In 1560, Richard Cosen was fined £10 for 'blasphemy'. In 1562, he was arrested for praising the duc de Guise and spreading rumours that the queen had died in childbirth. During the ensuing investigation, Cosen's servants testified that he and his wife spoke hopefully of the restoration of the monasteries, deplored the current dominance of the 'Genevans' in Colchester, and in a nice domestic touch, that the couple sat by the fire singing the mass together.[123] While Cosen's intransigence certainly contributed to his problems, it is still difficult to avoid the conclusion that he was being harassed.

The Elizabethan career of Benjamin Clere is even more revealing. He survived the purge of the city officials that ended Maynard's political career, thanks in part to his family connections – the Cleres were a political dynasty in sixteenth-century Colchester – and, in part, to his alliance with Thomas Upcher, a godly minister imposing a new moral order on Elizabethan Colchester. Upcher had gone into exile in Geneva in Mary's reign; he was a friend of John Foxe and the source of material that ended up in the *Acts and Monuments*.[124] The improbable alliance between Marian persecutor and Marian exile endured until 1575. However, that summer libels attacking the pair appeared. One of the libels denounced Clere for his role in the apprehension and execution of George Eagles. The libellers were arrested and tried in the Star Chamber, but the verdict is unknown. This reminder of Clere's Marian past was devastating. He lost his place on the common council in 1575 and was decisively defeated in an attempt to secure re-election in 1576.[125]

Undoubtedly the burnings in Colchester produced bitterness that lasted for years, and this bitterness would have persisted even had Mary lived past 1558. What the burnings did not produce, however, was riot or serious disorder. Even in Colchester, where the persecution was severe and there was a large and active Protestant minority, and even during a period of severe hardship caused by poor harvests and pestilence, the burnings posed no threat to the stability of the Marian regime.

As in Colchester, the burnings in London had a high percentage of victims – at least 20 of the 44 – who were residents of the city. But where the persecution in Colchester was administered with an iron hand, that in London proceeded more cautiously, if ultimately no less lethally. From the beginning, aware of the volatility and size of the crowds in the capital, the authorities seem to have been wary. The burning of John Rogers, the first victim of the persecution, cannot have reassured them. A vociferous crowd came out in support of Rogers, a well-known preacher in the city. (The Catholic polemicist Miles Hogarde penned a caustic description of over-enthusiastic spectators who seeing a flight of pigeons over the head of Rogers, hailed it as the Holy Spirit – in the form of a dove – descending on the martyr's head.[126])

The authorities' fear of disorder became very evident less than three months later when John Warne and John Cardmaker were condemned to die. Warne was an artisan and citizen of London, but it was Cardmaker who was the eye of the hurricane. Cardmaker had been vicar of St Bride's parish and a popular preacher. (No less than three Marian martyrs came from St Bride's, itself a mordant tribute to Cardmaker's effectiveness as an evangelist.) On 25 May 1555 he was condemned (along with other heretics) in the London consistory court with Bonner presiding. Almost certainly because of Cardmaker's presence (apart from Warne, the others being sentenced were from Essex), large crowds gathered, and they rushed forward as the prisoners were being led off to Newgate. Believing that this was the start of a riot, the members of the court fled for the safety of Bonner's residence. Bonner, less fleet than the others, found himself locked out and left to face a (fortunately for him nonexistent) hostile mob.[127] Further evidence of Bonner's anxiety in the run-up to Cardmaker's burning was the sermon delivered by Chedsey at Paul's Cross the day after the debacle at the consistory court. Defending Bonner against those in London (apparently a group vocal enough to be noticed) who criticized the bishop for the burnings, Chedsey took the remarkable of step of reading a letter aloud in which the queen reproved Bonner for being reluctant to try heretics. Chedsey assured his auditors (which included the lord mayor and the aldermen) that Bonner would obey the royal orders, but he also reassured them that Bonner 'will travayle and take payne with all that be of his iurisdiction for there amendment and sorye he is that anye is in prison for such matter'.[128] On 30 May, Cardmaker and Warne were burned before a large crowd. Rumours had been circulating that Cardmaker would recant, and when it became clear that he would not, the crowd went wild with excitement and yelled out their support.[129] The Venetian ambassador noted that Cardmaker had been held in great esteem in London and claimed that the burnings were becoming odious to many Londoners.[130]

When the time came for the next burning in Smithfield, on 1 July, the authorities were nervous. The victims were to be John Bradford, another celebrated London preacher, and John Leaf, a London apprentice. In an apparent attempt to reduce the number of spectators, the authorities manipulated the time of the execution. An enormous crowd had gathered in Smithfield by 4 am when it was rumoured that the execution would take place, but Bradford and Leaf were not taken from Newgate prison until 9 am, by which time the authorities apparently hoped the people would disperse. Yet in Foxe's words, 'in every corner of Smithfield there were some [people]'.[131] Mary Honeywood, a supporter of Bradford's, journeyed from Kent to watch his death. The press of the crowd was so great that her shoes were pulled from her feet and she had to walk back into the city barefoot.[132]

The reaction of this enormous crowd to the burnings of Bradford and Leaf has not been recorded, but it was not reassuring to Bonner. The next Londoners to be burned – Elizabeth Warne (John Warne's widow), George Tankerfield and Thomas Fust – were all burned outside the city: Tankerfield and Fust at different locations in Hertfordshire, and Warne at Stratford, a few miles east of London (see Map 10.1). The next burning in London was that of John Philpot, and it took place at the end of the year, on 18 December. Foxe does not describe the spectators' reaction, but an anonymous letter written to Bonner shortly afterwards referred to 'the harty love that the people shewed unto good M. Philpot at his goying to his death'.[133]

The scheduled burning at Smithfield of seven heretics in January 1556 gave the authorities further reason for concern. For the first time more than two people were to be burned together in London. In addition, these victims were likely to arouse sympathy on a variety of grounds. Five were Londoners. One of them, Bartlet Green, was of relatively high social status, having been a member of the Inner Temple. Two were women, and they were the first women to be burned in London in Mary's reign.[134] Two were young: John Tudson, an apprentice, was only 18, and Joan Lashford (the daughter of Elizabeth Warne and the step-daughter of John Warne) was about 20. Although the execution was to take place at the end of January, when the crowds could be expected to be smaller, elaborate measures were planned to eliminate the possibility of demonstrations in support of

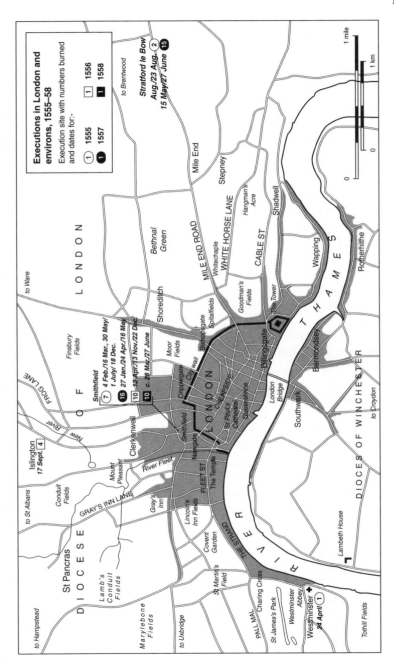

Map 10.1 Executions in London and environs 1555–8

the condemned or any other disturbance from the spectators. Less than a fortnight before the execution, the privy council sent a letter to the mayor and the sheriffs of London, ordering that when anyone was to be burned 'a good nombre of officers and other men appointed to be at the execucion, who may be charged to see suche as shall misuse themselves to the ill example of others, to be apprehended and comitted to warde'. The privy council also ordered that London householders were to be instructed not to allow their servants or apprentices outside while any burnings were taking place.[135] On 23 January 1556, four days before the seven were burned, the mayor ordered the aldermen to instruct the householders in their wards to keep their servants indoors until 10 am on the morning of the event. The mayor also ordered that the beadles of each ward were to be ready for duty at 6 am that morning; each to come armed with 'a good halberde'. The aldermen were warned that they would 'answear for the Contrarye at your peryll'.[136] The London diarist Henry Machyn noted that the night before the execution an order was issued that 'no yong folke should come ther', but that, despite the order, great numbers of young people were present at the burning of the seven.[137]

Despite their inability to reduce the size of the crowds, the authorities felt secure enough to burn another six people in Smithfield on 24 April. Their confidence was probably enhanced by the fact that none of the six was from the city of London. Only two Londoners were burned in the remainder of 1556, and the pair were burned together, not at Smithfield, but outside the city at Stratford. There was only one more burning at Smithfield in 1556, that of three women from Essex. Evidently the authorities were now being careful not to burn Londoners in Smithfield. Furthermore they were apparently trying to avoid provoking the city with too many burnings, even of non-Londoners, in Smithfield. When 13 people from Essex and Hertfordshire were burned together on 27 June, the execution took place at Stratford.

Yet even with the use of Stratford as a sort of safety valve, tensions still ran high. These tensions, and Bonner's acute awareness of them, surfaced when 22 accused heretics were sent from Colchester to London on 30 August 1556. Anticipating trouble, Bonner had ordered that the prisoners be brought to him 'very early' the next morning, 'to the intent they might quietlye come and be examined by me'. Whether the prisoners deliberately delayed (how?) their journey to the bishop's house, as Duffy maintains, or for some other reason, the group did not set out from Aldgate until 10 am. Furthermore they travelled through Cheapside, which was the most direct route, but which also took them through one of the busiest areas of the city. By the time they reached Bonner's house, a crowd which the bishop claimed numbered 1,000 people had gathered. Bonner decided to try the 22 in his relatively remote palace in rural Fulham, and sought Pole's permission do this, 'perceiving by my last doing that your grace was offended'.[138] (What had Bonner done to offend Pole? The phrase my 'last doing' suggests, in this context, that Pole was offended in some way about the burning of 13 people at Stratford the previous June. Duffy suggests that Pole was upset over Bonner's severity.[139] Another possibility – one which would better explain Bonner's raising the issue as part of request to try suspected heretics in Fulham – is that the bishop had moved the execution of the 13 out of London to Stratford and that Pole was displeased by this.) In the event, the 22 prisoners were neither tried nor executed. Pole, 'fearing belike least by the death of so many together some disturbance might rise' ordered that the prisoners be released after they agreed to a leniently phrased recantation. (Foxe maintains that the prisoners worded it themselves.[140]) Clearly, fears of the Londoners' reactions to the burnings were being felt at the highest levels of government.

On 12 April 1557, the authorities felt confident enough to burn three men and two women (one of them a Londoner) at Smithfield.[141] But caution soon prevailed again. The next burnings in Smithfield were not until November. In the meantime a couple from St Dunstan in the West was burned at Islington, along with two men from Essex. The November burning presented particular difficulties. Three men were burned together; all three were Londoners. One of the three, Richard Gibson, was from the upper reaches of London's civic elite. Gibson's maternal grandfather was Sir William Bayly, who had been mayor of London in 1524. Gibson's father, also named Richard, was a royal serjeant-at-arms, master of the Merchant Taylors, swordbearer and bailiff of Southwark, and MP for New Romney.[142] From the beginning, Gibson's status ensured that he was treated with kid gloves and that Bonner devoted a great of his personal time and energy in trying to secure his recantation. Gibson had originally been arrested in 1555 because of a massive debt. He attracted the authorities' attention during his imprisonment when he had refused to make confession or attend mass. In October 1556, he submitted a very cautiously worded recantation to Bonner and cagily answered articles that the bishop sent to him. Under increased pressure from the bishop, Gibson supplied answers more conformable with Catholic orthodoxy. But at some point he must have withdrawn his recantation. In April 1557 he wrote to Bonner denouncing Catholic teachings and practices, and admonishing him on how a bishop should behave. Gibson's responses to another set of articles presented on 8 May are unknown, but they cannot have been satisfactory. He was examined by Bonner and his officials on 5 and 6 November and was finally condemned.[143] Gibson and two others were supposed to be burned on 12 November, but at the last moment the execution was delayed while John Feckenham tried to win them over. He failed, and on 13 November the three prisoners were burned at Smithfield.[144]

A month later, a number of Protestants meeting at a conventicle in Islington were arrested by Sir Henry Jerningham, the vice-chamberlain of Mary's household. One was John Rough, the leader of the largest (clandestine) Protestant congregation in London. These arrests triggered a rigorous investigation. Another of those arrested, Cuthbert Simpson, a deacon of Rough's congregation, was tortured, on the orders of the privy council, in an effort to compel him to produce written records of the congregation. Margaret Mearing, another member of the congregation, was arrested on 17 December. She and Rough were burned at Smithfield on 22 December.[145] The startling haste, and ruthlessness, of these trials and executions affords a sharp contrast to the caution with which heresy had hitherto been repressed in London. This may have been due to a determination not to let this opportunity slip. It may also reflect the involvement of privy councillors and those close to Mary in the proceedings; they may have pushed Bonner into acting with unusual alacrity. Simpson was burned at Smithfield along with two other Londoners around the end of March 1558.

The summer of 1558 brought further challenges to Bonner. Twenty-seven people were arrested attending another conventicle in Islington and seven of them were burned at Smithfield on 27 June. Once again, there was anxiety before the burning, with orders being issued that the spectators were neither to encourage the condemned nor demonstrate their support for them. Nevertheless Thomas Bentham, Rough's successor as leader of the London congregation, led the crowd in cheering the martyrs.[146] Bonner again grew apprehensive. There were another six members of the Islington conventicle who were due to be executed, and Bonner wrote to Pole urging that they be burned in Hammersmith instead of London, 'for than I can giff sentence against them here in the parishe church very quietly, and without tumult'.[147] In the event, the six were burned at Brentford, Middlesex, on 14 July, with no known protests or demonstrations. This was the last burning of Londoners and the last burning in London or its environs during Mary's reign.

From the outset, the burnings had presented problems in the governance of the capital that historians should not minimize. The Marian authorities certainly did not; in fact, Bonner approached the task of managing the burnings with the wariness of someone dismantling a bomb. Given the size and volatility of the London crowds, every burning was a possible source of disruption or worse. The number of victims and the fact that the burnings continued at periodic intervals greatly exacerbated the problem. At times, as when the 22 prisoners were sent in from Colchester or when 27 people were arrested at Islington, the number of those accused of heresy was large enough to threaten to overwhelm the process. The unanticipated and unforeseeable intensity of the persecution potentially threatened the stability of the capital. But the threat never materialized. While the Marian authorities could not prevent demonstrations at the burnings, these demonstrations never spread beyond the execution site and did not turn into serious disturbances, much less riots. As Duffy observes, no demonstration at any of the burnings was nearly as menacing as the anti-Catholic riot at Paul's Cross on 13 October 1553, which took place over a year before the heresy laws had been revived.[148] It should also be remembered that the continuing hostility to the burnings only arose in Colchester and London. There is no evidence to support claims that that the response to the burnings was 'hostile and immediate' throughout the south-east.[149]

Yet numerous scholars in the grip of a powerful conviction that because the burnings are repulsive to them, they must have been repulsive to Mary's subjects, have claimed that burnings actually undermined the stability of Mary's government.[150] Andrew Pettegree maintains that:

> By 1557 England was experiencing all the manifestations which in other countries would indicate that the social consensus underpinning support for the regime's religious policies was dangerously weak: open dissent at the place of execution,

the need for heavily armed guards to prevent tumult and protect those who were charged with executing the sentence, even daring prison raids to liberate imprisoned evangelicals.[151]

This statement deserves close attention. First of all, open dissent at the execution site and the need for heavily armed guards characterized many Tudor executions, including those of numerous Catholic priests during Elizabeth's reign. But it is the claim of 'daring prison raids' that is truly striking. Following Pettegree's notes we learn that this claim is based on a sentence in Susan Brigden's *London and the Reformation* which reads 'In September 1557 a prisoner was rescued from the Alderman's deputy in Blackfriars.'[152] Brigden's mention of the incident occurs in a discussion of the unpopularity of the burnings in London, so it is understandable to assume (and Brigden may herself have assumed) that this was indeed the rescue of a Protestant. Her source, the records of the Court of Aldermn, however, does not indicate who the prisoner was, why he was in custody or who rescued him; it simply states that a group of people forcibly rescued a man who was in the custody of an alderman's deputy as they were going through the street.[153] There is absolutely no evidence that religious motivations were involved in either the prisoner's arrest or his rescue. Nor is the episode a 'prison raid'; a group of people simply overpowered a single deputy on the street. And it is a single episode, not a series of 'raids'.

Claims that there was a universal reaction against the burnings are therefore exaggerated. Claims that the burnings seriously weakened or damaged the Marian regime are unsupported by any convincing evidence. The most severe tumults of Mary's reign occurred *before* the burnings started. But simply to maintain that a policy did not do much harm is not the same thing as maintaining that it was a complete success. The burnings provided opportunities for Protestants to reap favourable propaganda. They created lasting bitterness in Colchester and greatly complicated the relations between the government and the capital. All of these were manageable problems and, for the most part, they were successfully managed. Nevertheless, they were, in policy terms, the costs of the persecution. (Of course, there were enormous human costs as well, but to the Marian regime, the martyrs were criminals receiving their just punishment, and the only reasons for not trying or burning them would have been policy considerations.) Were there, again from the perspective of policy, benefits to the persecution that outweighed these costs?

Conclusion

The persecution was succeeding in that it was attaining its objectives up until Mary's death. The Protestant leaders and their most devoted loyalists were executed, driven overseas or driven underground. One by one, the conventicles were being uprooted and destroyed. The declining number of those burned in 1558 shows that the numbers of those refusing to conform was itself diminishing. Yet although the persecution was succeeding, that does not necessarily mean that it was the wisest policy for the government to pursue. What other options were realistically available to Mary's government for dealing with a religious minority, some of whose members were willing to defy it at all costs?

Toleration of all religious opinions was, in sixteenth-century eyes, not a realistic option. No English government had ever practised it and the only European governments that accepted the existence of dissident religious minorities did so out of necessity, because they were too weak to crush them. One point on which all sixteenth-century Christians agreed was that only one of the major confessions – Catholic, Protestant or Anabaptist – was the True Church. The others were diabolical heresies leading humanity into error and damnation. To tolerate heretics in one's midst was to risk provoking God, as innumerable Biblical examples demonstrated. It was also to permit the presence of a group of subjects whose complete allegiance to a ruler of a different faith could not be relied on. Both consequences were to be avoided if at all possible. For Mary and her ministers, any tolerance of heresy would be repudiating the divine providence that had miraculously raised her to the throne. Tolerance of religious dissenters, moreover, meant tolerating those who prayed for the failure of her religious policies, if not her actual death. And tolerance would mean abandoning the souls of at least some of her subjects to damnation.

Mary's position was strong enough for her to reject this unpalatable option. English Protestants were a small minority, clustered in one corner of the kingdom and without support from all but a handful of nobles. Yet if religious tolerance was not an option, were there realistic alternatives to a campaign of widespread violent repression? The most obvious alternative would have been not to revive the heresy laws and to deal with religious opponents only if they committed other offences. There would have been several problems with this approach, however.

Pettegree, after criticizing the persecution as 'clumsy and ill-thought-out', has admitted that it was essential for the Marian government to isolate the Protestant leadership from potential followers.[154] The Marian authorities did not ignore the exiles, as Sir John Cheke discovered. But the more immediate problem was presented by the Protestant leaders who remained in England. A few of the leading Edwardine clerics, such as Cranmer and Ridley, could have been executed for treason. But most had committed no crime. Almost all of the key Edwardine clerics were deprived of their livings for being married. But they remained in their communities as influential figures and vociferous opponents of the Catholic restoration. The heresy laws made many of these leaders heroic martyrs to their adherents, but, in ensuring their executions, they also isolated them from potential followers in the most permanent possible manner.

Many of the activities that led to charges of heresy were activities that were legal, or at worst mildly criminal; for example, heckling Catholics as they went to mass, or showing irreverence to the Host. To moderns, such actions appear to relatively harmless instances of gesture politics, which the Marian authorities could have, and should have, ignored. To a sixteenth-century Catholic the Host was God and irreverence towards it was naked blasphemy, which could not go unpunished. If the Marian regime disregarded open defiance, even sacrilege, it would appear weak and incapable of performing the duties that were expected of an early modern monarch. (Those who argue that Mary should have turned a blind eye to covert non-conformity, as Elizabeth was to do, ignore that much of the Protestant resistance to Mary was anything but covert.) To tolerate, or even ignore heretics, would have hindered, perhaps crippled the restoration of Catholicism.

Neither the regime nor its opponents were interested in co-existence, and persecution was therefore the only viable option – given sixteenth-century attitudes and values – in combating this hard core of dissenters. In dealing with the challenge of heresy, Mary turned to the traditional solution. It was one that had generally worked in the past, and the available evidence indicates that it was succeeding by the end of Mary's reign. The burning of Protestants was a policy that ultimately failed, and in its failure it did enormous damage to English Catholicism. But the policy was probably the best realistic option for dealing with a considerable problem. The persecution failed for the same reasons that the restoration of Catholicism failed: the sudden death of Mary and the accession of a Protestant successor.

Acknowledgements

A significant portion of the research for this chapter was done while I was a short-term fellow at the Folger Shakespeare Library in Washington DC. I would like to thank the Library for its support and hospitality. I would also like to thank Sue Doran, Eamon Duffy, Peter Marshall and Alec Ryrie for reading and commenting on earlier drafts of this chapter.

11

Reassessing Mary Tudor: Some Concluding Points

Judith M. Richards

In the late seventeenth century, William Joyner was so anxious about publishing his study of Cardinal Reginald Pole, Mary Tudor's archbishop of Canterbury, that he compared praising Pole in England with praising Scipio in Carthage or Hannibal in Rome.[1] Until recently, it has been even more hazardous to offer a discussion of Mary herself if it meant a significant reworking of the traditional Protestant accounts of the sixteenth-century English Reformations. That tradition long made it almost impossible to question Mary's reputation for religious bigotry and cruelty. Consequently, England's first queen regnant is still defined primarily by reference to the hundreds of burnings that took place in her reign, and therefore still most easily recognized as 'Bloody Mary'. That is often the only label that enables non-historians – and some historians – to distinguish the little-known Mary Tudor from the widely known and apparently much more romantic Mary Queen of Scots.

Just how enduring the hostility was to England's Catholic queen was demonstrated in the 1840s, at a time when the first English moves to Catholic emancipation had been made, and when, moreover, there was another female monarch on the throne. Within her multi-volume *Lives of the queens of England*, Agnes Strickland included a fresh account of Mary's reign, written by her sister Elizabeth and drawing on the first new historical sources made available since the sixteenth century. As well as primary sources, she drew on F. E. Madden's *The privy purse expenses of the Princess Mary* (1831) and P. F. Tytler's

England under the reigns of Edward VI and Mary (1839). But the historian found almost all that fresh material to be directly contradictory to the inherited assessment of England's first queen regnant, and therefore dangerous, because, she feared, to present a more complex account could easily be mistaken for a desire to excuse the agreed cruelty in Mary's religious and civil government. That such anxiety was well founded was confirmed by the uproar after the publication of that volume, derided as the work of a 'papistical sympathiser'. Some clergy thought the whole project so dangerous that it should be kept from the hands of 'young persons'.[2] Such popular sensitivity hardly changed through the rest of the nineteenth century. Any more nuanced view of Mary's reign simply could not compete with, for example, the vicarious thrills of reading the nineteenth-century versions of John Foxe's 'Book of Martyrs' which, as so many Victorian memoirs recall, was one of the few works sanctioned for Sunday reading. So it is not surprising that Foxe's 'Martyrs' remained potent in the popular imagination at least until the 1930s, and was frequently invoked by fiction writers who felt no need to explain the reference.[3]

Although the Protestant burnings were the primary reason that Mary Tudor has been judged a defective ruler, her reign was almost as infamous for the loss to France of Calais, the final remnant of England's once-great European possessions. That the English continental possessions had been diminishing for a considerable time, and had continued to do so during the two previous reigns, was not considered relevant. Nor was the much-publicized report that Mary shared her people's fury and distress at the loss of England's one remaining continental toehold. John Foxe may have shown a moment of compassion for her when he repeated the story of Mary's deathbed sighing for the loss of Calais and her declaration that the loss was her 'greatest wound'.[4] But he also shared what became the common view, that the loss itself was yet more evidence of the punishments God had visited upon her for her wilful enforcement of papal authority and false religion. More academic historical verdicts on Mary and her reign have also remained predominantly hostile, though the grounds for that hostility shifted. G. R. Elton, the pre-eminent Tudor historian in the second half of the twentieth century, declared her to be 'arrogant, assertive, [an authorial aside here: surely any reader might be pardoned for thinking that assertiveness was a necessary quality in an early-modern monarch?] bigoted, stubborn, suspicious and (not to put too fine a point upon it) rather stupid'.[5] Mary has more recently been declared to be pathetic,[6] which sounds as dismal a failure as a monarch could be, perhaps like the hapless Henry VI. In 1990, she was considered to lack 'subtlety and intelligence', and in 2000 there were still doubts as to whether she had the astuteness and intelligence to benefit from her excellent humanist education, as both of her more admirable royal siblings had done.[7] That is substantively how majority opinion stands: England's first queen regnant lacked intelligence, sense and judgement. Even her piety counted against her for a long time, since she was indubitably pious but in quite the wrong Christian tradition.

In the last few years, however, a considerable amount of work has gone into reassessing aspects of her reign, particularly the renewal of Catholicism. Curiously Mary herself remains substantially absent from many of the studies. If she had been a male monarch, it seems unlikely she would have been so sidelined, but she was female, and that, combined with her general reputation for being very uninteresting and/or incompetent, may explain why she is still so frequently left in the background.[8] We might even think that, given the number of feminist historians now active, Mary should have emerged as an interesting study simply by virtue of filling a role unprecedented in English history as the first queen regnant. Such attention, however, has more usually gone to Elizabeth, itself a striking indication of just how comprehensively Mary Tudor has been written out of history. In the dominant tradition, this is once again explained in part by reference to Mary's personal inadequacies. Traditional accounts of Mary present her as seared by her experiences at the hands of her father in the mid-1530s and thereafter starved of affection, increasingly stubborn, religiously conservative and bigoted, and – always of very uncertain health – given to 'hysterical' tendencies.[9] Given that personality assessment, it is perhaps not surprising that she has indeed been judged quite unprepared and/or unfit to rule the realm.

Since Mary's was indeed a personal monarchy, any reassessment of her reign needs to begin with a reconsideration of traditional interpretations of her character. It is also desirable that her reign should be discussed in terms that treat her as if she was as much a monarch as her male forebears had been and her half-sister was to be, a proposal which requires assessing her reign by comparable criteria. There is a pervasive expectation still that any essay about Mary, whatever its focus, must include a discussion of the number of Protestant martyrs during her regime, that being the primary reason she is known at all. But there is much less attention paid to the more than 300 Catholic martyrs who died during the reign of Henry VIII and Elizabeth – and that is before we consider the many monks in Ireland who died without any trial at the hands of Elizabethan troops.[10] To privilege those deaths under Mary alone is surely to reinforce the old Protestant polemics, rather than to assess her as one among several Tudor monarchs. There has been some suggestion that historians might excuse at least some of Mary's failings on gendered grounds: 'Mary's limitations as a ruler were largely those which were imposed by her sex.'[11] Mary herself would have found that an offensive view. Her family history offered several demonstrations that a woman's office or status could transcend her gender, as it had in the cases of her paternal great-grandmother, Margaret Beaufort, and her maternal grandmother, Isabella of Castile. Like her mother, Mary accepted that male heirs took precedence, but females were also fully competent to exercise full regal authority. Although Mary was England's first female monarch, her accession proclamation explicitly reassured all her 'good and faithful subjects that . . . they shall find us their benign and gracious sovereign lady, as others our noble progenitors have heretofore been'.[12] That gender mix may read confusingly, but the intended meaning is clear enough. Any remaining doubt was explicitly addressed in the act passed in April 1554, 'declaring that the Regal power of this realm is in the Queen's Majesty as fully and absolutely as ever it was in any her most noble progenitors kings of this realm'.[13]

Mary's capacity to rule as fully as a male was constantly – and sometimes unexpectedly – reiterated throughout her reign. There is, for example, the matter of her exercising the royal touch, that medieval and early-modern marker of true royalty in both France and England. Serious doubts had previously been raised about any female's capacity to exercise that power. It became a contentious issue in the later fourteenth century, when Edward III seemed likely to make good his claim through his mother to the French throne. That was when – and why – prominent French authorities set out many justifications for the Salic law which, they had fortuitously 'remembered', barred not only females, but also males with a claim through the female line, from the French throne. Among their arguments against women was that (like the English) French monarchs had the power to exercise the 'royal touch', that distinctive royal healing capacity. French polemicists argued that such a power was semi-priestly, derived from the coronation consecration. Since it was a semi-priestly power, the French authorities added, obviously women were disqualified from performing the royal touch – and therefore they were also incompetent to take the throne.[14] Mary, however, the first female monarch to face the issue directly, never doubted her capacity to exercise that healing capacity – and she revived blessing cramp rings as well. Indeed, cramp rings went by the hundreds to friends and relations across Europe. Elizabeth was to abandon the cramp rings again, but continued touching for the king's evil. Towards the end of the sixteenth century, Elizabeth's power to do so was invoked in print as a decisive proof she was indeed a legitimate monarch, whatever Catholic dissidents might suggest.[15]

If Mary could – and did – perform that quasi-sacral act, it is perhaps less surprising that she could also exercise her powers as Supreme Head of the Church, when the need arose, and whatever her general distaste for the title. In March 1554 she felt entirely competent to issue articles or injunctions to all her bishops, with a notably imperious set of instructions, and it was only in her capacity as Supreme Head of the Church that she could do that.[16] Her distaste for the title of Supreme Head was a consequence of her decision, at some stage during the previous reign, that the papacy was crucial to the maintenance of orthodox religion. But that was almost certainly a fresh decision, newly arrived at, not an old one stubbornly adhered to since the 1530s. Her earlier repudiation of papal supremacy, albeit first forced on her by her father, is the less surprising when it is remembered that there was then ambiguity about the ultimate authority of the papacy in secular matters – as French monarchs also demonstrated. In her brother's reign, however, Mary had been an increasingly unhappy witness to the many doctrinal changes progressively introduced and elaborated. There was, for her as for other religious conservatives, no way of knowing just where the religious changes would end. After all, significant variations on the preferred evangelical doctrine were still being extensively debated when Edward died. Such doctrinal uncertainty and disputation must have made an ultimate arbiter of orthodoxy like the pope an increasingly attractive authority – a view Stephen Gardiner, bishop of Winchester, also shared, despite his vehement earlier repudiations of papal claims.[17]

Much more has been said about the prosecutions and burnings of Marian heretics in Thomas S. Freeman's chapter, but there are three points that particularly bear on re-examining Mary's role in those dismaying deaths. The first is that hers was a world in which almost everyone – including many of those who suffered death by burning themselves – believed that burning persistent and obstinate heretics was the appropriate response to their obstinacy.[18] Mary's views in principle were conventional enough. The second point is that there should arguably be some uncertainty about exactly at what level Mary's responsibility for those burnings is assessed. Indisputably, as monarch and ultimate secular authority, she sanctioned and promoted the process, but many others actively collaborated and the prosecutions were actively initiated and pursued by a wide spectrum of her English subjects. As Gina Alexander pointed out three decades ago:

> the history of the persecution is not just of the edicts of Queen and Council, but of the active co-operation of the respectable and responsible members of society carrying out government decisions.... [The] courts were filled with suspected heretics because the Council, the commissioners, the justices and the jurors placed them there.[19]

The third point about the Marian burnings is that they are better understood when set in the wider context of related sixteenth-century burnings across much of western Christendom, as Catholic authorities struggled to suppress the new theologies. It is now generally agreed that in the half-century from 1523 some 3,000 Protestants were judicially executed as heretics in Europe.[20] In England, those deaths included Protestants of varying degrees of radicalism under Henry VIII, and two overly radical Protestants under Edward, but by far the greatest number of them occurred during Mary's reign. She presided over a large number of judicial deaths by any criterion, but Mary, uniquely among her Catholic peers, confronted the problem of restoring orthodox Catholicism to a realm which had officially adopted an increasingly advanced Protestantism under the previous regime. At least all the religious victims of her regime were formally tried, and almost all had an opportunity to recant.[21] Along with the other Tudor monarchs, Mary at least avoided the indiscriminate religious massacres which marred the history of sixteenth-century Netherlands and France.

To reiterate the starting point of this chapter, the weight of inherited tradition, insisting on Mary's stubbornness, emotional instability and general obtuseness, is due for reassessment. Redefining the monarchy of Mary implies not only invoking common criteria when assessing her against other early-modern monarchs, but also taking seriously the possibility that the choices Mary made were rational choices, rather than the predictable consequences of her self-evident inadequacies. As Quentin Skinner has written, 'unless we begin by assuming the agent's rationality, we leave ourselves with no means of explaining his (her?) behaviour, or even of seeing exactly what there is to explain about it, if . . . he (she?) is not acting rationally'.[22] Whatever those rational criteria are, there should surely be a consistency when applying them, for example, to Tudor monarchs. And indeed, even the historians most critical of her reign accept that there were several moments when Mary indisputably took the initiative, either without or against the advice of her usual counsellors.

These agreed moments of initiative include Mary's decision to make a stand against 'Queen Jane' in July 1553, and proclaim herself the true successor to Edward VI, her decision to marry Philip of Spain, her decision to take a stand in London against Wyatt's forces rather than retreat to Windsor, and her decision to declare war against France in 1557. Two out of four of those occasions have standardly been judged successful – her initial decision to make a bid for the throne, and her decision to make a stand to defend it against Wyatt in London – but those two are also often judged atypical.

There has been almost universal agreement that one decision she got wrong was her choice of marriage partner, an issue to be revisited later in this chapter. Her other most commonly asserted error, declaring war against France, led to the loss of Calais, England's last toehold on the continent. Since there is no room to discuss that fully in this chapter, only two points will be made here. The first is that Henri II of France, for reasons which seemed good to him, had sought to undermine Mary since before her accession, from Northumberland's attempt to install Jane Grey to Stafford's abortive raid on Scarborough Castle, the timing of which helped swing Mary's council to favouring a declaration of war. The French king had supported several plots and attempted coups against Mary between those events, so she had good reason to respond to his repeated efforts at destabilization.

Moreover, it is not clear that the English unanimously saw the loss of Calais as disastrous. One tradition, which Harbison found plausible, was that among the inducements Northumberland offered Henry to support the accession of Jane Grey after Edward's death was the return of Calais.[23] The Venetian ambassador reported in February 1558 that some parliamentarians were resisting further efforts to recover Calais, saying that 'if the French have taken Calais they thus took nothing from the English but recovered what was their own'. Mary herself deeply regretted the loss of Calais, but it seems not all her subjects felt the same, although the loss did subsequently make another useful rod with which to beat her reputation. In Elizabethan times there were some complaints about the revenues lost with the loss of Calais, but what was ignored was that the taxes and customs paid by the Calais merchant community usually covered, but occasionally fell short of, the costs of maintaining the garrison.[24] The overall financial loss, therefore, may not have been significant once garrison costs are factored in.

Mary is the one Tudor monarch for whom, despite her excellent humanist education and considerable classical skills, there is an almost universal doubt about her intelligence. That is not necessarily a problem, for no monarch has ever been required to take an IQ test before taking the throne. But her intelligence has sometimes been doubted in distinctively gendered terms which could hardly be applied to a male monarch. Most typical of that is the extent to which Mary has been deemed almost, if not actually, hysterical. Mary's tendency to hysteria has been adduced from two different kinds of evidence. One source was a report in April 1531. Mary was apparently seriously ill with what, in a nineteenth-century English translation of the sixteenth-century Italian text, reads as a condition 'the physicians call hysteria'. What the Venetian ambassador actually wrote was that the doctors believed Mary was suffering from a malfunction of her womb.[25] It is the nineteenth-century translation that calls it hysteria.[26] In the sixteenth century, blaming the womb was a response that could be made to almost any condition that appeared in a female. Still-influential ancient Greek medical texts attributed some 500 distinct disorders in women to womb malfunction; as late as 1636, John Sadler wrote in his *The sick woman's private looking-glass* that 'the 'evil qualities' of an 'ill-affected womb' could impact seriously on 'the heart, the liver and the brain', giving rise to problems which included 'convulsions, epilepsies, apoplexies, palseys, hectic fevers, dropsies, malignant ulcers, and, to be short, there is no disease so ill but may proceed from the evil quality of it'. It would seem likely, then, that the report from the Venetian ambassador is not a strong foundation for those historians who point to aspects of her behaviour and murmur 'almost hysterical'.

Given that Mary's medical problems might have actually been almost any condition, even one shared with males, what other interpretation might be offered for her recurrent illnesses, which so frequently occurred at times of great stress? They are conventionally characterized as menstrual, hysterical or psychosomatic. That may, of course, be true, at least some of the time. On the other hand, she herself wrote that one of her recurrent afflictions always occurred 'at the fall of the leaf',[27] which surely suggests that among other problems she may have suffered a seasonal allergic reaction. On occasion she was indeed seriously ill; on those occasions, while he was alive, her father sometimes sent his own physicians to her. But, during Edward's reign and at least in the early days of her own reign there is strong evidence that her illness was often feigned, for reasons of political expedience. The evidence that this was the case comes from the Imperial ambassador of the day, who often mentioned such occurrences in his reports; he often also mentioned the specific issue that had driven her to her putative illness. On the balance of probabilities, this was a tactic she resorted to even when the Imperial ambassador was not around to report it. So it is a plausible proposition that Mary was neither necessarily hysterical nor much given to psychosomatic illnesses, but did practise politically strategic illnesses at intervals throughout her life.

There is another consequence of Mary's imputed hysterical tendencies to be discussed, her false pregnancies, and how to understand them. Because of important advances in women's histories in recent years, it is now much better understood that in early-modern times diagnosing pregnancy was a precarious business. Indeed, as one scholar has noted, 'signs of pregnancy and even the signs of having given birth could be ambiguous ones. Nothing was certain until a child was born.'[28] Given that, Mary's experience might already be less risible than some have found it. But the matter of her so-called 'hysterical pregnancy' is worth considering further. It was Hippocrates who first recorded accounts of phantom pregnancy (pseudocyesis) as a recognized medical phenomenon. One of the more recent reports on pseudocyesis appeared in the *British Medical Journal* in 1985. That recorded a number of patients still presenting in that decade with objective signs of pregnancy, including enlargement of the abdomen, milk secretion and foetal movement – even though the patients were, in fact, not pregnant.[29]

Even more relevant to the case of Mary Tudor, there is considerable evidence that other elite women in mid-Tudor England experienced the same phenomenon. Katherine of Aragon may have undergone a phantom pregnancy in 1510.[30] Perhaps the best-known case is that of the wife of the governor of Calais, Arthur Plantagenet. Lady Lisle already had children by a previous marriage, but still believed she was probably pregnant again between November 1536 and August 1537. Modern commentators have referred to both Lady Lisle and Mary Tudor as clinging to their 'pathetic delusions' of pregnancy. There is no firm evidence of that in the case of Mary Tudor. She was, however, almost certainly guilty of a too-prolonged acceptance of the advice of her midwives and medical advisers, who said they had just got the date wrong. In the case of Lady Lisle we know much more certainly that the remark about 'pathetic delusions' is seriously misplaced, a determinedly modern misreading of the available evidence. Another significant feature of the Lisle story is the number of reports to Lady Lisle from other women in court circles who had themselves, or knew of others who had, experienced a similar problem and misdiagnosis at some stage.[31]

Since it seems pseudocyesis may have been a relatively common condition, contemporaries could have understood that in Mary's case too, but of course the disaffected exiles rejoiced at her apparent embarrassment and disappointment. With the passage of time, their pleasure – and relief – has become another stick with which to belabour the queen. Indeed, if a recent entry in Wikipedia is any guide, two major aspects of criticisms of her have become conflated, since that source – admittedly not authoritative – reports that it was the failure of her pregnancy which gave rise to her notorious prosecution of heretics.

There are, then, some good grounds for exploring another version of Mary Tudor, one which presents her as frequently rational, often resourceful in protecting her interests against an increasingly hostile regime, and – though this point will not be developed here – at least as well prepared to govern the realm as Henry VII, possibly Henry VIII, and Elizabeth. Edward was certainly better prepared to rule, but died before he could fully do so. This alternative version of Mary starts with her last years in her father's court, a period which for her had, on the whole, been serene. Her father insisted on her presence at his court for much of the time, even during his marriage to Katherine Howard – and two more dissimilar women it is difficult to imagine. This version of Mary was by then fully in accord with her father's preferred form of religion and showed few if any signs of hankering for the return of papal authority to England. She was in high favour at court, well-enough informed to be able to keep others in touch with her father's likely policy turns, and valued as an ornament to the court. She was an accomplished musician and dancer, and richly praised as translator of part of Erasmus's *Paraphrases*, a project dear to the heart, and under the patronage, of her close friend Queen Katherine Parr. Together the two talked fashion, collected paintings and studied classical texts, with Mary the better educated and perhaps guide and mentor in that enterprise.

Immediately after her father's death, the omens continued to look good for her. While the major European powers hesitated to recognize Edward, waiting to see whether Mary would make a claim to the throne, she made no move to do so. Whatever continental Catholics thought about the illegitimacy of Edward as well as Elizabeth, Mary entirely accepted her father's arrangements in the succession, as in religion. As Jeri McIntosh has so persuasively demonstrated, after her acquiescence in the rearrangements made to Edward's council, Mary was transformed into one of the wealthiest landowners in England.[32] She may have accepted the changes to the council more readily because the newly created duke of Somerset was married to a woman Mary had known most of her life, who had been in her mother's household and to whom she wrote in the friendliest terms. But after a promising start, that serene world rapidly deteriorated for Mary. Not only did her close friend, Queen Katherine, remarry with unseemly haste so soon after the death of Henry, but even more significantly, the evangelical nature of the new regime started to emerge. Within months Mary was writing furiously to Somerset about the religious changes. It seems likely that an undated enraged letter drafted in her hand, which Ellis dated to 1551, may belong to that earlier time; certainly it is possible to see from Somerset's reply that she wrote in similar terms, attacking those men 'whom the king my father ... made in this world of nothing', and who had now broken his will, and taken a usurped authority 'in making (as they call it) laws both clean contrary to his proceedings and will and against the custom of all Christendom and (in my conscience) against the law of God'.[33] If that was not an early draft of her letter to him, Somerset's scornful reply makes it clear those were the issues she had then addressed.

From the start of Edward's reign, Mary's most obvious allies in defending her father's religious settlement were disappearing fast out of the council, like Southampton, and/or into prison, like Gardiner. Mary had always shared her father's deep attachment to the traditional mass. From early 1547 there were already doubts being publicly expressed about the nature of that mass by the more evangelically minded. The extent to which Mary came to be distanced from the men in power as religious changes came fast upon each other is illustrated by the point that when Somerset finally came to trial in 1551, one of the charges against him was that he was too sympathetic to Mary. Her developing hostility to the Edwardine religious changes is notorious – and indisputable. It is less clear, however, that her (often derided) insistence that all religious changes made before Edward came of age were *ipso facto* illegal was as misjudged as is often assumed. Her argument that while the king was a minor he could neither exercise his status as God's immediate vice-regent on earth himself, nor delegate it to any one else to adjudicate religious changes on his behalf, was certainly politically inconvenient for the new regime. It may also have been logically consistent with the Henrician claims that the king alone was ultimate arbiter on religious matters.

Given Mary's early and increasing isolation from Englishmen of power and authority in the Edwardine years, it may have been quite rational for her to accept the protection of Charles V from 1547, and to write to him in what modern readers would find astonishingly submissive and ingratiating terms. Deference was expected in such a relationship, and to be delivered if the relationship was to endure. Of course her apparent dependency fell in with Charles's interests as well, giving him a point of access from which to intervene in English politics. For Mary, on the other hand, it gave her a protector who would at least threaten to defend her right to practise her own religion, even as she did so in the most public form of private observance possible. She has been faulted for looking beyond England for protection, but she was not going to find it within the realm. Moreover, in an era when dynastic realms were still the norm (on what other grounds did England still hold Calais?), appeals to nationalism are too often a historical stalking horse. We can presumably agree how dangerous it is to project an ideology based on nineteenth-century political formations back to the sixteenth century. Then it was much more accurate to speak of the primacy of loyalty to a prince or lord, rather than loyalty to an abstract concept of a nation. In 1569, for example, after the northern uprising, Elizabethan polemicists still battled to persuade northerners that they did indeed have on obligation to their monarch which took precedence even over their obligations to a Percy or a Neville.[34]

On the international scene it was a fact of mid-sixteenth-century life that the two major players in Europe were the Habsburg imperial interests on the one hand, and the steadily consolidating French realm on the other. In the divided realm of mid-Tudor England it was usual for contending parties to seek assistance from one or the other of the dominant powers. Once Dudley became Northumberland and was in the ascendancy, he moved to a closer alliance with France. Then it followed that the constraints on Mary's religious practice tightened so much that it seems likely she was, for at least some of the time, forbidden to hear mass at all. That surely is one indicator of just how sensible she had been to take advantage of Charles's protection for as long as that was possible. Without it, she was without any politically

potent supporters at all. Northumberland turned to the French even
more explicitly to help in his scheme to promote his daughter-in-law
as queen. Such resort to aid from beyond the realm makes the success
of Mary in taking the throne – an entirely English affair – the more
extraordinary. It was all over well before Northumberland could bring
across the proffered help from the French, or the Habsburgs could
recover from their ostentatiously neutral position. And once it was
clear that Mary's husband was to be Philip of Spain, then opponents
to that marriage again turned to France for assistance. They got it, but
not quickly enough or generously enough to forestall the marriage.
Nevertheless French support for what emerged as the Wyatt rebellion was important for enabling the plotters to proceed. The French
worked actively with their English partners to spread the rumours
that abounded as the plotted uprisings took shape. The ones about
the vast army Philip would bring with him to subdue England to
his will were particularly potent. Moreover, however difficult it is to
gauge just how much support Wyatt and his co-conspirators had in
England, it is generally agreed that Mary's speech to the Londoners at
the Guildhall was effective in rallying support to her side at the most
crucial stage of the attack on London.[35]

One point which has seldom been remarked about Mary is the
extent to which that queen – included, in recent years, in the
pantheon of the 100 bloodiest tyrants in the world in a Discovery
Channel series – was a monarch who conscientiously sought to operate through the rule of law. In that, she was a product of her age, for
her age included an increasing consciousness of the scope and public
recognition of statute law. The status of statute law was reaffirmed
by the early-Tudor disputes about the relative power of statute and
proclamation, by which it was agreed that royal proclamations could
not override statute. Statute law was, moreover, becoming more
widely accessible, being regularly written in English from 1483 and
quite standardly published in print from the end of the fifteenth century. It is widely agreed that the scope of statute law was considerably
expanded in the reign of Henry VIII, but its status was still subject to
challenge.

Mary's consciousness of the importance of the law was undoubtedly
strengthened by the Edwardine doctrinal changes in 1547. A significant number of those innovations, which she deplored, were initially
enforced by non-parliamentary means, and legally heresy, for months
before new laws could be passed by Edward's first parliament. It is
the case that, even after the first Edwardine changes were enacted

by parliament at the end of 1547, Mary continued to resist them. Her stated ground for continuing opposition even after the successive changes were written into statute law was that those laws were themselves illegitimate, being transacted on behalf of an under-age king and an authority that had been usurped. Gardiner may have thought that a constitutionally dangerous position, but many besides Mary adopted that position to justify resisting the innovations. After Mary's accession, her public attitude to the religious divisions she inherited contrasts with the early strategies of the Edwardine regime. Rather than covertly enforcing changes, she permitted, but did not enforce, her preferred religion. The proclamation issued in her name on 18 August 1553 made it clear that her own preference was for the religion 'she hath ever professed from her infancy'. Nevertheless, provided her subjects would forgo preaching and 'live together in quiet sort and Christian charity', they could live without religious compulsion, until 'such time as further order by common assent may be taken therein'.[36] That order was settled by the first parliament of her reign, the elections for which Jennifer Loach, in her study of the Marian parliaments, thought remarkably free of royal intervention.

Later, Mary's resistance to Pole's demands that those church lands expropriated since the mid-1530s should be returned to their original owner was also grounded in large part on the legal impossibility of doing so, though she was also much more aware than Pole of the political impossibility of doing so.[37] Although she became again a member of the Catholic Church, she was unswayed several times by suggestions that the authority of the pope should be invoked to override English statute. Parliamentary reaffirmation of the legality of her parents' marriage was one example of that. A similar concern with upholding the law can be seen in that much debated 1554 Act confirming that queens regnant, like male monarchs, were fully invested with the 'kingly or regal office of the realm'. Fleetwood's explanation, some years later, has Mary deeply dismayed by a suggestion that, because in all statutes the reference was to a king, as a queen she was freed from all statutory restraints on her power.[38] That explanation may be apocryphal, but it has some credibility since it surfaced first in Elizabeth's reign, not a period in which many anecdotes favourable to Mary appear. And whatever its origins, the bill explicitly insisted that all existing statutes that restricted kings also restricted queens. So this reassessment argues that Mary, for a monarch, was unusually committed to using her 'ordinary' authority in accordance with law. (Like any early-modern monarch, and necessarily, she retained the right to exercise 'extraordinary' authority, as the royal power to override normal legal process came to be defined in the next century.) And finally, this reassessment turns to another traditional critique of Mary's reign, her marriage to the Catholic Habsburg prince, who later became Philip II of Spain. Despite her age, all her advisers except Reginald Pole were agreed that she should marry; Pole thought it better that she should remain single and leave the matter of her successor in the hands of God. Her other advisers saw that as one more evidence of Pole's unworldliness, not least because, as matters stood, that successor would be her half-sister Elizabeth. The younger daughter's illegitimacy, first established by her father, had been reinforced when Mary's illegitimate status was reversed by her first parliament; Mary always suspected her sister's religion, as she did most other aspects of her character. Given her views of her likely heir, it is not surprising that Mary much preferred to follow the path of all her predecessors for at least 500 years and marry. The long-standing principle (if not always the practice) was the realm's ruler was chosen by the principle of dynastic succession. The importance of there being an identifiable heir was repeatedly demonstrated in the reign of Elizabeth; in 1569 Thomas Norton spoke for many before and after him when he prayed earnestly for Elizabeth's preservation since 'without or after [her] there is great daunger and small hope'.[39] That second queen regnant's reign proved indeed to be one marked by recurrent fears of an aspiring heir, sustained by religious difference, and after the first decade by threatened rebellion, assassination and invasion. The often intense anxiety about an unsettled succession continued until Elizabeth was on her deathbed; it even led to proposals for effectively bypassing the monarch's power to name the heir, thereby threatening the very basis of traditional royal authority.

The disruptive consequences of Elizabeth's reluctance to provide or nominate an heir might help modern readers understand why Mary faced such pressure to marry. Her private preference, she insisted, was to remain single; that (admittedly dubious) claim was publicly celebrated in a prayer for her safety, published when the birth of her heir was believed to be imminent: 'Thou Lord ... knowest that thy servant never lusted after man ... but she consented to take an husband with thy feare ... not for carnal pleasure, but only for the love & desire of posteritie, wherein thy name might be blessed for ever.'[40] There were other, more explicitly gendered reasons for urging her marriage. Charles V spoke for many, both English and foreign, when he wrote that 'it is important that she have heirs, and still more

important that some one may be by her side to assist her in the conduct of her affairs'.[41] There was general agreement that she should
have 'some one at her side to assist her'. That belief also gave rise
to considerable pressure from her English advisers for her to marry
within her realm and avoid more foreign influence. It was, however,
more usual for European monarchs to marry for diplomatic advantage, and Mary had particular need of such diplomatic support. As
previously discussed, she had faced French hostility throughout her
brother's reign and in the move to install Lady Jane Grey as successor
to Edward VI. Mary's main protector during those years had been her
cousin, the Emperor Charles V, also the dominant international threat
to French interests. She continued to face French hostility after her
accession, and her marriage to his son would ensure that Habsburg
protection continued, and thereby inevitably – and problematically –
French hostility was reinforced.

Whomsoever Mary decided to marry, there were other anxieties. The biblical injunctions that wives should be subject to their
husbands was widely understood to be a mainstay of good public
and domestic order. This gave rise to widespread expectations that
Mary, of indisputable piety, would submit to her husband's authority.
But wifely submission was never an immutable rule in England. To
develop further a point already made, in that very hierarchic society
status took precedence even over gender, and there were numerous occasions when women took precedence over their husbands.
Henry Parker, Lord Morley, who had been present at a feast given by
Margaret Beaufort, mother of Henry VII, recorded the details of the
occasion. Beaufort sat with a surviving daughter of Edward IV under
a cloth of state while also 'syttyng at her table the erle of Derby her
[i.e. Margaret Beaufort's] husband, the Vicount Wellys, the olde Lorde
Hastings, the byshoppe of Lincolne'.[42] The two royal ladies outranked
them all. There were also precedents of women governing countries;
the more distant rule of Isabella of Castile, mother of Katharine of
Aragon, may have slipped from public memory, but Mary of Hungary
was governor of the Netherlands, a major trading partner for English
interests, in 1554, as she had been for more than 20 years. Nevertheless, it was apparently surprising to many at court as it became
known that when Mary decided she would marry, she added that she
would, of course, love and obey her new husband, 'but if he wished
to encroach in the government of the kingdom, she would be unable
to permit it'.[43] Her council appears to have understood her conditions, for in December 1533, it wrote to Nicholas Wotton, Mary's

ambassador in France, that 'if the marriage took place the government of the realm should always remain in her Majesty and not in the prince'.[44] That statement that she would rule was, however, also written into the final marriage treaties, the terms of which were widely published but apparently neither widely believed nor understood.

The preferred English candidate for Mary's hand was Edward Courtenay. On paper he was eligible enough. He was the only son of Mary's close friend the marchioness of Exeter, and his father was a direct descendant of Edward IV. The failure of his candidacy stemmed in part from Mary's stated reluctance to marry a subject, a reluctance that was well founded. Edward IV's marriage to Elizabeth Woodville and Henry VIII's marriages into the Boleyn, Howard and Seymour families had all produced considerable political tensions, irrespective of the success or otherwise of the marriages themselves. Courtenay's association with Gardiner added a new element of partisanship to this debate. Furthermore Courtenay was unsuitable, less because he was some ten years younger than Mary, more because he had spent his most formative years – from the age of 12 for almost 15 years – in the Tower, as one more victim of Henry VIII. It followed that his worldly experience could only be described as seriously limited. And available evidence already indicated what was soon to become only too obvious, that Courtenay was not a particularly stable or reliable person. But when it was clear that Mary was determined to marry Philip, there was a conspiracy by (mainly Protestant) conspirators with French backing, ostensibly to thwart Mary's Habsburg marriage, probably actually to depose Mary and put Elizabeth, married to Courtenay, on the throne. Courtenay, however, confessed it all to Mary's lord chancellor, Gardiner, and the conspiracy failed, despite an alarming few hours when Wyatt and his men entered London and there was fighting in the streets.

Given that she accepted the need to marry to secure a (Catholic) successor, Mary essentially had to choose between a Valois or a Habsburg candidate. Every aspect of her past history and the current diplomatic situation committed Mary to marrying a Habsburg. That this decision quickly gave rise to plots and a rebellion against her owed as much to the expectation that her marriage would reinforce Catholicism (still very much the majority religion in England) as it did to anxiety about her marrying a foreigner, although the two issues were always difficult to separate. Undeniably this opposition was serious; but whatever candidate she had chosen would have provoked significant opposition.

Mary addressed a large crowd at London's Guildhall before Wyatt's rebellion was suppressed. In a remarkable speech she promised not to marry unless her subjects sanctioned her choice – in itself not a promise that male English monarchs were in the habit of making. Despite one historian's declaration that her whole speech was a 'series of deliberate, unequivocal lies',[45] Mary's marriage treaty was subsequently submitted to parliament, and both houses approved it, thereby also approving the marriage. Since it was generally accepted that 'the consent of Parliament is taken to be everie mans consent',[46] Mary kept her word. It is difficult to see how else she might have identified her subjects' agreement. In another unprecedented move, the terms of the marriage treaties were also proclaimed across her realm. Well before the marriage took place, for those who were still having difficulty in comprehending the status of a married queen regnant, two other laws passed through parliament to address anxieties about a married female monarch, and both were published. One already discussed emphasized that each English monarch, either male or female, was invested with full regal powers, despite the traditional usage of 'king' for monarchs. The other act, passed in the same parliamentary session, confirmed that Mary remained 'solye and a sole quene' with complete sovereignty after as before her marriage.[47]

Mary's husband's position was always unclear. Despite his stated wishes, he was never crowned, and from his arrival in England, even during the marriage service, the surrounding ceremonial reiterated his subordinate position.[48] Philip spent more time out of England than in it, during his marriage to Mary. That is one reason that it is a complex project to quantify how much influence he exercised in England during Mary's reign. Moreover, even while he was there, he faced increasing demands from his responsibilities elsewhere, as he gradually gained more control over his father's domains. But he did work with Mary on her main projects, and he did do much to restore to royal favour the men of such families as Dudley and Sidney, previously compromised by their support for Lady Jane Grey after the death of Edward VI. Their progressive restoration was signalled in part by their participation in jousts arranged by Philip, and was sufficiently successful for a number to fight with him in France, even while Mary was resisting being drawn in to that war. What finally drew Mary into it, as already discussed earlier in this chapter, was the bizarre attempt by Thomas Stafford to seize the rather decrepit Scarborough Castle as a first step to claiming the throne.

Mary's marriage to Philip has been criticized by later historians who believed that Philip played a dominant role in her government and influenced a number of her most controversial decisions, especially the burnings and entry into the war with the French. Two considerations have done much to shape that discussion. One is the absence of many of Philip's papers for the period. The second is the hostility towards Spain on religious and national grounds, which began in Elizabeth's reign and has continued to prejudice historical narratives for centuries. It may, however, be a suggestive comment on the substance of the contemporary Protestant critiques that a few years later the marriage partner preferred by William Cecil and others among Elizabeth's advisers was another Catholic Habsburg. Moreover, there were also suggestions that the terms for Mary's marriage to Philip would provide a satisfactory basis for the second female Tudor marriage to a foreigner. That more dispassionate approach might indicate that, even so soon after the event, Mary's marriage was not seen as quite the disaster her religious opponents had argued that it was. Those advisers, after all, had also lived through Mary's reign, and most of them had remained in the country during it.

Necessarily, this has been a chapter about clearing away more of the residue from the sixteenth-century wars of religion which has so profoundly coloured the English version of Mary's reputation ever since. The reassessing of Mary, still a work in progress, currently suggests a more rational, less bloody, less reactionary, less tyrannical monarch than popular mythology – and rather too much history – still has her. She is also far from the reactionary Catholic of Protestant polemic. Perhaps most importantly, she addressed with considerable care and success a variety of problems confronting her as England's first queen regnant. In that, Mary was an important paradigm-breaker, who set a number of important precedents for the next – and much more long-lived – queen regnant to follow. That, too, is a matter which is now being better recognized, though there is likely to be a very long wait for a study that reverses the historical standing commonly accorded to Queen Mary and to Queen Elizabeth respectively.

Appendix: The Marian martyrs

A considerable amount of imprecision is present in nearly all discussions of the Marian martyrs. No one is sure of exactly how many people died in the course of the persecution, nor has anyone hitherto compiled a list of all the martyrs. The list below should remedy this deficiency and also provide some basic background information about them, at least to the extent that this is available. Yet while I have tried to make this list as complete and accurate as possible, it is far from definitive. Even the exact number of the martyrs must remain uncertain. First of all, there is the problem of definition. I have included those who were arrested for religious offences and who died in prison, as well as those who were executed for heresy. Some researchers may prefer to consider only those who were burned. (The column headed 'manner of death' has been added to enable readers to separate rapidly those who expired in prison from those who were consumed by the flames.) Also I have not included John Tooley, a robber who was posthumously tried for heresy, as he had already been executed for theft. However, George Eagles is on the list, although he was convicted on a charge of sedition. I have numbered him among the martyrs because he was pursued by the authorities for his clandestine preaching. These editorial decisions are subjective and researchers should feel free to modify this list accordingly if they disagree with them. Second, the very existence of some of the martyrs I have tallied – notably numbers 169, 175, 177, 212, 213 and 251 on this list – is open to question. I have given my reasons for believing that these martyrdoms actually occurred in my notes; researchers can make their own judgements. Conversely, although there is evidence that Isabel Denye was burned in Gloucestershire (see the discussion in note 86), I have not found it convincing enough to include her on this list. The chronological order of the executions is quite important, and I have tried to replicate it, but in some cases – notably, but not exclusively, numbers 167, 171, 172, 193, 232 and 300 on the list – this proved impossible to do with absolute certainty. Again the problems involved are discussed in my notes, and readers are invited to come to their own conclusions.

Given the problems involved in identifying the martyrs and dating their deaths, I should say a few words about the sources upon which this list is based. Paramount among these is Foxe's *Acts and Monuments*; indeed all of the information on the list below, except where the notes indicate otherwise, is derived from Foxe. However, as a look at the list reveals, Foxe overlooked some martyrs and made mistakes – particularly chronological errors – about others. Therefore it has been necessary to consult a variety of sources. The obvious place to look is in diocesan records. However, for the Marian persecution these are extremely limited. In some cases the diocesan register does not survive or (e.g. the register of Maurice Griffith, the Marian bishop of Rochester) survives in fragments. More frequently, the registers survive intact but reveal little about the trials of the martyrs. This is because the volume of heresy trials in some dioceses led to such records being kept in court books. These have not survived. (A unique exception to this is Nicholas Harpsfield's courtbook as vicar-general of London in 1554, but this covered a period before the burnings began.) A major reason for this is that these books were used by Foxe and his assistants in their researches, and once the relevant information had been extracted from them, they were – partly through carelessness and laziness, but also from a desire to destroy embarrassing evidence, particularly about the beliefs of the martyrs – allowed to perish. Copies of documents in these books, and occasionally pages torn or cut from them, survive among Foxe's papers in BL Harley MSS 421 and 425. (On rare occasions papers in Foxe's collection were recorded by the early eighteenth-century ecclesiastical historian John Strype – who had access to these papers – and yet have subsequently gone missing).

However, the disappearance of diocesan records cannot be laid entirely at the doors of Foxe and his colleagues. Foxe – as he complained – had very limited access to the diocesan records of Chichester, but the same absence of Marian records exists there. It is possible that the destruction of some of the episcopal records of the persecution was undertaken by those who did not wish to see compromised the Marian officials who were active in the trials and survived into Elizabeth's reign. A happy exception to the dearth of diocesan records of Marian heresy trials occurs in Ely, where the bishop's register survives and the meagre number of martyrs (three) ensured that a separate court book was not kept. For two of the three martyrs condemned in the diocese, records of their trials survive (see notes 9 and 10 below). There is also one type of official document that provides limited, but important, information on the Marian martyrs. The heresy statutes mandated that a writ be sent to Chancery recording the excommunication and transference to the secular arm of a condemned heretic. Many, but not all, of these writs for the Marian period survive in the Chancery records in the National Archive at Kew. By the mid-sixteenth century, these writs were largely formulaic; in fact, they contain little – beyond standard statements of the heresies for which the individual or individuals was sentenced – apart from names, places of origin, sometimes the ages and occasionally the occupations of those condemned. But with the more shadowy of the martyrs these nuggets of information can often be quite valuable.

Apart from the *Acts and Monuments*, the most important sources are three lists of the Marian martyrs that were each printed in 1559. One of these lists followed an anonymous 'A briefe exhortation to England' which itself was printed at the end of John Knox's *The copie of an epistle . . . unto the inhabitants of Newcastle and Barwick* (Geneva, 1559), STC 15064. The 'Brief exhortation' was dated 12 January 1559. A list of the Marian martyrs also appeared in Crowley's *Chronicle*. Knox's list and Crowley's list do have minor variations, but they are nevertheless quite similar; it is likely that they both were drawing on a common list of martyrs, circulating among Protestants in England and on the Continent. The same cannot be said for the third list, Thomas Brice's *A compendious register in metre* (London, 1559), STC 3726. This was a poem in doggerel verse, listing the Marian martyrs along with where and when they died. Brice's *Register* is sufficiently different from Crowley and Knox to suggest that he compiled his list independently of them. This makes the *Register* valuable in corroborating the other two lists, and this value is increased by Brice's hard-won knowledge of Marian Protestantism in Essex and Kent. (For Brice's activities during Mary's reign, see the article on him in the *ODNB*.) But Brice's dates are often wrong and his knowledge decreases sharply for events outside the south-east. Each of these sources, however, contains information not to be found in the *Acts and Monuments*. This is also occasionally true of the two contemporary London 'diarists', Henry Machyn and Charles Wriothesley. Machyn, in particular, took an interest in executions for heresy and records many of the ones that took place in or near the capital.

This table lists the Marian martyrs in chronological order, or as close to chronological order as the imprecision of dates given in Foxe and other sources permits. The martyrs' names are given, followed by the dates of their deaths as closely as they can be determined. The manner of their deaths (with one exception, that of George Eagles, no. 236, these will be either burning at the stake or dying while incarcerated) are given next, followed by the reason for arrest (that is, the reason, where it is known, that the individual came to the attention of the authorities). This is followed by their occupations. (For clergymen, only a few of their more important livings are listed.) For women, with rare exceptions, their occupations in this period would have been as wives, therefore, where it is known, I have tried in this table to convey both their marital status and the occupation and status of their husband. Where nothing is known about these, this space is left blank.

The next heading is the 'instigator(s) of arrests'. This tries to convey an idea of who was responsible for the apprehension or capture of a martyr. This can be an extremely uncertain category, as many people might be involved in the arrest of a particular martyr. In this table I have tried to focus on those who denounced a particular martyr, and also on the magistrate responsible for sending the martyr to the ecclesiastical authorities. Many of these were active heresy hunters. Some of them may simply have been compelled by circumstances to deal with an accused heretic brought before them. The next category is that of the ecclesiastical official who condemned a particular prisoner to death; usually this was either the bishop himself or his chancellor.

In all cases, the capacity in which the official was acting, as well as his name, is given.

Another heading shows the place of death of the martyrs. It should be noted that the differences between sixteenth-century and twenty-first century London have complicated this list. In the sixteenth century the city of London was essentially bounded by the Temple in the west and the Tower in the east, and was entirely on the north bank of the Thames. Communities such as Islington, Stratford and Westminster, which are now part of Greater London, were, in Mary's reign, separate towns or villages. A particularly important boundary was that of the river Thames, because Southwark was not only outside the municipal jurisdiction of the city of London, it was also in a separate diocese, that of Winchester. This list therefore presents the sixteenth-century locations where the executions took place, and thus Islington, Stratford, Westminster and Southwark are considered to be independent communities. (See the map of the London area and the burnings that took place there.)

The place of origin also needs a few words of explanation. This is not the place where the martyrs were born, but the area where they had been living before death, or with which they were most closely associated. This criterion, while necessary for purposes of clarity, is occasionally unduly restrictive. For example, it is important to note that Elizabeth Folkes (no. 242) was born and raised in the staunchly Protestant village of Stoke Nayland. Clergymen present particular problems for this category, as they could hold livings in quite widely scattered areas. Four cases are particularly worthy of note: those of Laurence Saunders (no. 2), George Marsh (no. 16), John Cardmaker (no. 18) and John Bradford (no. 27). Saunders held livings in Northampton, Leicestershire, Coventry and London. I decided to give his London parish as his place of origin. A somewhat similar situation applies to his curate, George Marsh. However, because Marsh was largely active in his native Lancashire and does not seem to have been very involved with his London living, I decided to give the former as his place of origin. John Cardmaker was from Devon and was made chancellor of Wells. Moreover the last appointment was not a sinecure; Cardmaker spent the last years of Edward VI's reign in Somerset. But his period of greatest evangelical activity was as vicar of St Bride's parish in London. John Bradford neatly falls on both prongs of the dilemma, being active in both his native Lancashire and London. I decided to give London as his place of origin because, like Saunders, he was arrested because of his activities in the capital.

Much of the research for this list was done on a British Academy Short Term Grant in 2004.

	Name	Date of death	Manner of death	Reason for arrest	Occupation	Instigator(s) of arrest	Official condemning	Place of death	Origin
1	Rogers, John	4 Feb 1555	B	Preached a sermon attacking Catholicism	Clergyman, prebendary	Privy council	Stephen Gardiner, Lord Chancellor	Smithfield, London	London
2	Saunders, Laurence	8 Feb 1555	B	Preached a sermon attacking Catholicism	Clergyman, prebendary	Sir John Mordaunt	Stephen Gardiner, Lord Chancellor	Coventry, Works	All Hallows, Bread Street, London
3	Hooper, John	9 Feb 1555	B	Arrested as a leading Edwardine cleric	BP of Gloucester & Worcester	Privy council	Stephen Gardiner, Lord Chancellor	Gloucester	Gloucester
4	Taylor, Rowland	9 Feb 1555	B	Tried to prevent the celebration of a mass	AD of Bury St Edmunds; rector of Hadleigh	Sir Henry Doyle	Stephen Gardiner, Lord Chancellor	Hadleigh, Suffolk	Peripatetic but associated with Hadleigh, Suffolk
5	White, Rawlins	March 1555	B	U	Fisherman	U	Anthony Kitchin, BP Llandaff	Cardiff	Cardiff
6	Tomkins, Thomas	16 March 1555	B	U	Weaver	U	Edmund Bonner, BP London	Smithfield, London	Shoreditch, London
7	Causton, Thomas	26 March 1555	B	U	Gentleman	U	Edmund Bonner, BP London	Rayleigh, Essex	Horndon on Hill, Essex

	Name	Date of death	Manner of death	Reason for arrest	Occupation	Instigator(s) of arrest	Official condemning	Place of death	Origin
8	Higbed, Thomas	26 March 1555	B	U	Gentleman	U	Edmund Bonner, BP London	Horndon on Hill, Essex	Thundersley, Essex
9	Hunter, William	26 March 1555	B	Reading an English-language Bible; denied transubstantiation	Apprentice silk-weaver	Thomas Wood (vicar of South Weald, Essex); Sir Anthony Browne	Edmund Bonner, BP London	Brentwood, Essex	Brentwood, Essex
10	Knight, Steven	28 March 1555	B	U	Barber	U	Edmund Bonner, BP London	Maldon, Essex	U
11	Pygot, William	28 March 1555	B	U	Butcher	U	Edmund Bonner, BP London	Braintree, Essex	Essex
12	Dighel, William[1]	28 March 1555	B	U	U	U	U	Danbury, Essex?	U
13	Laurence, John	29 March 1555	B	U	Clergyman	U	Edmund Bonner, BP London	Colchester, Essex	In Sudbury Convent (at dissolution in 1538)
14	Ferrar, Robert	30 March 1555	B	U	Bishop of St David's	Privy council	Henry Morgan, BP St David's	Carmarthen	Yorkshire
15	Alcock, John[2]	2 April 1555	P	Led Protestant services, refused to join procession	Shearman	Sir Henry Doyle	None	Newgate prison, London	Hadleigh, Suffolk

No.	Name	Date		Offense	Occupation	Accuser	Examiner	Trial	Execution
16	Marsh, George	24 April 1555	B	Clandestine preaching	Curate	Earl of Derby	George Coates, BP Chester	Chester, Cheshire	Dean, Lancashire
17	Flower, William	24 April 1555	B	Assaulted priest celebrating mass	Ex-monk, schoolteacher, surgeon	Privy council	Edmund Bonner, BP London	Westminster, Middlesex	Cambridgeshire
18	Cardmaker, John	30 May 1555	B	Prominent Edwardine preacher, tried to flee England	Ex-Franciscan, vicar of St Brides, London, CH of Wells	Privy council	Edmund Bonner, BP London	Smithfield, London	St. Bride's, London
19	Warne, John	30 May 1555	B	Arrested attending a conventicle	Clothworker and upholsterer	U	Edmund Bonner, BP London	Smithfield, London	St. John Walbrook, London
20	Hawkes/Haukes, Thomas	10 June 1555	B	Refused to allow son a Catholic baptism	Gentleman	Earl of Oxford	Edmund Bonner, BP London	Coggeshall, Essex	Colne, Essex
21	Wats, Thomas	c. 10 June 1555	B	Failure to attend church	Linen draper	Lord Rich	Edmund Bonner, BP London	Chelmsford, Essex	Billericay, Essex
22	Ardeley, John	11 June 1555	B	U	Husbandman	U	Edmund Bonner, BP London	Rochford, Essex	Great Wigborough, Essex
23	Simpson, John	11 June 1555	B	U	Husbandman	U	Edmund Bonner, BP London	Rayleigh, Essex	Great Wigbrough, Essex
24	Chamberlain, Nicholas	14 June 1555	B	Refused to receive sacrament	Weaver	Earl of Oxford; Sir Philip Paris	Edmund Bonner, BP London	Colchester, Essex	Coggeshall, Essex

	Name	Date of death	Manner of death	Reason for arrest	Occupation	Instigator(s) of arrest	Official condemning	Place of death	Origin
25	Bamford (alias Butler), William	15 June 1555	B	Refused to receive sacrament	Weaver	Earl of Oxford; Sir Philip Paris	Edmund Bonner, BP London	Harwich, Essex	Coggeshall, Essex
26	Osmund, Thomas	15 June 1555	B	Refused to receive sacrament	Fuller	Earl of Oxford; Sir Philip Paris	Edmund Bonner, BP London	Manningtree, Essex	Coggeshall, Essex
27	Bradford, John	1 July 1555	B	Alleged seditious preaching	Prebendary; royal chaplain	Privy council	Stephen Gardiner, Lord Chancellor	Smithfield, London	London
28	Leaf, John	1 July 1555	B	U	Apprentice	London alderman	Edmund Bonner, BP London	Smithfield, London	London
29	Minge, William	2 July 1555	P	U	Priest	U	None	Maidstone prison, Kent	U
30	Bland, John	12 July 1555	B	Denounced mass	Curate of Adisham, Kent	Thomas Austen, Sir Thomas Moyle	Richard Thornden, BP Dover	Canterbury, Kent	Adisham, Kent
31	Sheterden, Nicholas	12 July 1555	B	U	U	U	Richard Thornden, BP Dover	Canterbury, Kent	Pluckley, Kent
32	Frankesh, John	12 July 1555	B	U	Vicar of Rolvendon, Kent	U	Richard Thornden, BP Dover	Canterbury, Kent	Rolvenden, Kent

	Name	Date		Circumstances	Occupation	Accuser	Condemned by	Trial	Origin
33	Middleton, Humphrey	12 July 1555	B	U	U	U	Richard Thornden, BP Dover	Canterbury, Kent	Ashford, Kent
34	Hall, Nicholas	c.19 July 1555	B	U	Bricklayer	U	Maurice Griffith, BP Rochester	Rochester, Kent, Kent	Dartford, Kent
35	Wade, Christopher	Prob. July 1555	B	U	Linen weaver	U	Maurice Griffith, BP Rochester	Dartford, Kent	Dartford, Kent
36	Polley, Margery [F]	Prob. July 1555	B	U	Wife of Richard Polley	U	Maurice Griffith, BP Rochester	Dartford, Kent	Pepeling, Calais
37	Carver, Derick	22 July 1555	B	Arrested attending a conventicle	Beer brewer	Edward Gage	Edmund Bonner, BP London	Lewes, Sussex	Dilsem, Liège; Brighton, Sussex
38	Launder, John	23 July 1555	B	Arrested attending a conventicle	Husbandman	Edward Gage	Edmund Bonner, BP London	Steyning, Sussex	Godstone, Surrey
39	Iveson, Thomas	July 1555	B	Arrested attending a conventicle	Carpenter	Edward Gage	Edmund Bonner, BP London	Chichester, Sussex	Godstone, Surrey
40	Aleworth, John	July 1555	P	U	U	U	None	Reading gaol	U
41	Abbes, James	2 Aug 1555	B	Publicly recanted previous recantation	Shoemaker	Privy council?	John Hopton, BP Norwich	Bury St Edmunds, Suffolk	Stoke Nayland, Suffolk[3]

	Name	Date of death	Manner of death	Reason for arrest	Occupation	Instigator(s) of arrest	Official condemning	Place of death	Origin
42	Denley, John	8 Aug 1555	B	Possessed incriminating letters[4]	Gentleman	Edmund Tyrrel	Edmund Bonner, BP London	Uxbridge, Middlesex	Maidstone, Kent
43	Newman, John	31 Aug 1555	B	Possessed incriminating letters	Pewterer	Edmund Tyrrel	Edmund Bonner, BP London	Saffron Walden, Essex	Maidstone, Kent
44	Patchingham, Patrick	c. 28 Aug 1555	B	U	U	U	Edmund Bonner, BP London	Uxbridge, Middlesex	Southwark[5]
45	Coker, William	23 Aug 1555	B	U	U	U	Richard Thornden, BP Dover	Canterbury, Kent	U
46	Hopper, William	23 Aug 1555	B	U	U	U	Richard Thornden, BP Dover	Canterbury, Kent	Cranbrook, Kent
47	Laurence, Henry	23 Aug 1555	B	Failure to display reverence to the sacrament	U	U	Richard Thornden, BP Dover	Canterbury, Kent	U
48	Colliar, Richard	23 Aug 1555	B	U	U	U	Richard Thornden, BP Dover	Canterbury, Kent	U
49	Wright, Richard	23 Aug 1555	B	U	U	U	Richard Thornden, BP Dover	Canterbury, Kent	Ashford, Kent

No.	Name	Date	B/P	Charge	Occupation	Accuser	Bishop/Examiner	Place	Residence
50	Stere, William	23 Aug 1555	B	U	U	U	Richard Thornden, BP Dover	Canterbury, Kent	Ashford, Kent
51	Hues (alias Curryer), Roger[6]	24 Aug 1555	B	U	U	U	Gilbert Bourne, BP Bath & Wells	Taunton, Somerset	Taunton, Somerset
52	Warne, Elizabeth [F]	23 Aug 1555	B	Arrested attending a conventicle	Widow (husband burned on 30 May 1555)	U	Edmund Bonner, BP London	Stratford le Bow, Essex	St John Walbrook, London
53	Tankerfield, George	26 Aug 1555	B	Denounced mass	Cook	Thomas Beard	Edmund Bonner, BP London	St Albans, Herts.	London
54	Smith, Robert	8 Aug 1555	B	U	Clerk	Privy council	Edmund Bonner, BP London	Uxbridge, Middlesex	Windsor, Berks
55	Harwood, Stephen	Aug 1555	B	U	Brewer	U	Edmund Bonner, BP London	Stratford le Bow, Essex	U
56	Fust, Thomas	Aug 1555	B	Denied the Real Presence[7]	Hosier	U	Edmund Bonner, BP London	Ware, Herts	St Brides, London
57	Hale, William	Late Aug 1555	B	U	U	U	Edmund Bonner, BP London	Barnet, Herts	Thorpe-le-Soken, Essex
58	King, George	After 2 July 1555	P	U	U	U	None	Lollard's Tower, London	U

	Name	Date of death	Manner of death	Reason for arrest	Occupation	Instigator(s) of arrest	Official condemning	Place of death	Origin
59	Leyes, Thomas	After 2 July 1555	P	U	U	U	None	Lollard's Tower, London	Thorpe-le-Soken, Essex
60	Andrew, William	After 12 July 1555	P	U	Carpenter	Lord Rich	None	Newgate	Thorpe-le-Soken, Essex
61	Samuel, Robert	31 Aug 1555	B	Ex-priest caught secretly visiting his wife	Curate	William Foster	John Hopton, BP Norwich	Ipswich, Suffolk	East Bergholt, Suffolk; Ipswich, Suffolk
62	Allen, William	Early Sept 1555	B	Refused to follow cross in procession	Labourer, servant	U	John Hopton, BP Norwich	Walsingham, Suffolk	Somerton, Suffolk
63	Coo, Roger	Sept 1555	B	U	Shearman	U	John Hopton, BP Norwich	Yoxford, Suffolk	Long Melford, Suffolk
64	Cob, Thomas	Sept 1555	B	U	Butcher	U	John Hopton, BP Norwich	Thetford, Norfolk	Haverhill, Suffolk
65	Catmer, George	6 Sept 1555	B	U	U	U	Richard Thornden, BP Dover	Canterbury, Kent	Hythe, Kent
66	Streater, Robert	6 Sept 1555	B	U	U	U	Richard Thornden, BP Dover	Canterbury, Kent	Hythe, Kent

67	Burward, Anthony	6 Sept 1555	B	U	U	U	Richard Thornden, BP Dover	Canterbury, Kent	Isle of Thanet, Kent
68	Brodbridge, George	6 Sept 1555	B	U	U	U	Richard Thornden, BP Dover	Canterbury, Kent	Bromfield, Kent
69	Tutty, James	6 Sept 1555	B	U	U	U	Richard Thornden, BP Dover	Canterbury, Kent	Brenchley, Kent
70	Glover, Robert	19 Sept 1555	B	Arrested as outspoken local Protestant	Gentleman	Ralph Baynes, BP Lichfield	Ralph Baynes, BP Lichfield	Coventry, Warks	Baxterley, Warks
71	Bungey, Cornelius	19 Sept 1555	B	U	Capper	U	Ralph Baynes, BP Lichfield	Coventry, Warks	Coventry, Warks
72	Haywood, Thomas	Sept 1555	B	U	U	U	Ralph Baynes, BP Lichfield	Lichfield, Staffs	U
73	Goreway, John	Sept 1555	B	U	U	U	Ralph Baynes, BP Lichfield	Lichfield, Staffs	Coventry, Warks
74	Tingle, ?	Sept 1555[8]	P	U	U	U	None	Newgate prison, London	U
75	Wolsey, William	16 Oct 1555	B	Denounced mass, failed to attend church[9]	Constable	Richard Everard	John Fuller, CH Ely	Ely, Cambs	Wisbech, Cambs

	Name	Date of death	Manner of death	Reason for arrest	Occupation	Instigator(s) of arrest	Official condemning	Place of death	Origin
76	Pygott, Robert	16 Oct 1555	B	Failed to attend church[10]	Painter	Informers; Sir Clement Higham	John Fuller, CH Ely	Ely, Cambs	Wisbech, Cambs
77	Latimer, Hugh	16 Oct 1555	B	Arrested as a leading Edwardine cleric	Preacher, former bishop	Privy council	John White, BP Lincoln; James Brookes, BP Gloucester; John Holyman, BP Bristol	Oxford	Baxterley, Warks
78	Ridley, Nicholas	16 Oct 1555	B	Treason	Bishop of London	Privy council	John White, BP Lincoln; James Brookes, BP Gloucester; John Holyman, BP Bristol	Oxford	London
79	Webbe, John[11]	30 Nov 1555	B	U	Gentleman	U	Richard Thornden, BP Dover, or Harpsfield	Canterbury, Kent	U
80	Roper, George	30 Nov 1555	B	U	U	U	Richard Thornden, BP Dover or Harpsfield	Canterbury, Kent	U

#	Name	Date	Cat.	Offence	Occupation	Accuser	Condemned by	Place of execution	Origin
81	Parke, Gregory	30 Nov 1555	B	U	U	U	Richard Thornden, BP Dover or Harpsfield	Canterbury, Kent	U
82	Gore, James[12]	7 Dec 1555	P	U	U	U	None	Colchester Prison	Essex?
83	Wiseman, William	13 Dec 1555	P	U	Clothworker	U	None	Lollards' Tower, London	London
84	Philpot, John	18 Dec 1555	B	Wrote an anti-Catholic account of 1553 convocation	AD of Winchester	Stephen Gardiner, Lord Chancellor	Edmund Bonner, BP London	Smithfield, London	Hampshire
85	Whittle, Thomas	27 Jan 1556[13]	B	Clandestine preaching, retracted his recantation	Vicar of Kirkby-le-Soken[14]	Informer	Edmund Bonner, BP London	Smithfield, London	Kirkby-le-Soken, Essex
86	Green, Bartlet	27 Jan 1556	B	Distributing seditious literature[15]	Lawyer of Inner Temple	Privy council	Edmund Bonner, BP London	Smithfield, London	St Michael's Basinghall, London
87	Brown, Robert	27 Jan 1556	B	Failure to attend church	U	Constable of St Bride's	Edmund Bonner, BP London	Smithfield, London	St Brides, London
88	Tudson, John	27 Jan 1556	B	U	Apprentice	Sir Roger Cholmley, Dr John Story	Edmund Bonner, BP London	Smithfield, London	St Mary Botolph, London
89	Went, John	27 Jan 1556	B	U	Shearman	U	Edmund Bonner, BP London	Smithfield, London	Langham, Essex

	Name	Date of death	Manner of death	Reason for arrest	Occupation	Instigator(s) of arrest	Official condemning	Place of death	Origin
90	Foster, Isabel [F]	27 Jan 1556	B	U[16]	Wife of a cutler	U	Edmund Bonner, BP London	Smithfield, London	St Brides, London
91	Lashford, Joan [F]	27 Jan 1556	B	Arrested visiting her parents in prison	Unmarried	U	Edmund Bonner, BP London	Smithfield, London	All Hallows the Less, London
92	Lomes, John	31 Jan 1556	B	U	U	U	Richard Fawcet, Canon	Canterbury, Kent	Tenterden, Kent
93	Snoth, Ages [F]	31 Jan 1556	B	U	Widow	U	Richard Fawcet, Canon	Canterbury, Kent	Smarden, Kent
94	Albright, Anne [F]	31 Jan 1556	B	U	U	U	Richard Fawcet, Canon	Canterbury, Kent	U
95	Sole, Joan [F]	31 Jan 1556	B	U	Wife	U	Richard Fawcet, Canon	Canterbury, Kent	Horton, Kent
96	Catmer, Joan [F]	31 Jan 1556	B	U	Widow of George Catmer	U	Richard Fawcet, Canon	Canterbury, Kent	Hythe, Kent
97	Potten, Agnes [F]	19 Feb 1556	B	U	Wife of Richard Potten	U	John Hopton, BP Norwich	Ipswich, Suffolk	Ipswich, Suffolk

241

98	Trunchfield, Joan [F]	19 Feb 1556	B	U	Wife of Michael Trunchfield	U	John Hopton, BP Norwich	Ipswich, Suffolk	Ipswich, Suffolk
99	Cranmer, Thomas	21 Mar 1556	B	Treason	Archbishop of Canterbury	Privy council	Thomas Thirlby, BP Ely; Edmund Bonner, BP London	Oxford	Canterbury, Kent
100	Maundrel, John	24 Mar 1556	B	Publicly denounced Catholic 'idolatry'	Husbandman	Vicar	William Geffre, CH Salisbury	Somewhere between Salisbury & Wilton	Wiltshire
101	Coberly, William	24 Mar 1556	B	Publicly denounced Catholic 'idolatry'	Tailor	Vicar	William Geffre, CH Salisbury	Somewhere between Salisbury & Wilton	Salisbury
102	Spicer, John	24 Mar 1556	B	Publicly denounced Catholic 'idolatry'	Mason	Vicar	William Geffre, CH Salisbury	Somewhere between Salisbury & Wilton	Salisbury
103	Harpole, John	1 April 1556	B	U	U	U	Maurice Griffith, BP Rochesters	Rochester, Kent, Kent	Tonbridge, Kent[17]
104	Beach, Joan [F]	1 April 1556	B	Denounced by fellow parishioners	Widow	U	Maurice Griffith, BP Rochester	Rochester, Kent, Kent	Tonbridge, Kent
105	Hullier, John	c. 2 April 1556	B	Quarrelled publicly over religion with Catholics	Curate	U	John Fuller, CH Ely	Cambridge	Babraham, Cambs

	Name	Date of death	Manner of death	Reason for arrest	Occupation	Instigator(s) of arrest	Official condemning	Place of death	Origin
106	Tyms, William	24 April 1556	B	Preached at a conventicle	Curate	Lord Rich	Edmund Bonner, BP London	Smithfield, London	Hockley, Essex
107	Drakes, Robert	24 April 1556	B	U	Rector	Lord Rich	Edmund Bonner, BP London	Smithfield, London	Thundersley, Essex
108	Spurge, Richard	24 April 1556	B	Failure to attend church	Shearman	Lord Rich	Edmund Bonner, BP London	Smithfield, London	Bocking, Essex
109	Spurge, Thomas	24 April 1556	B	U	Fuller		Edmund Bonner, BP London	Smithfield, London	Bocking, Essex
110	Ambrose, George	24 April 1556	B	U	Fuller	U	Edmund Bonner, BP London	Smithfield, London	Essex
111	Cavel, John	24 April 1556	B	U	Weaver	U	Edmund Bonner, BP London	Smithfield, London	Essex
112	Lyster, Christopher	28 April 1556	B	U	Husbandman	Earl of Oxford	Edmund Bonner, BP London	Colchester, Essex	Dagenham, Essex
113	Mace, John	28 April 1556	B	U	Apothecary	U	Edmund Bonner, BP London	Colchester, Essex	Colchester, Essex
114	Spencer, John	28 April 1556	B	U	Weaver	U	Edmund Bonner, BP London	Colchester, Essex	Colchester, Essex

No.	Name	Date		Status	Occupation	Accuser	Condemned by		
115	Joyne, Simon	28 April 1556	B	U	Sawyer		Edmund Bonner, BP London	Colchester, Essex	Colchester, Essex
116	Nichols, Richard	28 April 1556	B	U	Weaver		Edmund Bonner, BP London	Colchester, Essex	Colchester, Essex
117	Hammond, John	28 April 1556	B	U	Tanner		Edmund Bonner, BP London	Colchester, Essex	Colchester, Essex
118	Laverock, Hugh	15 May 1556	B	U	Painter		Edmund Bonner, BP London	Stratford le Bow, Essex	All Hallows Barking, London
119	Apprice, John	15 May 1556	B	U	Clothworker		Edmund Bonner, BP London	Stratford le Bow, Essex	St Thomas Apostle, London
120	Drowry, Thomas	15 May 1556	B	Relapsed heretic[18]	None as he was blind		John Williams, CH Gloucester	Gloucester	Gloucester
121	Crocket, John[19]	15 May 1556	B	U	Bricklayer		John Williams, CH Gloucester	Gloucester	Highnam, Glos[20]
122	Hut, Katherine [F]	16 May 1556	B	U	Widow	Sir John Mordaunt, Edmund Tyrrel	Edmund Bonner, BP London	Smithfield, London	Bocking, Essex
123	Thackvel, Elizabeth [F]	16 May 1556	B	U		Sir John Mordaunt, Edmund Tyrrel	Edmund Bonner, BP London	Smithfield, London	Great Burstead, Essex
124	Horns, Joan [F]	16 May 1556	B	U		Sir John Mordaunt, Edmund Tyrrel	Edmund Bonner, BP London	Smithfield, London	Billericay, Essex

	Name	Date of death	Manner of death	Reason for arrest	Occupation	Instigator(s) of arrest	Official condemning	Place of death	Origin
125	Ellis, Margaret [F]	Before 16 May 1556	P	Refused to receive the sacrament		Sir John Mordaunt, Edmund Tyrrel	None	Newgate prison, London	Billericay, Essex
126	Spicer, Thomas	21 May 1556	B	Failure to attend church[21]	Labourer	Sir John Tyrrel	Miles Dunning, CH Norwich	Beccles, Suffolk	Winston, Suffolk
127	Denny, John	21 May 1556	B	U	Tailor[22]	Hopton, BP Norwich visitation	Miles Dunning, CH Norwich	Beccles, Suffolk	Earl Soham, Suffolk[23]
128	Poole, Edmund	21 May 1556	B	U	Tailor[24]	Hopton, BP Norwich visitation	Miles Dunning, CH Norwich	Beccles, Suffolk	Needham, Suffolk[25]
129	Slech, William	31 May 1556	P	U	U	U	None	King's Bench, Southwark	U
130	Harland, Thomas	6 June 1556	B	Failure to attend church	Carpenter	U	Edmund Bonner, BP London	Lewes, Sussex	Woodmancoat, Sussex
131	Oswald, John	6 June 1556	B	U	Husbandman	U	Edmund Bonner, BP London	Lewes, Sussex	Woodmancoat, Sussex
132	Read, Thomas	6 June 1556	B	Unspecified disorderly conduct[26]	U	U	Edmund Bonner, BP London	Lewes, Sussex	U

#	Name	Date							
133	Avington, John	6 June 1556	B	U	Turner	U	Edmund Bonner, BP London	Lewes, Sussex	Ardingley, Sussex
134	Whood, Thomas	c. 20 June 1556	B	U	Minister	U	Probably George Day, BP Chichester	Lewes, Sussex	U
135	Milles, John[27]	c. 20 June 1556	B	U	U	U	George Day, BP Chichester	Lewes, Sussex	Hellingley, Suffolk
136	Adherall, William	24 June 1556	P	U	Minister	U	None	King's Bench, Southwark	U
137	Clement, John	25 June 1556	P	U	Wheelwright	U	None	King's Bench, Southwark	Redhill, Surrey
138	Moor, Thomas	26 June 1556	B	Denying the real presence[28]	Servant	Pole visitation	John White, BP Lincoln	Leicester	Holwell, Leicestershire
139	Adlington, Henry	27 June 1556	B	Arrested visiting Stephen Gratwick in prison	Sawyer	Jailor	Thomas Darbyshire, CH London	Stratford le Bow, Middlesex	Grinstead, Sussex
140	Parnam, Laurence	27 June 1556	B	Failure to attend church	Blacksmith	U	Thomas Darbyshire, CH London	Stratford le Bow, Middlesex	Hoddesden, Herts.
141	Wye, Henry	27 June 1556	B	Arrested as servant to Thomas Higbed	Brewer	Lord Rich	Thomas Darbyshire, CH London	Stratford le Bow, Middlesex	Stanford le Hope, Essex
142	Hallywel, William	27 June 1556	B	U	Blacksmith	U	Thomas Darbyshire, CH London	Stratford le Bow, Middlesex	Waltham Cross, Herts

	Name	Date of death	Manner of death	Reason for arrest	Occupation	Instigator(s) of arrest	Official condemning	Place of death	Origin
143	Bowyer, Thomas	27 June 1556	B	U	Weaver	John Wiseman of Felsted	Thomas Darbyshire, CH London	Stratford le Bow, Middlesex	Great Dunmow, Essex
144	Searles, George	27 June 1556	B	U	Tailor	U	Thomas Darbyshire, CH London	Stratford le Bow, Middlesex	White Notley, Essex
145	Hurst, Edmund	27 June 1556	B	U	Labourer	U	Thomas Darbyshire, CH London	Stratford le Bow, Middlesex	Colchester, Essex
146	à Coise, Lyon	27 June 1556	B	U	Merchant	U	Thomas Darbyshire, CH London	Stratford le Bow, Middlesex	Flanders
147	Jackson, Ralph	27 June 1556	B	U	Servant	U	Thomas Darbyshire, CH London	Stratford le Bow, Middlesex	Chipping Ongar, Essex
148	Derfall, John	27 June 1556	B	U	Labourer	Lord Rich, Thomas Mildmay of Chelmsford	Thomas Darbyshire, CH London	Stratford le Bow, Middlesex	Rettendon, Essex
149	Routh, John	27 June 1556	B	U	Labourer	Lord Rich	Thomas Darbyshire, CH London	Stratford le Bow, Middlesex	Wix, Essex
150	Pepper, Elizabeth [F]	27 June 1556	B	Failure to attend church	Wife of a weaver, Thomas Pepper	Constables and aldermen	Thomas Darbyshire, CH London	Stratford le Bow, Middlesex	Colchester, Essex

151	George, Agnes [F]	27 June 1556	B	U	Wife of husbandman, Richard George	Robert Maynard	Thomas Darbyshire, CH London	Stratford le Bow, Middlesex	Possibly Berechurch parish, Colchester, Essex
152	Parrett, Thomas	27 June 1556	P	U	U	U	None	King's Bench, Southwark, Surrey	U
153	Hunt, Martin	29 June 1556	P	U	U	U	None	King's Bench, Southwark, Surrey	U
154	Norice, John	29 June 1556	P	U	U	U	None	King's Bench, Southwark, Surrey	U
155	Bernard, Roger	30 June 1556	B	Failure to attend church	Labourer	U	John Hopton, BP Norwich	Bury St Edmunds, Suffolk	Framsden, Suffolk
156	Careless, John	1 July 1556	P	Unspecified disorderly conduct[29]	Weaver	Mayor of Coventry	None	King's Bench, Southwark, Surrey	Coventry, Warks
157	Palmer, Julins	17 July 1556	B	Incriminating MSS found in study	Fellow, Magdalen College; schoolmaster	Thomas Thackham	William Geffre, CH Salisbury	Newbury, Berks	Coventry, Warks
158	Gwin, John	17 July 1556	B	U	Shoemaker[30]	U	William Geffre, CH Salisbury	Newbury, Berks	U

	Name	Date of death	Manner of death	Reason for arrest	Occupation	Instigator(s) of arrest	Official condemning	Place of death	Origin
159	Askin [alias Roberts], Thomas	17 July 1556	B	U	U	U	William Geffre, CH Salisbury	Newbury, Berks	U
160	Cauches, Catherine [F]	17 July 1556	B	Failure to attend church[31]	Widow?	U	Jacques Amy, Dean of Guernsey	St Peter Port, Guernsey	St Peter Port, Guernsey
161	Massy, Perotine [F]	17 July 1556	B	Failure to attend church	Pawnbroker	U	Jacques Amy, Dean of Guernsey	St Peter Port, Guernsey	St Peter Port, Guernsey
162	Gilbert, Guillemine [F]	17 July 1556	B	Failure to attend church	U	U	Jacques Amy, Dean of Guernsey	St Peter Port, Guernsey	St Peter Port, Guernsey
163	Dungate, Thomas	18 July 1556	B	U	U	U	U	Grinstead, Sussex	East Grinstead, Sussex
164	Foreman, John	18 July 1556	B	U	U	U	U	Grinstead, Sussex	East Grinstead, Sussex
165	Tree, Anne [F]	18 July 1556	B	Failure to attend church[32]	U	U	Richard Brisley, CH Chichester[33]	Grinstead, Sussex	East Grinstead, Sussex
166	Waste, Joan [F]	1 Aug 1556	B	Failure to attend church	Spinner; daughter of William Waster, rope maker and barber	U	Ralph Baynes, BP Lichfield	Derby	Derby

167 Hook, Richard	Aug? 1556[34]	B	U	U[35]	U	George Day, BP Chichester[36]	Chichester, Sussex	Alfriston, Sussex[37]
168 Sharp, Edward	Early Sep. 1556	B	U	U	U	U	Bristol	Wiltshire; Bristol
169 Pencell, Rose [F][38]	18 Sep 1556	B	U	–	U	William Dalby, CH Bristol	Bristol	Bristol
170 Saxton, William	18 Sep 1556	B	U	Weaver	U	William Dalby, CH Bristol	Bristol	Bristol
171 Kurde, John	20 Sep 1556?[39]	B	U	Shoemaker	U	William Brinsley, CH Peterborough	Northampton	Syresham, Northants
172 Noyes, John	22 Sep 1556[40]	B	U	Shoemaker	Francis Nunn	John Hopton, BP Norwich	Laxfield, Suffolk	Laxfield, Suffolk
173 Ravensdale, Thomas	24 Sep 1556	B	U	Shoemaker[41]	U	U	Mayfield, Sussex	Rye, Kent
174 Hart, John	24 Sep 1556	B	U	U	U	U	Mayfield, Sussex	Withyam, Sussex
175 ?[42]	24 Sep 1556	B	U	Currier	U	U	Mayfield, Sussex	U
176 Holden, Nicholas[43]	24 Sep 1556	B	Unliscensed preaching[44]	Weaver	U	U	Mayfield, Sussex	Withyam, Sussex
177 ?	25 Sep 1556	B	U	Carpenter[45]	U	William Dalby?, CH Bristol	Bristol	Bristol
178 Clark, John	Nov 1556	P	U	U	U	None	Canterbury Castle	Headcorn, Kent?

	Name	Date of death	Manner of death	Reason for arrest	Occupation	Instigator(s) of arrest	Official condemning	Place of death	Origin
179	Chittenden, Dunstan	Nov 1556	P	U	U	U	None	Canterbury Castle	Ashford, Kent?
180	Foster, William	Nov 1556	P	Failure to attend church	Labourer	Sir Thomas Moyle	U	Canterbury Castle	Stone, Kent
181	Potkins, Alice [F]	Nov 1556	P	Refused to confess or receive the sacrament	Wife	John Roberts of Cranbrook	U	Canterbury Castle	Stapleherst, Kent
182	Archer, John	Nov 1556	P	U	Weaver	Sir John Guildford	U	Canterbury Castle	Cranbrook, Kent
183	Philpot, John [of Tenterden]	Jan 1557	B	U	U	Nicholas Harpsfield, AD Canterbury	Richard Thornden, BP Dover; Nicholas Harpsfield, AD Canterbury	Wye, Kent	Tenterden, Kent
184	Stephens, Thomas	Jan 1557	B	U	U	U	Richard Thornden, BP Dover; Nicholas Harpsfield, AD Canterbury	Wye, Kent	Biddenden, Kent
185	Kempe, Stephen	c. 15 Jan 1557	B	Refused to receive the sacrament[46]	U	U	Richard Thornden, BP Dover; Nicholas Harpsfield, AD Canterbury	Canterbury, Kent	Canterbury, Kent

186	Waterer, William	c. 15 Jan 1557	B	U	U	U	Richard Thornden, BP Dover; Nicholas Harpsfield, AD Canterbury	Canterbury, Kent	Biddenden, Kent
187	Prowting, Stephen	c. 15 Jan 1557	B	U	Sawyer[47]	U	Richard Thornden, BP Dover; Nicholas Harpsfield, AD Canterbury	Canterbury, Kent	Thurnham, Kent
188	Lowick, William	c. 15 Jan 1557	B	U	U	U	Richard Thornden, BP Dover; Nicholas Harpsfield, AD Canterbury	Canterbury, Kent	Cranbrook, Kent
189	Hudson, Thomas	c. 15 Jan 1557	B	U	U	U	Richard Thornden, BP Dover; Nicholas Harpsfield	Canterbury, Kent	Selling, Kent
190	Hay, William	c. 15 Jan 1557	B	U	U	U	Richard Thornden, BP Dover; Nicholas Harpsfield, AD Canterbury	Canterbury, Kent	Hythe, Kent
191	Final, Nicholas	16 Jan 1557	B	U	U	U	Richard Thornden, BP Dover; Nicholas Harpsfield, AD Canterbury	Ashford, Kent	Tenterden, Kent
192	Bradbridge, Matthew	16 Jan 1557	B	U	Servant to Nicholas Final?	U	Richard Thornden, BP Dover; Nicholas Harpsfield, AD Canterbury	Ashford, Kent	Tenterden, Kent
193	Carman, William[48]	After 18 Feb. 1557, before 6 Oct. 1557	B	U	Ploughwright[49]	U	Michael Dunning, CH Norwich	Norwich, Norfolk	Hingham, Norfolk

	Name	Date of death	Manner of death	Reason for arrest	Occupation	Instigator(s) of arrest	Official condemning	Place of death	Origin
194	Loseby, Thomas	12 April 1557	B	U	U	U	Edmund Bonner, BP London	Smithfield, London	U
195	Ramsey, Henry	12 April 1557	B	U	U	U	Edmund Bonner, BP London	Smithfield, London	U
196	Thirtle, Thomas	12 April 1557	B	U	U	U	Edmund Bonner, BP London	Smithfield, London	U
197	Hide, Margaret [F]	12 April 1557	B	U	Wife of innkeeper[50]	U	Edmund Bonner, BP London	Smithfield, London	London[51]
198	Stanley, Agnes [F]	12 April 1557	B	U	Wife	Lord Rich?	Edmund Bonner, BP London	Smithfield, London	Leigh, Essex[52]
199	Sharp, Richard	7 May 1557	B	U	Weaver	U	William Dalby, CH Bristol	Bristol	Bristol
200	Hale, Thomas	7 May 1557	B	U	Shoemaker	David Harris	William Dalby, CH Bristol	Bristol	Bristol
201	Gratwick, Stephen	28 May 1557[53]	B	U	U	U	John White, BP Winchester	Suffolk	Brighton, Sussex
202	Morant, William	28 May 1557	B	U	U	U	John White, BP Winchester	Suffolk	U

203	King, Thomas[54]	28 May 1557	B	U	U	U	John White, BP Winchester	Suffolk	U
204	Thurston, John	May 1557	P	U[55]	U	Edmund Tyrrel	None	Colchester Castle	Colchester, Essex
205	Bradbridge, Joan [F]	18 June 1557	B	U	–	U	Nicholas Harpsfield, AD Canterbury[56]	Maidstone, Kent	Staplehurst, Kent
206	Appleby, Walter	18 June 1557	B	U	Weaver[57]	U	Nicholas Harpsfield, AD Canterbury	Maidstone, Kent	Maidstone, Kent
207	Appleby, Petronil [F]	18 June 1557	B	U	Wife of Walter Appleby, weaver	U	Nicholas Harpsfield, AD Canterbury	Maidstone, Kent	Maidstone, Kent
208	Allin, Edmund	18 June 1557	B	Read scriptures publicly and preached	Miller	Sir John Baker	Nicholas Harpsfield, AD Canterbury	Maidstone, Kent	Frittenden, Kent
209	Allin, Katherine [F]	18 June 1557	B	U	Wife of Edmund Allen, miller	Sir John Baker	Nicholas Harpsfield, AD Canterbury	Maidstone, Kent	Frittenden, Kent
210	Manning, Joan [F]	18 June 1557	B	U	Wife of Robert Manning[58]	U	Nicholas Harpsfield, AD Canterbury	Maidstone, Kent	Maidstone, Kent
211	Lewes, Elizabeth [F][59]	18 June 1557	B	U	Probably unmarried	U	Nicholas Harpsfield?, AD Canterbury	Maidstone, Kent	U
212	?[60]	18 June 1557	B	U	U	U	U	Suffolk	U

	Name	Date of death	Manner of death	Reason for arrest	Occupation	Instigator(s) of arrest	Official condemning	Place of death	Origin
213	?[61]	18 June 1557	B	U	U	U	U	Suffolk	U
214	Fishcock, John	19 June 1557	B	U[62]	U	U	Richard Thornden?, BP Dover[63]	Canterbury, Kent	Headcorn, Kent
215	White, Nicholas	19 June 1557	B	U	U	U	Richard Thornden?, BP Dover	Canterbury, Kent	U
216	Pardue, Nicholas	19 June 1557	B	U	U	U	Richard Thornden?, BP Dover	Canterbury, Kent	U
217	Final, Barbara [F]	19 June 1557	B	U	Widow	U	Richard Thornden?, BP Dover	Canterbury, Kent	Tenterden, Kent
218	Bradbridge, ? [F]	19 June 1557	B	U	Widow	U	Richard Thornden?, BP Dover	Canterbury, Kent	Tenterden, Kent?
219	Wilson, ? [F]	19 June 1557	B	U	Wife	U	Richard Thornden?, BP Dover	Canterbury, Kent	U
220	Benden, Alice [F]	19 June 1557	B	Failure to attend church	Wife of Edmund Benden	John Roberts of Cranbrook; Sir John Guildford	Richard Thornden?, BP Dover	Canterbury, Kent	Staplehurst, Kent

	Name	Date		Denounced a priest during service; clandestine preaching	Owner of iron forge	Edward Gage	Nicholas Harpsfield, AD Canterbury	Lewes, Sussex	
221	Woodman, Richard	22 June 1557	B	U	U	U	Nicholas Harpsfield, AD Canterbury	Lewes, Sussex	Buxted, Sussex; Warbleton, Sussex
222	Stephens, George	22 June 1557	B	U	U	U	U	Lewes, Sussex	U
223	Maynard, William	22 June 1557	B	Clandestine preaching[64]	U	U	U	Lewes, Sussex	Ashridge, Kent
224	Hosman, William	22 June 1557	B	U	Servant to William Maynard	U	U	Lewes, Sussex	Ashridge, Kent
225	a Wood, Thomasin [F]	22 June 1557	B	U	Servant to William Maynard	U	U	Lewes, Sussex	Ashridge, Kent
226	Moris, Margery [F]	22 June 1557	B	U	–	U	U	Lewes, Sussex	Heathfield, Sussex
227	Moris, James	22 June 1557	B	U	U	U	U	Lewes, Sussex	Heathfield, Sussex
228	Burgis, Dennis	22 June 1557	B	U	U	U	U	Lewes, Sussex	Buxted, Sussex
229	Ashdon, ? [F]	22 June 1557	B	U	Wife[65]	U	U	Lewes, Sussex	Catsfield, Sussex?
230	Groves [or Grover], Christian [F]	22 June 1557	B	U	Wife	U	U	Lewes, Sussex	In the archdeaconry of Lewes, Sussex
231	Ambrose, ?	June 1557	P	U	U	U	None	Maidstone prison	U

	Name	Date of death	Manner of death	Reason for arrest	Occupation	Instigator(s) of arrest	Official condemning	Place of death	Origin
232	Foster, Adam	June 1557[66]	B	U	Tailor	Sir John Tyrell	John Hopton, BP Norwich	Bury St Edmunds, Suffolk	Mendlesham, Suffolk
233	Lawson, Robert	June 1557	B	U	Linen weaver	Sir John Tyrell	John Hopton, BP Norwich	Bury St Edmunds, Suffolk	Bedfield, Suffolk
234	Miller, Simon	c. 13 July 1557	B	U	Yeoman	U	Michael Dunning, CH Norwich	Norwich, Norfolk	Middleton, Norfolk
235	Cooper, Elizabeth [F]	c. 13 July 1557	B	Publicly recanted an earlier recantation	Wife of John Cooper, pewterer	Thomas Sommerton; Bacon	Michael Dunning, CH Norwich	Norwich, Norfolk	Norwich, Norfolk
236	Eagles, George	c. 2 Aug 1557	Hung, drawn and quartered	Preaching sedition; clandestine preaching	Tailor; itinerant preacher	Benjamin Clere	Sir Anthony Browne, JP	Chelmsford, Essex	Colchester, Essex
237	Bongeor, William	2 Aug 1557	B	Relapsed after recantation[67]	Glazier	Privy council	William Chedsey, AD Middlesex	Colchester, Essex	Colchester, Essex
238	Purcas [or Purchase], William [Robert]	2 Aug 1557	B	U	Fuller	U	William Chedsey, AD Middlesex	Colchester, Essex	Bocking, Essex
239	Benold, Thomas	2 Aug 1557	B	U	Tallow-chandler	U	William Chedsey, AD Middlesex	Colchester, Essex	Colchester, Essex

No.	Name	Date			Occupation/Status	Accuser	Condemner		
240	Silverside, Agnes, née Smith [F]	2 Aug 1557	B	U	Widow of Thomas Silverside, priest[68]	U	William Chedsey, AD Middlesex	Colchester, Essex	Colchester, Essex
241	Ewring, Helen [F]	2 Aug 1557	B	Relapsed after recantation[69]	Wife of John Ewring, miller	Robert Maynard	William Chedsey, AD Middlesex	Colchester, Essex	Colchester, Essex
242	Folkes, Elizabeth [F]	2 Aug 1557	B	U	Servant	U	William Chedsey, AD Middlesex	Colchester, Essex	Colchester, Essex
243	Munt, William	2 Aug 1557	B	Relapsed after recantation	Husbandman	Edmund Tyrrel	William Chedsey, AD Middlesex	Colchester, Essex	Great Bentley, Essex
244	Munt, Alice [F]	2 Aug 1557	B	Relapsed after recantation	Wife of William Munt, husbandman	Edmund Tyrrel	William Chedsey, AD Middlesex	Colchester, Essex	Great Bentley, Essex
245	Allin, Rose [F]	2 Aug 1557	B	Relapsed after recantation	Spinner	Edmund Tyrrel	William Chedsey, AD Middlesex	Colchester, Essex	Great Bentley, Essex
246	Johnson [alias Aliker], John	2 Aug 1557	B	34	Labourer	U	William Chedsey, AD Middlesex	Colchester, Essex	Thorpe le Soken, Essex
247	Crashfield, Richard	5 Aug 1557	B	U	Tailor	U	Michael Dunning, CH Norwich	Norwich, Norfolk	Wymondham, Norfolk
248	Frier, Robert[70]	Aug 1557	B	U	U	U	Maurice Griffith, BP Rochester	Rochester, Kent	Tonbridge, Kent[71]
249	Stevenson, Robert[72]	Aug 1557	B	U	U	U	Maurice Griffith, BP Rochester	Rochester, Kent	Stone, Kent
250	? [F][73]	Aug 1557	B	U	–	U	Maurice Griffith?, BP Rochester	Rochester, Kent	U

	Name	Date of death	Manner of death	Reason for arrest	Occupation	Instigator(s) of arrest	Official condemning	Place of death	Origin
251	? [F][74]	Aug 1557	B	U	–	U	Maurice Griffith?, BP Rochester	Rochester, Kent	U
252	Benion, Thomas	27 Aug 1557	B	U	Weaver	A constable of Bristol	William Dalby, CH Bristol	Bristol	Bristol
253	Lewes, Joyce [F]	10 Sep 1557	B	Turned her back as holy water was cast during mass	Gentlewoman	Ralph Baynes, BP Lichfield	Ralph Baynes, BP Lichfield	Lichfield, Staffordshire	Mancetter, Warwicks.
254	Allerton, Ralph	17 Sep 1557	B	Relapsed after recantation; clandestine preaching	U	Lord Darcy; Thomas Tye	Edmund Bonner, BP London	Islington, Middlesex	Great Bentley, Essex
255	Austoo, James	17 Sep 1557	B	Refused to receive the Eucharist	U	U	Edmund Bonner, BP London	Islington, Middlesex	St Dunstan in the East, London[75]
256	Austoo, Margery [F]	17 Sep 1557	B	U	Wife of James Austoo	U	Edmund Bonner, BP London	Islington, Middlesex	St Dunstan in the East, London[76]
257	Roth, Richard	17 Sep 1557	B	Relapsed after recantation; led conventicles	U	U	Edmund Bonner, BP London	Islington, Middlesex	Essex

258	Bongeor, Anges [F]	17 Sep 1557	B	U	Wife of Richard Bongeor, a currier of Colchester	U	William Chedsey, AD Middlesex	Colchester, Essex	Colchester, Essex
259	Thurston, Margaret [F]	17 Sep 1557	B	At Munt house when they were arrested; withdrew recantation.	Wife of John Thurston of Colchester	U	William Chedsey, AD Middlesex	Colchester, Essex	Colchester, Essex
260	Ormes, Cecily [F]	23 Sep 1557	B	Demonstrated in support of Simon Miller and Elizabeth Cooper at their burning	Wife of Edmund Ormes, weaver; daughter of a tailor	John Corbet (a Norwich alderman)	Michael Dunning, CH Norwich	Norwich, Norfolk	Norwich, Norfolk
261	Spurdance, Thomas	Nov 1557	B	U	Royal servant	Robert Gosnald (JP)	Michael Dunning, CH Norwich	Bury St Edmunds, Suffolk	Cottenham, Suffolk[77]
262	Hallingdale, John	13 Nov 1557	B	U	U	U	Edmund Bonner, BP London	Smithfield, London	St Leonard's, London
263	Sparrow, William	13 Nov 1557	B	Relapsed after recantation; selling 'blasphemous' ballads	U	U	Edmund Bonner, BP London	Smithfield, London	St Leonard's, London
264	Gibson, Richard	13 Nov 1557	B	Refusal to attend mass or confession[78]	Gentleman	U	Edmund Bonner, BP London	Smithfield, London	St Leonard's, London
265	Rough, John	22 Dec 1557	B	Leader of the largest conventicle in London	Minister, ex-Dominican	Roger Sergeant; Sir Henry Jerningham	Edmund Bonner, BP London	Smithfield, London	London

	Name	Date of death	Manner of death	Reason for arrest	Occupation	Instigator(s) of arrest	Official condemning	Place of death	Origin
266	Mearing, Margaret [F]	22 Dec 1557	B	Member of Rough's conventicle	Wife of James Mearing, London cobbler	U	Edmund Bonner, BP London	Smithfield, London	Aldgate, London
267	Lawton, Robert[79]	Feb or March 1558	B	U	U	U	Thomas Watson, BP Lincoln	Huntingdon	U
268	Dale, John	March 1558?	P	Denounced celebration of mass	Weaver	John Nowell (rector of Hadleigh)	None	Bury St Edmunds' jail	Hadleigh, Suffolk
269	Simpson, Cuthbert	c. 28 March 1558	B	Deacon of Rough's conventicle	Tailor	Roger Sergeant; Sir Henry Jerningham	Edmund Bonner, BP London	Smithfield, London	London
270	Foxe, Hugh	c. 28 March 1558	B	Member of Rough's conventicle	Hosier	Roger Sergeant; Sir Henry Jerningham	Edmund Bonner, BP London	Smithfield, London	Wood Street, London
271	Devenish, John	c. 28 March 1558	B	Member of Rough's conventicle	Wool winder[80]	Roger Sergeant; Sir Henry Jerningham	Edmund Bonner, BP London	Smithfield, London	London
272	Nichol, William	9 April 1558	B	Publicly denouncing Catholicism	U	U	U	Haverfordwest, Pembs	U
273	Seamen, William	19 May 1558	B	U	Husbandman	Sir John Tyrrel	John Hopton, BP Norwich	Norwich, Norfolk	Mendlesham, Suffolk

	Name	Date		Reason		Arrested by	Examiner	Imprisoned/Executed	Origin
274	Hudson, Thomas[81]	19 May 1558	B	Refused to attend mass	Glover	Berry (vicar of Aylsham, Norfolk)	John Hopton, BP Norwich	Norwich, Norfolk	Aylsham, Norfolk
275	Carman, Richard[82]	19 May 1558	B	Demonstrated support for Richard Crashfield at his execution	U	U	John Hopton, BP Norwich	Norwich, Norfolk	Raydon, Suffolk
276	Harris, William	26 May 1558	B	U	U	U	William Chedsey, AD Middlesex	Colchester, Essex	Colchester, Essex?
277	Day, Richard	26 May 1558	B	U	U	U	William Chedsey, AD Middlesex	Colchester, Essex	U
278	George, Christian [F]	26 May 1558	B	U	Wife of Richard George, husbandman	U	William Chedsey, AD Middlesex	Colchester, Essex	Berechurch parish, Colchester, Essex?
279	Wythers, Matthew	Early June 1558	P	Arrested attending a conventicle	U	Islington, Middlesex town constable	None	Newgate prison, London	U
280	Tyler, Thomas[83]	Early June 1558	P	Arrested attending a conventicle	U	Islington, Middlesex town constable	None	Newgate prison, London	U
281	Pond, Henry	27 June 1558	B	Arrested attending a conventicle	Saddler[84]	Islington, Middlesex town constable	Edmund Bonner, BP London	Smithfield, London	U
282	Eastland, Reinald	27 June 1558	B	Arrested attending a conventicle	U	Islington, Middlesex town constable	Edmund Bonner, BP London	Smithfield, London	U

	Name	Date of death	Manner of death	Reason for arrest	Occupation	Instigator(s) of arrest	Official condemning	Place of death	Origin
283	Southam, Robert	27 June 1558	B	Arrested attending a conventicle	U	Islington, Middlesex town constable	Edmund Bonner, BP London	Smithfield, London	St Dunstan in the West, London
284	Ricarby, Matthew	27 June 1558	B	Arrested attending a conventicle	U	Islington, Middlesex town constable	Edmund Bonner, BP London	Smithfield, London	U
285	Floyd, John	27 June 1558	B	Arrested attending a conventicle	U	Islington, Middlesex town constable	Edmund Bonner, BP London	Smithfield, London	U
286	Holiday, John	27 June 1558	B	Arrested attending a conventicle	U	Islington, Middlesex town constable	Edmund Bonner, BP London	Smithfield, London	U
287	Holland, Roger	27 June 1558	B	Arrested attending a conventicle	Merchant tailor	Islington, Middlesex town constable	Edmund Bonner, BP London	Smithfield, London	London
288	Yeoman, Richard	10 July 1558	B	Clandestine preaching	Curate of Hadleigh, Suffolk	Sir Thomas Moyle, John Nowell	John Hopton, BP Norwich	Norwich, Norfolk	Hadleigh, Suffolk
289	Milles, Robert	14 July 1558	B	Arrested attending a conventicle	U	Islington town constable	William Darbyshire, CH London	Brentford, Middlesex	London
290	Cotton, Stephen	14 July 1558	B	Arrested attending a conventicle	U	Islington town constable	William Darbyshire, CH London	Brentford, Middlesex	London?
291	Dynes, Robert	14 July 1558	B	Arrested attending a conventicle	U	Islington town constable	William Darbyshire, CH London	Brentford, Middlesex	London?

292	Wight, Stephen	14 July 1558	B	Arrested attending a conventicle	U	Islington town constable	William Darbyshire, CH London	Brentford, Middlesex	London?
293	Slade, John	14 July 1558	B	Arrested attending a conventicle	U	Islington town constable	William Darbyshire, CH London	Brentford, Middlesex	London?
294	Pikes, William	14 July 1558	B	Arrested attending a conventicle	U	Islington town constable	William Darbyshire, CH London	Brentford, Middlesex	Ipswich, Suffolk
295	Cooke, John	Beg. Aug 1558	B	U	Sawyer	U	John Hopton, BP Norwich	Bury St Edmunds, Suffolk	Stoke Nayland, Suffolk[85]
296	Miles [alias Plummer], Robert	Beg. Aug 1558	B	U	Shearman	U	John Hopton, BP Norwich	Bury St Edmunds, Suffolk	Stoke Nayland, Suffolk
297	Lane, Alexander	Beg. Aug 1558	B	U	Wheelwright	U	John Hopton, BP Norwich	Bury St Edmunds, Suffolk	Stoke Nayland, Suffolk
298	Ashley, James	Beg. Aug 1558	B	U	U	U	John Hopton, BP Norwich	Bury St Edmunds, Suffolk	Stoke Nayland, Suffolk
299	Bembridge, Thomas	5 Aug 1558	B	U	Gentleman	U	John White, BP Winchester	Hampshire	Hampshire
300	Horne, Edward[86]	Sep 1558	B	Refusal to attend mass	Labourer	U	John Williams, CH Gloucester	Newent, Glos	Newent, Glos
301	Snell, Richard[87]	9 Sept 1558	B	U	U	U	John Dakyn, AD East Riding[88]	Richmond, East Riding	Bedale, East Riding

	Name	Date of death	Manner of death	Reason for arrest	Occupation	Instigator(s) of arrest	Official condemning	Place of death	Origin
302	Gouch, Alexander	c. 7 Nov 1558[89]	B	U	Weaver	Francis Nunn	Miles Spenser, CH Norwich	Ipswich, Suffolk	Woodbridge, Suffolk
303	Driver, Margaret [F][90]	c. 7 Nov 1558[91]	B	U	Wife of Nicholas Driver, a husbandman	Francis Nunn	Miles Spenser, CH Norwich	Ipswich, Suffolk	Grundisburgh, Suffolk
304	Humfrey, Philip	Nov 1558	B	U	Tailor[92]	U	Miles Spenser, CH Norwich	Bury St Edmunds, Suffolk	Onehouse, Suffolk[93]
305	David [also Davye],[94] John	Nov 1558	B	U	Shearman[95]	U	Miles Spenser, CH Norwich	Bury St Edmunds, Suffolk	Stradishall, Suffolk
306	David [also Davye],[96] Henry	Nov 1558	B	U	Carpenter[97]	U	Miles Spenser, CH Norwich	Bury St Edmunds, Suffolk	Stradishall, Suffolk
307	Prest, Agnes [F][98]	Some time in 1558	B	Left her husband when he tried to force her to attend mass	Wife of one Prest, spinner	U	James Turberville, BP Exeter	Exeter, Devon	Region of Launceston, Cornwall
308	Corneford, John	10 Nov 1558	B	U	U	U	Reginald Pole, Archbishop of Canterbury	Canterbury, Kent	Wrotham, Kent

309	Brown, Christopher	10 Nov 1558	B	U	U	Reginald Pole, Archbishop of Canterbury	Canterbury, Kent	Maidstone, Kent
310	Herst, John	10 Nov 1558	B	U	U	Reginald Pole, Archbishop of Canterbury	Canterbury, Kent	Ashford, Kent
311	Snoth, Alice [F]	10 Nov 1558	B	U	–	Reginald Pole, Archbishop of Canterbury	Canterbury, Kent	Biddenden, Kent
312	Knight [alias Tynley], Katherine [F]	10 Nov 1558	B	U	–	Reginald Pole, Archbishop of Canterbury	Canterbury, Kent	Thurnham, Kent
313	Dangerfield, Joan [F]	U	P	U	Wife of William Dangerfield	James Brookes, BP Gloucester	None	Gloucester Jail	Wotton Under Edge, Glos

Key: [F] denotes a female martyr; B = burned, P = died in prison, BP = bishop, CH = chancellor of a diocese, AD = archdeacon, U = unknown.

1 According to Brice (Register, sig. C1v), one 'Diggil' was burned on 27 March 1555 (no first name or place of execution was supplied). According to Knox (Epistle, p. 110) and Crowley (Crowley Chronicle, sig. 4G2), William Dighel was burned on 28 March 1555 at Danbury. In his first account of the Marian persecution. Rerum in ecclesia gestarum ... Commentarii ([Basel, 1559], p. 428), Foxe stated that William Dighel was burned at 'Dauburiae' on 28 March 1555. In the first edition of the Acts and Monuments (A&M [1563], p. 1238), Foxe changed the location of Dighel's death to Banbury. (Almost certainly, this was a mistake. Danbury, a village in Essex five miles from Chelmsford, is a much more likely scene for an execution early in 1555 than Banbury.) Dighel was not mentioned again in any subsequent edition of Foxe's martyrology. Almost certainly this omission was inadvertent and William Dighel belongs in the list of martyrs.

2 In the first edition of the A&M Foxe had a brief account of a 'John Awcock' dying in prison on 2 April 1555 (A&M [1563], p. 1117. This account would be reprinted in all subsequent unabridged editions of the work. However, at another place in the first edition, Foxe supplied a very confused account of the ordeals of John Alcock, a shearman of Hadleigh, who was arrested for publicly challenging the vicar of the town. This account inconsistently related in one passage that Alcock was burned at Smithfield and in another that he died in prison. This account also identified John Alcock with the 'John Awcock' previously mentioned (A&M [1563], pp. 1662–3). In the second edition of the A&M, Foxe deleted the second account of Alcock, probably because of its errors and inconsistencies. While this deletion removed the incorrect assertion that Alcock was burned, it also removed the passage identifying Alcock as 'Awcock'. A misleading impression was thus inadvertently created that John Alcock and John Awcock were two different people.

3 See TNA C/85/141/4.

4 A confession of faith was found when Denley was arrested. Eamon Duffy suggests that the confession of faith was being carried by Denley because he had previously recanted and wished to buttress his readiness to die for the gospel with such a document (*Fires of faith: Catholic England under Mary Tudor* [New Haven and London, 2009], pp. 136–7). This gesture would be made by others who were burned, and for precisely this reason. However, there is no evidence that Denley had ever been arrested or even questioned as a heretic. We know that Newman, who was arrested with Denley (Duffy has apparently confused the pair) had previously been examined for heresy; we do not know if he recanted or why he was released at all (*A&M* [1583], p. 1246). This suggests that Denley and Newman were journeying in Essex, where they were arrested, on their way to meet Simpson and Ardley, carrying messages from co-religionists in Kent. They may also have intended to show the confession of faith to Simpson and Ardley for their comments.

5 See TNA C/85/127/11.

6 Foxe never mentioned a Roger Hues or a Roger Curryer. However there is ample evidence that Roger Hues was indeed burned. Brice states that 'Roger Corriar' was executed on 24 August 1555 (*Register*, sig. C3r). Crowley states that 'Roger Corierus' was burned at Taunton on 24 August 1555 (Crowley's *Chronicle*, sig. 4G4r) and Knox concurred with Crowley (*Epistle*, p. 113). On 21 June 1555, Gilbert Bourne, bishop of Bath and Wells, condemned 'Roger Hues or Curryer' of St Mary Magdalen parish, Taunton, as a heretic (TNA C/85/42/7). Moreover the eighth article charged against Richard Lush of Chew Stoke, who was also condemned for heresy on November 1558, reads, 'Item, thou didst affyrme and obstinatlie defend that men burned of late in this realme for heresye, viz. Cranmer, Latimer, Ridlye, Cardmaker, Frythe, and Roger Hues and such lyke …'. (BL, Harley MS 416, fo. 112r).

7 On 12 November 1554, Thomas Fust was summoned before Nicholas Harpsfield (in his capacity as vicar-general of London) and charged with not believing the Catholic doctrines. Fust admitted to not believing in Christ's Real Presence in the Sacrament (LMA, DL/C/614, fo. 4r). Although the court book where this is recorded does not state what happened to Fust, it is very likely that this frank admission of heresy led to his arrest.

8 Foxe mentions that one Tingle, imprisoned as a Protestant, died in Newgate (*A&M* [1583], p. 2075), but he does not say when this happened. The date of September 1555 is given by Knox (*Epistle*, p. 115) and Crowley (*Chronicle*, sig. 4G1v).

9 See Ely Diocesan Records G 1/8, fo. 81r.

10 *A&M* [1583], p. 1715. Pygott admitted that he had not attended church for three months prior to his arrest (Ely Diocesan Records G 1/8, fo. 83r).

11 Eric Ives is incorrect when he identifies this martyr with the John Webbe who was presented to a clerical living by the Marquis of Dorset (Eric Ives, *Lady Jane Grey: A Tudor mystery* (Chichester, 2009), p. 72).

12 In his first edition, Foxe stated that 'James Gore' died in prison on 7 January 1555 (*A&M* [1563], p. 1022). But in the same edition, Foxe also stated that 'James Gore' died in prison in Colchester on 7 December 1555 (*A&M* [1563], p. 1387). Both passages were reprinted in all subsequent editions, which creates the impression that Gorge and Gore were separate people. However, they are almost certainly one person, whose names and dates were taken from different sources and never collated. The December date, after the persecution was well under way is more likely than the January date.

13 Different dates are given for the executions of Whittle, Green and the five others who suffered with them. Foxe states that they were burned on 27 January 1556 (*A&M* [1583], p. 1844) and this date is confirmed by Wriothesley (*Wriothesley* II, p. 132). However, Machyn gives the date as 22 January (*Machyn*, p. 99). A letter from Bartlett Green survives which settles the matter (BL, Additional MS 19400, fos. 63r–64r). The letter is dated 27 January 1556, confirming that, in this instance Machyn is incorrect.

14 Foxe does not indicate what Whittle's living was; this information comes from the writ of Whittle's excommunication (TNA C/85/127/16). Whittle had been instituted as vicar of Kirkby-le-Soken on 18 April 1550 (Newcourt, *Reportorium* II, p. 353). He was deprived for marriage on 23 June 1555 (GL, MS 9531/12, fo. 457r).

15 See P. M. Took, 'The government and the printing trade, 1540–1560' (Ph.D. thesis, University of London, 1978), pp. 279–81.

267

16 Isabel Foster had been warned by the authorities in November 1554 to attend church (LMA, DLC/614, fo. 16v).

17 See TNA C/85/144/34–5.

18 Drowry had already abjured in consistory court in Gloucester on 28 March 1556 (Gloucester Diocesan Records 11, p. 207).

19 Foxe calls him 'Thomas Croker', but the writ of his excommunication states that his name was John Crocket (TNA C/85/203/2).

20 See TNA C/85/203/2.

21 Spicer was described as a relapsed heretic when sentenced, so he must have been arrested for heresy previously (Norfolk County Record Office, Register of Ordinations/1, fo. 15r).

22 NCRO, Reg. Ordinations/1, fo. 15r.

23 NCRO, Reg. Ordinations/1, fo. 15r.

24 NCRO, Reg. Ordinations/1, fo. 15r.

25 NCRO, Reg. Ordinations/1, fo. 15r.

26 Read's arrest was ordered by the privy council in April 1555 because he had been 'the chief mover of a lewd tumult at Waldron' (APC V, pp. 28, 115 and 120). The nature and purpose of this tumult are not stated.

27 On a single page, Foxe refers to this martyr both as 'Thomas' Milles and as 'John' Milles (*A&M* [1583], p. 2024). The sentence condemning Milles survives and gives his first name as John (BL, Harley MS 421, fos. 105v–106r).

28 See John Strype, *Ecclesiastical memorials* (3 vols. in 6 parts, Oxford, 1822), III, 2, p. 390.

29 APC IV, p. 368.

30 Foxe does not supply Gwin's occupation but Knox (*Epistle*, p. 120) and Crowley (*Chronicle*, sig. 4G2r) both describe him as a shoemaker.

31 Cauches and her daughters denied the Real Presence and denounced veneration of the Virgin Mary and the saints along with feast days (D. M. Ogier, *Reformation and society in Guernsey* [Woodbridge, 1996], p. 58).

32 BL Harley MS 421, fos. 109r–110v.

33 BL Harley MS 421, fos. 109r–110v.

34 There is some confusion about when Hook was executed. At one point, Foxe stated that Richard Hook was burned at Chichester about August 1555 (*A&M* [1583], p. 1688). Foxe may have been following Knox (*Epistle*, p. 112) or Brice (*Register*, sig. C2v), who both describe Hook as being executed in Chichester in July. Moreover, this date is apparently confirmed by a list, compiled in Elizabeth's reign, of those burned by the sheriffs of Surrey and Sussex during the previous reign, which has Hook burned when John Covert was sheriff (Folger Shakespeare Library MS L.b.246), and Covert's term of office ended in the autumn of 1555. However, in another place, Foxe notes that Hook was burned in 'Chester' (i.e. Chichester) sometime in 1556 (*A&M* [1583], p. 1954). Both entries were reprinted in all unabridged editions of the *A&M*, further adding to the confusion. The writ of Hook's excommunication (TNA C/85/48/19) shows that he was condemned on 14 October 1555, so he must have been burned after that date, probably in the summer of 1556.

35 Both Knox (*Epistle*, p. 112) and Brice (*Register*, sig. C2v) describe Hook as being lame.

36 TNA C/85/148/19.

37 TNA C/85/148/19.

38 The only direct evidence of her existence is a nineteenth-century work reporting that a seventeenth-century Bristol calendar, which no longer survives, states that a Rose Pencell was burned along with 'William Shapton' on 17 October 1555 (K. G. Powell, *The Marian martyrs and Bristol* [Bristol, 1972], p. 13). This is clearly incorrect; Shaxton

was burned on 18 September 1556 (*A&M* [1583], p. 2149). Yet it is striking that this account not only named the martyr but gave a hitherto unknown name. I suspect that there is some basis for this account.

39 At one point, Foxe declares that a shoemaker was burned at Northampton in October 1556 (*A&M* [1583], p. 1954). Knox (*Epistle*, p. 121), Crowley (*Chronicle*, sig. 4G2v) and Brice (*Register*, sig. C8v) all agree that a man was burned at Northampton; Knox also identifies him as a shoemaker. Later in the *A&M*, Foxe states that he learned from an informant that the shoemaker's name was John Kurde and that he was burned on 20 September 1557. This is followed by a fairly detailed account of Kurde's trial and execution. According to Foxe's informant, the burning was overseen by Sir Thomas Tresham, the sheriff of Northamptonshire (*A&M* [1583], p. 2021). However, Tresham was sheriff in 1555–6, not 1557. The most likely explanation is that Foxe's informant was correct in most of his details, but erred about the date of Kurde's execution.

40 Foxe vaguely states that John Noyes was burned on 22 September of either 1556 or 1557 and arrested the previous April (*A&M* [1583], p. 2021). Foxe also states that John Sulyard was sheriff of Norfolk and Suffolk when John Noyes of Laxfield was arrested (*A&M* [1583], p. 2021). Sulyard was sheriff in 1555–6, so Noyes must have been arrested in April 1556. The condemnation of John Moyes of Laxfield (clearly John Noyes) survives among Foxe's papers and is dated 15 May 1556 (BL, Harley MS 421, fos. 159r–160r). The writ of Noyes's excommunication (TNA C/85/141/19) is, a little confusingly, dated 6 May 1556. Was this an error for 16 May? In any case, all the evidence points to Noyes's arrest and execution taking place in 1556.

41 See note 43 below.

42 See note 43 below.

43 There is universal agreement that a group of men was burned at Mayfield, Sussex, on 24 September 1556, but the consensus ends there. Foxe states that John Hart, Thomas Ravensdale, a currier and shoemaker were burned together at Mayfield (*A&M* [1583], p. 1593). Brice claims that Ravensdale and *two* others were burned at Mayfield (*Register*, sig. C8r). Crowley declares that John Hart, 'Thomas Ravesdale', Nicholas Holden and *two* others were burned at Mayfield (*Chronicle*, sig. 4G2v). Knox may provide the most reliable version of events. He maintains that John Hart, Thomas Ravensdale (a shoemaker), plus an unnamed currier and Nicholas Holden (a weaver) were burned together (*Epistle*, p. 121). Clearly, Hart, Ravensdale and Holden were burned along with an unnamed currier. Only Crowley maintains that there was an additional person burned at Mayfield. This was very probably a mistake and I have not listed this fifth martyr.

44 In April 1555 the privy council ordered Holden's arrest for seditious preaching (APC V, p. 110).

45 According to Foxe an unnamed *carpenter* was burned in Bristol on 25 September 1556 (*A&M* [1583], p. 1593). Knox (*Epistle*, p. 121), Crowley (*Chronicle*, sig. 4G2v) and Brice (*Register*, sig. C8r) all state that an unnamed *glover* was burned at Bristol on 25 September 1556.

46 Strype, *EM* I, 1, p. 443.

47 BL, Harley MS 421, fo. 94r.

48 Foxe does not mention a William Carman. (Foxe states that a 'Thomas Carman' was burned in Norwich, but this was a confusion with Richard Carman: see note 82 below.) Nor do Knox, Crowley or Brice mention William Carman. Yet there is conclusive evidence that William Carman was tried for heresy, condemned and then executed in Norwich. Among Foxe's papers is a copy of the sentence, dated 18 February 1557, against William Carman (BL, Harley MS 421, fos. 157r–158r). The writ of William Carman's excommunication, also dated 18 February 1557, survives (TNA C/85/141/27). Francis Blomefield, an eighteenth-century antiquary, claimed that one of the city court books – still extant in his time, but now lost – contained an entry reading 'Mr Sotherton, sheriff, delyvr'd in court 4 bookes that were one William Carman's an herytyke lately brent, a Byble, a Testament and 3 Salters, which remain in the old Counsail House' (Francis Blomefield, *An essay towards a topographical history of the county of Norfolk*, eds F. B. and Charles Parkin [8 vols, London, 1805–10], III, p. 272). Furthermore among the articles charged against Thomas Wolman of Norwich, on 6 October 1557, was the charge that Wolman had said that 'Carman who was brent for heresye dyed well for that he did affirme and saye that he ded beleve that Christ was not put in

the sacrament of thaltar' (BL, Harley MS 421, fos. 151r and 154r). Although Wolman did not supply a first name for the Carman he was referring to, it had to be William, since Wolman's remark was made before 6 October 1557 and Richard Carman was burned in 1558.

49 BL, Harley MS 421, fo. 157r.

50 Machyn, *Diary*, p. 131.

51 Strype, *EM*, III, 2, p. 2.

52 Essex Record Office Q/SR/12/16.

53 Machyn, *Diary*, p. 137.

54 Foxe does not give King's first name but Knox (*Epistle*, p. 122) supplies it.

55 John Thurston and his wife Margaret were arrested in the house of William Munt (who would be burned in August 1557) by Edmund Tyrell (*A&M* [1583], pp. 2007 and 2009).

56 Harpsfield condemned Bradbridge, Walter and Petronil Appleby, Edmund and Katherine Allin, Joan Manning and Elizabeth Lewes (BL, Harley MS 590, fos. 78v–79r).

57 Appleby's occupation is given by Knox (*Epistle*, p. 122) and Crowley (*Chronicle*, sig. 4G3v).

58 BL, Harley MS 416, fo. 132r.

59 Foxe does not give Lewes's last name; it is found in BL, Harley MS 416, fo. 123r.

60 Machyn (*Diary*, p. 139) reports that two unnamed people were burned in Southwark for heresy on 18 June 1557. These deaths are not mentioned by Foxe, Brice, Crowley, Knox or Wriothesley. It is surprising, but possible, that they all could have overlooked a double burning. It is also possible that Machyn confused the date for the burnings of Gratwick, Morant and King on 18 *May* 1557, but if so, it is very surprising that he also got the number of those burned wrong.

61 See n. 59.

62 At one point during Fishcock's examinations, he went so far as to declare that he accepted Cardinal Pole's judgement on the Eucharist (BL, Harley MS 421, fos. 101r–103r). Presumably Fishcock withdrew or recanted this statement.

63 Foxe states that Fishcock, White, Pardue, Final, Bradbridge, Wilson and Benden were tried by an unnamed bishop (*A&M* [1583], pp. 1981–2). This was, considering the jurisdiction, almost certainly Richard Thornden, the suffragan bishop of Dover.

64 See APC V, p. 110.

65 According to Folger Shakespeare Library MS L.b.246, she was the wife of Thomas Ashdon.

66 Foxe states that Adam Foster was burned in June 1556 (*A&M* [1583], pp. 1917–18). However, this must be an error since Foster was condemned on 1 December 1556 (BL, Harley MS 421, fos. 179r–180r) and the writ of his excommunication was dated 3 December 1556 (TNA C/85/141/23). Foster, therefore could not have been executed until 1557, presumably in June.

67 Bongeor was one of 22 prisoners from Colchester who was released after signing a qualified statement of belief in the Eucharist in 1556 (*A&M* [1583], pp. 1973–4). On 17 November 1556, the privy council ordered Bonner to proceed against Bongeor as he had relapsed since his recantation (APC VI, p. 19).

68 Essex Record Office, CR 116/22/6.

69 Ewring was one of 22 prisoners from Colchester who was released after signing a qualified statement of belief in the Eucharist in 1556 (*A&M* [1583], pp. 1973–4). On 17 November 1556, the privy council ordered Bonner to proceed against Ewring as she had relapsed since her recantation (APC VI, p. 19).

70 Foxe does not give Frier's first name, but it is found in the writ of his excommunication; see TNA, C/85/144/36.

71 See TNA, C/85/144/36.

72 According to Foxe, Frier and a woman who was George Eagles's sister, were the only people burned in Rochester in August 1557 (A&M [1583], p. 2012). In fact, Foxe never mentions Robert Stevenson at all. Although Brice has two women and Frier burned in Rochester in August 1557, he agrees with Foxe in presenting Frier as the only male burned in the city that month (Register, sig. D2v). However, Crowley and Knox state that Frier was burned along with another man as well as two women on 20 August 1557 (Crowley's Chronicle, sig. 4G3v and Epistle, p. 124). The inconsistencies remain, but the writ, dated 11 June 1557, providing notification of the excommunications of both Robert Frier and Robert Stevenson, survives (TNA C/85/144/36). Unless Stevenson was released or died in prison in just over two months, Knox and Crowley were correct and Foxe and Brice overlooked him.

73 Foxe states that a woman burned in Rochester in August 1557 was the sister of George Eagles, the itinerant preacher glorified by Foxe as a martyr (A&M [1583], p. 2012).

74 Foxe states that only one woman – whom he identifies as George Eagle's sister – was burned in Rochester in August 1557. Brice, Crowley and Knox, however, all agree that two women were burned in Rochester that month (see n. 72). It is quite possible that Crowley and Knox are drawing on – and repeating – the same source, but the addition of Brice's testimony makes it likely that, in this case, Foxe overlooked a martyr.

75 Machyn, Diary, p. 152.

76 Machyn, Diary, p. 152.

77 Spurdance's place of origin is given as Crowfield, Suffolk in the writ of his excommunication (TNA C/85/141/26). The writ also reveals that it was Dunning who condemned Spurdance.

78 Gibson had originally been imprisoned for debt and drew suspicion upon himself by his refusal to attend Mass or receive confession (A&M [1563], p. 1643). Bonner handled this case carefully and from the autumn of 1556 until the autumn of 1557 there ensued a minuet of interrogations, guarded recantations and withdrawn recantations until Gibson was condemned on 6 November 1557. (See A&M [1563], pp. 1640–5 as well as BL, Harley MS 425, fos. 99r and 122r, Strype, Ecclesiastical Memorials III, 2, pp. 46–7 and TNA C/85/127).

79 Foxe does not mention Lawton and neither does Brice. But Crowley states that Lawton was burned in Huntingdon in February 1558 (Chronicle, sig. 4G4v). Knox also states that Lawton was burned in Huntingdon but in March 1558 (Epistle, p. 125). The writ of Lawton's excommunication also shows that on 1 October 1557, Thomas Watson, the bishop of Lincoln, condemned Robert Lawton for heresy and delivered him to the sheriff of Huntington to be burned (TNA C/85/116/11).

80 See Knox, Epistle, p. 125.

81 His name is given as Thomas 'Hodgeson' in TNA C/85/141/36 and BL, Harley MS 421, fos. 144r–145r and 147r.

82 Foxe refers to this martyr as Thomas Carman but his name is given as Richard in the articles charged against him (BL, Harley MS 421, fo. 147r), the sentence pronounced against him (BL, Harley MS 421, fo. 144r) and the writ announcing his excommunication (TNA C/85/141/36).

83 Foxe does not supply Taylor's first name; this is given by Knox (Epistle, p. 126), Crowley (Chronicle, sig. 4G5r) and Brice (Register, sig. D4r).

84 Pond's occupation is given by Crowley (Chronicle, sig. 4G5r).

85 The places of origin for John Cooke, Robert Miles, Alexander Lane and James Ashley are given on the writs of their excommunication (TNA C/85/141/25 and 26).

86 Foxe claimed that on 27 September 1556 'John' Horne and a woman were burned at Wotton-under-Edge (A&M [1583], p. 1951). Previously Knox and Crowley had declared that 'John' Horne was burned at Newent in September 1556 and that during that same month, an unnamed woman was burned at Wotton-under-hedge (Epistle, p. 121 and Crowley's Chronicle, sig. 4G2v). Brice, on the other hand, declared that 'John' Horne and a woman were executed together at 'Newton under hedge' on 26 September 1556 (Register, sig. C8r). All of this is confusing enough but it is made more confusing by the fact that while Newent and Wotton-under-Edge are both villages in Gloucestershire, they are at opposite corners of the county. In a letter written around 1638 (probably to one of Foxe's sons), John Deighton, a local informant, stated that Edward (not John) Horne was burned in Newent, not Wotton, and that this happened eight weeks before Mary Tudor died (i.e. in September 1558, rather than 1556). Deighton declared that

he had heard this from Christopher Horne, Edward's son, who was born about three months before his father's execution. Deighton added that Horne informed him that his mother was condemned along with his father, but that she saved herself by recanting (BL, Harley MS 425, fo. 121r). A writ notifying Chancery of the excommunication of Edward (not John) Horne, labourer, of Newent, and Isabella Denye of Wotton-under-Edge, reveals that they were condemned to death on 10 August 1556. Further information, although it is not necessarily reliable, comes from Samuel Rudder, an eighteenth-century Gloucestershire antiquarian, who drew on a manuscript – which no longer survives – then in the possession of the rector of Newent, which related anecdotes concerning the history of the village. According to Rudder, Edward Horne refused to go to Mass and was taken before the bishop of Gloucester. He escaped from detention in Gloucester and returned home, where he remained concealed. However when his child (Christopher?) was baptised, his wife saved a cutting of meat from the feast and sent it to him. This was observed by the midwife, who reported it to the town constable. A search was launched and Horne was discovered and executed (Samuel Rudder, *A new history of Gloucestershire* [Cirencester, 1779], pp. 561–4). A few facts stand clear from this. Horne was burned and his first name was Edward, not John. Beyond this, there is a great deal of confusion, which will probably never be completely cleared away. But reconciling the different accounts, it would seem that Horne was arrested and condemned in 1556, but escaped and was eventually recaptured as described by Rudder. He was then burned in September in 1558. There is no evidence that Horne's wife was even tried, much less condemned or executed. As for Isabel Denye, despite the reports of Brice, Crowley and Knox, there is no evidence that she was actually executed, although she was certainly sentenced to death for heresy. Moreover, Deighton declared that no one was burned for heresy in Wotton-under-Edge during Mary's reign (BL, Harley MS 421, fo. 121r).

87 Whether due to uncertainty or merely garbled syntax, Foxe, in his account of the ordeals of Richard and John Snell, was unclear which one of the two brothers was burned. Fortunately, the parish register for Richmond survives and supplies the exact identity of the martyr as well as the date of his death (A. G. Dickens, *The Marian persecution in the Diocese of York* [2 vols., York, 1957], II, p. 15).

88 Dakyn had been given a commission by the bishop of Chester to investigate and try heresy in the Richmond area.

89 Foxe states that Gooch and Driver were burned on 4 November 1558, and that this was the Monday after All Saint's Day 1558. Actually, 7 November was the Monday following All Saint's Day in 1558. Foxe may have got the date of 4 November from Brice (*Register*, sig. D4v).

90 Foxe gives Driver's first name as Alice, but the writs (there were two) of her excommunication give her first name as Margaret (TNA, C/85/141/37–38).

91 See note 88 above.

92 See TNA, C/85/141/37–38.

93 See TNA, C/85/141/37–38.

94 The writs of excommunication give his last name as Daye (TNA, C/85/141/37–38).

95 See TNA, C/85/141/37–38.

96 See note 94 above.

97 TNA, C/85/141/137–38.

98 Foxe does not give Prest's first name, but their contemporary, the Exeter antiquarian John Hooker (also Vowell) gives her name as Agnes (John Hooker, *A catalog of the bishops of Exceter* [London, 1584], STC 24885, sig. 12v).

Notes

Introduction

1. G. R. Elton, *Reform and Reformation, England 1509–1558* (London, 1977), p. 395.
2. A. G. Dickens, 'The early expansion of Protestantism in England 1520–1558', *Archiv für Reformationsgerichte* 78 (1987), pp. 219–20.
3. Eamon Duffy, *Fires of faith: Catholic England under Mary Tudor* (New Haven, Conn., 2009), pp. 168–70. See the list of martyrs in the Appendix which supports Duffy's point.
4. Christopher Haigh, *English Reformations: Religion, politics and society under the Tudors* (Oxford, 1993), p. 235.
5. W. C. Sellars and R. J. Yeatman, *1066 and all that* (London, 1930), p. 65.
6. See also A. G. Dickens, *The English Reformation*, 2nd edn (London, 1989), pp. 314–5.
7. Andrew Pettegree, *Marian Protestantism: Six studies* (Aldershot, 1996), pp. 152–3.
8. Mark Greengrass, *The French Reformation* (Oxford, 1987), p. 54.
9. For a discussion of this see Alec Ryrie, 'Counting sheep, counting shepherds: the problem of allegiance in the English Reformation' in *The beginnings of English Protestantism*, eds Peter Marshall and Alec Ryrie (Cambridge, 2002), pp. 84–110.
10. John Craig, *Reformation, politics and polemics: The growth of Protestantism in East Anglian market towns, 1500–1610* (Aldershot and Burlington, Vt., 2001), pp. 152–75.
11. Mark Byford, 'The birth of a Protestant town: The process of reformation in Tudor Colchester 1530–80' in *The Reformation in English towns, 1500–1640*, eds Patrick Collinson and John Craig (Basingstoke, 1998), p. 26.
12. See Peter Clark, *English provincial society from the Reformation to the Revolution: Religion, politics and society in Kent 1500–1670* (Hassocks, 1977), p. 100.
13. Michael Zell, 'The establishment of a Protestant Church', in *Early modern Kent 1540–1640*, ed. Michael Zell (Woodbridge, 2000), p. 217.
14. Ryrie, 'Counting sheep, counting shepherds', p. 95.
15. This point is discussed in J. H. M. Salmon, *Society in crisis: France in the sixteenth century* (London and New York, 1975), p. 124.

16. See James D. Tracy, *Holland under Habsburg rule, 1506–1566* (Berkeley, Calif., 1990), pp. 147–75, 200–7; and Alistair Duke, 'Building heaven in hell's despite: The early history of the Reformation in the towns of the Low Countries' in *Reformation and revolt in the Low Countries* (London, 1990), p. 76.

17. William Monter, 'Religious persecution and warfare' in *Palgrave advances in the European Reformations*, ed. Alec Ryrie (Basingstoke, 2006), pp. 284–5.

18. Pettegree, *Marian studies*, p. 153 (both quotations).

19. English Protestants had long associated Catholicism with 'feminine' attributes of irrationality and carnality, and perceived an affinity between the weaker sex and the false religion. See Frances E. Dolan, *Whores of Babylon: Catholicism, gender and seventeenth-century print culture* (Ithaca, N.Y., 1999), esp. pp. 47–60 and 72–76, and Katherine Dean, 'The gendered language of anti-papist polemic in England, 1603–1702' (Ph.D. thesis, University of Cambridge, 2000). For English Protestant constructions of Catholicism as being based on ignorance and carnality, see Peter Lake, 'Anti-popery: The structure of a prejudice' in *Conflict in early Stuart England*, eds Richard Cust and Ann Hughes (London and New York, 1989), pp. 74–7.

20. See Chapters 5 and 11 in this volume.

21. Elton, *Reform and Reformation*, pp. 376, 381.

22. For the assessments of Froude and Pollard on Mary, see Chapter 5 in this volume. Also on Froude, see Eamon Duffy's introduction in J. A. Froude, *The reign of Mary Tudor: Introduced and selected by Eamon Duffy* (London, 2009), pp. 1–21.

23. Dickens, 'The early expansion of Protestantism', p. 220.

24. Loades (1989), pp. 91–2, 266, 320, 327; Loades (1992), pp. 320, 327; Duffy and Loades (2006), p. 26.

25. Peter Mack, 'Elizabethan parliamentary oratory', *Huntington Library Quarterly*, 64 (2001), p. 43.

26. *A&M* [1583], pp. 2098–9.

27. See also Susan Doran, 'Holinsheds' Tudors' in *The Oxford handbook to Holinshed's chronicles,* eds Paulina Kewes, Felicity Heal and Ian Archer (Oxford, forthcoming).

28. R. H. Pogson, 'Revival and reform in Mary Tudor's Church: A question of money', *Journal of Ecclesiastical History* 25 (1974), pp. 249–65, and 'Reginald Pole and the priorities of government in Mary Tudor's Church', *HJ* 18 (1975), pp. 3–20.

29. Jennifer Loach, 'Pamphlets and politics, 1553–8', *Bulletin of the Institute of Historical Research* 48 (1975), pp. 31–44; 'The Marian establishment and the printing press', *EHR* 101 (1986), pp. 135–48.

30. Ann Weikel, 'The Marian council revisited' in *The mid-Tudor polity c. 1540–1560*, eds Jennifer Loach and Robert Tittler (London and Basingstoke, 1980), pp. 52–73.

31. C. S. L. Davies, 'England and the French war' in *Mid-Tudor polity*, pp. 159–85.
32. Jennifer Loach, *Parliament and the crown in the reign of Mary Tudor* (Oxford, 1986), especially pp. 232–5.
33. Robert Tittler, *The reign of Mary I* (Harlow, 1983), p. 83.
34. *The English Reformation revised*, ed. Christopher Haigh (Cambridge, 1987), in particular the chapters by Gina Alexander, Ronald Hutton and D. M. Palliser.
35. Eamon Duffy, *The stripping of the altars: Traditional religion in England 1400–1580* (New Haven, Conn., 1992), pp. 524–64.
36. Haigh, *English Reformations*, pp. 203–18, the quotation is at p. 234.
37. Thomas F. Mayer, *Reginald Pole: Prince and prophet* (Cambridge, 2000).
38. Lucy E. C. Wooding, *Rethinking Tudor Catholicism in Reformation England* (Oxford, 2000), pp. 114–51, and William Wizeman, *The theology and spirituality of Mary Tudor's Church* (Aldershot, 2006), p. 251.
39. *Reforming Catholicism in the England of Mary Tudor: The achievement of Friar Bartolomé Carranza*, eds John Edwards and Ronald Truman (Aldershot, 2005).
40. Duffy and Loades (2006), particularly the chapters by Claire Cross, Eamon Duffy, John Edwards, Thomas Mayer, William Wizeman and Lucy Wooding.
41. Duffy, *Fires of faith*, p. 83.
42. Elizabeth Russell, 'Mary Tudor and Mr. Jorkins', *Historical Research* 63 (1990), pp. 263–76.
43. Russell, 'Mary Tudor and Mr. Jorkins', p. 276.
44. Judith M. Richards, 'Mary Tudor as "sole queene"? Gendering Tudor monarchy', *HJ* 40 (4) (1997), pp. 895–924, and '"To promote a woman to beare rule": Talking of queens in mid-Tudor England', *SCJ* 28 (1997), pp. 101–21. See also 'Gender difference and the Tudor monarchy: The significance of Queen Mary', *Parergon* 21 (2004), pp. 27–46, and 'Mary Tudor: Renaissance Queen of England', in *'High and mighty queens' of early modern England: Realities and representations,* eds Carole Levin, Jo Eldridge Carney and Debra Garret-Graves (New York, 2003), pp. 27–43.
45. J. L. Mcintosh, *From heads of household to heads of state: The pre-accession households of Mary and Elizabeth Tudor, 1516–58* (New York, 2009).
46. Anna Whitelock, *Mary Tudor: England's first queen* (London, 2007), pp. 187, 199.
47. Whitelock, *Mary Tudor*, p. 309. See also her 'Mary Tudor, the first queen of England' in *The rituals and rhetoric of queenship, medieval to early modern*, eds Liz Oakley-Brown and Louise J. Wilkinson (Dublin, 2009), pp. 59–73.
48. Linda Porter, *Mary Tudor: The first queen* (London, 2007), pp. 369–78.
49. Loades (2006), p. 12.

50. Whitelock, *Mary Tudor*, p. 309.
51. Porter, *Mary Tudor*, pp. 74, 102–4, 158, 342–3, 346, 379–80.
52. Loades (2006), pp. 8, 212.
53. Loades (2006), pp. 210–5.
54. Alan Cromartie, *The constitutionalist revolution: An essay on the history of England, 1450–1642* (Cambridge, 2006), p. 91. We would like to thank Paulina Kewes for bringing this passage to our attention.
55. Eric Ives, *Lady Jane Grey: A Tudor mystery* (Oxford, 2009), pp. 86, 78.
56. Andrew Pettegree, 'A. G. Dickens and his critics: a new narrative of the English Reformation', *Historical Research* 77 (2004), pp. 55–7.
57. *The myth of Elizabeth*, eds Susan Doran and Thomas S. Freeman (Basingstoke, 2003).
58. Apart from Judith Richards's work (see n. 44), see Louis A. Montrose, *The subject of Elizabeth: Authority, gender and representation* (Chicago and London, 2006), pp. 43–56, and Paulina Kewes, 'Godly queens: The royal iconographies of Mary and Elizabeth' in *Tudor queenship: The reigns of Mary and Elizabeth*, eds Alice Hunt and Anna Whitelock (Basingstoke and New York, 2010), pp. 47–62.
59. See Haigh, *English Reformations*, pp. 210–16 and William Wizeman's chapter in this volume.
60. See, in particular, Eamon Duffy, 'Cardinal Pole preaching: St Andrew's Day 1557', in Duffy and Loades (2006), pp. 176–200.

1. A 'Sharp Rod' of Chastisement

1. John Strype, *The life and acts of Matthew Parker* (London, 1709), pp. 33–4.
2. *Cooper's chronicle*, fols 373v, 376v.
3. John Stow, *A summarie of Englyshe chronicles...* (London, 1565), STC 23319, p. 238.
4. Crowley's *Chronicle* (1559), sig. Ggggg4. See also William Samuel, *The love of God. Here is declared if you wyll rede that god doth love this land in dede by felynge his rod* (1559?), STC (2nd edn) 21690.4.
5. Edwin Sandys, *Sermons made by the most reverend Father in God, Edwin, Archbishop of Yorke, primate of Englande and metropolitane* (London, 1585), STC 21713, p. 45.
6. Edward Hake, *An oration conteyning an expostulation...* (London, 1587), STC 12608, sig. B3.
7. William Baldwin, *The funeralles of king Edward the sixt. Wherin are declared the causes of his death* (London, 1560), STC 1243, sig. C2.
8. Samuel, *The love of God*, pp. 7–8.
9. Strype, *Life of Parker*, pp. 132–3.
10. Alexandra Walsham, 'A very Deborah? The myth of Elizabeth as a providential monarch' in *The myth of Elizabeth I*, eds Susan

Doran and Thomas S. Freeman (Basingstoke, 2003), pp. 143–68; Peter McCullough, *Sermons at court: Politics and religion in Elizabethan and Jacobean preaching* (Cambridge, 1998), pp. 35–6, 81, 84–8; Patrick Collinson, 'A mirror of Elizabethan Puritanism: The life and letters of Edward Dering' in *Godly people: Essays on English Protestantism and Puritanism* (1983), pp. 302–4; Margaret Christian, 'Elizabeth's preachers and the government of women: Defining and correcting a queen', *SCJ* 24 (1999), pp. 561–76.

11. Strype, *Life of Parker*, p. 95; John Jewel, *Certaine sermons preached before the Queenes Maiestie, and at St Paul's Cross* (London, 1583), STC 14596, sig. K2v.

12. Edward Dering, *A sermon preached before the Quenes Majestie* . . . (London, 1569), STC 6699, sig. A4–5.

13. *Proceedings in the parliaments of Elizabeth I, 1558–1581*, ed. T. E. Hartley (3 vols, Leicester, 1981), I, p. 95.

14. For an alternative viewpoint, see A. N. McLaren, *Political culture in the reign of Elizabeth: Queen and commonwealth 1558–1585* (Cambridge, 1999), pp. 26, 105–33.

15. 'Puritans' like Foxe never defended the right of resistance but did advocate disobedience to unchristian laws and therefore implicitly to the rulers who tried to enforce them. Megan Hickerson, *Making women martyrs in Tudor England* (Basingstoke, 2005), p. 142.

16. Catholic polemic influenced both Thomas Bilson, *The true difference betweene Christian subiection and unchristian rebellion* (London, 1585), STC 307, and John Bridges, *The supremacie of Christian princes* . . . (London, 1573), STC 3737.

17. Bilson, *The true difference*, pp. 511–6. Goodman had indeed retracted his book, excusing himself on the grounds that he had been moved to write by 'the extremity of the time' and certainly did not mean that 'the people of their own authority may lawfully punish their magistrates': John Strype, *Annals of the Reformation and establishment of religion* . . . (4 vols, Oxford, 1709–38), I(i), pp. 184–5.

18. It is worth noting that an investigation was launched into the loss of Calais and some of the men thought responsible were put on trial.

19. Quotations from John Stubbs, *The discoverie of a gaping gulph with letters and other relevant documents*, ed. Lloyd E. Berry (Charlottesville, Va, 1968), p. 47. *Coopers chronicle*, fol. 276r.

20. Hake, *An oration*, sig. B3.

21. John Strype, *The life of the learned Sir Thomas Smith* (Oxford, 1820), Appendix 3, pp. 245–6.

22. *The prose works of Fulke Greville, Lord Brooke*, ed. John Gouws (Oxford, 1986), pp. 28–9.

23. Stubbs, *The discoverie of a gaping gulph*, p. 48.

24. Stubbs, *The discoverie of a gaping gulph*, pp. 47, 74–5.

25. Even Sir Thomas Smith admitted this.
26. Holinshed's *Chronicles* (1577), p. 1767.
27. Lord Keeper Bacon's speech to the 1559 parliament, *Proceedings in the parliaments of Elizabeth I*, I, p. 36.
28. *Proceedings in the parliaments of Elizabeth I*, I, pp. 131–3.
29. Unusually, John Hales did call Mary 'this wicked Athalia' in his hard-hitting 1559 oration to Elizabeth in which he urged her to glorify God and purify his Church. BL Harley MS 149, fol. 147r. Foxe printed the oration in full in the 1576 edition of the *Acts and Monuments*.
30. John Aylmer, *An harborowe for faithfull and trewe subiectes against the late blowne blast concerninge the government of wemen* (London, 1559), STC 1005, sigs D3v, E2, Fv, L2v.
31. Aylmer, *An harborowe*, sig. B2.
32. *A&M* [1583], pp. 1785, 1786 Gardiner is called 'this Vipers byrd' and 'a cruell persecutour'. Bonner is 'bloody Bonner' throughout the text. Foxe did not see Pole in the same light; note, for example his gloss 'Card Poole a Papiste but no bloudy Papist', *A&M* [1570], p. 2158.
33. David Loades, 'John Foxe and the Godly Commonwealth' in *John Foxe: Essays, I* (Oxford, 2001), p. 11.
34. *A&M* [1570], p. 1570.
35. Hickerson, *Women martyrs*, pp. 144–7, 150–4. For the text see *A&M* [1583], p. 2048.
36. *A&M* [1570], pp. 1568, 1569, 1579, 1679 (this particular gloss was a paraphrase of one of Hooper's answers but read as a statement of fact), 1754, 2155.
37. *A&M* [1570], pp. 2297–8.
38. He called Gardiner the 'blouddie tyrant', a 'bloudie, burning' persecutor, 'capitall enimie to ladie Elizabeth' and 'this wretched Achitophell'. Holinshed's *Chronicles* (1587), pp. 1130, 1101, 1159. See also Alec Ryrie and Michael Riordan, 'Stephen Gardiner and the making of a Protestant villain', *SCJ* 34 (2003), pp. 1039–63.
39. *A&M* [1570], p. 2298.
40. Holinshed's *Chronicles*, pp. 1160–2. This passage only appeared in the 1587 edition, and follows closely the words of Foxe in *A&M* [1570], p. 2298.
41. Thomas S. Freeman, 'Providence and prescription: The account of Elizabeth in Foxe's 'Book of Martyrs' in *The myth of Elizabeth*, p. 38.
42. Arthur Golding, *A briefe treatise concerning the burnynge of Bucer and Phagius at Cambridge...* (London, 1562), STC 3966, sig. J2.
43. Bridges, *The supremacie of Christian princes*, p. 223.
44. 'The Queene beyng perswaded of the clergie that she coulde not prosper so longe as she kepte in hir handes the revenew of the churche...', *Cooper's chronicle*, fol. 371v.

45. *The Harleian miscellany*, ed. Thomas Park (10 vols, London, 1818–13), X (1813), p. 263.
46. Richard Bancroft, *Dangerous positions and proceedings* . . . (London, 1640), STC 1345, p. 63.
47. John Clapham, *Elizabeth of England: Certain observations concerning the life and reign of Queen Elizabeth*, eds Evelyn Plummer Read and Conyers Read (Philadelphia, 1951), p. 56.
48. Thomas Broke, *An epitaphe declaring the lyfe and end of D. Edmund Boner* (London, 1569), STC 3817.4.
49. *Coopers chronicle*, fol. 360r. Contrast this with Foxe: 'but Peter Martyr was suffered to returne whence he came', *A&M* II [1571].
50. Richard Grafton, *A chronicle at large . . . of the affayres of Englande from the creation of the worlde, unto the first yeare of Queene Elizabeth* (London, 1568), STC 12147, pp. 1325–6, 1342.
51. *The chronicle of Fabian* . . ., ed. Henry Ellis (London, 1811), p. 714. This incident appeared in other chronicles, albeit without the effusive praise, while Holinshed and Foxe lowered the number to 240. Holinshed's *Chronicles* (1577), p. 1734. *A&M* [1570], p. 1637.
52. Holinshed's *Chronicles* (1587), p. 1732.
53. Grafton, *A chronicle*; *Cooper's chronicle*, fols 374v, 376.
54. Crowley's *Chronicle* (1559), sig Gggg 2–3.
55. *Cooper's chronicle*, fol. 362 r; Grafton, *A chronicle*, p. 1331.
56. Grafton, *A chronicle*, pp. 1331–3; 1336. See also Holinshed's *Chronicles* (1577), p. 1731.
57. Holinshed's *Chronicles* (1587), pp. 1096–9, 1102.
58. 10 February 1559, *Elizabeth I: Collected works*, eds Leah S. Marcus, Janel Mueller and Mary Beth Rose (Chicago, 2000), pp. 56–7.
59. *Erasmus' flores sententiarum* tr. R. Taverner (London, 1540), sig. A6.
60. Lemake Avale (pseud.), *A commemoration or dirige of bastarde Edmonde Boner* . . . (London, 1569). STC 977. The only reference to Mary was when he wrote of 'the daies of Queene Marie' in the sixth lesson.
61. John Prime, *The consolations of David, briefly applied to Queene Elizabeth in a sermon preached in Oxford the 17 November 1588* (Oxford, 1588), STC 20368, sig. B2, B4v.
62. John Rainolds, *A sermon upon part of the prophesie of Obadiah* . . . (Oxford, 1584), STC 20619, p. 28.
63. Thomas Brice, *A compendiou[s regi]ster in metre contei[ning the] names, and pacient suffry[ngs of the] membres of Iesus Christ* . . . (London, 1559), STC 3726.
64. Gyles Godet, 'Brief abstract of the genealogie of all the kynges of England' (1560?), STC 566.07, p. 26.
65. For accessible reproductions see Louis Montrose, *The subject of Elizabeth: Authority, gender and representation* (Chicago, 2006), pp. 59. 65.
66. This quotation is from the 1675 translation: *The history of the most renowned and victorious princess Elizabeth, late Queen of England* (London,

1675), STC [Wing] C362, sig. C2. Earlier translations offer different English wording but the sentiments are similar: see *Annales the true and royall history of the famous empresse Elizabeth* ... (London, 1625) STC 4497, sig. (a)2v. All translations, though, write of Mary's inveterate hatred for her sister.

67. Christopher Lever, *The historie of the defendors of the catholique faith*... (London, 1627), STC 15537, pp. 193–9, 207, 127–8.

2. Her Majesty, who is Now in Heaven

1. John Strype, *Ecclesiastical memorials* (3 vols, London, 1721), III, pp. 465–6. The text of the sermon is preserved in BL, Sloane MS 1578. For the reaction to his use of the phrase 'better a live dog than a dead lion', see *ODNB* 'John White'.

2. White's sermon was sufficiently persuasive to play a decisive part in the conversion of Edward Fenton some 50 years later, as testified in *The responsa scholarum of the English College, Rome*, ed. Anthony Kenny, Catholic Record Society (henceforward CRS), 54–5 (2 vols, London, 1962–63), I, pp. 231, 233.

3. 'Deus bonorum fidem tentare, malorum cogitations patefacere decrevisset', 'Report to Cardinal Moroni on the change of religion in 1558–9 [1561]', ed. J. H. Pollen, *Miscellanea I*, CRS, 1 (London, 1905), pp. 1–47: p. 1 (Latin) and p. 24 (English translation by Francis R. Ward).

4. '[S]i in locum infernorum [vellent sese ipsi] praecipitare', pp. 2 and 25.

5. Nicholas Sander, *De origine ac progressus schismatis Anglicani, liber... editus & auctus per Edouardum Rishtonum* (Cologne, 1585); enlarged edition *De origine ac progressu schismatis Anglicani, libri tres... aucti per Edouardum Rishtonum.... nunc iterum locupletius & castigatius editi* (Rome, 1586, and Ingolstadt, 1588); *The rise and growth of the Anglican schism*, trans. David Lewis (London, 1877; rpt. Rockford, IL, 1988), an English translation of the 1585 edition. This translation will be referred to as 'Lewis'.

6. '[H]ora Satanae & potestas tenebrarum Angliam uniuersam occupauit' ('[Then came] the hour of Satan, and the power of darkness took possession of the whole of England'), fol. 142r in the 1585 edition, p. 359 (1586); Lewis III.ii, p. 233.

7. 'Quando (inquit) tua excellentia suffragium quod antea dabat & debebat Ecclesiae & Catholicae fidei defensioni, commendabat haereticis ad religionis destructionem, non meminit puto, quod sua illustrissima familia & persona per haereticos pene extincta & perdita, per sanctissimae memoriae Reginam Mariam fuerit restituta, atque in hunc excelsum dignitatis gradum quem nunc tenet, euecta; sed quia hoc fecisti, & dilexisti magis gloriam hominum quam Dei, Deus te, reliquamque nobilitatem antiquam huius peccati participem, puniet per istos nouos hominess & haereticos.' Lewis IV.iii, pp. 260–1; fol. 155r–v

in 1585 edition; p. 378 (1586). On Norfolk, see *ODNB* 'Thomas Howard, fourth duke of Norfolk'.

8. Lewis I.ii, pp. 8–9; fols 5v–6r in 1585 edition.
9. Anne Dillon, *The construction of martyrdom in the English Catholic community, 1535–1603* (Aldershot, 2002), pp. 329–37.
10. Nicholas Sander, *A treatise of the images of Christ, and of his saints*, STC 21696 (Louvain, 1567), sigs ******1v–2r.
11. Nicholas Sander, *The supper of our Lord*, STC 21695 (Louvain, 1566), Preface 'To the body and blood of our Saviour Jesus Christ', *ad finem*.
12. Victor Houliston, 'Breuis dialogismus [text, with translation, commentary, and textual notes]', *English Literary Renaissance* 23 (1993), pp. 382–427.
13. Francis Edwards, *Robert Persons: The biography of an Elizabethan Jesuit* (St Louis, Mi., 1995), pp. 27–30.
14. *ODNB* 'Thomas Goldwell'.
15. 'Some correspondence of Cardinal Allen, 1579–85; from the Jesuit Archives', ed. Patrick Ryan, in *Miscellanea* VII, CRS, 9 (London, 1911), pp. 58–61, who suggests Goldwell; the anonymous reviewer of this essay suggests Anthony Kitchin of Llandaff.
16. J. H. Pollen, *The English Catholics in the reign of Queen Elizabeth: A study of their politics, civil life and government. 1558–1580: from the fall of the old Church to the advent of the Counter-Reformation* (London, 1920), pp. 236–7, 285, 332. See also Edwards, *Robert Persons*, p. 45.
17. Anne C. Parkinson, 'The rising of the northern earls', *Recusant History* 27 (2004–5), pp. 333–45, esp. p. 339.
18. Cf. Bodl. MS. Lyell empt. 13, 'A true and plaine declaration of the horrible treasons, practised by William Parry', which includes an apocryphal episode where the pope visits Philip II and encourages him to resume protection of England. This item is described as ' "The seventeenth of November", a poem written by a Roman Catholic shortly after William Parry's execution on 2 March 1585' in the *Catalogue of the collection of medieval manuscripts bequeathed to the Bodleian Library Oxford by James P. R. Lyell*, ed. Albinia de la Mare (Oxford, 1971). See Henry Kamen, *Philip of Spain* (New Haven, Conn. and London, 1997), pp. 72–3.
19. De Feria to Philip II, 21 Nov 1558, *CSPSp* 1 (1558–67), p. 1.
20. J. H. Pollen, *English Catholics in the reign of Elizabeth*, pp. 47–83.
21. Charles Arundel, *The copie of a leter, wryten by a master of arte of Cambridge*, STC 5742.9 (n.p., 1584). For a modern edition with a reliable discussion of the authorship, see *Leicester's commonwealth: 'The copy of a letter written by a Master of Art of Cambridge' (1584) and related documents*, ed. D. C. Peck (Athens, Oh., 1985). The work is often, but probably erroneously, attributed to Robert Persons.
22. *The Ven. Philip Howard earl of Arundel 1557–1595: English martyrs vol. II*, ed. J. H. Pollen and W. Macmahon, CRS, 21 (London, 1919),

pp. 59–60, based on *CSPD* 28, fol. 371b; cf. *Leicester's commonwealth*, ed. Peck, pp. 172–3.

23. *Unpublished documents relating to the English martyrs, Vol. I: 1584–1603*, ed. J. H. Pollen, CRS, 5 (London, 1908), p. 185.
24. BL MS Sloane 1786, item 16, fols 51–2. See also Paul Arblaster, *Antwerp & the world: Richard Verstegan and the international culture of Catholic reformation* (Leuven, 2004), pp. 41–2.
25. T. E. Bridgett and T. F. Knox, *The true story of the Catholic hierarchy deposed by Queen Elizabeth: With fuller memoirs of its last two survivors* (London, 1889), pp. 83–5.
26. *ODNB* 'Edmund Bonner'.
27. Nicholas Sander, 'Report to Cardinal Moroni', p. 39 (English translation). Thanks to Dr Tom Freeman for alerting me to this reference.
28. Thomas Stapleton, *A fortresse of the faith first planted amonge us englishmen, and continued hitherto in the universall church of Christ*, STC 23232 (Antwerp, 1565).
29. Nicholas Harpsfield, *Dialogi sex contra Summi Pontificatus, monasticae vitae, sanctorum, sacrarum imaginum oppugnatores, et pseudomartyres* (Antwerp, 1566).
30. Francis Hastings, *A watchword to all religious, and true hearted Englishmen* (London, 1598), STC 12927; Matthew Sutcliffe, *A briefe replie to a certaine odious and slanderous libel lately published by a seditious Jesuite, calling himselfe N. D. . . . entitled A temperate ward-word* (London, 1600), STC 23453; Robert Persons, *A treatise of three conversions of England from paganisme to Christian religion* (3 vols, St Omer, 1603–04), STC 19416. Persons worked with the 1596 edition of the *Acts and Monuments*.
31. *A treatise of three conversions of England*, II, p. 228.
32. 'The memoirs of Father Robert Persons', ed. J. H. Pollen, in *Miscellanea* II, CRS, 2 (London, 1906), pp. 54–7, 188–9.
33. Arnold Pritchard, *Catholic loyalism in Elizabethan England* (London, 1979), pp. 130–74, Michael L. Carrafiello, *Robert Persons and English Catholicism, 1580–1610* (Selinsgrove and London, 1998), pp. 88–102.
34. John Knox, *The first blast of the trumpet against the monstrous regiment of woman* (Geneva, 1558), STC 15070. See Sharon L. Jansen, *The monstrous regiment of women: Female rulers in early modern Europe* (Basingstoke, 2002).
35. R. Doleman (pseud.), *A conference about the next succession to the crowne of Ingland* (Antwerp 1594, *vere* 1595), STC 19398.
36. 'Pero yo confio en Nuestro Señor que su divina Providencia aya reservado esta empresa gloriosa para V. A.' Robert Persons to Isabella Clara Eugenia, 10 June 1601, in *Letters and memorials of William Cardinal Allen (1532–1594)*, ed. Fathers of the congregation of the London Oratory, introd. T. F. Knox (London, 1882), pp. 394–5.
37. First published as *The Jesuit's memorial, for the intended reformation of England under their first popish prince*, ed. Edward Gee, STC [Wing] P569 (London, 1690).

38. See Stephen Mullaney, 'Reforming resistance: Class, gender, and legitimacy in Foxe's *Book of Martyrs*', in *Print, manuscript, and performance: The changing relations of the media in early modern England*, ed. Arthur F. Marotti and Michael D. Bristol (Columbus, Oh., 2000), pp. 235–51, who argues that Mary Tudor 'seemed oblivious to this aspect of the cultural logic behind the official ritual, and as a consequence aided the Protestant cause by making heresy seem almost an everyday matter rather than an extraordinary one' (p. 241). This seems to me to overstate the case.
39. Andreas Philopater (pseud.), *Elizabethae Angliae Reginae haeresim Caluinianum propugnantis, saeuissimum in Catholicos sui regni edictum ... Cum responsione ad singula capita* (Antwerp, 1592), pp. 215–16. This work was also published in Lyon (1592), Rome and Cologne (1593).
40. See, for example, William Wizeman, *The theology and spirituality of Mary Tudor's Church* (Aldershot, 2006) and Duffy and Loades (2006).
41. See John Edwards, 'Introduction: Carranza in England', in *Reforming Catholicism in the England of Mary Tudor: The achievement of Friar Bartholomé Carranza*, eds. John Edwards and Ronald Truman (Aldershot, 2005), pp. 1–20, esp. pp. 18–19.
42. Works by Luis de Granada included *A memorial of a Christian life*, trans. Richard Hopkins (Rouen, 1586), STC 16903; *Of prayer, and meditation*, trans. Richard Hopkins (Paris, 1582), STC 16907. Robert Persons's influential *First booke of the Christian exercise, appertayning to resolution* (Rouen, 1582), STC 19353, revised as the *Christian directory* (Rouen, 1585), STC 19354.1 and (St Omer, 1607), STC 19354.5, was largely based on the Guia de Pecadores (Salamanca, 1556–7, 1567).
43. See T. E. Birrell, 'William Carter (c. 1549–84): recusant printer, publisher, binder, stationer, scribe – and martyr', *Recusant History* 28 (2006–07), pp. 23–42, esp. p. 34.
44. Antonio de Guevara, *The diall of princes* (London, 1557), STC 12427; (London, 1568), STC 12428; (London, 1582), STC 12429.
45. Donna B. Hamilton, *Anthony Munday and the Catholics, 1560–1633* (Aldershot, 2005), p. 100. Thomas Alfield, *A true reporte of the death & martyrdom of M. Campion Jesuite and preiste* (London, 1582), STC 4537. On Vallenger, see A. G. Petti, 'Stephen Vallenger (1541–1591)', *Recusant History* 6 (1962), pp. 248–64, esp. p. 259.
46. Thomas Stapleton, *A counterblast to M. Hornes vayne blaste against M. Fekenham ... touching, the othe of the supremacy* (Louvain, 1567), STC 23231. See Marvin R. O'Connell, *Thomas Stapleton and the Counter Reformation* (New Haven, Conn. and London, 1964), pp. 154–83.
47. 'Father Augustine Baker's treatise of the English Benedictine mission, 1635–6' in *Memorials of Father Augustine Baker and other documents relating to the English Benedictines*, ed. Dom Justin McCann and Dom Hugh Connolly, CRS, 33 (London, 1933), pp. 155, 159, 178, 181.

48. 'A preface, written by Father Robert Parsons, S. J., to the history of the wanderings of Syon', in Dom Adam Hamilton, *The angel of Syon: The life and martyrdom of Blessed Richard Reynolds, Bridgettine monk of Syon, martyred at Tyburn, May 4, 1535* (Edinburgh, 1905), pp. 102–4, 108–9.
49. 'Father Persons' memoirs (concluded) . . . Punti per la missione d'Inghilterra', ed. and trans. J. H. Pollen, in *Miscellanea* IV, CRS, 4 (London, 1907), pp. 104–7.
50. Persons, *A briefe apologie, or defence of the Catholike ecclesiastical hierarchie, & subordination in England* (Antwerp, 1601), STC 13391.5, pp. 196–7, cited by Edwards, *Robert Persons*, p. 9.
51. Pritchard, *Catholic loyalism in Elizabethan England*, pp. 78–101.
52. 'Bedingfeld papers', ed. J. H. Pollen in *Miscellanea* VI, CRS, 7 (London, 1909), p. 23.
53. 'Erat enim tunc temporis Curia Anglicana schola virtutum, puritatis altrix, domicilium pietatis. Regina ipsa omni virtutum genere instar Lunae splendebat, de cuius laudibus omnes historiae loquuntur; Dominae, ac puellae suae ut stellae rutilabant. . . . O foelicem Aulam talibus Aulicis, & beatam Angliam tali Aula, quae morum honestate vix multis claustris cedebat, & ex qua, tanquam ex fonte riui, in omnes Angliae prouincias pietatis exampla decurrebant. Durasset utinam haec in virginibus nostris Aulicis puritas, ac floruisset ipsius parens Religio Catholica, non ita graui laborasset Aula Angliae lasciuiae infamia.' Richard Smith, *Vita illustrissimae, ac piissimae dominae Magdalenae Montis-acuti in Anglia vice comitissae* (Rome, 1609), pp. 18–19, trans. C[uthbert] F[ursdon] as *The life of the most honourable and vertuous lady the La. Magdalen Viscountesse Montague* (St Omer, 1627), STC 22811, pp. 6–7. See *An Elizabethan recusant house: Comprising The life of the Lady Magdalen, Viscountess Montague (1538–1608)*, ed. A. C. Southern (London, 1954), pp. 12–13.
54. 'John Heywood's ingenious discription of Queen Mary I at 18 years of age', item 30 in BL Harl MS 1703, fol. 108b. This description dates from Mary's reign but is included in the papers of William Forrest (*fl.* 1530–76).

3. The Exclusion Crisis of 1553 and the Elizabethan Succession

1. See, for example, Sir John Harington, *A tract on the succession to the crown (A.D. 1602)*, ed. with notes and an intro. by Clements R. Markham (London, 1880), pp. 101–2.
2. William Covell, *Polimanteia, or, The means lawful and unlawful, to judge of the fall of a common-wealth* (Cambridge, 1595), STC 5884, sigs Dd2v–Dd3r; Sir Thomas Craig, *Concerning the right of succession to the kingdom of England* (London, 1703), p. 44; John Hayward, *An answer to the first*

part of a certain conference, concerning succession, published not long since under the name of R. Dolman (London, 1603) STC 12988, sig. O3r.

3. David Loades, *John Dudley, duke of Northumberland, 1504–1553* (Oxford, 1996), pp. 231ff; Diarmaid MacCulloch, *Tudor church militant: Edward VI and the Protestant Reformation* (London, 1999), pp. 39–41; Dale Hoak, 'The succession crisis of 1553', forthcoming. I am grateful to Professor Hoak for sharing his work with me in advance of its publication. See also Judith M. Richards, *Mary Tudor* (Routledge, 2008), pp. 111 *passim*.

4. Mortimer Levine, *Tudor dynastic problems, 1460–1571* (London, 1973), pp. 83–4 (Levine attributes responsibility for the scheme to Northumberland); Loades, *John Dudley*, pp. 240–1; Hoak, 'The succession crisis of 1553'; Howard Nenner, *The right to be king: The succession to the crown of England, 1603–1714* (Basingstoke, 1995), pp. 4, 44, 57, 21. Cf. Eric Ives, 'Tudor dynastic problems revisited', *Historical Research* 81 (2008), pp. 255–79, which appeared after this essay had gone to press.

5. See, *inter alia*, S. T. Bindoff, 'A kingdom at stake, 1553', *History Today* 3 (1953), pp. 642–48; Hester Chapman, *Lady Jane Grey* (London, 1962).

6. Hoak, 'The succession crisis of 1553'.

7. For an argument that there was support for Jane in the localities, see Robert Tittler, 'The local community and the crown in 1553: The accession of Mary Tudor revisited', *Bulletin of the Institute of Historical Research* 57 (1984), pp. 131–9.

8. See *The copie of a pistel or letter sent to Gilbard Potter in the tyme When he was in prison, for speaking on our most true queens part the Lady mary before he had his eares cut of. The .xiij. of Julye* (London, 1 Aug. 1553), STC 20188.

9. Paulina Kewes, 'Two queens, one inventory: The lives of Mary and Elizabeth Tudor' in *Writing lives: Biography and textuality, identity and representation in early modern England*, eds Kevin Sharpe and Steven N. Zwicker (Oxford, 2008), pp. 187–207; and *Drama, history, and politics in Elizabethan England*, forthcoming.

10. See, *inter alia*, 'The *Vita Mariae Angliae Reginae* of Robert Wingfield of Brantham', ed. and trans. Diarmaid MacCulloch, *Camden Miscellany*, 28, Camden Society, fourth series 29 (1984), pp. 245–50.

11. See Richard Beard, *A godly psalm, of Mary Queen, which brought us comfort all, through God, whom we of duty praise, that gives her foes a fall* (London, 1553), STC 1655; *Narratio historica vicissitudinis rerum* ([Wittenberg,] 1553) translated into English as *Historical narration of certain events that took place in the kingdom of Great Britain in the month of July, in the year of our Lord 1553*, trans. J. B. Inglis, ed. J. Ph. Berjeau (London, 1865).

12. *How superior powers ought to be obeyed of their subjects* (Geneva, 1558), STC 12020, p. 54.

13. John Knox, *The first blast of the trumpet against the monstrous regiment of women*, in *On rebellion*, ed. Roger A. Mason (Cambridge, 1994), pp. 3–47.

14. John Ponet, *A short treatise of politic power, and of the true obedience which subjects owe to kings and other civil governors* ([Strasbourg] 1556), STC 20178, sigs. D7r–D8 r. Ponet stresses Jane's innocence and reluctance to assume the crown.
15. Wingfield, *Vita*, pp. 254 ff.
16. Crowley's *Chronicle*, fol. 296r ff.
17. For an account of the historiography of the coup, see Jesse Freedman, ' "A realm most miserable": John Stow and the succession crisis of 1553' (M.St. thesis University of Oxford, 2007).
18. Patrick Collinson, 'The Elizabethan exclusion crisis and the Elizabethan polity', *Proceedings of the British Academy* 84 (1993), pp. 51–92. See also Mortimer Levine, *The early Elizabethan succession question, 1558–1568* (Stanford, 1966); Stephen Alford, *The early Elizabethan polity: William Cecil and the British succession crisis, 1558–1569* (Cambridge, 1998); Susan Doran, *Monarchy and matrimony: The courtships of Elizabeth I* (London, 1996); Marie Axton, *The queen's two bodies: Drama and the Elizabethan succession* (London, 1977); Henry James and Greg Walker, 'The politics of *Gorboduc*', *EHR* 110 (1995), pp. 109–21; Norman L. Jones and Paul Whitfield White, '*Gorboduc* and royal marriage politics: An Elizabethan playgoer's report of the premiere performance', *ELR* 26 (1996), pp. 3–17; Gerald Bowler, ' "An axe or an acte": The parliament of 1572 and resistance theory in early Elizabethan England', *Canadian Journal of History* 19 (1984), pp. 349–59.
19. On the authenticity of the will, see E. W. Ives, 'Henry VIII's will: a forensic conundrum', *HJ* 35 (1992), pp. 779–804.
20. *A declaration of the succession of the crown imperial of England, made by J. Hales, 1563*, in George Harbin, *The hereditary right of the crown of England asserted; the history of the succession since the Conquest cleared; and the true English constitution vindicated from the misrepresentations of Dr. Higden's view and defence* (London, 1713), STC 17449, pp. xx–xli.
21. *A&M* [1583]: http://www.hrionline.ac.uk/johnfoxe/main/5_1583, p. 1407.
22. On Foxe's views of kingship and the succession, see my *Drama, history, and politics*.
23. *A defence of the honour of the right high, mighty and noble princess Mary queen of Scotland and dowager of France with a declaration as well of her right, title & interest to the succession of the crown of England, as that the regiment of women is conformable to the law of God and nature* (London [i.e. Rheims], 1569), STC 15505, fol. 23r. For a stimulating account of Leslie's pamphlet, see Tricia A. McElroy, 'Executing Mary Queen of Scots: Strategies of representation in early modern Scotland' (D.Phil. thesis, University of Oxford, 2005).
24. Leslie, *A defence*, fol. 55r.
25. 'Sir Ralph Sadler's speech on the succession', in *Proceedings in the parliaments of Elizabeth I*, 3 vols, ed. T. E. Hartley (London, 1981–95), I, p. 86.

There is no certainty whether, and if so when, the speech was delivered; its tenor, however, is reflective of the views shared by the majority in the Lower and Upper Houses (Hartley, *Proceedings*, I, p. 55).

26. Alford, *The early Elizabethan polity*, pp. 112–17, 157.
27. *Select statutes and other constitutional documents*, 3rd edn, ed. G. W. Prothero (Oxford, 1906), p. 60.
28. *Leicester's commonwealth: The copy of a letter written by a master of art of Cambridge (1584) and related documents*, ed. Dwight C. Peck (Athens, Ga. and London, 1985); Peter Lake, 'From Leicester his commonwealth to Sejanus his fall: Ben Jonson and the politics of Roman (Catholic) virtue', in *Catholics and the 'Protestant nation': Religious politics and identity in early modern England*, ed. Ethan H. Shagan (Manchester, 2005), pp. 128–61, at p. 142.
29. Peter Holmes, *Resistance and compromise: The political thought of the Elizabethan Catholics* (Cambridge, 1982), pp. 133–4.
30. Collinson, 'The Elizabethan exclusion crisis', and 'The monarchical republic of Queen Elizabeth I' in *Elizabethan essays* (London, 1994), pp. 31–56; Edward Vallance, 'Loyal or rebellious? Protestant associations in England, 1584–1696', *The Seventeenth Century* 17 (2002), pp. 1–23; David Cressy, 'Binding the nation: The bonds of association, 1584 and 1696', in Delloyd J. Guth and John W. McKenna (eds), *Tudor rule and revolution: Essays for G. R. Elton from his American friends* (Cambridge, 1982), pp. 217–34.
31. Holinshed's *Chronicles*. For discussion, see my *Drama, history, and politics.* A wide-ranging reassessment of the late Elizabethan succession crisis will be appearing in *The question of succession in late Elizabethan England*, eds Susan Doran and Paulina Kewes.
32. *Admonition to the nobility and people of England and Ireland concerning the present wars made for the execution of his holiness sentence, by the high and mighty king catholic of Spain* ([Antwerp,] 1588), STC 368.
33. On Persons's political thought in the *Conference*, see Nenner, *The right to be king*, pp. 33 ff; Holmes, *Resistance and compromise*, pp. 150 ff; Peter Lake, 'The king, (the queen) and the Jesuit: James Stuart's *True law of free monarchies* in context/s', *TRHS*, 6th series, 14 (2004), pp. 243–60.
34. ([Antwerp], 1593), STC 22994, fol. 35v. The *News* was a clever reworking of an earlier Catholic pamphlet, *A Treatise of treasons against Q. Elizabeth* ([Louvain], 1572), STC 7601.
35. Susan Doran, 'Revenge her foul and most unnatural murder? The impact of Mary Stewart's execution on Anglo-Scottish relations', *History* 85 (2000), pp. 589–612; Susan Doran, 'Loving and affectionate cousins? The relationship between Elizabeth I and James VI of Scotland 1586–1603' in *Tudor England and its neighbours*, eds Susan Doran and

Glenn Richardson (Basingstoke, 2005), pp. 203–34; Nicholas Tyacke, 'Puritan politicians and King James VI and I, 1587–1604' in *Politics, religion and popularity in early Stuart Britain: Essays in honour of Conrad Russell*, eds Thomas Cogswell, Richard Cust and Peter Lake (Cambridge, 2002), pp. 21–44; Patrick Collinson, 'The religious factor' in *The struggle for the succession in late Elizabethan England: Politics, polemics and cultural representations*, ed. Jean-Christophe Mayer (Montpellier, 2004), pp. 243–73; J. E. Neale, 'Peter Wentworth: I', *EHR* 39 (1924), pp. 36–54; J. E. Neale, 'Peter Wentworth: II', *EHR* 39 (1924), pp. 175–205; J. E. Neale, *Elizabeth and her parliaments*, 2 vols (London, 1957), II, pp. 251–66; Hartley, *Proceedings*, III, pp. 42–4; *ODNB* 'Peter Wentworth'.

36. *Albion's England: The third time corrected and augmented* (London, 1592), STC 25081, pp. 176–8. It is worth comparing Warner's treatment of Mary with Thomas Chaloner's in his earlier neo-Latin elegy for Jane. Chaloner bluntly asserted that the queen had been providentially punished for her excessive cruelty towards her innocent cousin: see his 'Deploratio acerbae necis heroidis præstantissimæ D. Janæ Grayæ', printed posthumously in *De republica Anglorum instauranda libri decem* (London, 1579), STC 4938, sigs T4v–T6r. I am grateful to Scott Lucas for drawing Chaloner's poem to my attention and to Armand D'Angour for help with the translation.

37. Warner, *Albion*, p. 178.

38. Warner, *Albion*, p. 185.

39. On Wyatt's possible connection to three lost plays (*1–2 Lady Jane* by Henry Chettle, Thomas Dekker, Thomas Heywood, Wentworth Smith and John Webster and the anonymous *The overthrow of rebels*) and to Heywood's *If you know not me*, see Cyrus Hoy, Introductions, notes, and commentaries to texts in *The dramatic works of Thomas Dekker*, ed. Fredson Bowers, 4 vols (Cambridge, 1980), I, p. 311; Mary Forster Martin, '*If you know not me you know nobody*, and *The famous history of Sir Thomas Wyat*', *The Library* 13 (1932), pp. 272–81. For the play's topical commentary on the Essex rebellion, see Julia Gasper, *The dragon and the dove: The plays of Thomas Dekker* (Oxford, 1990), pp. 44–61.

40. *The famous history of Sir Thomas Wyatt with the coronation of Queen Mary, and the coming in of King Philip* (London, 1607), STC 6537, sigs B2v, A3v.

41. *Sir Thomas Wyatt*, sigs B1r, A3v.

42. *Sir Thomas Wyatt*, sig. B3r.

43. *Correspondence of King James VI of Scotland with Sir Robert Cecil and others in England, during the reign of queen Elizabeth. With an appendix containing papers illustrative of transactions between king James and Robert, earl of Essex*, ed. John Bruce, Camden Society, original series 78 (London, 1861), pp. 5, 6, 7, 8. Alexander Courtney has provided a compelling corrective

to earlier assessments of the Cecil–James correspondence, showing that Cecil was hardly an all-powerful mastermind behind the Stuart succession. See his 'The accession of James VI to the English throne, 1601–1603', unpublished M. Phil. thesis (University of Cambridge, 2004). I am grateful to Mr Courtney for sending me a copy of his thesis.

4. 'Thus Like a Nun, Not Like a Princess Born'

1. [John Reynolds], *Vox coeli or Newes from heaven*, written by S. R. N. T. (Elisium [i.e. London]: n. p., 1624), STC 22094. Margot Heinemann notes that the STC attribution of this work to Thomas Scott is a mistake (*Renaissance Quarterly* 41 (1988), pp. 352–6 (pp. 355–6). As she points out, the anonymous nature of the pamphlet did not protect its author from the two years' imprisonment which was his reward for being too outspoken with regard to royal policy in this and another pamphlet, *Votivae Angliae: ODNB* 'Reynolds, John (b. *c.* 1588, d. after 1655)'.
2. *Vox coeli*, p. 4.
3. *Vox coeli*, p. 59.
4. The dramatic response to the Spanish match was first systematically analysed by Jerzy Limon in *Dangerous matter: English drama and politics 1623–24* (Cambridge, 1986). For more recent work discussing the cultural politics of the match, see Thomas Cogswell, 'England and the Spanish match' in *Conflict in early Stuart England: Studies in religion and politics, 1603–1642*, eds Richard Cust and Ann Hughes (London, 1989), pp. 107–33, and Glyn Redworth, *The prince and the infanta: The cultural politics of the Spanish match* (New Haven, Conn., 2004).
5. This chapter deals mainly with *Sir Thomas Wyatt* as I have written on the other plays elsewhere – see Teresa Grant, 'Drama queen: Staging Elizabeth in *If you know not me you know nobody*' in *The myth of Elizabeth*, eds Susan Doran and Thomas S. Freeman (Basingstoke, 2003), pp. 120–42, and 'History in the making: The case of Samuel Rowley's *When you see me, you know me* (1604/5)' in *English historical drama 1500–1660: Forms outside the canon*, eds Teresa Grant and Barbara Ravelhofer (Basingstoke, 2007), pp. 125–57.
6. Thomas Dekker (et al.), *The famous history of Sir Thomas Wyat, With the coronation of Queen Mary and the coming in of King Philip* (London, 1607), STC 6537; Thomas Dekker (et al.), *The famous history of Sir Thomas Wyat, With the coronation of Queen Mary and the coming in of King Philip* (London, 1612), STC 6538. In 1602 Henslowe paid Chettle, Dekker, Heywood, Wentworth Smith and Webster for the two parts of the 'playe called Ladey Jane' and made payments for the costumes for the (probably related) lost *The overthrow of rebels*. See Cyrus Hoy, *Introductions, notes, and commentaries to texts in 'The dramatic works of Thomas Dekker', edited by Fredson Bowers* (4 vols Cambridge, 1980), I, pp. 311–50 (p. 311).

Critics have come to accept *Sir Thomas Wyatt* as some compilation and adjustment of this material to make a revised play.

7. A. M. Clark, *Thomas Heywood* (Oxford, 1931), pp. 30–4.

8. For the textual relationship see Mary Forster Martin, '*If you know not me you know nobodie*, and *The famous history of Sir Thomas Wyat*', *The Library* 13 (1932), pp. 272–81, esp. p. 274 and p. 281.

9. Julia Gasper, *The dragon and the dove: The plays of Thomas Dekker* (Oxford, 1990), pp. 44–61. She notes, for instance, that Dekker promotes Wyatt unhistorically to the privy council, and makes him an especial friend to London, both attributes actually borrowed from the earl of Essex in order to reinforce the parallels.

10. All quotations from the play are from Fredson Bowers (ed.), *Sir Thomas Wyatt*, pp. 398–469 in *The dramatic works of Thomas Dekker* (3 vols Cambridge, 1970), I, p. 399.

11. *A&M* [1583], p. 1406. Foxe adds bleakly, 'which indeed afterward came to passe, as by the course and sequele of this story may well appeare'.

12. See Susan Doran, 'Revenge her foul and most unnatural murder? The impact of Mary Stewart's execution on Anglo-Scottish relations', *History* 85 (2000), pp. 589–612, esp. p. 604, p. 606.

13. This is a point he insists upon in his first speech to parliament, where he speaks of 'my Birth-right and lineall descent . . . out of the loynes of Henry the seaventh . . . reunited and confirmed in me the Union of the 2 princely Roses of the 2 Houses of Lancaster and Yorke . . ., which, as it was first setled and united in him, so is it now reunited and confirmed in me, being justly and lineally descended not onely of that happy conjunction, but of both the Branches thereof many times before.' John Stow, *The annales, or generall chronicle of England, begun first by maister John Stow*, ed. and supp. Edward Howes (London, 1615), STC 23338, pp. 837–8.

14. This is a ploy that Elizabeth used to her advantage during Mary's reign – she appeared in public in as simple and unostentatious clothes (usually black or white) as she could in order to throw Mary's jewels and 'extravagance' into unfavourable relief. Patrick Collinson notes that this was part of her assumption of a 'new persona of a demure and respectable young woman who dressed plainly and eschewed ostentatious jewellery' (*ODNB* 'Elizabeth I (1533–1603)'). Lady Jane Grey also adopted what became the Protestant fashion, rejecting a rich gown, a gift from Mary of Guise, saying 'it were a shame to follow my Lady Mary against God's word and leave my Lady Elizabeth which followeth God's word' (*ODNB* 'Grey, Lady Jane (1537–1554)').

15. See Grant, 'Drama queen', pp. 124–5. All quotations from *If you know not me 1* are from Thomas Heywood, *If you know not me you know nobody Part 1* (London, 1606), STC 13328, ed. Madeleine Doran (Oxford, 1934/5). This is assuming that the speech as we have it in the 1607 edition is roughly as it was written in 1602; if not, then someone is

paraphrasing or parodying the last scene of *If you know not me 1* in the bad quarto of *Sir Thomas Wyatt*.

16. For the relationship of ballads and chronicles to the Foxe-based plays of the early seventeenth century see Grant, 'History in the making', esp. pp. 136–41.

17. See, for instance, Peter Lake, 'Anti-popery: The structure of a prejudice', in *Conflict in early Stuart England*, eds Richard Cust and Ann Hughes (London and New York, 1989), pp. 72–106.

18. Again, note that the errors of Catholicism rather than the Marian persecution of the Protestants are in the forefront of the dramatists' minds.

19. No one was, of course, by then still urging the queen to marry, though her refusal to nominate a successor had become a significant issue and people might have reflected ruefully on the lost chance of direct heirs her virginity had dictated.

20. This is, of course, based on the marriage of the Church and Christ in Revelation. For a Protestant playwright as eschatologically attuned as Dekker, Mary's attempt to marry her corrupt Catholic Church to the Lord provides irony and a reminder to the Elect of their (Protestant) God's promised punishment of Catholics at the Apocalypse, imminent as it was considered to be (see, for instance, Jane E. A. Dawson, 'The apocalyptic thinking of the Marian exiles', in *Prophecy and eschatology*, ed. Michael Wilks, Studies in Church History, Subsidia 10 (1994), pp. 75–91).

21. As Alison Plowden makes clear, Jane's marriage to Dudley was no more than a political expedient, and she herself noted that she 'had been deceived by the duke [of Northumberland] and the council and ill-treated by my husband and his mother' (*ODNB* 'Lady Jane Grey').

22. Grant, 'Drama queen', p. 125.

23. James had mentioned the very issue of Catholic loyalty in his maiden speech to parliament in 1604, opining that the two stumbling blocks were Catholics' insistence on the supremacy of the pope who 'claimes to have an Imperiall civill power over all kings and Emperors', and what might be seen as a concomitant dispensation to the Papal flock to assassinate rulers who did not conform to Catholicism (Stow, *Annales*, p. 841). In the wake of the Gunpowder plot, of course, this dispensation was alive with possibilities as rumours persisted about special papal absolution for the conspirators. Such an eventuality was dramatized in Part 2 of *If you know not me*, as Dr Parry reveals of his attempted assassination of Elizabeth: 'I have tane the Sacrament to doo't, confe'rd / With Cardinal Cemo about it, and receiv'd / Full absolution from his Holynes.' (Thomas Heywood, *If you know not me you know nobody, Part 2* (London, 1607), STC 13336, ed. Madeleine Doran (Oxford, 1934/5), ll. 2286–8. All quotations are from this edition.)

24. *Vox coeli*, p. 52.
25. *Vox coeli*, p. 53.
26. See Gasper, *Dragon and dove*, pp. 48–50 and Teresa Grant and Barbara Ravelhofer, 'Introduction' in *English historical drama*, pp. 8–9.
27. See *ODNB* 'Devereux, Robert, second earl of Essex (1565–1601)'.
28. See note 23.
29. James Ellison, '*Measure for Measure* and the executions of Catholics in 1604', *English Literary Renaissance* 33 (2003), pp. 44–87.
30. All quotations are from Samuel Rowley, *When you see me you know me* (London, 1605), STC 21417, ed. F. P. Wilson (Oxford, 1952).
31. For a full treatment of the way Heywood contrasts Elizabeth and Mary in this play see Grant, *Drama queen*.
32. See Susan E. Krantz, 'Thomas Dekker's political commentary in *The whore of Babylon*', *Studies in English Literature 1500–1900* 35 (1995), pp. 271–91.
33. Krantz, 'Thomas Dekker's political commentary', p. 275 ff. By 1624, of course, the accusations had become even more vociferous and Reynolds's *Vox coeli* is typically forthright. Despite Mary Tudor's denials, all the other members of her family insist on the involvement of the Spanish in 'that execrable and damnable plot of treason', Anne of Denmark going so far as to suggest that the only thing the Spaniards hated about the Plot was its failure (at pp. 55–6).
34. Cf Ellison, '*Measure for Measure*'.

5. Inventing Bloody Mary

1. Thomas Fuller, *The Church history of Britain*, ed. J. S. Brewer (6 vols, Oxford, 1855), IV, pp. 200 and 247–8.
2. Peter Heylyn, *Ecclesia restaurata* (London, 1661), STC [Wing] H1701, pp. 81 and 83–4.
3. Admittedly, the duke of York's actions as *de facto* viceroy in Scotland in 1679–82 had alarmed many; see Tim Harris, *Restoration: Charles II and his kingdoms, 1660–1685* (London and New York, 2005), pp. 333–59. However, opposition to the prospect of his rule antedated his actions in Scotland and it was ultimately based on anti-Catholic prejudices and fears.
4. 'Vox populi, vox dei', in *A collection of scarce and valuable tracts... selected from... libraries, particularly, that of... Lord Somers*, ed. Walter Scott (13 vols, London, 1809–15), VIII, p. 302.[Hereafter this series will be referred to as *Somers's tracts*].
5. Elkanah Settle, *The character of a popish successor* (London, 1681), STC [Wing] S2670, p. 13.
6. Robert Ferguson, 'A representation of the threatening dangers impending over Protestants in Great Britain', in *Somers's tracts*, IX, p. 331.

7. See Harris, *Restoration*, pp. 150–1 and John Miller, *Popery and politics in England 1660–1688* (Cambridge, 1973), pp. 72–6.

8. 'J. D.', *The coronation of Queen Elizabeth* (London, 1680), STC [Wing] D31, pp. 3–5.

9. Quoted in Melinda S. Zook, *Radical whigs and conspiratorial politics in late Stuart England* (University Park, Pa., 1999), p. 101.

10. 'Plain dealing is a jewel and honesty the best policy', in *Somers's tracts*, VIII, p. 261.

11. John Smith, *The narrative of . . . a further discovery of the late horrid and popish-plot* (London, 1679), STC [Wing] S4217, p. 4.

12. 'J. D.', *Coronation*, pp. 5–6.

13. Nicholas Billingsley, *The infancy of the world* (London, 1658), STC [Wing] B2912, p. 76.

14. Thomas Deloney, *The royal garland of love* (London, 1674), STC [Wing] D967, sig. A7r.

15. Benjamin Harris, *The Protestant tutor* (London, 1679), STC [Wing] P3843, pp. 111, 113, 115.

16. The term 'whig' carries a number of different meanings. I am using it to describe those who, in the years 1678–83, sought to exclude the duke of York from the succession, and in later years to denote someone who was opposed to popery and supported the English constitution against absolute rule. I have eschewed the term 'Whig' to avoid confusion with the political party of that name.

17. See Zook, *Radical whigs*, passim, and Mark Goldie, 'Priestcraft and the birth of whiggism' in *Political discourse in early modern Britain*, eds Nicholas Phillipson and Quentin Skinner (Cambridge, 1993), pp. 209–31.

18. See Richard Cust, *Charles I: A political life* (Harlow, 2005), pp. 145–7 and 254; also see Caroline M. Hibbard, *Charles I and the Popish Plot* (Chapel Hill, N. C., 1983), especially, pp. 168–71.

19. Miller, *Popery and politics*, p. 169.

20. John Kenyon, *The Popish Plot* (London, 2000), p. 24. The whig playwright and pamphleteer Elkanah Settle argued that a Catholic monarch of England had to be a tyrant, as Catholicism could only be established and maintained by arbitrary power and not by the limited powers of the British monarchy. (Settle, *Character of a popish successor*, pp. 18–20).

21. Dr Williams's Library, Morrice MS F, p. 75.

22. Gilbert Burnet, *The history of the Reformation of the Church of England*, ed. Nicholas Pocock (7 vols, Oxford, 1865), II, p. 406.

23. T. S., 'An account of Queen Mary's methods', in *Somers's tracts*, VIII, pp. 324–7.

24. Gilbert Burnet, *A letter writ by the . . . Bishop of Salisbury to the . . . Bishop of Cov and Lichfield* (London, 1693), STC [Wing] B5824, pp. 2–3.

25. Burnet, *History of the Reformation*, II, p. 591.

26. Burnet, *History of the Reformation*, III, pp. 31–3.
27. Jeremy Collier, *An ecclesiastical history of Great Britain* (2 vols, London, 1708–14), II, p. 404, 406.
28. Collier, *Ecclesiastical history*, II, p. 406.
29. For a look at the dissemination of such fears on a popular level, see Jeremy Black, 'The Catholic threat and the press in the 1720s and 1730s', *Journal of Religious History* 12 (1983), pp. 364–81.
30. William Prior, *Popery not Christianity* (London, 1750), pp. 33–4.
31. *A select history of the principal English Protestant martyrs* (London, 1746), unpaginated preface.
32. This declaration was accurate. The first 63 pages of *A select history* cover the pre-Marian martyrs; the remaining 255 are devoted solely to those who died in Mary's reign.
33. *The curse of popery and popish princes* (London, 1716), p. xiv.
34. Devorah Greenberg has recently, and rather counter-intuitively, argued that the eighteenth-century abridgements of Foxe were not necessarily anti-Catholic but were often intended to promote tolerance, due process of law, and unity among all denominations. (See Devorah Greenberg, 'In a tradition of learned ministry: Wesley's "Foxe" ', *Journal of Ecclesiastical History* 59 (2008), pp. 227–31). A few points should however be borne in mind. The first is that Greenberg's chief, indeed virtually exclusive, example is John Wesley's multi-volume abridgement of Foxe in his 50-volume Christian Library (1751). The format, printing history and purposes of this edition (to provide examples extolling a learned ministry) were entirely atypical. It is true that many eighteenth-century editions of Foxe contain appeals to dissenters, but this is in order, not to promote toleration, but to unify all British Protestants against Catholics. Thus the most popular abridgement of Foxe began with a preface that claimed that the 'Book of Martyrs' had 'been long recommended by Protestant divines of every denomination', and took care to list the celebrated Methodist preachers George Whitefield, John Wesley and Martin Madan among them. But the book opened with a vehement denunciation of the 'strange, unscriptural and inhuman maxims, tenets and carnal observances of Roman Catholicism' (*Fox's original and complete Book of Martyrs*, ed. Paul Wright (London, 1782), sig. A1r and p. 1).
35. See John N. King, 'Eighteenth-century folio publication of Foxe's *Book of Martyrs*', *Reformation* 10 (2005), pp. 102–3 as well as Elizabeth Evenden and Thomas S. Freeman, *Religion and the book in early modern England: The making of Foxe's 'Book of Martyrs'*, cap. 9 (forthcoming, Cambridge).
36. *The Book of Martyrs or, the history of paganism and popery* (Coventry, 1764), pp. 331 and 333.
37. Henry Southwell, *The new Book of Martyrs* (London, 1780?), pp. 263 and 367.

38. Laurence Echard, *The history of England* (3 vols, London, 1707–18), I, pp. 756, 787.
39. On Rapin and his historical writing see Hugh Trevor-Roper, 'A Huguenot historian: Paul Rapin', in *Huguenots in Britain and their French background*, ed. Irene Scouloudi (Totowa, N. J., 1987), pp. 3–19.
40. Paul de Rapin de Thoyras, *The history of England*, trans. N. Tindal (15 vols, London, 1725–31), VIII, p. 215.
41. John Oldmixon, *The history of England* (London, 1739), p. 213.
42. Linda Colley, *In defence of oligarchy: The Tory Party 1714–60* (Cambridge, 1982), p. 87. For Carte's political and religious sympathies see the article on him in the *ODNB*.
43. Thomas Carte, *A general history of England* (4 vols, London, 1747–1755), III, pp. 353–4.
44. Tobias Smollett, *A complete history of England* (4 vols, London, 1757–8), II, p. 708.
45. See Trevor-Roper, 'Huguenot historian', p. 17 for discussion of Hume's history as response to Rapin's work.
46. David Hume, *A history of England* (8 vols, Dublin, 1788), IV, pp. 462–3.
47. Nicholas Phillipson, *Hume* (London, 1989), p. 137; and T. E. Jessop, *A bibliography of David Hume and Scottish philosophy* (London, 1938), pp. 29–32.
48. D. R. Woolf, 'A feminine past? Gender, genre and historical knowledge in England, 1500–1800', *American Historical Review* 102 (1997), pp. 665–7.
49. Mrs Markham, *A history of England*, 13th edn (London, 1853), p. iii. The dependence of Mrs Markham's history on Hume's work did not escape contemporaries; see Francis Palgrave, 'Hume and his influence upon history', *Quarterly Review* 73 (1843), p. 591.
50. Markham, *History of England*, p. iii.
51. Markham, *History of England*, pp. 291, 294.
52. Markham, *History of England*, p. 291.
53. Maria Collcott, *Little Arthur's history of England* (2 vols, London, 1835), II, pp. 93, 96.
54. Collcott, *Little Arthur's history*, II, p. 94.
55. For other examples see Edward Baldwin, *The history of England for the use of schools and young persons*, 2nd edn (London, 1826), pp. 95–6; W. J. Hart, *The epitome of English history* (London, 1822), p. 157; William Cooper, *Cooper's history of England* (London, 1843), p. 54.
56. Charles Dodd, *The Church history of England* (3 vols, Brussels, 1737–42), I, pp. 464–6. The quotation is on p. 464.
57. Dodd, *Church history*, pp. 464–6.
58. John Lingard, *The history of England*, 6th edn (10 vols, London, 1854–5), V, p. 259.

59. Lingard, *History*, V, p. 259.
60. Edwin Jones, *John Lingard and the pursuit of historical truth* (Brighton, 2001), pp. 79–81.
61. See Rohan Maitzen, ' "This feminine preserve": historical biography by Victorian women', *Victorian Studies* 38 (1995), pp. 371–93; Anne Laurence, 'Women historians and documentary research: Lucy Aiken, Agnes Strickland, Mary Anne Everett Green and Lucy Toulmin Smith', in *Women, scholarship and criticisms: Gender and knowledge, c. 1790–1900*, eds Joan Bellamy, Anne Laurence and Gill Perry (Manchester and New York, 2000), pp. 125–41. See Woolf, 'A feminine past?', pp. 645–79 for the background to these developments.
62. At Elizabeth's request, it was Agnes's name alone that appeared on the *Lives of the queens of England*. Nevertheless about half of the individual biographies within the work, including the one of Mary, were written by Elizabeth. See Jane Strickland, *Life of Agnes Strickland* (Edinburgh and London, 1887), pp. 18–23, 64–5 as well as Una Pope-Hennessy, *Agnes Strickland: Biographer of the queens of England, 1796–1874* (London, 1940), pp. 105–10, 319.
63. Agnes Strickland, *Lives of the queens of England* (12 vols, London, 1840–48), V, pp. 449–50 for Elizabeth Strickland's declaration that her account of Mary was based on 'the rich mass of documents largely edited by our great historical antiquarians, Madden and Tytler'.
64. Strickland, *Lives*, V, p. 210.
65. Strickland, *Lives*, V, pp. 213–18, 427–8, 431.
66. Strickland, *Lives*, V, p. 431.
67. Jane Strickland, *Life*, pp. 68–9; Pope-Hennessy, *Agnes Strickland*, pp. 105–6, 109, 237–8.
68. Charles Dickens, *The complete works of Charles Dickens* (21 vols, London, 1906), vol. XIII, p. 227. (The capitalization in this quotation reproduces that in the text.) *A child's history* was first serialized in *Household Words* in 1851–3.
69. Anne Rodwell, *The child's first steps to English history* (London, 1844), p. 127.
70. William Legge, *A reading book of English history and biography* (London, 1863), p. 131.
71. Henry Ince and James Gilbert, *Outlines of English history*, 6th edn (London, 1870), pp. 94–5.
72. H. F. M. Prescott, *Spanish Tudor: The life of Bloody Mary* (New York, 1940), pp. 110–11, 218–19, 373–4.
73. Strickland, *Lives*, V, p. 450.
74. Strickland, *Lives*, V, p. 411.
75. Strickland, *Lives*, V, pp. 305–8, 359–61, 410–12, 429–30, 433, 442.
76. Henry Hallam, *The constitutional history of England*, 5th edn (New York, 1847), p. 70.

77. John Milner, *The history civil and ecclesiastical...of Winchester* (2 vols, London, 1798), I, p. 355.
78. Milner, *History...of Winchester*, I, pp. 355–7. Milner repeated the charge that Protestants provoked their persecution in *Letters to a prebendary*, 2nd edn (London, 1801), p. 145.
79. Thomas Flannagan, *A short catechism of English history, ecclesiastical and civil, for children* (London, 1851), pp. 34–5.
80. On Mary's 'hysteria' and her false pregnancies see Judith M. Richards' chapter in this volume.
81. J. A. Froude, *History of England from the fall of Wolsey to the Spanish Armada* (12 vols, London, 1872–5), VI, pp. 96–7.
82. Froude, *History of England*, V, pp. 520–3.
83. Froude, *History of England*, VI, p. 97.
84. W. F. Collier, *History of the British Empire* (London, 1870), p. 173.
85. Osmund Airy, *Text-book of English history* (London, 1981), p. 211.
86. A. F. Pollard, *The history of England from the accession of Edward VI to the death of Elizabeth* (London, 1910), pp. 172–3.
87. Pollard, *History of England*, p. 174.
88. Pollard, *History of England*, p. 172.
89. Pollard, *History of England*, p. 174.
90. Pollard, *History of England*, p. 172.
91. Robert Tittler, *The reign of Mary I* (London and New York, 1983), p. 80.
92. Prescott, *Spanish Tudors*, pp. 401, 420.
93. David Loades, *Mary Tudor: The tragical history of the first queen of England* (Kew, 2006); Anna Whitelock, *Mary Tudor, England's first queen* (London, 2009), p. 309.
94. Prescott, *Spanish Tudor*, p. 498.

6. *'Ad Omne Virtutum Genus'?*

1. G. R. Elton, *Reform and Reformation: England 1509–1558* (London, 1977), p. 376.
2. Maria Dowling, *Humanism in the age of Henry VIII* (London, 1986), pp. 20–1.
3. Susan E. James, *Kateryn Parr: The making of a queen* (Aldershot, 1999), distilled into *ODNB* 'Katherine Parr'.
4. For example, David Loades, 'The personal religion of Mary I', in Duffy and Loades (2006), pp. 1–29.
5. Loades (1989), p. 43.
6. Desiderius Erasmus, *The education of a Christian prince*, trans. Neil M. Cheshire and Michael J. Heath, ed. Lisa Jardine (Cambridge, 1997), p. 5.
7. See Aysha Pollnitz, 'Princely education in sixteenth-century Britain' (Ph.D. dissertation, University of Cambridge, 2006).

8. See *The Cambridge companion to Renaissance humanism*, ed. Jill Kraye (Cambridge, 1996), and particularly P. O. Kristeller, 'Humanism', in *The Cambridge history of Renaissance philosophy*, eds C. B. Schmitt, Q. Skinner and E. Kessler (Cambridge, 1988), pp. 113–37.

9. Gloria Kaufman, 'Juan Luis Vives on the education of Women', *Signs* 3 (1978), pp. 891–6.

10. Judith M. Richards, ' "To promote a woman to beare rule": Talking of queens in mid-Tudor England', *SCJ* 28 (1997), pp. 101–21 (at pp. 101–2); 'Mary Tudor as "sole quene"? Gendering Tudor monarchy', *HJ* 40 (1997), pp. 895–924 (at p. 904).

11. J. L. Vives, *De institutione feminae Christianae: Liber primus, SWV*, V, pp. 37–9.

12. *Epistola* I (for Mary), dated from Oxford, October 1523; *Epistola* II (to Charles Blount), dated from London, 1523. Cp Vives, *De Institutione*, p. xii, which gives the date as October 1524.

13. Juan Luis Vives, *De subventione pauperum sive de humanis necessitatibus Libri II, SWV*, IV, p. xii.

14. Thomas Linacre, *Rudimenta grammatices* (London, c.1523), STC 15637, sig. A1v; D. F. S. Thomson, 'Linacre's Latin grammars', in *Linacre studies: Essays on the life and work of Thomas Linacre c. 1460–1524*, eds Francis Maddison, Margaret Pelling and Charles Webster (Oxford, 1977), pp. 24–35.

15. *Rudimenta grammatices Thomae Linacri ex anglico sermone in latinum versa, interprete Georgio Buchanano Scoto* (Paris, 1533).

16. Loades (1989), p. 36; Beverley A. Murphy, *Bastard prince: Henry VIII's lost son* (Stroud, 2001).

17. BL Cotton MS Vitellius C. i., fol. 23; quoted from Loades (1989), p. 42.

18. Dedication of the *De ratione studii puerilis* to Catherine, dated October 1523.

19. Loades (1989), pp. 71, 73; if Fetherston composed a tract against the divorce, it is not extant.

20. Giles Duwes, *Introductorie for to lerne to rede, to pronounce and to speke French trewly* (London, [1533?]), STC 7377, although written several years before; modern edition in *L'éclaircissement de la langue française ... la grammaire de Gilles Du Guez*, ed. F. Génin (Paris, 1852), pp. 891–1079. H. S. Bennett, *English books and readers 1475 to 1557* (Cambridge, 1969), pp. 94–5, considers French 'freely spoken' at court, whereas Loades (1989) sees it as an aristocratic accomplishment of diminished utility (p. 43).

21. Gordon Kipling, *The triumph of honour: Burgundian origins of the Elizabethan Renaissance* (Leiden, 1977), pp. 24–5.

22. Hazel Pierce, *Margaret Pole, countess of Salisbury, 1473–1541: Loyalty, lineage and leadership* (Cardiff, 2003), pp. 97–9.

23. *CSPVen*, VI, 1055.
24. Henry Ellis, *Original letters illustrative of English history* (3 vols, London, 1824), II, pp. 19–20; John E. Paul, *Catherine of Aragon and her friends* (London, 1966).
25. Loades (1989), p. 43.
26. Kristian Jenson, 'The humanist reform of Latin and Latin teaching' in *The Cambridge companion to Renaissance humanism*, pp. 63–81.
27. Loades (1989), p. 49.
28. Loades (1989), p. 118.
29. Vives, *Epistola I*, sig. R.iiv–iiir.
30. James Kelsey McConica, *English humanists and reformation politics under Henry VIII and Edward VI* (Oxford, 1965), p. 156.
31. For letters to Margaret to the age of 16, see *The correspondence of Sir Thomas More*, ed. Elizabeth Frances Rogers (Princeton, 1947), letters 69, 70, 76, 106–8.
32. BL Add. MS 17012, fols 192v–194r: 'The prayor of Saynt Thomas of aquune translaytd oute of Latyn ynto Englyshe by ye most excelent Prynses [deleted] Mary, doughter to the moste hygh and myghty Prynce and Pryncess Kyng Henry the viii and Quene Kateryne hys wyfe [deleted] in the yere of our Lorde God ml cccc xxvii: and the xi yere of here age'.
33. BL Royal MS 17 C.XVI. See James P. Carley, 'The writings of Henry Parker, Lord Morley: A bibliographical survey', in '*Triumphs of English': Henry Parker Lord Morley: translator to the Tudor court*, eds Marie Axton and James P. Carley (London, 2000), pp. 27–68. For Morley's preface, see *Forty-six lives translated from Boccaccio's De Claris Mulieribus by Henry Parker, Lord Morley*, ed. H. G. Wright, EETS original series 214 (London, 1943 [for 1940]), pp. 172–3.
34. Loades, 'Personal religion', p. 8; Loades (1989), p. 43.
35. Morley's *Somnium Scipionis* (BL Royal MS 18 A.LX, fol. 1v). See Jeremy Maule, 'What did Morley give when he gave a "Plutarch" life?', in *Triumphs of English*, pp. 107–30, and David R. Carlson, 'Morley's translations from Roman philosophers and English courtier literature', in *Triumphs of English*, pp. 131–51.
36. Desiderius Erasmus, *Opus epistolarum Desiderii Roterodami*, ed. P. S. Allen (12 vols, Oxford, 1906–47), VII, Ep. 2023 (Basle, 13 August 1528), ll. 12–21. The letter appeared in *Adagiorum opus* (1528), sig. ee8v, to fill the final page.
37. *En magnis impendiis, summisque laboribus damus amice lector T. Liuii Patauini Latinae historiae*, ed. Desiderius Erasmus (Basle, 1531); Erasmus, *Opus epistolarum*, IX, p. 143, Ep. 2435 (1 March 1531) and X, p. 201, Ep. 2794 (20 April 1533).
38. Vives, *Epistola I*, sig. R.iiiv.

39. Vives, *Epistola I*, sig. S.iir.
40. Vives, *Epistola I*, sig. S.iir.
41. Vives, *Epistola II*, sig. T.iv.
42. Erasmus, *Opus epistolarum*, IX, Ep. 2435, ll. 73–90.
43. Erasmus, *Opus epistolarum*, IX, Ep. 2431, ll. 24–7; quoted from Richard F. Hardin, 'The literary conventions of Erasmus' *Education of a Christian Prince*: Advice and aphorism', *Renaissance Quarterly* 35 (1982), pp. 151–63.
44. Lisa Jardine and Anthony Grafton, ' "Studied for action": How Gabriel Harvey read his Livy', *Past and Present* 129 (1990), pp. 30–78.
45. *De Institutione, SWV, VI*, pp. 42–53; Jerome, Letter 107.
46. Vives, *Epistola II*, sig. T.ivr.
47. CWE, vol. 24, p. 669; see Joan Simon, *Education and society in Tudor England* (Cambridge, 1967), ch. 3; Simon Goldhill, *Who needs Greek? Contests in the cultural history of Hellenism* (Cambridge, 2002), pp. 14–59.
48. Jane Stevenson, 'Women Catholics and Latin culture' in *Catholic culture in early modern England*, eds Ronald Corthell, Frances E. Dolan, Christopher Highley and Arthur F. Marotti (South Bend, Ind., 2007), pp. 52–72.
49. Vives, *De institutione*, SWV, VI, pp. 38–41.
50. Vives, *De institutione*, SWV, VI, pp. 38–41.
51. Loades (1989), p. 33.
52. 12 October 1541, *L&P*, XVI, 1253.
53. Loades (1989), p. 61.
54. Loades (1989), p. 113.
55. Loades (1989), p. 61.
56. Loades (1989), p. 91; 'Personal religion', pp. 9–12.
57. G. W. Bernard, 'The making of religious policy 1533–1546: Henry VIII and the search for the middle way', *HJ* 41 (1998), pp. 321–49; Susan Brigden, *London and the Reformation* (Oxford, 1989), p. 315.
58. Garrett Mattingly, *Catherine of Aragon* (London, 1942), p. 292.
59. Dowling, *Humanism*, p. 231; Chapuys to Erasmus, 1 February 1536, *Opus epistolarum*, XI, ep. 3090.
60. Bernard André, *Historia Regis Henrici Septimi*, ed. James Gairdner, Rolls Series (London, 1858), p. 43. See David R. Carlson, 'Royal tutors in the reign of Henry VII', *SCJ*, 22 (1991), pp. 253–79. For Erasmus' account of Henry's letters, see *Opus epistolarum*, Ep. 2143, VIII, p. 130.
61. London, BL Royal MS 17 C.XII, fols 3r and 2r.
62. The translation of '*bonae litterae*' (as well as '*litterae humaniores*') as 'literature' belies the complexity of the matter and methods of reading through which humanists articulated a liberal education.
63. John Leland, *Principium ac illustrium aliquot et eruditorum in Anglia virorum Encomia, Trophaea, Genethliaca, & Epithalamia*, ed. Thomas Newton (London, 1589), STC 15447, pp. 3, 74.

64. Leland, *Encomia*, p. 74.
65. Leland, *Encomia*, p. 51.
66. BL Royal MS 17 A.xxx. See Carley, 'Writings of Henry Parker, Lord Morley', pp. 34–7.
67. Leland, *Encomia*, p. 51.
68. Leland, *Encomia*, pp. 67–8.
69. Leland, *Encomia*, p. 58.
70. Leland, *Encomia*, p. 39 [recte 38].
71. Leland, *Encomia*, pp. 52–3.
72. J. K. Sowards, 'On education: More's debt to Erasmus', in *Miscellanea Moreana: Essays for Germain Marc'hadour*, eds Clare M. Murphy, Henri Gibaud and Mario A. Di Cesare, Moreana 100 (Binghamton NY, 1989), pp. 103–23.
73. 'Inventories of the wardrobes, plate, chapel stuff, etc. of Henry Fitzroy . . . and Katherine princess dowager', ed. J. G. Nichols, in *Camden Miscellany 3*, Camden Society, original series 61, (London, 1855), pp. 23–41; James P. Carley, *The books of King Henry VIII and his wives* (London, 2004), p. 120.
74. T. A. Birrell, *English monarchs and their books: From Henry VII to Charles II*, Panizzi Lectures 1986 (London, 1987), p. 21; Carley, 'Writings of Henry Parker, Lord Morley', p. 44.
75. Birrell, *English monarchs*, pp. 22–3.
76. Birrell, *English monarchs*, p. 23.
77. The work first appeared in 1528, and later in Paris '*de nouvel imprimé*' in 1538.
78. Diarmaid MacCulloch, *Suffolk and the Tudors: Politics and religion in an English county 1500–1600* (Oxford, 1986), pp. 170, 180–1; *ODNB* 'John Hopton'.
79. David Starkey, *Elizabeth: Apprenticeship* (London, 2000), p. 82; cf. Loades (1989), p. 332.
80. Michael K. Jones and Malcolm G. Underwood, *The king's mother: Lady Margaret Beaufort, countess of Richmond and Derby* (Cambridge, 1993); Susan Powell, 'Lady Margaret Beaufort and her books', *The Library* vi, series 20 (1998), pp. 197–239.
81. Loades (1989), pp. 331, 335; Carley, *Books*, p. 123.
82. Miles Hogarde, *A mirrour of loue* (London, 1555), STC 13559, sig. A2r.
83. McConica, *English humanists*, p. 242.
84. C. R. Thompson, 'Erasmus and Tudor England', in *Actes du Congrès Erasme, Rotterdam, 27–8 octobre 1969* (Amsterdam, 1971), pp. 29–68.
85. J. B. Trapp, *Erasmus, Colet and More: The early Tudor humanists and their books*, Panizzi Lectures 1990 (London, 1991), pp. 13–29; 'Christopher Urswick and his books: The reading of Henry VII's almoner', *Renaissance Studies*, 1 (1987), pp. 48–70.
86. Queens' College Cambridge, MS 13; M. R. James, *A descriptive catalogue of the western manuscripts in the library of Queens' College Cambridge*

(Cambridge, 1905), pp. 14–16. On Oxford, Bodleian Library, Douce MS 110, see Trapp, *Erasmus, Colet and More*, pp. 22–3.

87. McConica, *English humanists*, p. 132.
88. Respectively, BL Royal MS 18 A.XV, Royal MS 2 D.XXVIII, and Royal MS 17 C.XVI.
89. BL Royal MS 17 A.XLVI.
90. David Starkey, 'An attendant lord? Henry Parker, Lord Morley' in *Triumphs of English*, pp. 1–25; R. M. Warnicke, 'The Lady Margaret Beaufort, countess of Richmond (d. 1509) as seen by John Fisher and by Lord Morley', *Moreana* 19 (1982), pp. 47–55.
91. BL Royal MS 2 D.XXVIII.
92. Carley, 'Writings of Henry Parker', p. 50.
93. BL Add. MS 12060; Richard Rex, 'Morley and the papacy: Rome, regime, and religion' in *Triumphs of English*, pp. 87–105 (at pp. 93–100). Carley and Rex's edition of the text is Appendix 7, pp. 253–69.
94. Jones and Underwood, *The king's mother*, p. 158.
95. *Triumphs of English*, p. 263 Rex, *Triumphs*, p. 268, n.45, considers it likely that Morley was familiar with the quasi-hagiographical material in Fisher's memorial sermon (*A mornynge remembraunce had at the moneth mynde of the noble prynces Margarete countesse of Rychemonde & Darbye* (London, 1509), STC 10891), and that this later work has now been lost.
96. *Triumphs of English*, pp. 253–4.
97. See for example, Lucy Wooding, 'The Marian restoration and the language of Catholic reform' in *Reforming Catholicism in the England of Mary Tudor: The achievement of Friar Bartolomé Carranza*, eds John Edwards and Ronald Truman (Aldershot, 2005), pp. 49–64, who states that the Marian regime removed the *Paraphrases*; John Craig, 'Forming a Protestant consciousness? Erasmus' *Paraphrases* in English parishes, 1547–1666', in *Holy scripture speaks: The production and reception of Erasmus'* Paraphrases *on the New Testament*, eds Hilmar M. Pabel and Mark Vessey (Toronto, 2002), pp. 313–43 asserts that they remained and suggests that it was perceived as 'political folly' to attempt their removal. See Aysha Pollnitz's chapter in this volume.
98. John Standish, *A discourse wherin is debated whether it be expedient that the scripture should be in English for al men to reade that wyll* (London, 1554), STC 23207, sig. B.iiv. For Udall, see Desiderius Erasmus, *The first tome or volume of the Paraphrase of Erasmus upon the Newe Testamente* (London, 1548), STC 2854, sig. AAa.iir, i.e. fol. iir in John.
99. Standish, *Discourse*, sig. B.iiiv.
100. Robert Wingfield, 'The *Vita Mariae Angliae Reginae*, ed. and trans. Diarmaid MacCulloch, *Camden Miscellany* of Robert Wingfield of Brantham', 29 (28, Camden Society, fourth series 29, 1984), pp. 182, 223, 272.
101. For a survey with contrasting conclusions, see Lucy Wooding, *Rethinking Catholicism in Reformation England* (Oxford, 2000), ch. 4.

102. Wingfield, *Vita*, pp. 221, 270.
103. Anna Whitelock and Diarmaid MacCulloch, 'Princess Mary's household and the succession crisis, July 1553', *HJ* 50 (2007), pp. 265–87.
104. St Vincent of Lerins, *The waie home to Christ*, trans. John Proctor (London, 1554), STC 24754, sigs A.iiir and C.viiir.
105. John Aungel, *The agrement of the Holye Fathers, and doctors of the Churche, vpon the cheifest articles of Christian religion* (London, 1555), STC 634, sig. A.iiir.
106. See William Wizeman, *The theology and spirituality of Mary Tudor's Church* (Aldershot, 2006), pp. 43–7.
107. See Elizabeth I, *Collected works*, eds Leah S. Marcus, Janel Mueller and Mary Beth Rose (Chicago, 2000), Letter 6, p. 15; for the Latin originals, see Elizabeth I, *Autograph compositions and foreign language originals*, eds Janel Mueller and Leah S. Marcus (Chicago, 2003), pp. 13–15.
108. Elizabeth I, *Collected works*, pp. xxviii–xxix.
109. Roger Ascham, *Letters of Roger Ascham*, trans. Maurice Hatch and Alvin Vos, ed. Alvin Vos (New York, 1989), no. 37, to Johann Sturm, Greenwich, 14 September 1555, p. 210; *Æschinis et Demosthenis orationes duæ contrariæ. Commentariolum J. Sturmij in easdem Hecatommeres*, ed. Johann Sturm (Strasbourg, 1550).
110. See, for example, *Letters of Roger Ascham*, no. 39, p. 166, Ascham to Sturm, Cambridge, 4 April 1550.
111. Johann Sturm, *Ioannis Sturmii de periodis liber unus* (Strasbourg, 1550); Lawrence V. Ryan, *Roger Ascham* (Stanford, 1963), p. 144.
112. Trinity College, Cambridge II.12.21. Ryan states only that Sturm sent a copy of his *De periodis* to Elizabeth.
113. *Letters of Roger Ascham*, no. 40, pp. 169, 176.
114. BL Harley MS 1860.
115. *Letters of Roger Ascham*, no. 56 [London], 15 January 1554, p. 249.
116. BL Royal MS 13 B.X, fols 4v–5r. Dowling, *Humanism*, p. 222.
117. Cambridge, University Library, Ms. Dd.VI.56; see *Catalogue of manuscripts preserved in the library of the University of Cambridge* (5 vols, Cambridge, 1855–6), I, p. 309. John F. McDiarmaid, 'John Cheke's preface to De Superstitione', *Journal of Ecclesiastical History* 48 (1997), pp. 100–20.
118. Jane Stevenson, *Women Latin poets: Language, gender, and authority, from antiquity to the eighteenth century* (Oxford, 2005), pp. 258–61.

7. Religion and Translation at the Court of Henry VIII

1. Desiderius Erasmus, *The first tome or volume of the Paraphrases of Erasmus upon the Newe Testament*, trans. Nicholas Udall, Thomas Caius, Mary Tudor and Francis Mallett, ed. Nicholas Udall (London, 1548) STC 2854 variant. Hereafter, this edition is referred to as *Paraphrases* of Erasmus [1548] and the commentaries within it by the name of the relevant gospel, e.g. *Paraphrase on John* [1548] as signatures begin afresh with each.

2. *Visitation articles and injunctions of the period of the Reformation*, eds Walter Howard Frere and William McClure Kennedy (3 vols, London, 1910), II, pp. 117–18.

3. James K. McConica, *English humanists and Reformation politics under Henry VIII and Edward VI* (Oxford, 1965), p. 248; E. J. Devereux, 'Publication of the English *Paraphrases* of Erasmus', *Bulletin of the John Rylands Library* 51 (1969), pp. 348–67.

4. John Craig, 'Forming a Protestant consciousness? Erasmus' *Paraphrases* in English parishes, 1547–1666', in *Holy scripture speaks: The production and reception of Erasmus' 'Paraphrases on the New Testament'*, eds Hilmar M. Pabel and Mark Vessey (Toronto, 2002), pp. 313–60. For Harpsfield's visitation, see Philip Hughes, *The Reformation in England* (3 vols, London, 1953), II, p. 234 and Eamon Duffy, *The stripping of the altars: Traditional religion in England, c.1400–c.1580* (New Haven, Conn. and London, 1992), p. 530.

5. Erasmus, *The Paraphrase of Erasm[us] Roterdame upon [the] epistle of Sai[n]t Paule unto his discyple Titus*, trans. Leonard Cox (London, 1534) STC 10503; Stephen Gardiner, Letters to Edward Seymour, November 1547, in *Letters of Stephen Gardiner*, ed. James A. Muller (Cambridge, 1933), no. 130, pp. 381, 383–7, no. 131, pp. 402–3, no. 133, p. 412, no. 135, pp. 417–18, no.136, pp. 421–2.

6. John N. Wall, 'Godly and fruitful lessons: The English Bible, Erasmus' *Paraphrases*, and the Book of Homilies' in *The godly kingdom of Tudor England: Great books of the English Reformation*, ed. John E. Booty (Wilton, Conn., 1981), pp. 73–85; E. J. Devereux, 'Sixteenth-century translations of Erasmus' New Testament commentaries in English' in *CWE Paraphrases on Romans and Galatians*, ed. Robert D. Sider (Toronto, 1984), p. xxxiv.

7. Nicholas Udall, 'To the moste vertuous Ladie and moste gracious Quene Katherine' in *Paraphrase on John* [1548], sig. AAa2a–b.

8. Udall, 'To the most vertuous Ladie Quene Kateryne' in *Paraphrase on Acts* [1548], sig. AAA2a.

9. BL, Cotton MS Vespasian F.III, fol. 37r. Susan E. James's arguments for assigning the letter to 1547 are persuasive: *Kateryn Parr: The making of a queen* (Aldershot, 1999), p. 32 n.41.

10. James, *Kateryn Parr*, p. 134, 228; John King, 'Patronage and piety: The influence of Catherine Parr' in *Silent but for the word: Tudor women as patrons, translators, and writers of religious works*, ed. Margaret P. Hannay (Kent, Ohio, 1985), p. 48.

11. David Loades, 'The personal religion of Mary I' in Duffy and Loades (2006), p. 1.

12. Udall, 'To … Quene Katherine' in *Paraphrase on John* [1548], sig. AAa2a.

13. Udall, 'To the most vertuous Ladie and most gracious Quene Katherine' in *Paraphrase on Luke* [1548], sig. C6a.

14. Loades, 'The personal religion of Mary I', pp. 13–17.
15. Devereux, 'The publication of the English *Paraphrases* of Erasmus', p. 349; Wall, 'Godly and fruitful lessons', p. 75.
16. Erasmus, Epistle dedicatory to Cardinal Grimani, 13 November 1517, in *CWE Paraphrases on Romans and Galatians*, trans. John B. Payne et al., ed. Sider, p. 2.
17. See for instance Erasmus, 'To the most renoumed Prince Ferdinando Archduke of Austriege', in *Paraphrase on John* [1548], sigs AAa4a–AAa6b.
18. R. A. B. Mynors, 'The publication of the Latin *Paraphrases*' in *CWE Paraphrases on Romans and Galatians*, ed. Sider, pp. xx–xxix.
19. Noël Béda, *Annotationum libri duo* (Paris, 1526); see Erika Rummel, 'Why Noël Béda did not like Erasmus' *Paraphrases*' in *Holy scripture speaks*, eds Pabel and Vessey, pp. 265–78.
20. Juan Luis Vives, *De ratione studii puerilis, epistola I*, 2nd edn (Bruges, 1526), sig. Siia.
21. Richard Smyth, *Assertion and defence of the sacramente of the aulter* (London, 1546) STC 22815, sigs Biiib, Miib–Rviiib, and *Defence of the blessed masse, and the sacrifice therof* (London, 1547) STC 22820, fols 105r, 184r–187r; William Peryn, *Thre godly and notable sermons, of the moost honorable and blessed sacrament of the aulter* (London, 1546) STC 19786, sigs Aiib–Aiiia, Giiia, Mvib, Sviiia. I am grateful to Richard Rex for these references. See also his 'Role of English humanists in the Reformation up to 1559' in *The education of a Christian Society: Humanism and the Reformation in Britain and the Netherlands*, eds N. Scott Amos, Andrew Pettegree and Henk van Nierop (Aldershot, 1999), pp. 30–1.
22. BL, Royal MS 17 A. XLVI, fol. 1v; Richard Rex, 'Morley and the papacy: Rome, regime, and religion' in *The triumphs of English: Henry Parker, Lord Morley translator to the Tudor court*, eds Marie Axton and James P. Carley (London, 2000), pp. 87–106.
23. Cox, Epistle dedicatory in *Paraphrase of Erasm[us] . . . upon . . . Titus*, sigs Aia–Biia.
24. Craig, 'Forming a Protestant consciousness?', pp. 320–2, e.g. Udall, printed marginalia in *The first tome or volume of the Paraphrases of Erasmus upon the Newe Testament*, trans. Nicholas Udall, Thomas Caius, Mary Tudor and Francis Mallett, ed. Nicholas Udall (London, 1552) STC 2866, sig. GGG4a.
25. Udall, 'To the good Christian' in *First tome of the Paraphrases* (1552), sig. CC7b; McConica, *English humanists.*
26. [Henry VIII], *Necessary doctrine and erudicion for any Chrysten man* (London, 1543) STC 5170, sigs Aiiib, Fvb–Giva, Sviia–Uiib.
27. [Henry VIII], *Primer set foorth by the kinges maiestie and his clergie* (London, 1545) STC 16034, sig. **b.
28. Richard Rex, *Henry VIII and the English Reformation*, 2nd edn (Basingstoke, 2006), pp. 100, 103, 106, 127, 149.

29. Udall, 'To ... Quene Katherine' in *Paraphrase on Luke* [1548], sig. C2b.
30. Udall, 'To ... Quene Katherine' in *Paraphrase on Luke* [1548], sig. C3a.
31. *ODNB*, 'Caius, Thomas (c.1505–1572)' and *ODNB*, 'Mallett, Francis (d. 1570)'. The translators of Acts and Matthew are unknown.
32. Folger Shakespeare Library, Washington DC, MSS L. b. 26 and L. b. 302, fol. 6r.
33. Erasmus, *Novum Testamentatum paraphrases* (2 vols, Basel, 1524), BL 3913 k. 4. James P. Carley has identified the king's initials on the title page of vol. II: *The libraries of King Henry VIII* (London, 2000), p. xlix.
34. Henry's notations, Erasmus, *Novum Testamentum paraphrases* (1524) I, pp. 44, 47, 148–50; see Jane E. Phillips on Erasmus, *CWE Paraphrase on John*, trans. and ed. Jane E. Phillips (Toronto,1991), p. 49 n.37.
35. Henry's notations, Erasmus, *Novum Testamentum paraphrases* (1524), I, pp. 151–2.
36. Henry's notations, Erasmus, *Novum Testamentum paraphrases* (1524) I, p. 77; see Phillips, *CWE Paraphrase on John*, p. 86 n.69.
37. Loades, 'The personal religion of Mary I', p. 25.
38. BL, Cotton MS Vespasian F.XIII, fol. 72r.
39. Udall, 'To ... Quene Katherine' in *Paraphrase on John* [1548], sig. AAa1a.
40. Maria Dowling, *Humanism in the age of Henry VIII* (London, 1986), pp. 219–47; King, 'Patronage and piety', pp. 44, 264 n.1; Mary Ellen Lamb, 'The Cooke sisters: Attitudes toward learned women in the Renaissance' in *Silent but for the word*, ed. Hannay, p. 116.
41. Thomas à Kempis, *Full deuoute and gostely treatyse of the imytacion and followynge the blessyd lyfe of our most merciful savyour Cryst*, trans. William Atkinson and Margaret Beaufort (London, [1504] 1517) STC 23957, sig. C5b, drawing on Matthew 11:25, Luke 10:21 in addition to 1 Corinthians 1:20–24.
42. [Jacques de Gruytrode], *Mirroure of golde for the synfull soule*, trans. Margaret Beaufort (London, 1506) STC 6894.5; Michael K. Jones and Malcolm G. Underwood, *The king's mother: Lady Margaret Beaufort, countess of Richmond and Derby* (Cambridge, 1992), p. 184.
43. John Fisher, *Here after foloweth a mornynge remembrau[n]ce had at the moneth mynde of the noble prynces Margarete Countesse of Rychemonde [et] Darbye* (London, 1509) STC 10891, sig. Aiiia; Jones and Underwood, *King's mother*, pp. 184–5.
44. BL, Add. MS 17012, fols 192v–94r.
45. BL, Royal MS 17 C. XVI, fol. 2v.
46. BL, Add. MS 12060, fols. 9v, 20r–23v; James P. Carley, 'The writings of Henry Parker, Lord Morley' in *Triumphs of English*, eds Axton and Carley, p. 51.
47. While scholars have praised Parr's learning, she was not as comfortable with Latin as her step-daughters. There are no holograph records of her Latin and she claimed to find English 'aptest' for her intelligence: BL,

Lansdowne MS 1236, fol. 11r. Nor was she the 'anonymous' translator of the *Paraphrase on Matthew*, as James argues: *Kateryn Parr*, pp. 228–33. In his dedicatory letter to the *Paraphrase on Acts*, sig. AAA2a, Udall contrasted his unwillingness to meddle with Mary's attempt at John to his thorough revisions of the *Paraphrase on Matthew* and *Acts*. Had Parr parsed Matthew, Udall would have considered his intervention there equally improper.

48. Katherine Parr, *Prayers or medytacions, wherein the mynd is stirred, paciently to suffre all afflictions here* (London, 1545) STC 4818.5; C. Fenno Hoffman, Jr., 'Catherine Parr as a woman of letters', *Huntington Library Quarterly* 23 (1960), pp. 349–67.

49. Kimberly Anne Coles, *Religion, reform and women's writing in early modern England* (Cambridge and New York, 2008), p. 56 describes Parr's adaptation as combining 'traditional and emergent forms' of worship.

50. Janel Mueller, 'Devotion as difference: Intertextuality in Queen Katherine Parr's *Prayers or meditations* (1545)', *Huntington Library Quarterly* 53 (1990), pp. 171–91 (at pp. 176–7).

51. Juan Luis Vives, *De institutione feminae christianae*, SWV, V, pp. 2, 3.

52. James, *Kateryn Parr*, pp. 136, 156, 161, 219–20, 237.

53. Loades (1989), pp. 102–5, 116–17.

54. *CSPSp*, VI.ii, p. 459, VIII, p. 2; *LP*, XVIII.ii, no. 39, p. 19, no. 467, p. 254, no. 501, p. 269; XX.ii, no. 900, p. 438; Hatfield House, Cecil MS 147, fol. 6r–v; Loades (1989), pp. 102–17; James, *Kateryn Parr*, pp. 90, 111, 113, 117, 127–35.

55. *LP*, XIX.i, no. 118, p. 64; *CSPSp*, VII, p. 55.

56. *CSPSp*, VIII, p. 280; *LP*, XX.i, no. 862, p. 434; XX.ii, no. 899, p. 437, no. 900, pp. 437–38; A&M [1583], II, p. 1243.

57. TNA, LC2/2, fol. 45r; *LP*, XX ii no. 909 (47), p. 445.

58. *LP*, XX.ii App. 2, p. 549; TNA, E101/424/12, fol. 15r.

59. *LP*, XVI no. 1253, p. 536.

60. Loades (1989), p. 118.

61. Udall, 'To . . . Quene Katherine' in *Paraphrase on John* [1548], sig. AAa1a.

62. '*ut opus hoc Pulcherimum, atq[ue] utilissimum . . . summo Reipub[licae] bono suscepisti*': BL, Cotton MS Vespasian F.III, fol. 37r.

63. *Paraphrase on John* [1548], sig. IIi1a; see Phillips, *CWE Paraphrase on John*, p. 118 n.75.

64. Mary follows 1534's *nos* rather than 1535's *vos* in rendering 'stryuen against us': *Paraphrase on John* [1548], sig. MMm3a; Phillips, *CWE Paraphrase on John*, p. 167 n.1.

65. Udall echoes 1535's *sibi* rather than the earlier *tibi videntur* in 'thynke themselves'; and 1535's *perfectio* rather than the earlier *profectio* in 'euangelicall perfeccion': *Paraphrase on Luke* [1548], sigs S1a and S2b; see Phillips on Erasmus, *CWE Paraphrase on Luke*, trans. and ed. Jane E. Phillips (Toronto, 2003), pp. 66 n.26, 68 n.35.

66. Lori Chamberlain, 'Gender and the metaphorics of translation' in *Rethinking translation: Discourse, subjectivity, ideology*, ed. Lawrence Venuti (London, 1992), pp. 55–74; but see Suzanne Trill, 'Sixteenth-century women's writing: Mary Sidney's *Psalmes* and the 'femininity' of translation' in *Writing and the English Renaissance*, eds William Zunder and Suzanne Trill (London and New York, 1996), pp. 140–58.

67. Udall, 'To the moste vertuous Ladie Quene Katherine' in *Paraphrase on Matthew* [1548], sig. C8a; Udall, 'To the good Christian' in *First tome of the Paraphrases* (1552), sig. CC7b.

68. Erasmus, *Opus epistolarum*, eds P. S. Allen et al. (11 vols, Oxford, 1906–58), I, no. 188, pp. 418–19.

69. *Paraphrase on John* [1548], sigs BBb2a–b.

70. *Paraphrase on John* [1548], sig. BBb4a; see Phillips, *CWE Paraphrase on John*, p. 20 n.49.

71. *Paraphrase on John* [1548], sig. LLl1a.

72. *Paraphrase on John* [1548], sig. KKk2b; see Phillips, *CWE Paraphrase on John*, p. 136 n.40.

73. *Paraphrase on John* [1548], sig. CCc7a; see Phillips, *CWE Paraphrase on John*, p. 42 n.33.

74. *Paraphrasis in Ioannem* [1534], p. 224; *Paraphrase on John* [1548], sig. IIi5b.

75. *Paraphrasis in Ioannem* [1534], p. 160; *Paraphrase on John* [1548], sig. GGg2b.

76. *Paraphrase on John* [1548], sig. CCc5b; see Phillips, *CWE Paraphrase on John*, p. 38 n.4, locating the verb in Livy, *Ab urbe condita*, 1.57.8; 39.42.10, Tacitus, *Histories*, 4.29.1 and *Annals*, 11.37.2.

77. *Paraphrase on John* [1548], sig. DDd1a; see Phillips, *CWE Paraphrase on John*, p. 45 n.4, locating the figure in Cicero, *De inventione*, 1.20–2.

78. Erasmus, *CWE De copia/ De ratione studii*, trans. Betty I. Knott and Brian McGregor, ed. Craig Thompson (Toronto, 1978), pp. 302–3, 678–9.

79. *Paraphrasis in Ioannem* [1534], pp. 79, 225; *Paraphrase on John* [1548], sigs DDd1b, IIi6a.

80. *Paraphrasis in Ioannem* [1534], p. 115; *Paraphrase on John* [1548], sig. EEe4b.

81. E.g. BL, Lansdowne MS 96, fols 25r–26r.

82. Lucy E. C. Wooding, *Rethinking Catholicism in Reformation England* (Oxford, 2000), pp. 152–80; Duffy, *Stripping of the altars*, pp. 524–42.

83. *Paraphrase on John* [1548], sigs BBb6b, DDd8a, IIi8a–b, KKk7b, LLl3b, LLl5b, LLl7a, MMm5a.

84. Edmund Bonner, *Profytable and necessarye doctryne, with certayne homilies* (London, 1555) STC 3283.7 and 3285.9 (*Homelies*), Preface 3–4, sigs B1a–B2a, T2a–T4a; Thomas Watson, *Holsome and Catholyke doctryne concerninge the seven sacramentes* (London, 1558) STC 25114, fols ir, xxxvir–lxr, lxxr, cxlv. See William Wizeman, 'The theology and

spirituality of a Marian bishop: The pastoral and polemical sermons of Thomas Watson', in Duffy and Loades (2006), pp. 258–80.

85. Craig, 'Forming a Protestant consciousness?', pp. 326–28.
86. Folger Shakespeare Library, Washington DC, MSS L. b. 26 and L. b. 302, fol. 6r.
87. Erasmus, *Epistle of Erasmus Roterdamus, sent unto Conradus Pelicanus, concerning his opinion of the blessed Sacrament* (London, 1554) STC 10491, sig. A5a; Lucy Wooding, 'The Marian Restoration and the mass', in Duffy and Loades (2006), pp. 227–57.
88. *Paraphrase on John* [1548], sig. NNn3b.

8. Maids and Wives

1. Holinshed's *Chronicles* (1587), p. 1091.
2. For a discussion of Mary's various false pregnancies see Judith Richard's chapter in this collection.
3. Holinshed's *Chronicles* (1987), p. 1161.
4. G. R. Elton, *England under the Tudors* (London, 1955), p. 214.
5. *A&M* [1570], p. 1335.
6. Miles Hogarde, *The displaying of the protestantes* (London, 1556), STC 13557.
7. John Christopherson, *An exhortation to all men to beware rebellion* (London. 1554) STC 5207, sig. O4r.
8. James Brooks, *A sermon very notable, fruitful and godly* (London, 1553) STC 3838, sig. A3v.
9. Brooks, *A sermon*, sig. B3r.
10. John Proctor, 'The prologue to his deer brethren and naturall countree men of Englande', *The way home to Christ and truth leading from Antichrist and errour*, Vincent of Lerins (1556) STC 24754, Ab.
11. Eamon Duffy, *The stripping of the altars: Traditional religion in England 1400–1580* (New Haven, Conn. and London, 1992), p. 529.
12. Robert Carl Johnson has suggested in *John Heywood* (New York, 1970), p. 67, that the chief spider could represent a number of historical figures, Wolsey, Cromwell, Cranmer and Northumberland.
13. John Heywood, *The spider and the fly*, ed. John S. Farmer (London, 1908), p. 412.
14. Heywood, *The spider*, pp. 426–7.
15. Nicholas Udall, *Respublica*, ed. W. W. Greg (London, 1932). For a nuanced reading of this play see Greg Walker, *The politics of performance in early Renaissance drama* (Cambridge and New York, 1998), Chapter 5.
16. Udall, *Respublica*, p. 65.
17. Udall, *Respublica*, p. 66.
18. This view of the Edwardine Reformation can be directly related to the model of history in *Respublica*, which Douglas F. Rutledge has argued

is cyclical and 'designed to help society cope in a cohesive fashion with the threat of misrule'. Constructing history as a cycle implies a degree of repetition incompatible with the more confessional or Augustinian models of history favoured by Godly reformers, Protestant and Catholic. See 'Respublica: Rituals of status elevation and the political mythology of Mary Tudor', *Medieval and Renaissance drama in England* 5 (1991), pp. 53–68.

19. Walker, *Politics of performance*, p. 189.
20. William Forrest, *The history of Grisild the second* (London, 1875), p. 130.
21. Ursula Potter, 'Tales of patient Griselda and Henry VIII', *Early Theatre* 5 (2002), pp. 11–28, at p. 17.
22. Forrest, *Grisild*, p. 5.
23. David Aers and Lynn Staley, *The powers of the holy: Religion, politics, and gender in late medieval English culture* (University Park, Pa., 1996), pp. 239–40.
24. Forrest, *Grisild*, p. 5.
25. Forrest, *Grisild*, pp. 79–80.
26. A. G. Dickens, *The English Reformation*, 2nd edn (London, 1989), p. 313.
27. Forrest, *Grisild*, p. 125.
28. Forrest, *Grisild*, p. 127.
29. Duffy and Loades (2006), p. 199.
30. *The life of Fisher*, a late Marian text probably completed under Elizabeth, draws on very different historiographical traditions from Forrest's *The history* and in particular at times evokes More's *Richard III*. For a discussion of this work, see Thomas Betteridge, *Tudor histories and the English Reformations 1530–83* (Aldershot, 1999), chapter 3.
31. Forrest, *Grisild*, p. 150.
32. For this aspect of Edwardine literature, see Thomas Betteridge, *Literature and politics in the English Reformation* (Manchester, 2004) chapter 2.
33. John Guy, *Tudor England* (Oxford and New York, 1988), p. 239.

9. The Religious Policy of Mary I

1. Judith M. Richards, 'Mary Tudor: Renaissance queen of England' in *'High and mighty queens' of early modern England: Realities and representations*, eds Carole Levin, Jo Eldridge Carney and Debra Barrett-Graves (New York and Basingstoke, 2003), p. 37.
2. Matthew Hansen, ' "And a queen of England, too": The "Englishing" of Catherine of Aragon in sixteenth-century English literary and chronicle history', in *'High and mighty queens'*, p. 81. I wish to thank Susan Doran and Thomas S. Freeman for pointing out the latter issue to me.
3. See Mary's will in Loades (1989), pp. 372, 373, 377.
4. *CSPD: Mary I*, revised (London, 1998), pp. 5–6.
5. Christopher Haigh, *English Reformations* (Oxford, 1993), pp. 206–7.

6. Jennifer Loach, *Parliament and crown in the reign of Mary Tudor* (Oxford, 1986), pp. 77–8.
7. A. G. Dickens and Dorothy Carr (eds), *The Reformation in England to the accession of Elizabeth I: Documents of modern history* (New York, 1968), pp. 145–8.
8. Loach, *Parliament and crown in the reign of Mary*, pp. 76, 173.
9. *CSPSp*, 1554, pp. xxiv–xxviii; cf. Philip Hughes, *The Reformation in England* (3 vols, London, 1950–4), II, pp. 189–90; Elizabeth Russell, 'Mary Tudor and Mr Jorkins', *Historical Research* 63 (1990), p. 266.
10. *Visitation articles and injunctions of the period of the Reformation, 1536–1558*, eds W. H. Frere and W. M. Kennedy (3 vols, London, 1910), II, pp. 322–9.
11. *The correspondence of Reginald Pole*, ed. Thomas Mayer (4 vols, Aldershot, 2002–8), III, p. 545.
12. *The Anglican canons 1529–1947*, ed. Gerald Bray (Woodbridge, 1998), pp. 100–7; *The canons and decrees of the Council of Trent*, trans. H. J. Shroeder (Rockford, Ill., 1978), pp. 276–8. Regarding the most controversial activities of the Marian Catholic revival – the persecution of religious dissenters and the deprivation of married clergy – see the articles by Judith M. Richards and Thomas S. Freeman in this volume.
13. Eamon Duffy, *The stripping of the altars* (London, 1992), pp. 543–5; Haigh, *English Reformations*, pp. 214–16.
14. Gary Gibbs, 'Marking the days: Henry Machyn's manuscript and the mid-Tudor era', in Duffy and Loades (2006), p. 302. *Pace* Loades (1989), pp. 327–8 and John King, *Tudor royal iconography* (Princeton, 1989), p. 186.
15. For Philip II's restricted role in the Catholic revival of Marian England, see Alexander Samson, 'Changing places: The marriage and royal entry of Philip, Prince of Austria, and Mary Tudor, July–August 1554', *SCJ* 36 (2005), pp. 761–84.
16. *CSPD: Mary I*, pp. 337–8, 356.
17. *Pole Correspondence*, III, p. 544.
18. John O'Malley, *Tradition and transition: Historical perspectives on Vatican II* (Lima, Ohio, 2002), p. 154.
19. Duffy, *Stripping of the altars*, pp. 533–7.
20. Duffy and Loades (2006), pp. xix–xx.
21. *CSPD: Mary I*, pp. 334–5.
22. Thomas Mayer, 'The success of Cardinal Pole's final legation' in Duffy and Loades (2006), pp. 164–74.
23. *CSPD: Mary I*, pp. 355–6.
24. Andreas Löwe, *Richard Smyth and the language of orthodoxy: Re-imagining Tudor Catholic polemicism* (Leiden, 2003), pp. 51–7.
25. Loach, *Parliament and crown in the reign of Mary*, pp. 76, 172–7.
26. *CSPD: Mary I*, pp. 291, 331.

27. *CSPD: Mary I*, p. 331.
28. *Anglican canons*, ed. Bray, pp. 80–1.
29. Natalie Mears, 'Courts, courtiers, and culture in Tudor England', *HJ* 46 (2003), pp. 710–11; Gary Gibbs offers some interesting hypotheses regarding Mary's strategies as queen and Catholic reformer in 'Marking the days: Henry Machyn's manuscript', pp. 301–7.
30. *CSPD: Mary I*, pp. 365, 368, 372, 373, 375.
31. O'Malley, *Tradition and transition*, p. 154.
32. Loach, *Parliament and crown in the reign of Mary*, p. 173.
33. Thomas Mayer, *Reginald Pole: Prince and prophet* (Cambridge, 2000), pp. 282–9.
34. Pole credited Mary and Philip with the restoration of Westminster Abbey; see *Pole Correspondence* III, p. 305. See also Duffy and Loades (2006), pp. xxi–ii. In canonical terms, the pre-1536 houses had ceased to exist, according to the negotiations for England's reconciliation with Rome; therefore the Marian communities were new foundations. What Mary, Pole and the religious thought in this regard was probably another matter; see Mayer, *Pole*, p. 283.
35. For the restoration of St Peter's Abbey, Westminster, see C. S. Knighton, 'Westminster Abbey restored' in Duffy and Loades (2006), pp. 77–123.
36. *CSPD: Mary I*, p. 222.
37. Loades (1989), pp. 371–4, 377.
38. Diarmaid MacCulloch, *Tudor Church Militant: Edward VI and the Protestant Reformation* (London, 1999), p. 32.
39. Loades (1989), p. 142.
40. *CSPD: Mary I*, p. 228.
41. Claire Cross, 'The English universities, 1553–1558' in Duffy and Loades (2006), p. 62.
42. William Wizeman, *The theology and spirituality of Mary Tudor's Church* (Aldershot), p. 20.
43. Cross, 'The English universities', p. 72; Daniel Bennett Page, 'Uniform and catholic: Church music in the reign of Mary Tudor (1553–1558)' (Brandeis University Ph.D. thesis, 1996), p. 49.
44. Page, 'Uniform and catholic', pp. 311–17, 338–49.
45. *Pole Correspondence* III, pp. 489–90.
46. Andrew Hegarty, 'Carranza and the English universities', in *Reforming Catholicism in the England of Mary Tudor: The achievement of Friar Bartolomé Carranza*, eds John Edwards and Ronald Truman (Aldershot 2005), pp. 153–72.
47. Loades (1989), pp. 372–3, 377.
48. Cross, 'The English universities', pp. 72–3.
49. Jennifer Loach, 'Reformation controversies' in *The history of the University of Oxford*, ed. T. H. Aston (8 vols, Oxford, 1984–92), III, pp. 381–7.

50. T. A. Birrell, *English monarchs and their books: From Henry VII to Charles II*, Panizzi Lectures 1986 (London, 1987), p. 22.
51. Birrell, *English monarchs and their books*, pp. 21–3; Wizeman, *Theology and spirituality of Mary Tudor's Church*, pp. 209–11.
52. See Birrell, *English monarchs and their books*, pp. 21–2.
53. Judith M. Richards, 'Mary Tudor: Renaissance queen of England' in *'High and mighty queens' of early modern England*, p. 39.
54. 'Introduction' in *The book in Britain, 1400–1557*, eds Lotte Hellinga and J. B. Trapp vol. III of the *Cambridge history of the book in Britain* (Cambridge, 1999), pp. 4–5, 23–4.
55. See *The complete works of Miles Hogarde*, ed. William Wizeman (2009, Renaissance English Text Society).
56. Duffy, *Stripping of the altars*, p. 542.
57. William Wizeman, 'The pope, the saints and the dead: Uniformity of doctrine in Carranza's *Catechismo* and the printed works of the Marian theologians' in *Reforming Catholicism in the England of Mary Tudor*, pp. 115–16.
58. Wizeman, *Theology and spirituality of Mary Tudor's Church*, pp. 43–9.
59. Pamela Neville-Sington, 'Press, politics and religion' in *The book in Britain III*, p. 606.
60. Page, 'Uniform and catholic', pp. 26–7.
61. For a recent discussion of Trent's nuanced stance regarding sacred music, see Alexander Fisher, *Music and religious identity in Counter-Reformation Augsburg, 1580–1630* (Aldershot, 2004), pp. 18–21.
62. Page, 'Uniform and catholic', pp. 46–50.
63. Page, 'Uniform and catholic' pp. 68–94, 136–40.
64. Page, 'Uniform and catholic', pp. 171–7, 179, 184–7.
65. David Skinner, *Robert Fayrfax, the masses, the cardinall's musick*, CDGAX 353 (ASV 2001), programme notes, p. 1.
66. Page, 'Uniform and catholic', pp. 232–40, 243ff.
67. John Edwards, 'Corpus Christi at Kingston upon Thames: Bartolomé Carranza and the eucharist in Marian England' in *Reforming Catholicism in the England of Mary Tudor*, pp. 139–52.
68. Page, 'Uniform and catholic', p. 391.
69. John Irving, 'Philipus de Monte (1521–1603)' in *Renaissance masterpieces: The choir of New College, Oxford, CD 92433* (STEMRA, 1998), programme notes, p. 23.
70. Stanford Lehmburg, *The reformation of cathedrals: Cathedrals in English society, 1485–1603* (Princeton, 1998), pp. 124–31; Page, 'Uniform and catholic', pp. xii–xv.
71. Gary Gibbs, 'Marking the days: Henry Machyn's manuscript', pp. 299–308.
72. Wizeman, *The theology and spirituality of Mary Tudor's Church*, p. 48; and William Wizeman, 'The theology and spirituality of a Marian bishop:

The pastoral and polemical sermons of Thomas Watson' in Duffy and Loades (2006), pp. 258–61.

73. Page, 'Uniform and catholic', p. xii.
74. According to the *Grey Friars chronicle*, Mary provided the shrine and its altar with 'diverse jewels'; see Page, 'Uniform and catholic', p. 73.
75. Led by Mary, even the ambassadors of Muscovy came to the shrine; see Page, 'Uniform and catholic', p. 73; Knighton, 'Westminster Abbey', pp. 95–6.
76. Wizeman, *Theology and spirituality of Mary Tudor's Church*, pp. 219–50.
77. Page, 'Uniform and catholic', pp. 73–5. I wish to thank Susan Doran and Thomas Freeman for calling my attention to the last point.
78. Loades (1989), pp. 245, 310.
79. H. O. Evennett, *The spirit of the Counter-Reformation* (Cambridge, 1968), pp. 37–40.
80. Evennett, *Spirit of the Counter-Reformation*, p. 42.
81. Lorraine Attreed and Alexandra Winkler, 'Faith and forgiveness: Lessons in statecraft for Queen Mary Tudor', *SCJ* 36 (2005), pp. 971–89.
82. Timothy Elston, 'Tranformation or continuity? Sixteenth-century education and the legacy of Catherine of Aragon, Mary I, and Juan Luis Vives' in *'High and mighty queens'*, pp. 12–26.
83. Richards, 'Mary Tudor: Renaissance queen of England', pp. 29–31.
84. Haigh, *English Reformations*, p. 236; Cross, 'The English universities', p. 76.
85. For Newman and his times see Ian Ker, *John Henry Newman: A biography* (Oxford, 1988).
86. *Pace* John Bossy, *The English Catholic community, 1570–1850* (London, 1975), p. 397.
87. O'Malley, *Tradition and transition*, p. 37.

10. Burning Zeal

1. See Andrew Pettegree, *Marian Protestantism: Six studies* (Aldershot, 1996), pp. 161–3; Elton, *Reform and Reformation* (London, 1977), p. 377; David Loades, *The reign of Mary Tudor*, 2nd edn (Harlow, 1991), pp. 275 and 396 (hereafter this last work will be cited as Loades, *Reign*). In an important, but qualified caveat, Christopher Haigh maintains that while the burnings failed in that they made heroes of their victims, they nevertheless did little harm to Mary's government: *English Reformations: Religion, politics and society under the Tudors* (Oxford, 1993), p. 234.
2. Eamon Duffy, *Fires of faith: Catholic England under Mary Tudor* (New Haven, Conn. and London, 2009), pp. 79–170. (Hereafter this work will be cited as *FF*.)
3. Judith M. Richards, *Mary Tudor* (Abingdon and New York, 2008), pp. 197–202.
4. London Guildhall MS 9531/12, fol. 363r.

5. BL, Cotton MS Titus Bii, fol. 99r–v. Copies of this letter were probably also sent to JPs in other counties.
6. TNA, SP 14/190, fol. 133r–v.
7. Duffy argues that Mary was following Pole's lead on the burning of heretics and other religious matters (*FF*, pp. 94–95 and 114).
8. See Brad Gregory, *Salvation at stake: Christian martyrdom in early modern Europe* (Cambridge, Mass. and London, 1999), pp. 74–96; Benjamin Kaplan, *Divided by faith: Religious conflict and the practice of toleration in early modern Europe* (Cambridge, Mass. and London, 2007), pp. 15–47 and 99–124; and Alexandra Walsham, *Charitable hatred: Tolerance and intolerance in England, 1500–1700* (Manchester, 2006), pp. 39–56.
9. *FF*, pp. 155–70, esp. pp. 167–70.
10. See, for example, Pettegree, *Marian studies*, p. 161; Walsham, *Charitable hatred*, p. 77, Sarah Covington, *The trail of martyrdom: Persecution and resistance in sixteenth-century England* (Notre Dame, Ind., 2003), p. 12; and Michael Zell, 'The establishment of a Protestant Church' in *Early modern Kent, 1540–1640*, ed. Michael Zell (Woodbridge, 2000), p. 231.
11. *APC* VI, p. 135.
12. Loades, *Reign*, p. 297; Zell, 'Establishment', p. 231.
13. *A&M* [1583], p. 2012.
14. TNA C/85/141/26; *A&M* [1583], p. 2025.
15. *A&M* [1563], pp. 1631–2; *APC* VI, p. 144.
16. *A&M* [1583], p. 2020.
17. See Appendix numbers 103, 104, 248, 249, 250 and 251.
18. Martha C. Skeeters, *Community and clergy: Bristol and the Reformation c. 1530–c. 1570* (Oxford, 1993), pp. 132–33.
19. *A&M* [1583], p. 2052.
20. *A&M* [1583], p. 2052.
21. I. T. Shield, 'The Reformation in the diocese of Salisbury, 1547–1562' (B. Litt. dissertation, Oxford, 1960), pp. 223–4. Such a re-examination is curious. Perhaps the new hearing was needed to obtain the necessary writ from Chancery. If so, it would suggest that Geffrie, in his zeal, had cut some procedural corners and this might help explain Hungerford's reluctance to proceed with the burnings.
22. *A&M* [1583], pp. 2054–55.
23. On Geffrie's death halting heresy prosecution in Salisbury, see *A&M* [1583], p. 2100.
24. *A&M* [1583], pp. 2039–43.
25. *FF*, p. 187.
26. John Strype, *Ecclesiastical memorials* (3 vols. in 6 parts, Oxford, 1822), III, 2, pp. 125 and 127–8; and BL Harley MS 416, fol. 74r. Hereafter, *Ecclesiastical memorials* will be cited as *EM*.
27. Walsham, *Charitable hatred*, p. 77.

28. *A&M* [1583], pp. 1480, 1579–81, 1689.
29. *A&M* [1583], pp. 1971–4.
30. *A&M* [1583], pp. 2039–43.
31. *A&M* [1583], pp. 1916, 1972–4 and 2037 and Appendix, nos. 197, 237, 241, 243–5, 257.
32. *A&M* [1583], pp. 2206–7.
33. *A&M* [1583], pp. 2013–24 and 2016.
34. Elizabeth Cooper, Cicely Ormes and Richard Sharp; see *A&M* [1583], pp. 2005, 2023, 2052.
35. *The correspondence of Reginald Pole*, ed. Thomas F. Mayer (4 vols, Aldershot, 2002–2008), III, pp. 132–3.
36. *APC* VI, p. 144 and *A&M* [1563], p. 1631. Thurston was burned on 17 September 1557.
37. *A&M* [1583], 2047, *APC* VI, pp. 361 and 371–2; R. H. Fritze, 'Faith and local faction: Religious changes, national politics and the development of local factionalism in Hampshire' (Ph.D. dissertation, University of Cambridge, 1981), p. 342.
38. My estimate of the number of Henrician burnings is tallied from Foxe, J. A. F. Thomson, *The later Lollards, 1414–1520* (London, 1965) and John Fines, *Biographical register of early English Protestants, 1525–1558* (2 vols. The first volume was published in Abingdon in 1981. The second volume remains in typescript. I used the copy in the Cambridge University Library).
39. William Monter, *Judging the French Reformation: Heresy trials by sixteenth century parlements* (Cambridge, Mass., 1999), p. 35.
40. Monter, *Judging*, pp. 40–2, and James D. Tracey, *Holland and Habsburg rule, 1506–66* (Berkeley, Calif., 1990), pp. 160–70.
41. Monter, *Judging*, p. 53.
42. See Appendix. The list there compromises 313 names rather than 312 because I have included George Eagles in it, although he was technically neither arrested nor executed for heresy.
43. *Archdeacon Harpsfield's visitation, 1557*, ed. L. E. Whatmore, Catholic Record Society (2 vols, London, 1950–1), passim.
44. *Harpsfield's visitation*, II, pp. 176–83.
45. London Guildhall Library MS 9531/12, fol. 419r and *Interrogatories upon which ... churchwardens shal be charged* (London, 1557), STC 10117.
46. *A&M* [1583], pp. 2112–13.
47. *A&M* [1583]. p. 2071.
48. E. Cardwell, *Documentary annals of the Reformed Church of England* (2 vols, Oxford, 1839), I, pp. 109–13; Helen L. Parish, *Clerical marriage and the English Reformation: Precedent, policy and practice* (Aldershot, 2000), pp. 186–88.
49. Parish, *Clerical marriage*, pp. 188–9.
50. John Rogers, Laurence Saunders and John Bland were all married parish priests but they had been arrested and removed from their

livings before the deprivation of married priests began. John Frankesh, another martyr, was also a parish priest but it is not known if he was even married.

51. *A&M* [1583], p. 1895 and Richard Newcourt, *Repertorium: An ecclesiastical parochial history of the diocese of London* (2 vols, London, 1708–10), II, pp. 586–7.

52. William Hale, Thomas Leyes, William Andrew and John Johnson (see Appendix numbers 57, 59–60 and 246).

53. Newcourt, *Repertorium*, II, p. 586.

54. See Appendix numbers 21, 123, 124 and 125.

55. Brett Usher, 'Essex evangelicals under Edward VI: Richard Lord Rich, Richard Alvey and their circle' in *John Foxe at Home and Abroad*, ed. David Loades (Aldershot, 2004), pp. 53–4; and Newcourt, *Repertorium*, II, p. 384.

56. *A&M* [1583], pp. 1974–6.

57. Newcourt, *Repertorium*, II, pp. 50 and 106; London Guildhall Library MS 9531/12, fol. 473r.

58. *A&M* [1583], pp. 2005–7.

59. *A&M* [1583], pp. 2008–21.

60. *A&M* [1583], pp. 2015, 2016–18.

61. See *A&M* [1570], p. 2197; *A&M* [1583], pp. 1979–80, 2081–2.

62. *A&M* [1583], p. 2112, *Harpsfield's visitation*, I, p. 124; LPL Pole Register, fol. 377r.

63. J. S. Chamberlain, 'Staplehurst Register', *Archaeologia Cantiana* 28 (1909), p. 289 and *A&M* [1583], p. 1979. Potkins died in prison in November 1556, Benden was burned on 19 June 1557 and the Allins were burned on the preceding day (*A&M* [1583], pp. 1584, 1981,1979).

64. Jeri McIntosh, *From heads of household to heads of state: The pre-accession households of Mary and Elizabeth Tudor, 1516–1558* (New York, 2008), pp. 148–93; Anna Whitelock and Diarmaid MacCulloch, 'Princess Mary's household and the succession crisis, July 1553', *HJ* 50 (2007), pp. 265–87.

65. See Diarmaid MacCulloch, *Suffolk and the Tudors: Politics and religion in an English county, 1500–1600* (Oxford, 1985), pp. 232–4.

66. 'The *Vita Mariae Anglicanae Reginae* of Robert Wingfield of Brantham', ed. and trans. Diarmaid MacCulloch, *Camden Miscellany* 28, Camden Society, fourth series 29 (1984), p. 259 (hereafter cited as *Vita*); *A&M* [1563], p. 1698; *A&M* [1583], p. 2048.

67. For example *A&M* [1583], pp. 2049, 2099–2100.

68. Whitelock and MacCulloch, 'Princess Mary's household', pp. 281–3; Eric Ives, *Lady Jane Grey: A Tudor mystery* (Chichester, 2009), p. 229.

69. *A&M* [1583], pp. 1683, 1895–6, 1910–12, 1917, 2006–7; *FF*, pp. 95–6,136–7.

70. *A&M* [1583], p. 1683.
71. See 'Tyrell, Edmund' in *HoP.*
72. MacCulloch, *Suffolk and the Tudors*, pp. 178–9; BL Cotton MS Cleopatra E iv, fol. 124r.
73. G. Baskerville, 'Married clergy and pensioned religious in Norwich Diocese, 1555', *EHR* 33 (1948), p. 62; *A&M* [1583], p. 1913.
74. *A&M* [1583], pp. 1912, 1917–18, 2035–6.
75. *Vita*, pp. 255–6 and 258; also see 'Williams, Philip' in *HoP.*
76. *A&M* [1583], pp. 2089–90.
77. *Vita*, p. 257.
78. *A&M* [1583], pp. 1519, 1527.
79. MacCulloch, *Suffolk*, p. 233.
80. *A&M* [1583], p. 1703.
81. 'Darcy, Thomas', *ODNB.*
82. *A&M* [1563], pp. 1616–18; *APC* V, p. 132; *APC* VI, pp. 18–19.
83. *A&M* [1583], pp. 1971–2.
84. *A&M* [1583], pp. 1585, 1593,1601–3.
85. See Appendix numbers 21, 60, 106–8, 141, 148–9, 198.
86. *APC* V, p. 337.
87. *A&M* [1583], pp. 1594–6.
88. Peter Clark, *English provincial society from the Reformation to the Revolution: Religion, politics and society in Kent 1500–1640* (Hassocks, Sussex, 1977), pp. 49–64.
89. See Diarmaid MacCulloch, *Thomas Cranmer* (New Haven, Conn. and London, 1996), pp. 297–322; Michael Zell, 'The prebendaries plot of 1543: A reconsideration', *Journal of Ecclesiastical History* 27 (1976), pp. 241–53.
90. Clark, *English provincial society*, p. 98.
91. MacCulloch, *Thomas Cranmer*, pp. 303–8, 317, 322.
92. MacCulloch, *Thomas Cranmer*, p. 312.
93. *A&M* [1583], pp. 1665–73; 'Bland, John', *ODNB.*
94. Clark, *English provincial society*, pp. 54–55; 'Baker, John', *ODNB*; MacCulloch, *Thomas Cranmer*, pp. 307–10, 312, 314.
95. *A&M* [1563], pp. 1594, 2054.
96. BL Harley MS 416, fol. 124v, *A&M* [1570], p. 2197; *A&M* [1583], pp. 1979–80.
97. *A&M* [1583], pp. 2081–2.
98. See Appendix numbers 181, 182 and 220.
99. See the *ODNB* articles on Baker and Moyle.
100. *Harpsfield's visitation* I, pp. 123–4 and II, p. 183.
101. Thomas S. Freeman, 'Over their dead bodies: Concepts of martyrdom in late medieval and early modern England' in *Martyrs and martyrdoms in England, c. 1400–1700*, eds Thomas S. Freeman and Thomas F. Mayer (Woodbridge, 2007), pp. 15–19; Alec Ryrie, *The gospel and Henry VIII:*

Evangelicals in the early English Reformation (Cambridge, 2003), pp. 85–9; and Susan Wabuda, 'Equivocation and recantation during the English Reformation: The "subtle shadows" of Dr. Edward Crome', *Journal of Ecclesiastical History* 44 (1993), pp. 224–42.

102. *A&M* [1583], pp. 2005, 2035.
103. *A&M* [1583], pp. 2021–2.
104. Samuel Rudder, *A new history of Gloucestershire* (Cirencester, 1779), pp. 563–4. Rudder claimed that he drew this story from an older manuscript history of the parish and he does seem to be very well-informed regarding the details of Hornes's arrest and execution (see Appendix note 85).
105. *A&M* [1583], pp. 2012, 2035, 2048.
106. *A&M* [1583], p. 2049.
107. *FF*, pp. 171–87.
108. For London, I am only counting burnings in Smithfield and not including the burnings that took place in areas around London such as Islington, Stratford, Southwark, Westminster and Brentford.
109. That was Stephen Kempe who was burned in Canterbury in January 1557.
110. *A&M* [1583], p. 1543.
111. *APC* V, pp. 134,137.
112. *Narratives of the days of the Reformation*, ed. J. G. Nichols, Camden Society, original series 77 (London, 1859), p. 212.
113. BL Harley MS 416, fol. 74v.
114. *A&M* [1583], p. 1915.
115. *A&M* [1583], pp. 1915, 2007–8.
116. *A&M* [1583], p. 1971.
117. *A&M* [1563], pp. 1610, 1614–15. Duffy's suggestion that he may have played a role in the arrest of Elizabeth Folkes (*FF*, p. 166) seems to be based on his confusion of Nicholas Clere, Folkes's employer, with Nicholas's older brother Benjamin.
118. *A&M* [1583], pp. 1971–2. Foxe misdates the letter in which this information appears to 1557, but internal references show that it was written in 1556.
119. *A&M* [1583], p. 2006.
120. *A&M* [1583], pp. 1605, 2008.
121. *A&M* [1583], p. 2009.
122. BL Harley MS 416, fols 74r and 75r.
123. Laquita M. Higgs, *Godliness and Governance in Tudor Colchester* (Ann Arbor, Mich. 1988). pp. 191–2; 'Browne, Robert' in *HoP*; and Mark Byford, 'The price of Protestantism: Assessing the impact of religious change on Elizabethan Essex: The cases of Heydon and Colchester, 1558–1594' (Oxford University D.Phil. thesis, 1988), pp. 158–62.

124. On Upcher's career see C. H. Garrett, *The Marian exiles: A study of the origins of Elizabethan puritanism* (Cambridge, 1938), p. 268; Byford, 'Price of Protestantism', pp. 123 and 192–258. On Upcher's ties to Foxe see Thomas S. Freeman, 'Fate, faction and fiction in Foxe's Book of Martyrs', *HJ* 43 (2000), p. 612.

125. Byford, 'Price of Protestantism', pp. 225–58; Higgs, 'Godliness and governance', pp. 233–4.

126. Miles Hogarde, *The displaying of the Protestantes* (London, 1556), STC 13558, fol. 62v. On the support the crowd showed to Rogers also see *CSPD* XIII, p. 138.

127. *A&M* [1583], p. 1583.

128. *A&M* [1563], p. 1217.

129. *A&M* [1583], pp. 1579–80.

130. *CSP Ven.*, VI, 1, p. 94.

131. *A&M* [1583], p. 1605.

132. Thomas Fuller, *The history of the worthies of England*, ed. P. Austin Nuttall (3 vols, London, 1840), II, p. 86.

133. *A&M* [1583], p. 1843.

134. Elizabeth Warne, although a Londoner, was executed at Stratford.

135. *APC* V, p. 224.

136. LMA, COL/CC/01/01/016, fol. 367v.

137. *The diary of Henry Machyn, citizen and merchant-taylor of London, 1550–1563*, ed. J. G. Nichols, Camden Society, original series 42 (London, 1848), pp. 99–100 (hereafter *Machyn*).

138. *A&M* [1583], pp. 1972–3; *FF*, pp. 138–40.

139. *FF*, pp. 139–40.

140. *A&M* [1583], p. 1972. Foxe maintains that Pole was responsible for the qualified reprieve. One wonders. It seems to have been Bonner who was anxious to avoid provoking the London crowds with more burnings. Foxe's crediting Pole may well have been due to the martyrologist's profound reluctance to say or write anything favourable about Bonner.

141. Margaret Hide was a Londoner, Agnes Stanley was from Leigh, Essex and where the three men were from is unknown.

142. Bindoff, *HoP*, under 'Gibson, Richard'.

143. *A&M* [1563], pp. 1640–5; *A&M* [1583], pp. 2026–7; Strype, *EM*, III, 2, pp. 46–7; ECL MS 260, fols. 72r and 204r; BL Harley MS 425, fols 99r and 125r; BL Add. MS 19400, fol. 33r.

144. *Machyn*, pp. 157–8. Foxe incorrectly gave the date as 18 November (*A&M* [1583], p. 2025).

145. *A&M* [1583], pp. 2029–31 and *A&M* [1563], p. 1632 [recte 1652].

146. *A&M* [1583], pp. 2043 and 2074; also see BL Harley MS 416, fol. 63r–v.

147. Inner Temple Library Petyt MS 538/47, fol. 3r.

148. *FF*, p. 83.
149. A. G. Dickens, *The English Reformation*, 2nd edn (London, 1989), p. 297.
150. See note 1 above.
151. Pettegree, *Marian studies*, p. 161.
152. Susan Brigden, *London and the Reformation* (Oxford, 1989), p. 605.
153. LMA, COL/CA/01/01/014, fol. 539v.
154. Pettegree, *Marian studies*, pp. 162–3.

11. Reassessing Mary Tudor

1. Cited by Thomas F. Mayer, *Reginald Pole: Prince and prophet* (Cambridge, 2000), p. 1.
2. Una Pope-Hennessy, *Agnes Strickland, biographer of the queens of England 1796–1874* (London, 1940), p. 109. The section on Mary was written by Elizabeth Strickland, but published in Agnes's name.
3. See for example, L. M. Montgomery, *Anne of Windy Willows*, first published 1936 (London, 1972), pp. 70–1.
4. *A&M* [1583], p. 1988.
5. G. R. Elton, *England under the Tudors* (Cambridge, 1958), p. 214; *Reform and Reformation: England 1509–1558* (London, 1977), p. 376.
6. Loades (1989), p. 146.
7. Glyn Redworth, *In defence of the Church Catholic: The life of Stephen Gardiner* (Oxford, 1990), p. 315; Susan Brigden, *New worlds, lost worlds: The rule of the Tudors 1485–1603* (London, 2000), p. 199.
8. A recent exception to this rather surprising tradition is William Wizeman, *The theology and spirituality of Mary Tudor's Church* (Aldershot, 2006).
9. Mary has been defined as 'bigoted' from at least the eighteenth-century David Hume's *History of England* (5 vols, London, 1864), III, p. 19 to Elton, *Reform and Reformation*. Several historians, including her foremost biographer, David Loades, present Mary as 'almost hysterical'.
10. See Brad Gregory, *Salvation at stake: Christian martyrdom in early modern Europe* (Cambridge, Mass. and London, 1999), p. 6; William Monter, *Judging the French Reformation: Heresy trials by sixteenth-century parlements* (Cambridge, Mass. and London, 1999), p. 48.
11. Loades (1989), p. 8.
12. *Tudor royal proclamations*, eds Paul L. Hughes and James F. Larkin (3 vols, New Haven, Conn. and London, 1969), II, No. 388.
13. '*Anno Mariae Primo Actes made in the Parlyament*', April, 1554, Cap I (London, 1554), fol. ii and verso (STC 9943).
14. For a discussion of the history and implications of the fourteenth-century debates, see my 'Gender difference and Tudor monarchy: The significance of Queen Mary I', *Parergon* 21 (2004), pp. 27–46.

15. M. Bloch, trans J. E. Anderson, *The royal touch: Sacred monarchy and scrofula in England and France* (London, 1973), pp. 190–1.
16. See *Visitation articles and injunctions of the period of the Reformation*, eds W. H. Frere and W. M. Kennedy (3 vols, London, 1910), II, pp. 322 ff.
17. For an account of Gardiner's changing opinions, see Redworth, *In defence of the Church Catholic*, pp. 48–70, 311–29.
18. Diarmaid MacCulloch, *Thomas Cranmer: A life* (New Haven, Conn., 1996), pp. 474–7.
19. Gina Alexander, 'Bonner and the Marian persecutions', *History* 60 (1975), pp. 374–91.
20. Gregory, *Salvation at stake*, p. 6.
21. For further discussion of the burnings, and Mary's role in them, see T. S. Freeman's essay in this collection, and my *Mary Tudor* (London, 2008), pp. 197–202.
22. Quentin Skinner, 'Some problems in the analysis of political thought and action', *Political Theory* 2 (1974), pp. 277–303, esp. p. 295.
23. E. Harris Harbison, *Rival ambassadors at the court of Queen Mary* (Princeton, N. J., 1940), pp. 50–3.
24. David Grummit, *The Calais garrison: War and military service in England, 1436–1558* (Woodbridge, 2008), pp. 164–5.
25. CSPVen IV April, 1531, no. 664, p. 279. The analysis of her condition includes the explanation *è stata molto male de matre secundo medici dicono.*
26. 'Hysteria' comes from the Greek term for 'womb', and was adopted as a popular nineteenth-century descriptor of some specifically 'female' disorders. For a more detailed introduction to this area of study, see Sara Mendelson and Patricia Crawford, *Women in early modern England 1550–1720* (Oxford, 1998), pp. 18–30.
27. Mary to unknown recipient, 23 Nov. 1550, in, *England under the reigns of Edward VI and Mary*, ed. P. F. Tytler (2 vols, London, 1839), I. p. 347.
28. Laura Gowing, 'Secret births and infanticide in seventeenth-century England', *Past and Present* 156 (1997), pp. 87–115, 90.
29. James Owen Drife, 'Phantom pregnancy', *British Medical Journal* 291 (1985), pp. 183–8, cited in Catherine Mann, ' "My Lord Lysles man": Household and identity in sixteenth-century letters' (Ph.D. thesis, University of Melbourne, 2002).
30. I am grateful to Professor Sybil Jack for allowing me to make use of her unpublished paper on the medical history of sixteenth and seventeenth-century queens.
31. Lady Lisle's 'pregnancy' and responses to it are fully discussed in Mann, ' "My Lord Lysles Man" ', pp. 147–67.
32. J. L. McIntosh, 'Sovereign princesses: Mary and Elizabeth Tudor as heads of princely households and the accomplishment of the female

succession in Tudor England, 1516–1588' (Ph.D. thesis, Johns Hopkins University, 2002), pp. 207–19.

33. BL Lansdowne MS 1236 fol. 28. Also H. Ellis, *Original letters illustrative of English history* (3 vols, London, 1824–46), II, pp. 161–2.

34. See, for example, Thomas Norton, *To the queenes poore deceived subiectes of the North contreye* (London, 1569).

35. The fullest account of the French contributions is still to be found in David Loades, *Two Tudor conspiracies* (Cambridge, 1965).

36. *Tudor royal proclamations*, II, proclamation 390.

37. See, as one example, the letter from Julius III to Pole in which he reports Mary's view that to attempt to change existing property arrangements would produce greater confusion and concedes that point. Pole found it much harder to let the issue go. *CSPF*, 1553–8, no. 690, 20 Sept 1553.

38. J. D. Alsop, 'The act for the queen's legal power, 1554', *Parliamentary History* (1994), pp. 261–78.

39. Norton's Preface to R. Grafton, *A chronicle at large* (London, 1569), STC 12147.

40. 'A solemne prayer, made for King Phillip and Queene Maries childe', *A&M* [1583], p. 1481.

41. *CSPSp*, xi, Emperor to Renard, 10 Oct. 1553, p. 282.

42. *'Triumphs in English' Henry Parker, Lord Morley, translator to the Tudor court,* eds Marie Axton and James P. Carley (London, 2000), p. 263.

43. *CSPSp*, xi, Renard to the Emperor, 12 Oct. 1553, p. 288.

44. *CSPF* 1553–1558, Council to Dr Wotton, 7 Dec. 1553, p. 35.

45. David Starkey, *Elizabeth: Apprenticeship* (London, 2000), p. 131.

46. Sir Thomas Smith, *De republica Anglorum: A discourse on the commonwealth of England* (1583) (Cambridge, 1906), p. 49.

47. Both pieces of legislation were immediately published in *Anno Mariae Primo Actes made in the Parlyament*, April 1554 (STC 9943).

48. For more discussion of the ceremonial enactment of his lesser status, see my 'Mary Tudor as 'sole quene'? Gendering Tudor monarchy', *HJ* 40 (1997), pp. 895–942.

Further Reading

This is a guide to the most important recent works on Mary and aspects of her reign.

Biography

Until recently David Loades had pretty much cornered the market in biographies of the queen with his *Mary Tudor: A life* (Oxford, 1989) and the more recent *Mary Tudor: The tragical history of the first queen of England* (Kew, 2006). As explained in various chapters in this volume, Loades tends to see Mary as a tragic figure, ill-equipped for queenship, and it is left to Judith M. Richards's *Mary Tudor* (London, 2008) to provide a strong and well-judged defence of the queen against charges that she was hysterical, fanatical and just a little dull. Richards's biography combines scholarship with readability, and is an excellent starting point for students. For lively narratives they could also turn to Linda Porter, *Mary Tudor: The first queen* (London, 2009) or Anna Whitelock's *Mary Tudor: England's first queen* (London, 2009), both of which tell a dramatic story and are also keen to present Mary as a more sympathetic figure.

Mary's Education and Early Household

Maria Dowling recognized the humanist influences on Mary's education in *Humanism in the Age of Henry VIII* (London, 1986) and 'A woman's place? Learning and the wives of Henry VIII', *History Today*, 41 (1991), pp. 38–42. Several articles have built upon Dowling's pioneering work, including: Timothy G. Elston, 'Transformation or continuity? Sixteenth-century education and the legacy of Catherine of Aragon, Mary I, and Juan Luis Vives', in *'High and Mighty Queens' of Early Modern England: Realities and representations,* eds Carole Levin, Jo Eldridge Carney, and Debra Barrett-Graves (New York and Basingstoke, 2003), pp. 11–26; and Kathi Vosevich, 'The education of a prince(ss): tutoring the Tudors', in *Women, Writing, and the Reproduction of Culture in Tudor and Stuart Britain,* eds Elizabeth Mary Burke, Jane Donawerth, Linda L. Dove, and Karen L. Nelson (New York, 2000), pp. 61–76. Although the extent of Katherine Parr's influence on Mary is debated, there is no doubt that it was of some significance. Mary's time in Katherine's household and the relationship between the two women can be accessed in the standard biography of Henry's last queen: Susan E. James, *Kateryn Parr: The making of a queen* (Aldershot, 1999).

J. L. McIntosh's *From Heads of Household to Heads of State: The pre-accession households of Mary and Elizabeth Tudor 1516–1558* (New York, 2009) examines the role of Mary as the head of an independent household and major property owner before her accession.

The Accession Crisis of July 1553

The succession crisis of 1553 and short reign of Lady Jane Grey have lately been attracting considerable scholarly interest. Nonetheless, a short older survey that is still worth reading is S. T. Bindoff, 'A kingdom at stake, 1553', *History Today*, 3 (1953), pp. 642–8. Also of value, despite its age, is Mortimer Levine, *Tudor dynastic problems, 1460–1571* (London, 1973), which explains some of the legal and political issues surrounding Mary's exclusion from the throne.

A more recent analysis of some of the legal issues can be found in Eric Ives, 'Tudor dynastic problems revisited', *Historical Research*, 81 (2008), pp. 255–79. Ives goes on to provide a full study of the 1553 political crisis in *Lady Jane Grey: A Tudor mystery* (Oxford, 2009), in which he argues that Jane's claim was perfectly legal and it was not therefore surprising that she had the support of Edward VI's council. Support for Jane outside London is discussed in Robert Tittler and S. L. Battley, 'The local community and the crown in 1553: The accession of Mary Tudor revisited', *Bulletin of the Institute of Historical Research*, 57 (1984), pp. 131–9. Northumberland's role in the events of 1553 is discussed in David Loades, *John Dudley, duke of Northumberland 1504–1553* (Oxford, 1996).

Providing an eyewitness account of Mary's responses to the crisis of 1553, with an indispensable introduction, is 'The *Vita Mariae Angliae Reginae* of Robert Wingfield of Brantham', ed. and trans. Diarmaid MacCulloch, in *Camden Miscellany*, 28, Camden Society fourth series 29 (1984), pp. 181–301. Building largely on Wingfield's account, Anna Whitelock and Diarmaid MacCulloch trace the role of Mary's household in securing her success in 1553 in 'Princess Mary's household and the succession crisis, July 1553'. *HJ*, 50 (2007), pp. 265–87. Jeri McIntosh's, *From Heads of Household* (see above) covers similar ground.

Mary's Coronation

Two important studies of Mary's coronation are Dale Hoak, 'The coronations of Edward VI, Mary I, and Elizabeth I, and the transformation of the Tudor monarchy' in *Westminster Abbey reformed 1540–1640*, eds C. S. Knighton and Richard Mortimer (Aldershot and Burlington, Vt., 2003), pp. 114–51; and Alice Hunt, 'Legitimacy, ceremony and drama: Mary Tudor's coronation and *Respublica*', in *Interludes and Early Modern Society:*

Studies in gender, power and theatricality, eds Peter Happé and Wim Hüsken (Amsterdam and New York, 2007), pp. 331–51. Alice Hunt also has a chapter on Mary's coronation in her *The Drama of Coronation: Medieval ceremony in early modern England* (Cambridge, 2008).

Overviews of the Reign

A short and useful overview is provided in Robert Tittler, *The Reign of Mary I* (Harlow, 2nd edn, 1991). Far more substantial is David Loades, *The Reign of Mary Tudor: Politics, government and religion in England, 1553–58* (London, 1979, 2nd edn 1991). In a seminal and influential essay, Elizabeth Russell pointed to the need for a reassessment of the reign in 'Mary Tudor and Mr Jorkins', *Historical Research*, 63 (1990), pp. 263–76. Judith M. Richards has helped to provide it in her biography, *Mary Tudor* (London, 2008).

Mary's Marriage

Alexander Samson has been responsible for the latest work on Mary's marriage. In his 'Changing places: The marriage and royal entry of Philip, prince of Austria, and Mary Tudor, July–August 1554', *SCJ*, 36 (2005), pp. 761–84, Samson argues that there was a far greater willingness in England to accept Philip as king than was previously believed. However, in 'A fine romance: Anglo-Spanish relations in the sixteenth century', *Journal of Medieval and Early Modern Studies*, 39 (2009), pp 65–94, Samson draws attention to the suspicions that the marriage aroused within London as well as to tensions that existed between the English and Spanish households of the married couple. For a different kind of discussion, see also his 'Mapping the marriage: Thomas Geminus's "Britanniae Insulae Nova Descriptio" and "Nova Descriptio Hispaniae" (1555)', *Renaissance and Reformation*, 31 (2008), pp. 95–116. Samson's monograph on the Spanish marriage, *Mary Tudor and the Habsburg marriage: England and Spain 1553–1557*, is now in press.

Philip's role in the government of England is dealt with by David Loades in 'Philip II and the government of England' in *Law and Government under the Tudors: Essays presented to Sir Geoffrey Elton . . . on . . . his retirement*, eds Claire M. Cross, David Loades and J. J. Scarisbrick (Cambridge, 1988), pp. 177–94, and David Loades, 'King Philip of England'. *History Today*, 57 (2007), pp. 40–8.

Religion: Restoration and Persecution

Unsurprisingly, Mary's religious policy and the Marian church have attracted the most attention from historians. Thirty years ago, Rex Pogson did important work in focusing on the difficulties that the Marian regime faced in effecting a Catholic restoration; see his 'Revival and reform in Mary Tudor's church: A question of money', *Journal of Ecclesiastical History*, 25 (1974), pp. 249–65; 'Reginald Pole and the priorities of government in Mary Tudor's church', *Historical Journal*, 18 (1975), pp. 3–20; and 'The legacy of the schism: Confusion, continuity and change in the Marian clergy' in *The Mid-Tudor Polity, c. 1540–1560*, eds Jennifer Loach and Robert Tittler (Basingstoke, 1980), pp. 116–36.

Work on local parish records, however, demonstrated that despite financial and economic difficulties the Marian restoration was remarkably successful at a local level. Both Ronald Hutton's important essay, 'The local impact of the Tudor Reformations', in *The English Reformation Revised*, ed. Christopher Haigh (Cambridge, 1987), pp. 114–38, and Christopher Haigh's ground-breaking *English Reformations: Religion, politics and society under the Tudors* (Oxford, 1993) have led to a reassessment of traditional assumptions that the Marian counter-reformation was doomed to failure. Meanwhile, Eamon Duffy pointed to the spiritual vitality of the Marian Church in *The Stripping of the Altars: Traditional religion in England, c.1400–c.1580* (New Haven, Conn. and London, 1992). In an important study, *The Theology and Spirituality of Mary Tudor's Church* (Aldershot, 2006), William Wizeman SJ argues that the theology, spirituality and strategies of the Marian Church were not at all backward-looking, but rather reflected, and even anticipated, Counter-Reformation Catholicism, especially the reforms of the Council of Trent (1545–63).

Two recent collections of essays also testify to the strength of the Marian Church. *Reforming Catholicism in the England of Mary Tudor: The achievement of Friar Bartolomé Carranza*, eds John Edwards and Ronald Truman, (Aldershot, 2005) examines the reforming initiatives of the Marian Church through the career of a major Spanish churchman and Mary's confessor. This collection is particularly noteworthy for its essays on Cardinal Pole. *The Church of Mary Tudor*, eds Eamon Duffy and David Loades (Aldershot, 2006) contains a wealth of invaluable essays, including those by Claire Cross, Ralph Houlbrooke, William Wizeman, Lucy Wooding and the editors.

Apart from Stephen Gardiner and Cardinal Pole, relatively little work has been carried out on individual Marian bishops. Kenneth Carleton's *Bishops and Reform in the English Church, 1520–1559* (Woodbridge, 2001) looks at the bishops' role over a wide time-span, while David Loades examines the whole Marian episcopate in *The Church of Mary Tudor*, eds Eamon Duffy and David Loades (Aldershot, 2006), pp. 33–56. Gina Alexander, however, has published two groundbreaking studies on Bishop Bonner: 'Bonner and the Marian persecutions', *History*, 60 (1975), pp. 374–91 (also published in *The English Reformation Revised*, ed. Christopher Haigh (Cambridge, 1987), pp. 157–77); and 'Bishop Bonner and the parliament of 1559', *Bulletin of the Institute of Historical Research*, 56 (1983), pp. 164–79.

Stephen Gardiner has been the subject of some early biographies, notably the impressive James Arthur Muller, *Stephen Gardiner and the Tudor Reaction*

(New York, 1926, repr. 1970). The most recent one is Glyn Redworth, *In Defence of the Church Catholic: The life of Stephen Gardiner* (Oxford, 1990). For Gardiner's historical afterlife, see Alec Ryrie and Michael Riordan, 'Stephen Gardiner and the making of a Protestant villain', *SCJ*, 34 (2003), pp. 1039–63.

Virtually all the major recent work on Cardinal Pole and English religious affairs has been carried out by Thomas F. Mayer. Amongst his many monographs and essays, see *Reginald Pole: Prince and prophet* (Cambridge, 2000); *Cardinal Pole in European Context* (Aldershot, 2000); 'A test of wills: Cardinal Pole, Ignatius Loyola, and the Jesuits in England' in *The Reckoned Expense: Edmund Campion and the early English Jesuits,* ed. Thomas M. McCoog (Woodbridge, 1996), pp. 21–37; and 'Becket's bones burnt! Cardinal Pole and the invention and dissemination of an atrocity' in *Martyrs and Martyrdom in England, c.1400–1700*, eds Thomas S. Freeman and Thomas F. Mayer (Woodbridge, 2007), pp. 126–43. But also essential reading are Eamon Duffy's important essays in *The Church of Mary Tudor*, eds Eamon Duffy and David Loades (Aldershot, 2006) and *Fires of Faith: Catholic England under Mary Tudor* (New Haven, Conn. and London, 2009), pp. 29–56. *Fires of Faith* takes a thoroughly revisionist stance: arguing that Mary's regime was neither inept nor reactionary, Duffy highlights the propaganda achievements and tight organization of the Marian Church.

Until recently, little analytical work had been done on the Marian persecutions, though Megan Hickerson's *Making Women Martyrs in Tudor England* (Palgrave, 2005), which concentrates on the portrayal of female martyrs in John Foxe's *Acts and Monuments*, inevitably has a lot to say about some of the Marian martyrs, as does David Loades, *The Oxford Martyrs* (London, 1970, repr. 1992). Andrew Pettegree's *Marian Protestantism: Six studies* (Aldershot, 1996) contains a vigorously argued final chapter which provides a critical summary of the policy of Marian persecution. However, Eamon Duffy's new book *Fires of Faith* takes issue with this conclusion and judges the burnings to have been effective in subduing heresy. Two valuable detailed studies on the Marian persecutions in particular regions are Patrick Collinson, 'The persecution in Kent', and Ralph Houlbrooke, 'The clergy, the church courts and the Marian restoration in Norwich'; both are in *The Church of Mary Tudor*, eds Eamon Duffy and David Loades (Aldershot, 2006). A detailed examination of a handful of burnings and their local impact can be found in Thomas S. Freeman, 'Notes on a source for John Foxe's account of the Marian persecution in Kent and Sussex', *Historical Research* 67 (1994), pp. 203–11.

Gender

The pioneering work on gender was carried out by Judith M. Richards. In addition to her biography, the following articles are essential: 'Mary

Tudor as "sole quene"? Gendering Tudor monarchy', *HJ*, 40, 4 (1997), pp. 895–924;" To promote a woman to beare rule': Talking of queens in mid-Tudor England', *SCJ*, 28 (1997), pp. 101–21; 'Gender difference and Tudor monarchy: The significance of Queen Mary I', *Parergon*, 21 (2004), pp. 27–46; 'Mary Tudor: Renaissance queen of England', in *'High and Mighty Queens' of Early Modern England: Realities and representations*, eds Carole Levin, Jo Eldridge Carney and Debra Barrett-Graves (New York and Basingstoke, 2003), pp. 27–44.

Also important but with a different perspective is Glyn Redworth, ' "Matters impertinent to women": Male and female monarchy under Philip and Mary', *EHR*, 112 (1997), pp. 597–613. Charles Beem uses Mary as one of his four major case studies in his chronological survey of female monarchs, *The Lioness Roared: The problems of female rule in English history* (Basingstoke, 2006). Although he styles her rule a success, he conventionally casts Mary as 'deferential' in her exercise of power.

Representation

Specifically on representation but with a gender dimension, Louis A. Montrose, *The Subject of Elizabeth: Authority, gender and representation* (Chicago and London, 2006), pp. 43–56 provides a thoughtful and important reconsideration of Mary. Paulina Kewes is equally thought-provoking in arguing that Elizabeth learned from and adapted Mary's self-representation: 'Two queens, one inventory: the lives of Mary and Elizabeth Tudor', in *Writing Lives: Biography and textuality, identity and representation in early modern England*, eds Kevin Sharpe and Steven N. Zwicker (Oxford, 2008), pp. 187–207 and 'Godly queens: The royal iconographies of Mary and Elizabeth', in *Tudor queenship: The reigns of Mary and Elizabeth*, ed. Anna Whitelock and Alice Hunt (Basingstoke, 2010), pp. 47–62. By contrast, Kevin Sharpe, *Selling the Tudor Monarchy: Authority and image in sixteenth-century England* (New Haven, Conn. and London, 2009) is surprisingly traditional in its approach to Mary.

Governance and Parliament

In an online article, 'The Marian court and Tudor policy-making' (tudors.org), John Guy criticizes the approach and conclusions of many earlier works on Marian governance, arguing that they tend to focus on constitutional or administrative processes, and as a result obscure the nature of the political process. Amongst these earlier works are studies of the Marian privy council, including Dale Hoak, 'Two revolutions in Tudor government: the formation and organization of Mary I's Privy Council' in *Revolution Reassessed: Revisions in the history of Tudor government and administration*, eds Christopher Coleman and David Starkey (Oxford, 1986), pp. 87–115; and Ann Weikel, 'The Marian council revisited', in *The mid-Tudor polity*, *c. 1540–1560*, eds Jennifer Loach and Robert Tittler (Basingstoke, 1986), pp. 52–73. Other bureaucratic studies include L. Abbott, 'Public office and private profit: The legal establishment in the reign of Mary Tudor', also in *The Mid-Tudor Polity*, pp. 137–58.

For parliament, the best overview remains Jennifer Loach, *Parliament and the Crown in the Reign of Mary Tudor* (Oxford, 1986). The Upper House is examined in Michael A. Graves, *The House of Lords in the Parliaments of Edward VI and Mary I: An institutional study* (Cambridge, 1981). For detailed studies of particular statutes, see: Patrick Carter, 'Mary Tudor, parliament and the renunciation of first fruits, 1555', *Historical Research*, 69 (1996), pp. 340–6, and James D Alsop, 'The Act for the queen's regal power, 1554', *Parliamentary History*, 13 (1994), pp. 261–76.

Wyatt's Rebellion

Two useful articles on the causes and significance of the 1554 rebellion are Malcolm R. Thorp, 'Religion and the Wyatt Rebellion of 1554', *Church History*, 47 (1978), pp. 363–80, and W. B. Robison, 'The national and local significance of Wyatt's rebellion in Surrey', *HJ*, 30 (1987), pp. 769–90. David Loades provides a valuable narrative of both this rebellion and the Dudley conspiracy in *Two Tudor Conspiracies* (Cambridge, 1965).

Foreign Policy and the Loss of Calais

The best account of the French war is provided by C. S. L. Davies, 'England and the French war, 1557–9', in *The Mid-Tudor Polity, c. 1540–1560*, eds Jennifer Loach and Robert Tittler (Basingstoke, 1980), pp. 159–85. For French policy, see David Potter, 'The duc de Guise and the fall of Calais, 1557–1558', *EHR*, 98 (1983), pp. 481–512. Also see Potter's 'Mid-Tudor foreign policy and diplomacy', in *Tudor England and its neighbours*, eds Susan Doran and Glenn Richardson (Basingstoke, 2004), pp. 106–38.

For the financial cost of the maintaining the garrison at Calais and the implications of the town's loss, see David Grummitt, *The Calais Garrison: War and military service in England, 1436–1558* (Woodbridge, 2008).

Index